Multinational Enterprises and Human Rights

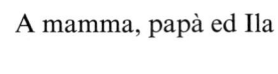

Multinational Enterprises and Human Rights

Obligations under EU Law and International Law

Alexandra Gatto

PhD, LLM, MA

Edward Elgar

Cheltenham, UK • Northampton, MA, USA

Published by
Edward Elgar Publishing Limited
The Lypiatts
15 Lansdown Road
Cheltenham
Glos GL50 2JA
UK

Edward Elgar Publishing, Inc.
William Pratt House
9 Dewey Court
Northampton
Massachusetts 01060
USA

A catalogue record for this book
is available from the British Library

Library of Congress Control Number: 2009941134

ISBN 978 1 84844 034 0

Typeset by Servis Filmsetting Ltd, Stockport, Cheshire
Printed and bound by MPG Books Group, UK

Contents

Acknowledgements

This book is the product of more than three years of research conducted mainly in the highly stimulating environment of the European University Institute in Florence. This book would not have been possible without a great deal of help from many people. I would like to reiterate my thanks to everyone who took time to review this book and make invaluable comments and suggestions.

First of all, I would like to express all my gratitude to my supervisor Professor Francioni for his continuous guidance, availability and support throughout the development and drafting of the PhD thesis on which this book is based. Special thanks go to Professor Olivier De Schutter and Professor Enzo Cannizzaro as members of the jury of my PhD defence, who provided insightful and thought-provoking comments on my work.

My warmest thanks go also to Professor Cremona for her stimulating observations on an early draft of this book and for her precious guidance until the completion of this work. I cannot fail to thank Professor Moreau, who helped me to define the object of my research at the beginning of this work, Professor G. de Bùrca and B. de Witte, who believed in this research project from the beginning and gave me the chance to present early excerpts of this work.

I am most grateful to Jean Pierre Laviec and Lucio Baccaro for allowing me to conduct research at the Institute for International Labour Studies of the International Labour Organisation in Geneva and to discuss an embryonic version of my book in that context. I would also like to thank Professor Peter Rosenbulm and Professor Mark Barenberg who provided a fresh new look on my research during my exchange at the Columbia University Law School. I am very thankful also to Jar for his support during the editing phase of this book.

However, it would not have been possible to accomplish this long term endeavour without their unconditional support. A special thank you goes to mamma, papà and Ila, who patiently stood by me and relentlessly encouraged me during these years.

Finally, life in Florence would not have been the same without the irreplaceable friendship and reliable presence of all my friends. To all of them, (and to all those I have forgotten to mention), goes my most sincere *grazie*!

Introduction

This book addresses the question of how the European Union can ensure that EU-based multinational enterprises (MNEs) respect human rights when operating in third countries. First, it identifies primary obligations on MNEs as developed by international law in order to tackle the above question. Secondly, on the basis of this theoretical framework it investigates how the European Union has acted to promote respect of human rights obligations by MNEs which are based on the territory of one of its Member States. Thirdly, the gap between the EU's commitment to the respect and promotion of human rights, the potential to regulate the conduct of MNEs and the EU's reluctance to impose human rights obligations on MNEs is explored. It is suggested that current human rights law should develop in the sense of considering companies as duty holders, together with States and other non-state actors, for the realisation of human rights. Moreover, a principle of graduation of responsibility is applied to MNEs, according to the specific human right involved, the proximity to the victim and the element of State authority exercised by the company in a particular situation. The above-depicted gradation of responsibility (from the obligation to *respect*, to the obligation to *promote* human rights) should be matched by a gradation of corresponding implementing mechanisms.

Applying this theoretical framework to the EU, three main recommendations have been formulated. First, the EU should more firmly link the promotion of MNEs' human rights obligations to international human rights law and support the constitution of an international law framework within the UN. Secondly, the EU should promote MNEs' human rights obligations, within the limits of its competence, both at the international and at an external level. It has been argued that a proactive attitude in this respect would not require the acquisition of new powers, but simply the recognition of a functional competence on the basis of Article 6 of the Treaty of European Union (TEU) in taking positive (and not merely negative) steps for the promotion of human rights in the areas of its competence occurring in international law and the international framework for MNEs' responsibility. Finally, the EU should not abandon the option of exploring non-binding and incentive measures, both at the international and external levels, to be encouraged as a viable complement to binding measures.

PART I

Multinational enterprises and human rights:
the international legal framework

1 Theoretical framework

1.1 INTRODUCTION

Multinational enterprises (MNEs) are very powerful actors in the current world order. The turnover of these multinationals is growing faster than the world social product. The universe of MNEs now spans 82 000 parent companies worldwide, with 810 000 foreign affiliates. And their combined value-added accounted for roughly 4 per cent of world GDP, a share that has remained relatively stable since 2000.[1] However, 85 per cent of the largest companies are based in the United States (US), the European Union (EU) and Japan. In particular 54 per cent of them are based in the EU.[2] About one-third of world trade takes place within groups of MNEs.

The economic power of MNEs has been strengthened by the process of globalization. What is commonly defined as globalization refers to a set of far-reaching changes in the global economy and in the regulation of international trade since the 1970s.[3] As a consequence of the collapse of the Bretton-Woods system and the oil crisis, the flexibility of exchange rates stimulated the growth in financial speculation and enhanced dependence on OPEC countries. At the same time, international trade barriers and exchange controls were loosened between North America and Western Europe, so that from the 1980s the integration of global capital and commodity markets intensified.[4]

The reduction of trade and non-trade barriers and the reduction of public control on foreign investment was followed by the reduction of governments' economic role through privatization of public enterprises. This ongoing process was reinforced by the development of

---

[1] See United Nations Conference on Trade and Development (UNCTAD), *World Investment Report 2009: Transnational Corporations, Agricultural Production and Development*, 2009, Geneva, United Nations Publications, at xxi.

[2] Ibid., p. 230.

[3] See C.A. Michalet, *Qu'Est-Ce Que la Mondialisation?* 2004, Paris, La Découverte, at 22.

[4] See G. Jones, *Multinationals and Global Capitalism: From the Nineteenth to the Twenty-First Century,* 2005, Oxford, Oxford University Press, at 60.

telecommunications and technologies which have allowed enterprises to overcome the former barriers of time and space and, in many respects, the boundaries of national markets.

One of the most important factors in relation to the globalization of the economy is foreign direct investment (FDI) by companies in foreign markets. The attitude towards FDI has deeply changed. Until the 1970s foreign investment was subject to restrictions and requirements concerning profit repatriation, technology transfer, exports, and domestic participation of MNEs.[5] This was due to the fact that foreign investors wanted to be protected against discrimination *vis-à-vis* domestic investors.[6] On the other hand, developing countries were concerned that MNEs might exploit the resources of host countries without giving much in return. Today, on the contrary, most governments have enacted regulatory changes in order to attract foreign investment. The settlement of MNEs in developing countries is perceived as beneficial to technology transfer, job creation and the flow of a strong currency.[7]

On the flip-side of the coin, the liberalization of international trade and the reinforcement of investors have provided MNEs with the option of taking advantage of lower human rights standards or weak systems of governance when they operate in developing countries.[8] In addition to exercising huge economic power, corporate influence has recently extended into areas previously regarded as the proper prerogative of government. In developing countries with poor infrastructure or otherwise ineffective government, MNEs often carry out governmental functions in regions where their plants and workers are located, for example in the creation of basic infrastructure such as streets, housing and medical assistance. In the Niger Delta, for instance, oil companies invest millions of dollars every year in building infrastructures.[9] Some MNEs even assume bureaucratic functions such as organizing elections for local committees.[10]

---

[5]   See ibid., at 65.

[6]   See M. Sornarajah, *The Settlement of Foreign Investment Disputes*, 2000, The Hague, Kluwer, at 8.

[7]   See P. Malanczuk, 'Globalization and the Future Role of Sovereign States', in F. Weiss et al. (eds), *International Economic Law with a Human Face*, 1998, The Hague, Kluwer, at 45.

[8]   See S. Joseph, 'Taming the Leviathans: Multinational Enterprises and Human Rights' (1999) 46 *Netherlands International Law Review* 171.

[9]   See A. Eide, et al. (eds), *Human Rights and the Oil Industry*, 2000, Antwerp, Groningen and Oxford, Intersentia.

[10]   See C. Hanley, 'The Abuse of Human Rights by European-Based Multinational Corporations: Effective Control Mechanisms for the EU' (LLM thesis on file at the European University Institute, Florence, 2001) at 2.

At the same time, while the risk of expropriation by governmental action is receding, the risk of private disturbance and violence increases, thus corporations become more and more involved in security measures, which may lead to human rights abuses. In the last two decades the role of companies that provide security is larger and different to what it has been since the foundation of the modern State. Private companies now provide more services and more kinds of services, including some that have been considered fundamental military capabilities in the modern era. Today, it is estimated that tens of thousands of private military company (PMC) employees in Iraq are operating on contracts with the Iraqi and US government, as well as with private business.

The rise of PMCs as significant actors in military affairs has been ascribed to a number of factors. After the end of the Cold War, the increased chances of internal conflict, combined with the reluctance of the key States to intervene in distant conflicts, caused weak or failing States to turn to the private sector to fill the security vacuum. Secondly, the demobilization that accompanied the end of superpower rivalry released a workforce of individuals trained by their national militaries but available to the private market. This coincided with a general enthusiasm for outsourcing, though the economic savings of using PMCs rather than maintaining a large standing army are under debate. Thirdly, in States unable or unwilling to provide security to non-state actors, PMCs may be the only option for private companies, multilateral organizations and, increasingly, non-governmental organizations (NGOs). This expansion of activity has been accompanied by a growing concern about the role of private commercial interests in military affairs, and in particular about the unregulated use of lethal violence through PMC personnel. The emergence of PMCs in military affairs poses challenges both to law and to thinking about international security. Regulation in this context has long been based on the assumption that States are the sole legitimate providers of security. Increasingly, however, activities are being outsourced to PMCs, though this outsourcing has not been accompanied by corresponding checks and oversight.[11]

Over the past few years corporate responsibility has become one of the major issues facing the international community, with initiatives mushrooming at international, regional and national level in recent years. The International Labour Organisation (ILO) Tripartite Declaration of

---

[11] See D.D. Avant, *The Market for Force: the Consequences of Privatizing Security*, 2005, Cambridge, Cambridge University Press, at 178–191.

Principles Concerning Transnational Enterprises and Social Policy first adopted in 1977,[12] has been revised in 2000 and in 2006. The Organisation for Economic Co-operation and Development (OECD) Guidelines for Multinational Enterprises,[13] drawn up in 1976 was revised most recently in 2000. In 2003, the United Nations (UN) Sub-Commission for the Promotion and Protection of Human Rights approved the Norms on the Responsibility of Transnational Corporations and Other Businesses Enterprises with Regard to Human Rights,[14] which identify a set of human rights principles for business enterprises[15] and have been linked to the UN voluntary initiative Global Compact.[16] Legislation covering corporate codes of conduct was introduced into both the Australian Parliament[17] and the Congress of the United States,[18] where 85 per cent of large companies have already adopted voluntary codes of conduct. Although the impact of self-regulation cannot be overestimated, these initiatives can be welcomed as the first sign of recognition by companies of responsibility towards a number of human rights and more in general towards society at large.

---

[12]   Tripartite Declaration of Principles concerning Multinational Enterprises and Social Policy, adopted by the Governing Body of the International Labour Office at its 204th Session (Geneva, November 1977) as amended at its 279th (November 2000) and 295th (March 2006) Sessions.

[13]   See Organisation for Economic Cooperation and Development (OECD), *The OECD Guidelines for Multinational Enterprises*, OCDE/GD 97/40 (2000), 2000, Paris, OECD, available at: http://www. oecd.org/daf/investment/guidlienes/mnetext.htm (accessed 5 April 2002).

[14]   See United Nations (UN), 'Norms on the Responsibilities of Transnational Corporations and Other Business Enterprises with Regard to Human Rights', E/CN.4/Sub.2/2003/12/Rev.2 (2003). Approved 13 August 2003, by UN Sub-Commission on the Promotion and Protection of Human Rights resolution 2003/16, E/CN.4/Sub.2/2003/L.11 (2003), at 52.

[15]   See UN, 'Draft Fundamental Human Rights Principles for Business', E/CN.4/Sub.2/2002X/Add, E/CN.4/Sub/2002/wg;2/wp.1/Add, available at: http://www.1umn.edu/humanrights/lnks/principles11-18-200.htm (accessed 14 March 2002).

[16]   See UN, *Guidelines for Cooperation between the United Nations and the Business Community*, available at: http://www.unglobalcompact.org (accessed 15 March 2006).

[17]   See 'The Corporate Code of Conduct Bill 2000' sponsored by Senator Vicky Bourne. See *Report on the Corporate Code of Conduct Bill 2000*, June 2001, Commonwealth of Australia.

[18]   Corporate Code of Conduct Act to require nationals of the United States that employ more than 20 persons in a foreign country to implement a Corporate Code of Conduct with respect to the employment of those persons, and for other purposes (H.R. 5377), introduced by Cynthia McKinney.

Recently a number of lawsuits pending before US[19] and UK[20] courts and consumer awareness campaigns[21] have brought to the attention of public opinion egregious human rights violations committed by US and European MNEs.

In the European context, the attention on the responsibility of MNEs in Europe dates back to the 1970s, within the realm of the European Economic Community (EEC). Apart from two isolated initiatives in the context of political cooperation, the interest in European MNEs' activities in third countries was not revived until 1993, when the President of the European Commission, Jacques Delors, called on business to take part in the fight against social exclusion. The appeal to European companies was strengthened at the European Council in Lisbon in March 2000,[22] when companies' social responsibility was linked to Europe's new strategic goal for 2010: to become the most competitive and dynamic knowledge-based economy in the world, capable of sustainable economic growth with more and better jobs and greater social cohesion. This goal was then articulated in the Commission's European Social Agenda,[23] which emphasized the role of Corporate Social Responsibility in addressing the employment and social consequences of economics and market integration. The subsequent

---

[19]   Cases pending before US courts under the Alien Tort Claims Act have been dealt with by B. Stephens, 'Corporate Liability: Enforcing Human Rights Through Domestic Litigation' (2001) 24 *Hastings International and Comparative Law Review* 401.

[20]   See for instance *Lubbe and Others v Cape* plc [2000] 4 All ER 268, [2000] 1 WLR 1545, [2000] 2 Lloyd's, Rep 383 (HL). An update on British cases is provided by R. Meeran, *Access to Courts for Corporate Accountability: Recent Developments,* available at: http://www.johnpickering.co.uk (accessed 11 November 2006).

[21]   A number of international human rights and environmental non-governmental organizations constantly monitor MNEs' activities worldwide. Consumer campaigns have proved effective in changing corporate policies in some cases, in particular on companies involved in the apparel and garment industries. A list of current campaigns can be found on www.corporatewatch.org and www.amanestyinternational.com. For an assessment of recent consumer campaigns see Chris Avery, 'Business and Human Rights in a Time of Change', in M.T. Kamminga and S. Zia Zafiri (eds), *Liability of Multinational Corporations under International Law*, 2000, The Hague, Kluwer Law International, at 17–73 and R. O' Brien, 'NGOs, Civil Society and Global Economic Regulation', in S. Picciotto and R. Mayne (eds), *Regulating International Business. Beyond Liberalisation*, 1999, London, Macmillan Press, at 257.

[22]   This development is traced in the European Union website, http://www.europa.eu.int/comm//employment_social/soc-dial/csr (accessed 5 May 2003).

[23]   See Communication from the Commission to the Council, the European Parliament and the Economic and Social Committee, *Social Policy Agenda* COM (2000) 379 final, 28 June 2000.

Commission Communication, Corporate Social Responsibility[24] recognized a role for the European Union in encouraging Corporate Social Responsibility and in setting up a framework to ensure that environmental and social considerations were integrated into companies' activities. In March 2006 the Commission of the European Union issued a Communication, Implementing The Partnership for Growth and Jobs: Making Europe a Pole of Excellence on Corporate Social Responsibility.[25] Through this initiative the Commission reaffirms its preference for non-binding initiatives and promotes the creation of a businesses alliance for Corporate Social Responsibility.

1.2   MNEs AND HUMAN RIGHTS

It is difficult to deny that MNEs exercise considerable influence and perhaps some power over the direction of economic and social policy. While MNEs cannot be said to have replaced the State as the unit of official power, it must be admitted that decisions and activities of MNEs carry considerable weight in national and international policy making.[26] Today's leadership of MNEs in economic affairs, especially in the fields of trade, investment and financial services is a culmination of an evolving process of policy development. Not only have MNEs enhanced the commercial aspects of traditional human endeavours in agriculture, health and medicine, transport and clothing, but in many countries of the world MNEs are also responsible for the provision of public services such as water, electricity, telephone, and household gas, leaving only a few, if any at all, aspects of human life untouched by corporate activities.[27]

At the same time, the expanding role of private corporations is taking place in a period of steady reduction of governmental involvement in commercial and social undertaking, for corporations now perform some of the tasks relinquished by governments. As a result, such is the power of MNEs that they can affect the economic policy of the countries in which they

---

[24]   *Communication from the Commission concerning Corporate Social Responsibility: a Business Contribution to Sustainable Development* COM (2002) 347 final, 2 July 2002.

[25]   *Communication from the Commission to the European Parliament, the Council and the European Economic and Social Committee, Implementing the Partnership for Growth and Jobs: Making Europe a Pole of Excellence on Corporate Social Responsibility* COM (2006) 136 final, 22 March 2006.

[26]   See Michalet, *supra* n. 3, at 78. See also Sornarajah, *supra* n. 6, at 8.

[27]   Michalet, *supra* n. 3 at 14.

operate. Consequently, their impact on human rights and development can be considered more significant than that of domestic firms.

The relationship between MNEs and human rights is a complex one. Three aspects can be distinguished. First, MNEs can be direct violators of human rights, for example, by making use of forced labour. Secondly, they can indirectly violate human rights by supporting a regime that violates human rights. An example of this is the intended investment by a subsidiary of the Dutch MNE IHC Caland in Myanmar.[28] Thirdly, besides the fact that they may threaten an effective enjoyment of human rights, they can also have a positive influence. In general, the presence of MNEs can raise the standard of living and improve respect for economic, social and cultural rights.[29]

1.2.1 MNEs as Violators of Human Rights

MNES can have a substantial impact on the enjoyment of economic, social and cultural rights. Their influence on the right to work, the right to just and favourable conditions of work and the right to form a trade union is evident. MNEs can breach labour rights by mistreating and exploiting their labour forces, by preventing the creation of trade unions, by the use of child labour and discriminatory practices in recruiting. However, they can also affect civil and political rights; for example, the prohibition of discrimination. Another example is the right to life. The accident with the subsidiary of the American MNE Union Carbide in Bhopal, India in 1984 is an example of the effect that MNEs can have on this right.[30] MNEs can cause environmental damage that can impact on the right to health, life, minority rights and the right to self-determination.[31] Inefficient rules on

---

[28] See N. Jägers, 'Multinational Corporations under international law', in M. Addo (ed.), *Human Rights Standards and the Responsibility of Transnational Corporations*, 1999, The Hague, Kluwer Law International, at 260.

[29] O. de Schutter, 'Transnational Corporations as Instruments of Human Development', in P. Alston and M. Robinson (eds), *Human Rights and Development: Towards Mutual Reinforcement*, 2005, Oxford, Oxford University Press, at 403–44.

[30] The accident, which was the result of inadequate safety measures, is the worst industrial disaster of the twentieth century. It killed over 8000 people in its immediate aftermath and caused injuries to over 500 000. See *Re Union Carbide Corporation Gas Plant Disaster* 809 F. 2d 195.

[31] See e.g. *Wiva Royal Dutch Shell Petroleum Co.* 226 F. 3d, 88 (2d Cir 2000). See also S. Joseph, 'An Overview of the Human Rights Accountability of Multinational Enterprises', in Kamminga and Zia-Zarifi, *supra* n. 21, 75 at 79.

workers' safety may threaten workers' right to the protection of health or their right to life.

In considering the responsibilities of business with regard to human rights, it is important to reiterate that States are the primary duty bearers of human rights. While business can affect the enjoyment of human rights significantly, business plays a distinct role in society, holds different objectives, and influences human rights differently to States. The responsibilities of States cannot therefore simply be transferred to business; the responsibilities of the latter must be defined separately, in proportion to its nature and activities.

The first two responsibilities – to 'respect' and to 'support' human rights – relate to the acts and omissions of the business entity itself. The third responsibility on business entities – to 'make sure they are not complicit' in human rights abuses – concerns the relationship between business entities and third parties.

A responsibility to 'respect' human rights is comparatively unproblematic and requires business to refrain from acts that could interfere with the enjoyment of human rights. For example, a private detention centre institution should refrain from inflicting cruel, inhuman and degrading treatment on people detained.

1.2.2   Corporate Complicity in Human Rights Violations Committed by State Authorities

Companies may also be responsible for participating in or assisting abuses committed by others, especially government authorities and armed groups, in which case they could be said to be complicit in the abuses. Three ways in which a company can support a regime which systematically violates human rights have been identified.[32] The firm can increase a regime's repressive capacity by producing products or by providing major sources of revenues or infrastructures – such as roads – that are used by the regime and enhance its repressive capacity. The firm may also provide international credibility to an otherwise discredited regime. Moreover, government abuses may benefit companies commercially in the case in which governments commit abuses to produce infrastructure designed for business use.

Four situations illustrate where an allegation of complicity might arise against a company. First, when the company actively assists, directly or

---

[32]   This distinction is suggested in A. Clapham and S. Jerbi, 'Categories of Corporate Complicity in Human Rights Abuses' (1994), 24 *Hastings International and Comparative Law Review* 329, at 339.

indirectly, others in committing human rights violations; secondly, when the company is in a partnership with a government and could reasonably foresee, or subsequently obtains knowledge, that the government is likely to commit abuses in carrying out the agreement; thirdly, when the company benefits from human rights violations, even if it does not positively assist or cause them; and fourthly, when the company is silent or inactive in the face of violations.[33] For example, Unocal in Burma[34] could be said to have benefited from forced labour, which was used to build the infrastructure for the Yadana Pipeline. In other cases, governments may rely on abuses to provide firms with resources or may accommodate their commercial interests by resorting to repression to forestall labour unrest.[35] Recently Security Council Resolution 1499 (2003)[36] set up a group of experts whose report recognizes that multinational companies operating in the area, especially in the development and exploitation of natural resources, have an unavoidable impact on the ongoing conflict because of the long term economic and trade relations established with the relevant political organizations controlling the territory, and demanded that multinational enterprises operate in accordance with the same corporate norms that they would follow in their home countries.[37]

---

[33] C. Forcese, *Putting Conscience into Commerce: Strategies for Making Human Rights Business as Usual*, International Centre for Human Rights and Democratic Development, 1997, Montreal, at 22–4, available at: http://www.ichrdd.ca/flash.html (accessed 25 February 2002).

[34] See *Burma v Unocal Inc.* 176 FRD 329, 345. See also S. Bottomley, *Corporations and Human Rights*, in Bottomley and Kinley, *supra* n. 17, 47 at 49.

[35] An exhaustive analysis of collusion and complicity between business and State authorities, applied to a real case, can be found in the Report of the South Africa Truth and Reconciliation Commission. South African Truth and Reconciliation Commission, *Report of the South African Truth and Reconciliation Commission*, Vol. 4, Ch.2, *Institutional Hearings, Business and Labour*, 1998, Cape Town, Juta.

[36] See UN Security Council Resolution 1499 (2003) [on extension of the mandate of the UN Expert Panel on the Illegal Exploitation of Natural Resources and Other Forms of Wealth in the Democratic Republic of the Congo] adopted by the Security Council at its 4807th meeting, on 13 August 2003, SC Res. 1499 (2003).

[37] See UN Final Report of the Panel of Experts on the Illegal Exploitation of Natural Resources and Other Forms of Wealth of the Democratic Republic of the Congo S/2002/1146, 16 October 2002; UN Final Report of the Panel of Experts on the Illegal Exploitation of Natural Resources and Other Forms of Wealth of the Democratic Republic of the Congo S/2003/1027, 23 October 2003. For a commentary on this case see A.M. Papaioannou, 'The Illegal Exploitation of Natural Resources in the Democratic Republic of Congo: A Case Study on Corporate Complicity in Human Rights Abuses', in O. de Schutter, *Transnational Corporations and Human Rights*, 2006, Oxford and Portland, Or., Hart, at 263.

The responsibility on business entities to make sure they are not complicit in human rights abuses raises complex issues. Corporations often act with other partners in joint ventures, or with national and local governments, which could lead to allegations of complicity if the partner itself has abused human rights. One definition of 'complicity' states that a company is complicit in human rights abuses if it authorizes, tolerates, or knowingly ignores human rights abuses committed by an entity associated with it, or if the company knowingly provides practical assistance or encouragement that has a substantial effect on the perpetration of human rights abuse.

As with the responsibility to 'support' human rights, the duty on business to act or not act in each of these situations might not always be clear. Questions arise as to the extent of knowledge that a business entity had or should have had in relation to the human rights abuse and the extent to which it assisted through its acts or omissions in the abuse.

National and international criminal law has elaborated the doctrine of complicity as a basis for criminal liability, including criminal liability for legal persons for their complicity in crimes. The doctrine of complicity under national and international criminal law could therefore provide guidance in the further elaboration of this responsibility.[38]

1.2.3   MNEs as Promoters of Human Rights

As stated above, MNEs cannot be seen exclusively as a threat to human rights. In some cases they can also have a positive influence by contributing to the economic growth of some countries. A corporation can act as a promoter of human rights if, for example, it takes steps to protect the human rights of the persons who are directly involved in the activities of the corporation, such as employees. It is also possible that the MNE seeks to promote the human rights of the persons outside the corporation who are connected to the corporation's activities, either directly or indirectly, or not at all.

More complex issues arise in relation to the responsibility to 'support' human rights. For example, the responsibility to 'support' human rights suggests that business entities carry positive responsibilities to promote

---

[38]   Under international criminal law, three elements must be met to show complicity: first, a crime must have been committed; second, the accomplice must contribute in a direct and substantial way to the crime; and, third, the accomplice must have had intent or knowledge or was reckless with regard to the commission of the crime. See International Peace Academy and Fafo AIS, *Business and International Crimes: Assessing the Liability of Business Entities for Grave Violations of International Law*, September 2004, at 23; available at: http://www.fafo.no/liabilities/index.htm (accessed 3 February 2007).

human rights. On the one hand, business entities have a great and sometimes unexploited potential to promote human rights through investment and promotion of economic growth and the underlying conditions
required for the enjoyment of human rights. A responsibility to 'support'
human rights could help channel this. On the other hand, accepting that
business has positive responsibilities to use its influence to promote human
rights could sit uneasily with the traditional discretion of States to make
appropriate choices and exercise balance in designing policies to fulfil
human rights. In this context, it is relevant to note that business entities already carry positive responsibilities in other areas of national law,
for example in the law of negligence when discharging a duty of care to
employees or local communities. This could provide guidance when clarifying the positive responsibilities on business to 'support' human rights.

Similarly, subdividing the responsibility to 'support' human rights
into subcategories of responsibilities could be helpful. For example, the
Committee on Economic, Social and Cultural Rights has subdivided the
obligations of States party to the International Covenant on Economic,
Social and Cultural Rights (ICESCR)[39] into obligations to respect, protect
and fulfil (promote, provide and facilitate) economic, social and cultural
rights. The responsibilities to 'support' human rights could therefore
be clarified by considering what business could do to protect, promote,
provide and facilitate human rights. These sub-responsibilities could then
be classified as 'essential', 'expected', or 'desirable' conduct of business
entities.

1.3 THE CHALLENGE OF ADDRESSING HUMAN RIGHTS VIOLATIONS BY MNEs

Whether we look at MNEs as violators of human rights, accomplices of
human rights violations perpetrated by State authorities or as promoters
of human rights, the features of MNEs pose peculiar problems in terms
of being the addressees of human rights obligations. MNEs have the
capacity, for example, to fragment their business activities in a variety of
foreign countries, while always remaining responsive to a decision making
centre located in the country of origin, where the parent company controls and oversees the strategy of the whole group.[40] On the one hand, the

---

[39]   See UNTS 3, 993, 19 December 1966 (entered into force 3 January 1976).
[40]   See D. Vagts, 'The Multinational Enterprise: a New Challenge for
Transnational Law' (1970) 83 *Harvard Law Review* 739 at 740; and P. Muchlinski,

decentralization of the MNEs' structure enables it to choose to operate in countries which have laxer human rights and social regulation. Although not necessarily a determinant the existence of lower standards may be one of the factors that influence companies' investment decisions. On the other hand, the MNE is able to retain control over subsidiaries by the reliable chain of corporate structure and vertical integration that ties together the foreign subsidiaries and the parent company in a coherent legal unit.

One of the main reasons for the difficulties of addressing human rights obligations on MNEs can be found in their structure and organization. First, MNEs are not created by a single law. Secondly, there is no one law that delineates the limits of their activities and the distribution of power. Control of MNEs is arranged in a way that defies territorial boundaries. They are characterized by having a profit-making motive, together with the ability to operate across national borders and outside the effective supervision of domestic and international law. In economic terms, MNEs differ from domestic enterprises: in their choice of locating productive facilities across national borders; in their ability to trade across frontiers with affiliates, thus maintaining a competitive advantage over local firms; in their know-how of foreign markets; and in the organization of their managerial structure globally, according to the most suitable line of authority.

MNEs are increasingly organizing themselves in the form of global networks and strategic alliances. It follows that diverse local sites may be advantageous for different stages of the production cycles. Outsourcing or global sourcing are the methods used by MNEs to transfer part of their production to other countries or regions of the world, in order to take advantage of lower wages or lower costs of real estate. As a result, MNEs may escape regulatory control by States because they are able to select countries offering them the most favourable terms as regards social, environmental or tax regulation.

As a result, MNEs operate freely from many of the constraints that were traditionally imposed on them. As pointed out by Moreau, MNEs pose a 'challenge to the traditional legal delimitations of time and space'.[41] In other words, MNEs act and take decisions within a framework that has been freed from national constraints through an extensive network of

---

Multinational Enterprises and the Law, 1999, Oxford, UK and Cambridge, Mass., USA Blackwell, at 13.

[41]   See M.A. Moreau and G. Trudeau, 'The Social Effects of Globalization on Labour Law International', in Industrial Relations Association, *Global Integration and Challenges for Industrial Relations and Human Resource Management in the Twenty-First Century*, World Congress on Industrial Relations, Tokyo, May 2000.

decision-making and operational structures formed by their headquarters, branches, subsidiaries and other forms of investment by independent company investment units in other parts of the world. In addition, MNEs enjoy great flexibility in moving production sites, as well as moving profits within the framework of the organization. Therefore, the effectiveness of any legal standards is challenged by the speed of corporate decision making and of the implementation of their decisions. In other words, a production unit can be shut down and relocated in a very short period of time.[42] Consequently, legal standards, in order to be effective, should be applied with reference to a similar framework that is supranational in scope.

For the time being, however, neither businesses nor States seem to be ready to define international standards for MNEs.

Corporations usually shield their responsibility behind the assumption that, being private entities, they are not bound by international law. Furthermore, they claim that human rights and business are two separate disciplines that do not overlap and that the protection of human rights is the exclusive concern of States.[43] The increased scrutiny of corporate behaviour and the immediacy of global communications have made business aware of the need for a policy on human rights.[44] Corporations, however, are not willing to accept an international status, unless the obligations they will be bound by are reasonable and the general effect of the status is to enhance their public position and facilitate their operations, rather than subjecting them to tiresome constraints inconsistent with economic efficiency. The business response to the need for greater human rights accountability has mainly been the adoption and support of voluntary initiatives[45] such as codes of conduct, social statements in annual accounts and label schemes.[46] On the other hand, a certain resistance

---

[42] On the overcoming of *rattachement territoriaux* by MNEs see M.A. Moreau, 'Le Territoire – Aspects Européens et Internationaux – Des Rattachements Territoriaux Nationaux à la Transnationalité des Normes du Travail' (2003), 1140 *Semaine Sociale Lamy* 82.

[43] This conservative approach to business has been expressed by M. Friedman, 'The Social Responsibility of Business is to Increase its Profits' (1970) 13/9 *New York Times Magazine* 122.

[44] See G. Chandler, 'Keynote Address: Crafting a Human Rights Agenda for Business', in Addo (ed.), *Human Rights Standards, supra* n. 28, at 28.

[45] See M. Urminsky, *Self-Regulation in the Workplace: Codes of Conduct, Social Labelling and Socially Responsible Investment*, MCC Working Paper, 1 Series on Management Systems and Corporate Citizenship, International Labour Organization (2001).

[46] For a critical appraisal of voluntary initiatives, D. Cassel, 'Corporate Initiatives: A Second Human Rights Revolution?' (1996) 19 *Fordham International*

has been expressed to the adoption of legally binding norms either at the international[47] or regional level. For instance, the business view in support of voluntary initiatives was made clear on the occasion of the debate over Corporate Social Responsibility launched by the European Commission.[48]

1.4   COMPLEXITY AND COMPLEMENTARITY: THE INTERPLAY AMONG DIFFERENT LEVELS OF RESPONSIBILITY

The legal response to address MNEs' responsibility for human rights norms preliminarily requires a critical look at the usefulness and relevance of the legal categories in which we have been educated. Indeed, the rise of MNEs throws into confusion classical legal notions such as: responsibility and accountability; self-regulation versus legal responsibility; international, national and extraterritorial levels of enforcement; and criminal and civil responsibility.

The terms responsibility and accountability are sometimes used interchangeably.[49] However, in the context of the debate over MNEs and human rights, the concepts of corporate responsibility and accountability are used to refer to two different legal approaches in addressing the role of business and MNEs in relation to human rights.[50] While responsibility indicates the condition of having a duty or an obligation, accountability

---

Law Journal 1963. See also A. Supiot, 'Du Nouveau au Self- Service Normatif: la Responsabilité Sociale des Entreprises', in *Etudes Offerts à Jean Pélissier, Analyse Juridique et Valeurs en Droit Social*, 2004, Paris, Dalloz, at 542. The academic community and civil society have expressed their criticism over voluntary initiatives in International Council on Human Rights Policy, *Beyond Voluntarism-Human Rights and the Developing International Legal Obligations of Companies*, February 2002, available at: www.ichrp.org (accessed 3 March 2006).

[47]   See D. Weissbrodt and M. Kruger, 'Norms on the Responsibilities of Transnational Corporations and Other Business Enterprises with Regard to Human Rights', (2003) 97 *American Journal of International Law* 901.

[48]   See *European Multi-Stakeholder Forum on Corporate Social Responsibility – Final Report*, June 2004, available at: http://forum.europa.eu.int/irc/empl/csr_ eu_multi_stakeholder_forum/info/data/en/csr%20ems%20forum.htm (accessed 23 September 2009).

[49]   It must be noted however that the two terms are used almost interchangeably in legal English. See F. De Franchis, *Dizionario Giuridico [Law Dictionary]*, 1996, Milan, Giuffrè.

[50]   See A. Clapham, *Human Rights Obligations of Non-State Actors,* 2006, Oxford, Oxford University Press, at 195.

refers to the possibility of being required or expected to justify actions or decisions.[51]

In stricter legal terms, corporate responsibility refers to the secondary obligations[52] arising from the breach of primary rules and substantive standards for the conduct of MNEs that go beyond what is required at the national level of the host state, to ensure corporate contributions to the protection of human rights. This is, for example, the approach underlying the 'Norms on the Responsibility of Transnational Corporations and other Business Enterprises With Regards to Human Rights' (UN Norms) adopted by the UN Commission on Human Rights, which specifically provide for transnational corporations and other business enterprises to carry out their activities: 'in respect of national sovereignty and human rights'.[53]

Corporate accountability, on the other hand, refers to the way in which public and private actors are considered responsible for their decisions and are expected to explain them. Thus, this means that they must be open in their decision-making processes in order for them to be examined by other interested parties. In this light, corporate accountability response to the current situation in which businesses can 'no longer count on the anonymity of the market place' to hide from scrutiny[54] makes reference to the existence of voluntary codes of conduct and procedural standards in terms of transparency, reporting and openness to the public, as indirect means of ensuring the socially responsible conduct of MNEs. This, for instance, is the approach of the Global Reporting Initiative and of the European Commission.

The question of defining MNEs' obligations in terms of accountability or responsibility, therefore, gives rise to the questions of which standards are used to measure corporate behaviour and which mechanisms are used to implement these standards. From this standpoint, three forms of accountability/responsibility can be distinguished: informal accountability; self regulation and legal responsibility.[55]

---

[51]   See *Oxford Dictionary of English*, 2003, Oxford, Oxford University Press.

[52]   While primary norms regulate the behaviour of subjects of international law, secondary norms regulate the primary rules: creation, modification, extinction, interpretation and operation. The distinction has its origin in Hart's legal theory; see H.L.A. Hart, *The Concept of Law*, (1961) 1994, Oxford and New York, Clarendon Press and Oxford University Press.

[53]   UN Norms, *supra* n. 14, para. E.

[54]   See N. Choucri, 'Corporate Strategy towards Sustainability', in W. Lang (ed.), *Sustainable Development and International Law*, 1995, London and Boston, Graham & Trotman and M. Nijhoff, 189, at 193.

[55]   See S. Joseph, *Corporations and Transnational Human Rights Litigation*, 2004, Oxford, Hart, at 8.

1.4.1   Informal Accountability

One of the most visible forms of accountability for human rights abuses has arisen in the informal non-governmental arena. Most noticeable for the public at large have been the protests and disruptions aimed at economic globalization in general, rather than MNEs in particular.

NGOs have become highly adept at mobilizing public opinion against unethical corporations. Many prominent corporations have suffered the wrath of exposure to negative NGO campaigns and boycotts, including Nestlé, Shell, McDonald's, Coca Cola and Nike. Grassroots activism may be the best known mechanism for encouraging MNEs to respect human rights. However, as noted by McCorquodale, such pressure and, consequently, its impact, have so far been piecemeal and inconsistent. Moreover, these initiatives tend to concentrate on high profile MNEs, only on certain visible sectors, such as the clothing industry, which are more respondent to consumer pressure, while they usually leave untouched, for instance, the extractive industry.[56] Finally, these campaigns mainly involve a limited section of consumers, notably well informed, ethically concerned consumers located mainly in Western countries.

Alongside activism designed to mobilize consumers, there are also initiatives designed to harness the power of investors to catalyse socially responsible conduct on the part of companies within investment portfolios. Socially responsible investment products, where companies are included or excluded on the basis of their social and/or environmental records, are widely available from many investment institutions. Social investment initiatives are flourishing throughout EU Member States.[57] Various reporting criteria have been formulated, such as those in the global reporting initiatives, which assist companies in producing social and environmental reports to market their credentials to socially responsible investment funds or to investors.

1.4.2   Self-regulation

A second trend to be analyzed is that of self-regulation. non-binding initiatives or voluntary undertakings by the business sector.[58] Self-regulation

---

[56]   R. McCorquodale, 'Human Rights and Global Business', in Bottomley and Kinley, *supra* n. 16, at 89–114.

[57]   See *Corporate Social Responsibility. National Public Policies in the European Union*, European Commission, Employment and Social Affairs (January 2004).

[58]   See Urminsky, *supra* n. 45. See also E.V.K. FitzGerald, *Regulating Large International Firms. United Nations Research Institute for Social Development*, United Nations Research Institute for Social Development, UNRISD PB/04/1,

includes a wide array of instruments, ranging from codes of conduct and social labels to transparency and disclosure requirements.[59] They all have in common the fact of being promoted and voluntarily adopted by businesses, together with a non-legally binding nature.

In some cases however, voluntarily adopted instruments such as codes of conduct or social labels, once voluntarily adopted, acquire a binding effect. Codes of conduct for instance are commitments by companies to respect fundamental standards, while social labels are addressed to consumers to indicate that the production of the goods concerned has taken place while respecting particular standards. Clearly worded codes can have a legal significance because they set out the values, ethical standards and expectations of the company concerned, and might be used as evidence in legal proceedings with suppliers, employees and consumers.[60]

The trustworthiness of some codes of conduct may be questioned by the use of unfair business practices. At the level of individual company codes, empirical evidence suggests that, though their number is growing, policies or codes of conduct specifically covering human rights are still an exception rather than the rule for companies.[61] Generally, the human rights addressed by industry-wide and individual company codes focus on workers' rights – conditions of employment, health and safety, freedom of association and non-discrimination – as well as the rights of children, particularly regarding their employment and education. However, there are many other relevant rights guaranteed by international human rights law, such as privacy, the rights of indigenous people, freedom of expression, cultural belief and practice, as well as the right to liberty and a fair trial, which are overlooked.

A number of codes, however, also express clear commitments to implement the Universal Declaration of Human Rights.[62] Most contain at least

---

Geneva (19 March 2004); C. Crook, 'A Survey of Corporate Social Responsibility', *The Economist* (3 January 2005).

[59]   See CSR Europe & Ashridge Center for Business and Society, *Exploring Business Dynamics. Mainstreaming Corporate Social Responsibility in a Company's Strategy, Management and Systems*, (2002) at 9.

[60]   See H.W. Baade, 'Codes of Conduct for Multinational Enterprises', in N. Horn (ed.), *Legal Problems of Codes of Conduct for Multinational Enterprises*, 1980, Deventer, Kluwer, 407.

[61]   Cassel, *supra* n. 46, at 163; for a parallel survey at a European level see P. Spicher, *Les Droits de l'Homme dans les Chartes d'étique Economique*, 1996, Bern and Fribourg, Commission Nationale Suisse Pour l'Unesco, Institut Interdisciplinaire d'Etique et des Droits de l'Homme de l'Université de Fribourg-Centre Info.

[62]   See UN, *Universal Declaration of Human Rights*, GA Res. 217a (III), UN Doc. A/180 (1948), available at: http:// www.unhchr.ch/udhr/index.htm (accessed 13 April 2006).

some specific commitments about the company's conduct towards groups with which it has a direct connection, such as employees, sub-contractors, suppliers and host governments. Many codes require a company's sub-contractors to comply with its provisions and may contain detailed descriptions of prohibited corrupt practices and make commitments to protect the environment and consult local communities affected by their operations.[63]

Social labels are words or symbols on products which seek to influence the purchasing decisions of consumers by providing an assurance about the ethical and social impact of a business process on other stakeholders. These may imply extra costs but also marketing advantages. The hope is that there will be a consumer premium concentrated in particular in niche markets. Certification has increased rapidly; nonetheless it still accounts for only a minority of products. This implies that such schemes have impact mainly in markets that are both discretionary and publicly visible, such as the garment industries. On the other hand, smaller enterprises may find it difficult to absorb the cost of certification and the proliferation of different certification schemes.

The concept of social disclosure is underscored by the notion that a corporation is responsible to the community at large for its actions and is placed in a position similar to that of a provider of a public service that is called on to explain and account for its action in the light of broad concepts of the public interest. This has resulted in a wider concept of disclosure than that needed by the financiers of a corporation, and includes disclosure to employees, the use of local value added statements and environmental disclosure. Many of the schemes listed above have associated monitoring and reporting arrangements. Yet, given their specific focus, these may well not capture a company's full social and environmental impact. A wider initiative in this area is the Global Reporting Initiative.[64]

Broader disclosure is likely to render more effective market mechanisms that steer companies towards responsible conduct. For example, an important requisite for consumer action is access to information about company activities and their impact. In the absence of appropriate disclosure, consumers or other stakeholders will be unaware of corporate human rights abuses. Unless the information available is sufficiently detailed and reliable, it will be impossible to identify which companies are

---

[63]   An assessment of the benefits and limitations of codes of conducts can be found in D. Spar, 'The Spotlight on the Bottom Line: How Multinationals Export Human Rights' (1988) 77 *Foreign Affairs* 7.

[64]   See http://www.globalreporting.org/ (accessed 2 February 2006).

the most serious offenders and to ensure that pressure from consumers and investors is appropriately targeted. It is now common for companies to disclose information over and above that required by law. The most popular subject is environmental performance. Although disclosure techniques in other areas are less advanced, there is no reason in principle why companies could not be made to report in all areas in which they have a relevant social impact. An alternative approach to formal publication of information is to allow public access to company records. External reporting might be a promising way of increasing managerial circumspection and activating social pressure.

Directive 2003/51/EC about annual accounts has recently been adopted,[65] and requires that EU-based listed companies should disclose an annual corporate governance statement as part of their annual report. The Directive states that within their corporate governance statement companies may also provide an analysis of environmental and social aspects necessary to understand their development, performance and position. While not mandating reporting on CSR issues, the Directive recognizes the relevance of environmental and social issues in the context of corporate governance.[66]

The value added statement is a financial device that seeks to show the production contribution made by the company in the course of an accounting period. The value-added statement reports on the calculation of value added and its application among the stakeholders in the group. For instance, the local value-added statement by the subsidiary of an MNE can show the overall contribution it has made to the economy of the host country. Such a statement may be of particular use to developing countries where the prime users of information about the operations of MNEs' subsidiaries are not investors but the government as principal economic planner and other groups concerned with the impact of the MNE on national development.[67] Value-added statements are common in European firms' annual reports, although there is no common European directive on this matter. An example of disclosure can be found in the

---

[65] See Directive 2003/51/EC of the European Parliament and of the Council of 18 June 2003 amending Directives 78/660/EEC, 83/349/EEC, 86/635/EEC and 91/674/EEC *on the annual and consolidated accounts of certain types of companies, banks and other financial institutions and insurance undertakings* [2003] OJ L 178/16.

[66] Ibid, recital 8.

[67] See Z. Rahman, 'The Local Value Added Statement: a Reporting Requirement of Multinationals in Developing Host Countries' (1990) 25 *International Journal of Accounting* 87 at 88.

Eco-Management and Audit Scheme (EMAS) ISO 19000, which encourages companies to voluntarily set up an environmental management and audit system.[68]

Self regulation is still considered to be inadequate. The main shortcomings are the vagueness of commitments, the lack of monitoring and compliance mechanisms and the absence of compensation schemes for victims of abuses. One of the main criticisms is that self-regulatory regimes are designed to give the appearance of regulation and thereby ward off criticism and the imposition of external regulation. In other words, MNEs' codes of conduct are often seen as public relations exercises. Most codes of conduct use aspirational language or state broad values of the organization, such as business integrity, openness, enriching the community, treating people with dignity and respect or conducting business responsibly.

Voluntary schemes can easily be flouted by less scrupulous MNEs. In addition, companies are generally reluctant to open their operations and activities to independent monitoring or verification of these codes. Furthermore, self-regulation and other voluntary approaches have limited impact on the actual performance of companies.[69] In the absence of legislative requirements, many companies do not even meet the minimum standard specified in international human rights law.

Although the impact of self-regulation cannot be overestimated, it represents an initial step by companies in acknowledging their role in addressing human rights issues. Codes of conduct may themselves be understood as an evolutionary step on the road to legally binding standards that carry the support of a responsible majority, while ensuring censure and accountability of wrongdoing companies.

On the other hand, despite the fact that there are no legal obstacles to imposing direct human rights duties on companies, these attempts have so far been unsuccessful. The main defeats for the definition of legally binding instruments can be seen in the failure of the Multilateral

---

[68]   See Regulation (EC) 761/2001 of the European Parliament and of the Council of 19 March 2001 Allowing Voluntary Participation by Organisations in a Community Eco-Management and Audit Scheme (EMAS) [2001] OJ L 114/1, repealed by Commission Regulation (EC) No 196/2006 of 3 February 2006 amending Annex I to Regulation (EC) No 761/2001 of the European Parliament and of the Council to take account of the European Standard EN ISO 14001:2004, and repealing Decision 97/265/EC [2006] OJ, L 032, pp. 4–12.

[69]   See OECD, *Voluntary Approaches for Environmental Policy: an Assessment,* 1999, Paris, OECD. This report highlighted that to be credible self-regulation must include credible regulatory threats, reliable monitoring and third-party participation and penalties for non-compliance.

Agreement on Investment (MAI),[70] the failure to introduce personal criminal liability for legal persons in the Rome Statute of the International Criminal Court level (ICC)[71] and at a European level, the limited follow up given to the European Parliament's Resolution on 'EU Standards for European Enterprises Operating in Developing Countries: Towards a European Code of Conduct'.[72]

---

[70]   M.T. Kamminga, 'Holding Multinational Corporations Accountable for Human Rights Abuses: A Challenge for the EC', in P. Alston et al. (eds), *The EU and Human Rights*, 1999, Oxford, Oxford University Press, 554 at 569.

[71]   The consultations held in Rome in 1998 for the setting up of the International Criminal Courts have shown on the one hand large agreement and recognition of the width of companies' involvement in human rights violations. Many of the delegations present notably referred to behaviour that once again is hard to tackle from a legal perspective. On the other hand the attempt to extend the jurisdiction of the Court over legal persons had failed in facing the issues of collective responsibility (and the risks this would have implied) and the disagreement on the definition itself of legal persons, which greatly differs in different law systems. Moreover, it must be recognized that great development in the field of international criminal law has followed the creation of International Criminal Tribunals and the corpus of case law they have created. On this point see A. Clapham, 'The Question of Jurisdiction under International Criminal Law over Legal Persons: Lessons from the Rome Conference on an International Criminal Court', in Kamminga and Zia-Zarifi (eds), *supra* n. 21, at 139. However, Art 25(3)d of the Statute of the ICC establishes individual criminal responsibility of a natural person who 'contribute to the commission of a crime by a group of persons acting for a common purpose'. The transferability however of the theory of individual criminal responsibility to the context of MNEs is limited. Francioni points out three difficulties in effectively addressing corporate human rights abuses through individual criminal responsibility. First, the case law on individual criminal responsibility refers to cases of individual complicity (or contiguity) with States in international crimes (see for instance *United States v Carl Krauch, et al, IC Farben,* Case 6, Nurberg Military Tribunals, vols. VII–VIII). As noted by de Schutter (2004), however, the establishment of a special Criminal Court for Sierra Leone seems not to exclude this possibility. Secondly, the scope of international crimes is much narrower than the category of human rights violations under international law. As a consequence the majority of possible human rights violations committed by MNEs could not be reached by punishing the responsible officers under international criminal liability. Finally, individual responsibility seems to provide an inadequate response to the need for remedial actions for the victims of human rights abuses and in particular in case of widespread violations of the right to health and the right to life. See F. Francioni, 'Alternative Perspectives on International Responsibility for Human Rights Violations by Multinational Corporations', in W. Benedek et al. (eds), *Economic Globalisation and Human Rights*, 2007, Cambridge, Cambridge University Press, 245–64.

[72]   See Resolution on EU standards for European enterprises operating in developing countries: Towards a European Code of Conduct, adopted by the European Parliament on 15 January 1999, A4-0508/1998, [1999] OJ C 104/176, Rapporteur Richard Howitt, Member of the European Parliament (MEP).

Voluntary initiatives can be regarded as a prompt and flexible solution to the present corporate deficit of MNEs' accountability. However, this does not imply the rejection of mandatory measures. On the contrary, voluntary initiatives are perceived as complementary to regulatory measures, as part of an overall strategy to hold MNEs accountable. A wider basis of consensus created by voluntary measures can be later translated into legal obligations. The development of legal regulation of environmental matters is a good example of this progressive development of social concern into legal obligations. Just as once few would have believed that environmental issues would be mainstreamed into corporate affairs to the extent that they now are, so today we find a wide range of human rights issues in boardroom discussions.

1.4.3   Legal Responsibility: Direct Obligations under International Law, Indirect Obligations by the Home State and the Host State

In addition to consumer pressures and voluntary initiatives, different ways of ensuring legal responsibility of MNEs can be identified. Different legal instruments, at the national, regional and international level, could be and are currently employed to ensure the contribution of MNEs to the promotion of human rights. Such instruments, for instance, encompass national laws enacted by the home State of an MNE or by the host State receiving foreign investment. Another possible option is that of the construction of a theory of legal liability of the corporation as such under public international law.

The first and most traditional way of addressing MNEs' responsibility, assumes that the responsibility to prevent and suppress human rights violations by multinational corporations falls upon the host State on whose territory the MNE's activities take place. National laws impose domestic human rights responsibilities on corporations, such as laws regarding anti-discrimination, sexual harassment, workplace relations and environmental standards. Criminal liability applies in some States to punish certain types of egregious human rights behaviour of legal persons.[73] Nevertheless, seeking redress for human rights abuses by MNEs at the home State level, may prove to be difficult.[74] As a result of the process of

---

[73]   See Crimes Amendment (Corporate Manslaughter) Bill 2003 (New South Wales, Australia).

[74]   See J. Woodroffe, 'Regulating Multinational Corporations in a World of Nation States', in Addo (ed.) *supra* n. 28, at 131. See also H. Ward, *Governing Multinationals: the Role of Foreign Direct Liability*, The Royal Institute of International Affairs, Briefing Paper, No. 18 February (2001).

globalization itself, reliance on the law of the host States, on whose territory the MNE's activities take place, may provide only illusory guarantees of human rights against corporate conduct.[75] First of all, the competition among States to attract finance capital and technology to support growth and development may render unrealistic the expectation that local authorities will exercise effective supervision and human rights monitoring over the activities of MNEs on their territory. Secondly, reducing human rights obligations exclusively to the respect of local law may introduce an element of relativism that is hardly compatible with the universal value of human rights. Recent cases brought before UK courts have shown how MNEs take advantage of lax and discriminatory labour laws and apply workers' safety measures which would be inadequate or illegal in their State of origin.[76] Finally, host countries may not be endowed with a judicial system as efficient or willing to deal with complex claims involving large groups of individuals. Local subsidiaries may be insolvent or uninsured, domestic legislation in the host country may preclude the possibility of bringing claims against an employee, and finally, in these countries insufficient or no legal aid altogether is provided.[77] The combination of these factors together with the complexity of the cases renders access to justice in host countries, in fact, impracticable.

The second option postulates the attribution of the responsibility for human rights violations to the State of origin of the MNE on the basis of a theory of effective control over the transnational network of corporate activities. States of origin ('home States') of MNEs, while being in a better position to assess MNEs conduct are nonetheless reluctant to take action. The home States of MNEs are closely linked by their own system of regulations, licences and administrative oversight to the MNEs based in their territory. They benefit from their world wide operations by way of tax revenues and the increase in wealth of their citizens. Therefore, they are in the best position to assess and manage the risk connected with the foreign activities that, because of their inherent danger or because of the modalities of their execution, may cause harm to people abroad. Nonetheless, home States allow corporations subject to their jurisdiction or control to commit human rights abuses abroad that are both impermissible and subject to sanctions at home. This double standard in the application of human rights is not consistent with the principle of the indivisibility of human rights as

---

[75] See Francioni, 'Alternative Perspectives', *supra* n. 71.

[76] See the case *Lubbe*, *supra* n. 20.

[77] R. Meeran, *The Unveiling of Transnational Corporations*, in Kamminga and Zia Zarifi (eds), *supra* n. 21, at 264.

proclaimed in the Vienna Declaration of 1993 and the principle of non-discrimination as proclaimed in the UN Charter, which requires that people are not discriminated against in the enjoyment of their international human rights simply because of their nationality or their place of residence at a given time. However, as a response to the difficulties inherent in suing in the host State, legal recourse to the parent company, based in the UK or the US and with substantial assets, has boomed.[78] This option is not devoid of obstacles either. To begin with, it is necessary to overcome the principle of the separation of corporate entity (the so called 'corporate veil' barrier) by showing that, despite the separation of personality, the parent company owes a duty of care to those affected by its subsidiary operations. Secondly, a jurisdictional problem can be raised by the application by UK and US courts of the principle of *forum non conveniens.*[79]

Another tool for the improvement of the human rights responsibility of MNEs is by the direct imposition on enterprises of obligations under international law. The status of MNEs and the scope of their responsibility has not yet been fully defined in international law. Even if international law does not seem to be adequately equipped to cope with MNEs' behaviour, the fast-moving changes in this area demonstrate that international actors (both State and non-state) acknowledge that this subject is not only one of international concern, but one in which more legal developments are desirable. The development of human rights obligations upon MNEs, however, is shown by three trends in international law: the expansion of State responsibility in the private sphere; the rise of individual duties; and direct international soft-law obligations on companies.

Attempts to establish an international legally binding document on the responsibilities of MNEs have so far proved unsuccessful, as demonstrated

---

[78]   See Stephens, *supra* n. 19.

[79]   This principle has been developed in the context of commercial cases with an aim to ensure that cases are tried in the country in which they can be litigated most cost-effectively. Generally when a defendant is based in England, English courts have jurisdiction to deal with the claim. However, the defendant can prove that even if jurisdiction has been found in England, there is another 'clearly and distinctly more appropriate forum' in another country where justice as between the parties can be done. In resolving jurisdiction disputes, courts take into consideration factors such as the most real and substantial connection of the claim with one jurisdiction, but also convenience factors such as the proximity of witnesses and documents. The principle is also applied, with some variations, in other common law jurisdictions, including in the United States and Australia. See the case *Spiliada Maritime Corp. v Cansulex Ltd* [1987] AC 460. In civil and commercial cases, however, the application of this principle has been excluded by Regulation 44/2001 in the realm of EU Member States.

by the failure of the negotiations of the MAI[80] and the difficulties encountered by the drafters of UN Norms.[81] Nevertheless, the direct responsibility of MNEs to secure international human rights would help to discourage complicity between corporate conduct and the host State's human rights abuses. In the long term it may help to redress the normative imbalance that exists today in international law: on the one hand a strong and far-reaching protection of the rights of MNEs under investment and arbitration treaties, and on the other hand a weak and very soft system of obligations on the MNE to comply with fundamental human rights and other norms of international law.

1.4.4   The Interaction between Binding and Non-Binding Instruments

While taking into account that the two approaches of accountability and responsibility are at different stages of development and acceptance at the international level, this book intends to frame MNEs' obligations in respect of human rights in terms of responsibility rather than accountability. Although controversy still surrounds the question of identifying substantive standards for corporate responsibility, the present analysis is mostly concerned with the identification of primary rules and substantive standards for the conduct of MNEs, rather than secondary obligations.

It must be added that a broad grey area is also developing. Indeed, a variety of instruments have been developed which, on the one hand, do not fall into the categories of legal responsibility as described above, nor within self-regulation.

With regard to international guidelines for MNEs and companies' codes of conduct, they are indeed neither entirely enforceable domestically, nor entirely non-binding internationally.[82] As a result of the interaction between self-regulation and legal instruments, at least three ways in which soft law may acquire a binding effect have been described.[83] Firstly,

---

[80]   See Kamminga, 'Holding Multinational Corporations Accountable', *supra* n. 70, at 557.

[81]   See D. Weissbrodt and M. Kruger 'The Norms on the Responsibilities of Transnational Corporations and Other Business Enterprises With Regard to Human Rights', in P. Alston, *Non-State Actors and Human Rights*, 2005, Oxford, Oxford University Press, at 315.

[82]   See N. Horn, 'Codes of Conduct for MNEs and Transnational Lex Mercatoria: an International Process of Learning and Law Making', in N. Horn (ed.), *Legal Problems of Code of Conduct for Multinational Enterprises*, 1980, Deventer, Kluwer, 45–81.

[83]   An exhaustive account of the possible legal effects of codes of conduct is provided by Baade, *supra* n. 60, at 407.

codes which originate in agreements within sectoral organizations may constitute legally binding contracts. Secondly, governments and international organizations may make compliance with codes a formal condition for tendering and performance in procurement contracts or in order to gain access to markets.[84] Finally, voluntarily adopted codes can be used by judges to give substantive content to vague normative standards: for instance to see what constitutes 'due diligence'.[85] In the EU context, the most distinctive example of this type of intermediate regulation is provided by the International Framework Agreements signed by MNEs and international trade unions associations, which set the standards against which the company will operate worldwide.

Against this background, it is suggested that two key concepts should be used in order to address the issue of MNEs' accountability for human rights violations.

The first concept is that of complexity. Addressing the responsibility of MNEs for human rights violations is complex because human rights obligations on MNEs are still unspecified and evolving, as they are adapted from the traditional realm of State obligations to obligations of non-state actors. Secondly, although international human rights law also binds MNEs, the scope of their obligations varies according to the context. Commentators usually refer to the notion of the sphere of influence of an MNE or to its proximity to the violations. Thirdly, when we deal with MNEs, we are faced with the myriad of connections that obscure the relationship between MNEs and the human rights victim. For instance, the sub-contracting of services or the support offered to rebel forces in one country pose complicated questions of responsibility.[86]

The second fundamental concept is that of complementarity among different levels of responsibility (international, national and extraterritorial). Applying the concept of complementarity is crucial in understanding that one MNE's behaviour may give rise to different levels of responsibility (for instance, under international human rights law, domestic civil or criminal law) and to the responsibility of several subjects (for instance an individual,

---

[84]   This option is explored by Hanley in the context of the EU. She suggests that access to EU public procurement may be subject to compliance with a European label. See Hanley, *supra* n. 10, at 33.

[85]   P. Muchlinski, 'Human Rights Social Responsibility and the Regulation of International Business: the Development of International Standards by Intergovernmental Organisations' (2003) 3 *Non-State Actors and International Law* 123, at 129.

[86]   These concepts have been developed and suggested in Clapham, *Human Rights Obligations, supra* n. 50 at 561ff.

the company he or she belongs to and, possibly, a State entity with which this organization is complicit) at the same time. These different levels of responsibility and the multiplicity of human rights offenders should not be understood as contradictory or mutually exclusive but rather as complementary. Similarly, complementarity is required among different types of implementing measures: binding and non-binding measures should be understood as complementary rather than mutually exclusive.

1.5 OBJECTIVES, SCOPE AND LIMITATIONS

Given the complexity of the subject matter, it is necessary from the outset to define the limitations and scope of this enquiry.

The objective of this book is threefold. First, corporate responsibility developments at the EU level are used to understand the main clashes outlined above: the intersection of different levels of accountability that range from legally binding to voluntary measures and intermediate initiatives. In order to do so, a tentative distinction between self-regulatory instruments, legal instruments and intermediate ones will be made. The objective of this assessment is not to produce a systematic evaluation of all the norms of EU law dealing with the responsibility of MNEs; neither is it to describe all the examples concerning self regulation within the EU Member States, since they are mushrooming every day. The idea is rather to identify the specific features of the EU legal order as opposed to the international and domestic level, and to explain how these features provide a unique potential to address the issue of MNEs' responsibility for human rights abuses.

Secondly, the gap between the EU's commitment to the respect and promotion of human rights, the potential to regulate the conduct of MNEs and the reluctance in taking steps in this respect will be explored. The normative paradigm I adopt is that, by virtue of its legal order, the EU is bound to respect human rights in all its policies and thus enjoy a certain measure of law-making power in this field. Secondly, the EU, as an international organization, has to act in the field of human rights in accordance with international human rights law. In addition, since the EC has the legal instruments to impose direct legal obligations on companies in certain branches of EU law, coherence and consistency arguments require that the EU regulate the conduct of MNEs based in the EU's Member States for the respect of human rights obligations when operating through their subsidiaries in third countries.

As we will examine, existing EU law indeed has the potential to take measures to hold MNEs accountable. First, the European Union has the capacity to enact legal rules applicable to individuals and enterprises, and it has the power to enforce compliance with such rules autonomously through levying fines and penalties; secondly it can use its external relations instruments to encourage developing countries to raise human rights standards and enforce them on MNEs operating in their countries. Finally, the EU can promote convergence on voluntary initiatives that go under the definition of Corporate Social Responsibility.[87]

Thirdly, proposals for legal reforms in the area of EU external relations will be advanced to allow more visibility to the impact of European MNEs on human rights matters and for the improvement of mechanisms for monitoring this impact. However, it must be pointed out that, in the case of regulation of MNEs, the traditional divide between internal and external action of the EU is also challenged. One of the main features of the regulation of undertakings and groups of undertakings by EU law, as opposed to international law, is that they are regarded as unitarian subjects, regardless of their legal definition. In addition, many branches of EU law, such as competition law, have developed in such a way as to apply to companies wherever they operate, if their activities may have an effect on the EC common market.

It must also be pointed out that, despite the fact that different areas of EU law such as company law and public procurement could be interpreted or revised with a view to contributing to the promotion of human rights, this book will place particular emphasis on the opportunities offered by the external relations of the European Union to raise human rights standards in developing countries and enforce them on MNEs. Several reasons point in this direction.

First, European multinationals have been increasingly subjected to stringent requirements from within, by EU laws that regulate the protection of worker rights, the environment and consumers. The situation changes dramatically where the activities of MNEs' subsidiaries in third countries are concerned. A vast number of cases brought before US and British courts have accused EU multinationals of violating the right to health, the right to life and the exploitation of forced labour and child labour in countries such as South Africa,[88] Nigeria[89] and Myanmar[90]. It

---

[87] See *Corporate Social Responsibility: a Business Contribution to Sustainable Development*, *supra* n. 24; *Implementing the Partnership for Growth and Jobs*, *supra* n. 25; *EU Multi-stakeholders Forum – Final Report*, *supra* n. 48.

[88] See case *Lubbe, supra* n. 20.

[89] See case *Wiva, supra* n. 31.

[90] See testimony by M. Simons for EarthRights International at the hearing of the Development and Co-Operation Committee of the European Parliament on European Oil Companies in Burma of 11 October 2001, available at: http://

is the impact of MNEs' activities that has a particular detrimental impact on third countries, as a result of the practice of delocalisation and out-sourcing of MNEs based in one of the EU Member States.

On the other hand, third countries are the addressees of the European Union development co-operation policy, which sets as its objectives to contribute to the general development and consolidation of democracy and the rule of law and to that of respecting human rights and funda-mental freedoms (Article 177) of the Treaty Establishing the European Communities (TEC). This objective became operational through the inclusion of human rights clauses within the present widespread system of co-operation, association agreements, technical assistance instruments and the Generalised System of Preferences (GSP).[91]

Given the strict link between the external relations of the EU and the promotion of universally recognized human rights, it is suggested that the area of external relations may provide the most useful instruments to improve the accountability of European MNEs operating in third coun-tries. It is suggested, in particular, that the European Union could use and improve existing external relations tools such as human rights clauses included in the external agreements and the human rights special incentive of the Generalised System of Preferences in order to encourage develop-ing countries to raise their human rights standards imposed to companies operating in their country. In this way, indirect human rights obligations of MNEs will be strengthened.

So far the European Union seems to have shown a preference for this pattern. Social and labour considerations are gaining weight in EC development and cooperation and commercial policies. Recently, a call for the respect of the OECD Guidelines for Multinational Enterprises[92] was introduced in the Joint Declaration annexed to the EU Association Agreement with Chile of 2000.[93] Similar considerations are likely to be

---

www.earthrights.org/burmafeature/testimony_at_the_hearing_of_the_develop-ment_committee_of_the_european_parliament.html (accessed 13 June 2005).

[91]   Council Regulation (EC) 980/2005 of 27 June 2005, applying a scheme of generalized tariff preferences [2005] OJ L 169/1 (the GSP Regulation).

[92]   See DAFFE/IME/WPG (2000) 15 final, available at: www.oecd.org/daf/investment/guidelines (accessed 8 March 2004).

[93]   Agreement establishing an association between the European Community and its Member States, of the one part, and the Republic of Chile, of the other part, [2002] OJ L 352/3 and 2005/106/EC: Council decision of 22 November 2004 on the signing and provisional application of an Additional Protocol to the Agreement establishing an association between the European Community and its Member States, of the one part, and the Republic of Chile, of the other part, to take account of the accession of the Czech Republic, the Republic of Estonia,

introduced in future EU agreements with African Caribbean and Pacific (ACP) countries and Latin American countries.[94]

This option has the advantage of building on an existing and well-known mechanism of EU external relations: the use of human rights clauses both in positive and negative terms. In addition, it presents a less controversial option from the standpoint of international human rights law, since it encourages governments to raise their standards and ensure that MNEs comply with them.

This hypothesis is not without criticism. The classic objections to conditionality as a protectionist or neo-colonialist tool can be raised. In addition, the effectiveness of such indirect obligations on the conduct of private actors in developing countries can be questioned. However, it is assumed that a rethinking of EU external relations in the light of international human rights norms could contribute to the improvement of MNEs' respect for human rights. Moreover, coherence and consistency[95] criteria argue in favour of an EU external policy that would balance the protection of economic interest with the promotion of human rights.

Among the different levels of action (international/regional/national) a strictly EU approach will be taken. The analysis will include only the options available to the EU legal framework in the different branches of the EU which affect the conduct of MNEs. Certainly this is not to affirm that the action of the EU can be placed in a void. Therefore, an overview of the international legal framework will also be provided. This is significant because the EU, as an addressee of international law, is said by the European Court of Justice (ECJ) to be bound by the general rules of international law in its conduct and that a violation of customary international law could be relevant to the determination that a piece of Community secondary legislation was invalid and inapplicable to an individual or a legal

---

the Republic of Cyprus, the Republic of Latvia, the Republic of Lithuania, the Republic of Hungary, the Republic of Malta, the Republic of Poland, the Republic of Slovenia and the Slovak Republic to the European Union, [2005] OJ L 38 pp. 1–2.

[94]   See European Commission Directorate-General for Trade Directorate F– WTO: *Sustainable Development, Investment, Standards, Intellectual Property, New Technologies. Bilateral Trade Relations Iv Investments, Standards & Certification, TBT, Note To 133 Committee, Corporate Social Responsibility and Trade Policy – Implementing CSR Practices and the OECD Guidelines for Multinational Enterprises in Developing Countries* Brussels, 7 June 2004.

[95]   See A. Clapham, 'Where is the EU Human Rights Common Foreign Policy and How is it Manifested in Multilateral Fora?', in Alston et al. (eds), *supra* n. 70, at 627.

person.[96] The EC's treaty relations include commitments to respect human rights in the context of relations with third States.[97] The assumption is that the Community considers the Universal Declaration of Human Rights as reflecting the principles of international law binding on the Community and the states with which it concludes such treaties.[98] There is no reason to believe that the EU is not similarly bound by the same international human rights obligations.

Aligning EU law with international human rights law would present several advantages. First, relying on international rather than exclusively on EU human rights instruments would limit the risk of allegations of imposing a European model on third countries or even accusations of using human rights for protectionist purposes. Secondly, the practice of the EU as a subject of international law can contribute to the creation or reinforcement of general principles of international law through its practice.[99] Finally, the EC plays a role in the major multilateral organizations such as the World Trade Organisation (WTO), International Labour Organisation (ILO) and the OECD, making the EU a key actor in North/ South relations.[100] It is an organization which wields enormous economic power on the international scene and great bargaining power in international organizations, such as the UN, the WTO and the OECD, which can

---

[96] See Case C-162/96 *Racke GmbH & Co v Hauptzollant Mainz* [1998] ECR I-3655. According to Tomuschat, the ECJ has become the guardian of legality not only with respect to the three Community treaties, but also with regard to international law in general: C. Tomuschat, 'The International Responsibility of the European Union', in E. Cannizzaro (ed.), *The European Union as an Actor in International Relations*, 2002, The Hague and London, Kluwer Law International, 177, at 187.

[97] See B. Brandtner and A. Rosas, 'Human Rights and the External Relations of the European Union: An Analysis of Doctrine and Practice' (1998) 9 *European Journal of International Law* 469, at 489.

[98] See A. Clapham, *Human Rights Obligations, supra* n. 50, at 177–93. Some authors go a step further and consider the EC bound by the main international instruments for the protection of human rights adopted either within the framework of the Council of Europe or within the United Nations when a significant number of Member States are parties to them. See O. de Schutter, 'The Implementation of the Charter of Fundamental Rights through the Open Method of Coordination', in O. De Schutter and S. Deakin (eds), *Social Rights and Market Forces. The Open Method of Coordination of Employment and Social Policies the Future of Social Europe?* 2004, Brussels, Bruylant, 243.

[99] See B. Simma and P. Alston, 'The Sources of Human Rights Law: Custom, Jus Cogens and General Principles' (1992) 12 *Australian Year Book of International Law* 82.

[100] See C. Bretherthon and J. Vogler, *The European Union as a Global Actor*, 2002, London and New York, Routledge, at 109.

promote the development of a coherent regime for the harmonization and enforcement of more effective mechanisms of accountability at the international level. It follows that the study of MNEs' accountability, although focused on the EU, cannot be limited exclusively to it. An overview of the trends and initiatives on this issue at the international level will provide a necessary background to ensure coherence between EU initiatives and the international framework. The international/EU interaction will be emphasized over the EU/national divide, also because the specific focus of this study is the ways and means of preventing or minimizing the possible negative impact of European MNEs when operating in third countries.

The distinction among different forms of implementation of MNEs' obligations (binding and non-binding measures and the interaction between these two) will be mirrored in the analysis of EU initiatives. The first category would include the use of human rights clauses in external agreements; examples of the second are the initiative on Corporate Social Responsibility and incentive measures, such as technical cooperation, contained in autonomous regulations and in external agreements. The Communication on CSR and the Parliamentary Resolution on a Code of Conduct for European Enterprises Operating in Developing Countries (the Howitt Resolution), enunciate a strategy for the development of an EU framework on corporate responsibility, mainly focused on voluntary initiatives, but without precluding the possibility of development towards a more binding framework. The EU has also been particularly creative in developing instruments targeted on the conduct of MNEs and which represent an interaction between legally binding rules and voluntary schemes. One example is given by the possibility of introducing social concerns, envisaged by the revised Public Procurement Directives.[101] While social clauses will be enshrined in a piece of national legislation as a condition for a public contract, it will be left to companies to decide whether to comply with social requirements in order to access public bids. A different way of interaction is provided by the International Framework Agreements (IFAs), signed by European MNEs and international associations of trade unions. Although these agreements are not legally binding, they are signed in the context of European Works Councils, whose formation is legally required rather than merely voluntary.

This book is primarily concerned with identifying primary obligations on MNEs, as are being developed by international law. Secondly,

---

[101] Directive 2004/18/EC of the European Parliament and of the Council of 31 March 2004, on the coordination of procedures for the award of public works contracts, public supply contracts and public service contracts [2004] OJ L 134/114.

it investigates how the European Union is acting to promote the respect of these obligations by the MNEs which are based on the territory of one of its Member States. This analysis will necessarily include different levels at which MNEs' responsibility can be tackled. A distinction will be made between EU measures addressed either directly to MNEs at the internal and at the external level and measures addressed to States which host European MNEs. Within this framework a further graduation of measures will be made with reference to their legal force. Therefore, a distinction between binding and non-binding, or 'mixed' measures, will be adopted.

1.6 WORK PLAN

This book is divided into four Parts. Part I assesses the scope of MNEs' responsibility for human rights in international law. Chapter 1 develops the conceptual framework against which the book question will be analysed. It draws attention, in particular, to the process of globalisation and to the specific features of MNEs, and the notion of human rights, in order to contextualize the enquiry. In Chapter 2, the option of invoking human rights obligations over MNEs will be examined. Even if the assertion that they have acquired a limited international subjectivity is controversial, they have acquired both substantive and formal protections under international legal instruments and practice. The normative paradigm I adopt is that the progressive acquisition of rights under international law also implies the acquisition of obligations. As human rights are a fundamental part of the general principles of international law, corporations invoking the protection of these principles should also respect human rights as part of those principles governing their transactions.

This inquiry is followed by an attempt to define the scope of the human rights obligations of MNEs (Chapter 3). A brief critical overview of trends in international law regarding the regulation of corporate behaviour will show that there are fast-moving changes in this area which demonstrate that the international actors (both State and non-State) acknowledge that the MNE is not only a subject of international concern, but one in which more legal developments are desirable. This overview, although not exhaustive, seeks to illustrate the main advantages and shortcomings of the options that are currently available in international law to hold MNEs accountable. It also serves as a background in order to understand the attitude of the European Union towards its MNEs operating in developing countries and the ongoing debate on Corporate Social Responsibility generated by the Green Paper 'Promoting a European framework for corporate social responsibility'[102] and the follow-up Communications on Corporate Social Responsibility.[103] The contribution of this part should be understood as providing the necessary framework for the analysis of the book topic. In particular, international standards on MNEs will serve as a benchmark to assess the divergences and similarities between the international and European approach to MNEs' responsibility.

Part II will bring the question of the human rights accountability of MNEs for their activities in developing countries within the European Union framework. First, the issue of the EC/EU's powers to act in the field of human rights will be addressed. Secondly, the question as to why the European Union should take steps to enhance accountability of its economic private actors operating abroad will be tackled. Thirdly, the main initiatives addressed directly to MNEs based in the European Union will be considered. These include the main initiatives both within the European Union and at the external level ranging from binding to non-binding initiatives. At the internal level, among binding initiatives, particular attention will be given to the possibility of introducing social concerns into public procurement. On the side of non-binding measures, the voluntary initiatives promoted by the European Commission that go under the label of 'Corporate Social Responsibility' will be examined. At the external level, the EU's measures addressed to MNEs mainly take the form of codes of conduct – such as the Code of Conduct for Companies Operating in South Africa and the European Union Code of Conduct on Arms Export and the proposal for a European Code of Conduct for European Multinational Enterprises (The Howitt Resolution).[104] In this context, International Framework Agreements (IFAs) can be regarded as one of the most interesting recent instruments developed at the EU level to address MNEs' responsibility for labour rights and human rights. These agreements are concluded between an MNE and a global union federation.[105] While they have the form of a contract between private parties, they have a potential global reach, since IFAs protect the

---

[102]   See Commission of the European Communities, *Green Paper – Promoting a European Framework for Corporate Social Responsibility* COM (2001) 366 final, 18 July 2001.

[103]   *A Business Contribution to Sustainable Development, supra* n. 24; *Implementing the Partnership for Growth, supra* n. 25.

[104]   See *EU Standards for European Enterprises Operating in Developing Countries, supra* n. 72.

[105]   Global Union Federations are the international representatives for unions organized in specific industry sectors or occupational groups.

fundamental social rights of the employees of the company concerned in all its operations.[106]

Part III focuses on measures addressed to States that host MNEs rather than measures addressed directly to MNEs. It suggests that a possible option to promote MNEs' respect for human rights in developing countries is to raise MNEs' human rights standards in developing countries. Governments in developing countries will in turn be encouraged to enforce human rights obligations on MNEs operating in their countries. In addition, the scrutiny of MNEs in developing countries could be enhanced by incentive measures aimed at strengthening local NGOs and increasing awareness about the conduct of MNEs directly at the host State level. Great potential in both respects is offered by the instruments available to the external relations of the European Union Two levels at which the EU can operate will be distinguished (Chapter 7). On the one hand, the EU can encourage governments in developing countries to raise their human rights standards by subjecting access to assistance and to trade to the respect of human rights (so-called conditionality).[107] In turn, governments can enforce such standards on MNEs operating in their countries (indirect obligations on MNEs). To this end, the impact of instruments such as human rights clauses in development and assistance programmes, in the Cotonou Agreement[108] (Chapter 8), the human rights arrangement of the GSP and the reference to the OECD Guidelines in the EC–Chile Agreement (Chapter 9) will be examined.

A Conclusion in Part IV proposes some drafting suggestions for an overall EC/EU policy for improving the human rights responsibility of European MNEs.

---

[106] IFAs are defined by the International Confederation of Free Trade Unions (ICFTU) as: 'A framework agreement is an agreement negotiated between a multinational company and a global union federation concerning the international activities of that company. The main purpose of a framework agreement is to establish a formal ongoing relationship between the multinational company and the global union federation which can solve problems and work in the interests of both parties.' See http://www.icftu.org (accessed 3 May 2006).

[107] See E. Fierro, *The EU's Approach to Human Rights Conditionality in Practice,* 2003, The Hague and London, M. Nijhoff, at 100–102.

[108] Partnership Agreement between the members of the African, Caribbean and Pacific Group of States (ACP) of the one part, and the European Community and its Member States, of the other part, signed in Cotonou on 23 June 2000, 2000/483/EC [2000] OJ L 317.

1.7 TERMINOLOGY

1.7.1 Multinational Enterprises

The essential feature of the MNE is that it has no coherent existence as a legal entity. It is a political and economic reality which articulates itself in a confusing variety of legal forms and devices.[109] Its main features, such as the complexity of its legal structure, the interplay of legal entities and relationships constituting its structure, make the MNE's power elusive and challenging to the political order and rule of law.

The terms multinational enterprise (MNE), transnational corporation (TNC) and multinational corporation (MNC) are generally taken to be interchangeable. Nevertheless, TNC or MNE does imply actual incorporation, while the term multinational enterprise encompasses both a cluster of 'corporations or unincorporated bodies of diverse nationality joined together by ties of common ownership and responsive to a common management strategy'.[110]

Regarding the adjective 'transnational', as opposed to 'multinational', the former emphasizes the company's ability to conduct operations across national borders and was originally reserved for enterprises which were jointly owned and controlled by entities from several countries.

According to the definition given by the OECD, MNEs are defined as 'companies or other entities whose ownership is private, State or mixed established in different countries and so linked that one or more of them may be able to exercise a significant influence over the activities of others, and in particular, to share knowledge and resources with others'. However, the OECD Guidelines revised in 2000 do not define the term 'multinational enterprises', a concept which embraces a diversity of situations found throughout the business world. Rather, they describe some general criteria covering a broad range of multinational activities and arrangements. These arrangements can include traditional international direct investment based on equity participation, or other means which do not necessarily include an equity capital element. Majority ownership is not the exclusive form of linkage between two companies in different countries which allows one to exercise a significant influence over the activities of others. Accordingly, an entity may be considered part of

---

[109] See P.I. Blumberg, *The Multinational Challenge to Corporation Law. The Search for a New Corporate Personality*, 1993, Oxford, Oxford University Press, at 232ff.

[110] See D. Vagts, 'The Multinational Enterprise: A New Challenge for Transnational Law' (1970) 83 *Harvard Law Review* 739, at 740.

a multinational enterprise without necessarily being a majority owned subsidiary. The sharing of knowledge and resources among companies or other entities does not in itself indicate that such companies or entities constitute a multinational enterprise.[111]

The ILO Tripartite Declaration specifies that:

> Multinational enterprises include enterprises, whether they are of public, mixed or private ownership, which own or control production, distribution, services or other facilities outside the country in which they are based. The degree of autonomy of entities within multinational enterprises in relation to each other varies widely from one such enterprise to another, depending on the nature of the links between such entities and their fields of activity and having regard to the great diversity in the form of ownership, in the size, in the nature and location of the operations of the enterprises concerned. Unless otherwise specified, the term 'multinational enterprise' is used in this Declaration to designate the various entities (parent companies or local entities or both or the organisation as a whole) according to the distribution of responsibilities among them, in the expectation that they will cooperate and provide assistance to one another as necessary to facilitate observance of the principles laid down in the Declaration.[112]

More recent UN documents and literature also refer more generically to the 'private sector', business or global businesses.[113] On the contrary the UN Norms adopt the most encompassing definition of transnational businesses. According to the Norms:

> The term 'transnational corporation' refers to an economic entity operating in more than one country or a cluster of economic entities operating in two or more countries – whatever their legal form, whether in their home country or country of activity, and whether taken individually or collectively. 21. The phrase 'other business enterprise' includes any business entity, regardless of the international or domestic nature of its activities, including a transnational corporation, contractor, subcontractor, supplier, licensee or distributor; the corporate, partnership, or other legal form used to establish the business entity; and the nature of the ownership of the entity.[114]

Whatever the precise definition, there are particular economic and legal features that differentiate these private economic actors (MNEs, TNCs, MNEs) from those with merely domestic activities.

---

[111] See OECD Guidelines, *supra* n. 13.
[112] See ILO Tripartite Declaration, *supra* n. 12, at para 6.
[113] Whereas the UN Global compact refers more generally to companies or businesses. See http://www.unglobalcompact.org/Portal/Default.asp? (accessed 4 July 2006).
[114] See UN Norms, *supra* n. 14.

For the purpose of this book the term 'multinational enterprise' will be used. While recognizing that the problem of responsibility involves all types of commercial enterprises and many of the legal and ethical considerations apply equally to multinational enterprises and to those with domestic operations, the present study will focus mainly on MNEs. A further argument in favour of limiting the scope of this study to MNEs is that it will focus on how the EU is dealing with the issue of the responsibility of European MNEs whose parent company is based or registered in one of the EU's Member States, and conducting business in one or more country outside the EU.

1.7.2 Human Rights

For the purpose of this chapter, the starting point for defining 'human rights' is the international law of human rights. Human rights can be approached from different angles and different levels of abstraction. Four planes of discussion may be distinguished: philosophical, sociological, political and normative. In tracing the origins of human rights Shestack[115] distinguishes the five groups of theories: religion, natural law, positivism, Marxism and the sociological approach.

Theories based on religious assumptions accept the existence of supra-positive law, the core of which is the divine being: since human beings were created in the image of God, a human being is a value in itself and each human being deserves inherent dignity originating from natural law.[116] According to the theory of natural law, human rights are vested in individuals by virtue of their social and rational nature and independently of legislative *fiat*.[117] A reaction of natural law theories was the emergence of legal positivism based on the methodological distinction between 'is' and 'ought to be', consequently the State legislator's will was recognized

---

[115] See J.J. Shestack, 'The Jurisprudence of Human Rights', in T. Meron (ed.), *Human Rights in International Law: Legal and Policy Issues*, 1984, Oxford, Clarendon Press, 69, at 70.

[116] See R. Cassin, 'From Ten Commandments to the Rights of Man', in H.H Cohn and S.G. Shoham (eds), *Essays in Honour of Haim Cohen*, 1971, Tel Aviv and New York, 13.

[117] The tradition of natural law concept dates back to ancient times and its roots may be found in the philosophies of both Stoics and Aristotle. It was continued in medieval times by Thomas Aquinas. From Grotius and Pufendorf a process of secularisation can easily be traced. John Locke reformulated the theory in the seventeenth century. In revised form natural rights philosophy had a renaissance in the aftermath of the Second World War. For an exposition of the theory of natural law see J. Maritain, *The Rights of Man and Natural Law*, 1980, London, UMI; J. Donnelly, 'Human Rights as Natural Rights' (1982) 4 *Human Rights Quarterly* 391.

as the only source of law.[118] The general assumption of Marx's theory states that particular social relations are the backbone of human rights as a historical category.[119] Treating human beings only on the basis of their historic presence, this theory does not provide a sufficient foundation for a universal account of human rights. Finally, in the sociological school of jurisprudence some withdrawal from both the apriorism of natural rights and the analytical school of jurisprudence can be noticed. According to this relativistic approach the interest forms the background of any law, so that the universality of human rights cannot be justified.

Even if it is undeniable that these theories have influenced the conceptualization of human rights, however, from the Second World War onwards the normative aspect of human rights has become the centre of interest and acquired inseparable connotations with the positivisation of international law that concentrated on the protection of individual rights. Nowadays, human rights are a defined area of international law laid down in international treaties and conventions and interpreted by international bodies and international courts.[120]

Human rights treaties have distinct characteristics. The treaties are arranged in a series of affirmations, each affirmation introducing a right that all individuals have by virtue of the fact that they are human. Therefore human rights law concentrates on the value of the persons themselves, who have the right to benefit from particular freedoms and forms of protection.[121] Consequently, human rights law is not limited to any particular sphere of activity. Human rights law should apply as much to economic issues as to political, social and environmental ones.

The basic foundation for international law on human rights is the Universal Declaration of Human Rights (UDHR)[122] of 1948, which

---

[118]   See H. Kelsen, *Principles of International Law*, 1959, New York, Rinehart. Positivist theory was partially revised in critical terms by Hart. See H.L.A. Hart, 'Positivism and the Separation of Law and Morals' (1955) 71 *Harvard Law Review* 593.

[119]   K. Marx, *Economic and Philosophic Manuscripts of 1844*, 1977, Moscow, Progress, at 153.

[120]   The historical development and the disruptive effect of human rights are described in A. Cassese, *Human Rights in a Changing World*, 1990, Cambridge, Polity Press. See, also N. Bobbio, *The Age of Rights*, 1996, Cambridge, UK: Polity Press; See H.J. Steiner and P. Alston, *International Human Rights in Context: Law, Politics, Morals*, 2000, Oxford and New York, Oxford University Press.

[121]   See G.C. Jonathan, 'Human Rights Covenants', in R. Bernhardt et al. (eds), *Encyclopaedia of Public International Law*, 2000, Amsterdam and New York, North-Holland and Elsevier, at 916.

[122]   See UN, GA Res. 217A (III), A/810 (1948), at 71.

contains both civil and political rights as well as economic, social and cultural rights. Certain aspects of the UDHR are considered customary law,[123] and two legally binding treaties have been developed to implement it: the International Covenant on Civil and Political Rights (ICCPR)[124] and the International Covenant on Economic, Social and Cultural Rights (ICESCR). In addition to these universal documents there are a broad range of treaties and declarations, some of which relate to specific rights or classes of persons including the convention Against Torture and other Cruel, Inhuman or Degrading Treatment and Punishment,[125] and the Convention on the Elimination of all Forms of Discrimination Against Women (CEDAW).[126] Other human rights treaties have been adopted at a regional level such as the European Convention on Human Rights (ECHR),[127] the American Convention on Human Rights (1969)[128] and the African Charter on Human and Peoples' Rights (1981).[129]

The ICCPR and the ICESCR have long been interpreted as imposing different legal obligations. Whereas the ICCPR requires each State party to respect and to ensure to all individuals within its jurisdiction the rights recognized in the Covenant,[130] parties to the ICESCR are required to merely undertake steps to the maximum available resources and to achieve progressively the full realization of the rights recognized in the Covenant.[131] Economic, social and cultural rights have for a long time been interpreted as objectives or programmatic rights rather than individual rights. This interpretation was based on the assumption that

---

[123]   See J.C. Salcedo, 'Human Rights Universal Declaration', in Bernhardt et al. (eds), *supra* n. 121, at 925.

[124]   See 19 December 1966, 999 UNTS 171 (entered into force 23 March 1976).

[125]   See UN, GA Res. 39/46, annex, 39 UN GAOR Supp. (No. 51), A/39/51 (1984), at 197 (entered into force 26 June 1987).

[126]   See UN, GA Res. 34/180, 34 UN GAOR Supp. (No. 46), A/34/46, at 193 (entered into force 3 September 1981).

[127]   See European Convention for the Protection of Human Rights and Fundamental Freedoms (ETS 5), 213 UNTS 222 (entered into force 3 September 1953, as amended by Protocols Nos 3, 5, and 8, which entered into force on 21 September 1970, 20 December 1971 and 1 January 1990 respectively).

[128]   See American Convention on Human Rights, 36 *OAS Treaty Series*, 1144 UNTS 123 (entered into force 18 July 1978), reprinted in *Basic Documents Pertaining to Human Rights in the Inter-American System*, OEA/Ser.L.V/II.82 doc.6 rev.1 (1992), at 25.

[129]   See African Charter on Human and Peoples' Rights, adopted 27 June, 1981, OAU Doc. CAB/LEG/67/3 rev. 5, (1982) 21 *International Legal Materials* 58, (entered into force 21 October 1986).

[130]   See Art 2(1) ICCPR.

[131]   See Art 2(1) ICESCR.

economic, social and cultural rights require action on the part of the State (so-called positive rights) and the availability of resources. Moreover, economic, social and cultural rights were often conceived as collective rather than individual rights.

If the protection of these two sets of rights in two different legal instruments was justified historically as being the residue of a long-term Western versus socialist divide, however, the prevalence of one of the categories of rights was not tenable either on theoretical and normative grounds.[132] Thus, civil and political rights often require positive measures for their realization, as well as economic, social and cultural rights; secondly, both categories of rights give rise to individual rights; thirdly most international human rights instruments such as the UDHR and the International Convention on the Elimination of all Forms of Racial Discrimination to quote but a few, are not structured in terms of the distinction between civil, political rights and economic, social and cultural rights.

The recognition of the indivisibility and interdependence of civil, political and economic social and cultural rights[133] is one of the most important features of the contemporary conception of human rights. According to the usual interpretation these principles point to the fact that one right cannot be accorded priority over other rights. Both categories of rights should be seen as complementary.[134] Although differences between both categories remain, it has been underlined that the realization of a group of rights largely depends on the enjoyment of the others. Individual development, indeed, requires appropriate social political, economic, cultural and ecological conditions. Moreover, ensuring a minimum in one of these is indispensable to developing or preventing degradation in another one; for example, ensuring minimal social standards is necessary for the enjoyment of political rights.[135]

---

[132] See A. Rosas and M. Sheinin, 'Categories and Beneficiaries of Human Rights', in R. Hanski and M. Suksi (eds), *An Introduction to the International Protection of Human Rights: a Textbook,* 1999, Turku/Åbo, Institute for Human Rights, Åbo Akademi University, 49.

[133] The progressive recognition that economic, social and cultural rights are on the same footing as civil and political rights is thoroughly described in A. Eide et al. (eds), *Economic, Social and Cultural Rights,* The Hague and Boston, M. Nijhoff, 2001, 250.

[134] See K. Drzewicki, 'Internationalization and Juridization of Human Rights', in Hanski and Suksi (eds), *supra* n. 132, at 42. On the justiciability of economic, social and cultural rights see A. Rosas and M. Scheinin, 'Economic and Social Rights as Legal Rights', in Eide, *supra* n. 133, at 41.

[135] See T. Van Boven, 'General Course on Human Rights' (1993) 4 *Collected Courses of the Academy of European Law* 1 at 50.

The principle of indivisibility and interrelation of all human rights as reaffirmed in the Vienna Declaration[136] is particularly relevant to the issue of MNEs' responsibility for breaches of human rights. In fact, the argument that economic and social rights prevail over civil and political rights has often been used by repressive governments, which claim to promote economic development of their citizens, while denying their basic civil and political rights. A similar argument is often put forward by MNEs to justify their presence in States with human rights abuse records, where companies defend their presence on the basis that they contribute to the production of wealth, and thus to the improvement of economic and social rights.[137] However, basic civil and political rights such as the right to life or freedom of expression are often overlooked.[138]

Another characteristic of human rights is their universality. Although the universality of human rights is still an object of criticism,[139] there has been a progressive globalization of human rights and an overwhelming majority of governments have formally committed themselves to respect them. As pointed out by Donnelly the *moral* universality of human rights has been translated into their international *normative* universality.[140]

---

[136] All human rights are universal, indivisible and interdependent and interrelated. The international community must treat human rights globally in a fair and equal manner, on the same footing, and with the same emphasis. While the significance of national and regional particularities and various historical, cultural and religious backgrounds must be borne in mind, it is the duty of States, regardless of their political, economic and cultural systems, to promote and protect all human rights and fundamental freedoms. See UN, *UN World Conference on Human Rights: Vienna Declaration and Programme of Action*, A/CONF.157/23 (1993).

[137] See R. Sullivan and D. Hogan, 'The Business Case for Human Rights – The Amnesty International Perspective', in Bottomley and Kinley *supra* n. 17, 69, at 74. See also Chandler, *supra* n. 44, at 39.

[138] See D. Aguirre, 'Multinational Corporations and the Realisation of Economic, Social and Cultural Rights' (2004) 35 *California Western International Law Journal* 53 at 61.

[139] See C. Brown, 'Universal Human Rights: A Critique' (1997) 1 *The International Journal of Human Rights* 41; H. Bielefeldt, 'Western Versus Islamic Human Rights Conceptions? A Critique of Cultural Essentialism in the Discussion of Human Rights' (2000) 1 *Political Theory* 90; B. Parekh, *Rethinking Multiculturalism Cultural Diversity and Political Theory*, 2000, London, Macmillan, at 264.

[140] See J. Donnelly, *Universal Human Rights in Theory and Practice*, 2003, Ithaca, Cornell University Press, at 2. The universality of human rights is upheld by the majority of commentators. Cassese maintains that: 'despite the differences . . . a core of values and criteria universally accepted by all States is gradually emerging'. See Cassese, *Human Rights*, *supra* n. 120, at 64. The universality of human rights is upheld by the majority of commentators. See also F. Capotorti, 'Human Rights the Hard Road Towards Universality', in R.St.J. Macdonald and D.M. Johnston

All States proclaim their acceptance of and adherence to international human rights norms and charges of human rights violations are among the strongest complaints that can be made in international relations. Three quarters of the worlds' States have undertaken international human rights obligations to implement these rights by becoming parties to international human rights covenants. Therefore, it can be said that human rights law provides if not a universal, at least the most widely accepted benchmark against which the action of States and individuals, including MNEs, can be measured worldwide.

While the primary sources of international human rights law is found in the United Nations Charter, the Universal Declaration, and UN human rights Treaties, there is no agreement over the formation of a general, non treaty-based, international law of human rights. Three main approaches may be distinguished. According to the customary law approach, constant State practice matched with *opinio iuris* contributed to substantiate human rights in terms of customary international law. This option, however, is fraught with controversy.[141] According to the authentic interpretation approach, the Universal Declaration and the body of rules and principles built upon it are to be considered an authoritative interpretation of the UN Charter. Others refer to human rights as being part of the concept of general principles of law.[142] The last option is usually favoured on the basis that it is better suited than customary law to meeting the requirements for the formation of *jus cogens*.[143]

Despite the debate over the sources, however, the proposition that a body of general international human rights law has emerged is today no longer seriously disputed with regard to some of the most fundamental human rights, which outlaw genocide, torture, slavery, racial discrimination and other large scale violations of human rights. Without expressly

---

(eds), *The Structure and Process of International Law: Essays in Legal Philosophy, Doctrine and Theory*, 1983, Leiden, Nijhoff, 977. C. Tomuschat, 'Is Universality of Human Rights Standards an Outdated and Utopian Concept?', in B. Roland and D. Nickel (eds), *Das Europa der zweiten Generation: Gedachtnisschrift für Christoph Sasse*, 1981, Kehl am Rein, NP Engel Verlag, at 585.

[141] See Simma and Alston *supra* n. 99, at 100.

[142] According to Article 38 of the Statute of the International Court of Justice, general principles of law constitute a third source of international law besides treaties and custom.

[143] Simma and Alston, *supra* n. 99 at 28 and B. Simma, 'International Human Rights and General International Law: A comparative Analysis' (1993) 4 *Collected Courses of the Academy of European Law* 163, at 228. In the same sense L. Henkin, *International Law: Politics and Values*, 1995, Dordrecht and Boston, M. Nijhoff, at 61–2.

using the notion of *jus cogens*,[144] the ICJ implied the existence of obligations *erga omnes* in the *Barcelona Traction* case.[145] The Court stated that such obligations derive from the outlawing of an act of aggression, and of genocide and rules concerning the basic rights of the human person.

Defining human rights as constituting an inherent part of international law and placing fundamental human rights at the top of the hierarchy of international law, would constitute the basic assumptions to individuate human rights obligations on MNEs.

Although these arguments will be explained in greater detail below, it is worth anticipating that estoppel arguments require that a subject that invokes international law to protect its rights would be equally bound by duties enshrined in international law in respect of these. In the case of MNEs, since they have not hesitated to invoke, for instance, the protection of property rights and investors' rights before international arbitration bodies[146] and even regional human rights courts,[147] they cannot claim to be absolved by international obligations when it comes to human rights abuses.

Secondly, human rights as a uniform and universally recognized body of law is particularly well suited to constitute a minimum core of obligations for subjects that can easily defy the boundaries of national law and are able to take advantage of weaker legislative and jurisdictional systems. Once admitted that at least a number of basic human rights are universally recognized and accepted, compliance with these standards should be ensured even in States with lax legislative and judiciary systems. The local law defence will not operate where the relevant area of law is not regulated or is clearly below internationally recognized human rights standards.[148]

Finally, the strict interdependence and interrelation of human rights militates in favour of not limiting aprioristically MNEs' responsibility to a *numerus clausus* of obligations. The most recent UN documents endorse this approach by mentioning all UN human rights treaties and declarations as reference texts for MNEs' behaviour.[149]

---

[144]   The notion of *jus cogens* refers to those norms of international law from which no derogation is possible. This notion finds its positive recognition under Art 53 of the Vienna Convention of the law of the treaties, a treaty is void if, at the time of its conclusion, it conflicts with a peremptory norm of general international law.

[145]   See Case *Barcelona Traction, Light and Power Co. Ltd. (Belgium v Spain)* (1970) ICJ Rep 3.

[146]   See Sornarajah, *supra* n. 5, at 151–170.

[147]   M. Addo, 'The Corporation as a Victim of Human Rights Violations' in Addo, *supra* n. 28, 187, at 194.

[148]   Joseph, 'Taming the Leviathans', *supra* n. 7, at 191.

[149]   UN Norms, *supra* n. 14.

The relevance of the principle of interrelation of human rights to the issue of MNEs' accountability is shown by the relationship between the right to elementary education and the prohibition of child labour. On the one hand, the enjoyment and fulfilment of the right to free and compulsory elementary education is primarily dependent on States' compliance with their international obligations. On the other hand, this right can be hampered by MNE failure to respect the prohibition of child labour. Moreover, as mentioned above, the impact of MNEs' activities has become so pervasive that they may virtually affect, either directly or indirectly, and in varying degrees, every aspect of human life, so that the ways and extent of their impact on human rights is difficult to foresee. For instance, in practice a lot of cases have witnessed the involvement of MNEs in breaches of human rights obligations that apparently seem not to be applicable to corporations but only *vis-à-vis* States, such as the right to fair trial.[150]

---

[150] See *Wiva* case, *supra* n. 31.

2 Multinational enterprises as addressees of international law

2.1 INTRODUCTION

The question of whether MNEs can be held accountable at the international level for human rights violations raises the difficult problem of whether corporations can acquire rights and duties under international law. As discussed above, MNEs pose challenges to traditional legal categories.[1] Firstly, the status of MNEs is not expressly recognized under international law. MNEs defines more an economic entity, rather than a legal one. Its branches, subsidiaries and shareholders can be spread across many States and create an economic unity. In addition, most of the distorting power of MNEs derives from decisions and activities taking place outside the particular country and therefore outside the control of the State.[2] This chapter argues that the concept of legal personality, as defined by recent development in international practice, doctrine and case law, is evidence of the fact that MNEs have increasingly become the addressees of norms under the international legal system.

2.2 THE CONCEPT OF LEGAL PERSONALITY

The concept of legal personality in international law,[3] as in all branches of law, means that a person possesses the capacity to be the subject of legally

---

[1] Henkin, *supra* Ch.1 n. 143, at 161.
[2] Ibid., at 103.
[3] Subject is used synonymously with the term legal personality. According to Mosler 'subjects and personality became interchangeable for two reasons: in classical international law States were, with some anomalous exceptions, the only subjects of international law [. . .]. The second reason is the still controversial question whether a minimum scope of capacity is needed for participation as a subject of international legal relations.' H. Mosler, 'Subjects of International Law', in Bernhardt et al. (eds), *Encyclopaedia of Public International Law*, *supra* Ch.1 n. 121, at 712. P.M. Dupuy is critical of the trend in North American doctrine to substitute the legal notion of 'international subjects' with that of actors in inter-

relevant situations. These situations may be rights or claims, duties or obligations, and they may be competences to act in an organized society.

While international law still refers above all to States, the international legal order has undergone a fundamental change since the Second World War, as the number of subjects of international law has increased. Two major developments have prompted this evolution. On the one hand, the landmark opinion by the International Court of Justice (ICJ) in the *Reparation for Injuries Suffered in the Service of the UN*[4] case reversed the dominant doctrine according to which there was no alternative to full international legal personality owned by States and paved the way for the possibility of enlarging the number of legal subjects, according to the social needs mirrored by the development of the international legal framework.[5] The Court, invited to examine the question of whether the United Nations had international legal personality, affirmed that legal subjects can have varying degrees of personality according to the needs of the community.

The second major development was the Universal Declaration of Human Rights of 1948, which launched the so-called human rights revolution.[6] By endowing the individual with rights and duties[7] at the international level, human rights law recognized a new central subject of international law. Thus, individuals, international organizations, insurgents and national liberation movements, and (more controversially) non-governmental organizations and companies have become relevant in certain fields of international law, by the acquisition of varying degrees of substantial and procedural rights and duties.

While many commentators still reaffirm that only sovereign States enjoy

---

national relations. See. P.M. Dupuy, *L'Unité de l'Ordre Juridique International, Cours Général de Droit International Public 2002*, Recueil des Cours, Académie de Droit International de La Hague (2003) at 107.

⁴ *Reparation for Injuries Suffered in the Service of the United Nations*, Advisory Opinion (1949) ICJ Rep 174, at 179. In the present case the ICJ held that according to this definition the United Nations is a subject of international law.

⁵ Ibid., at para. 109.

⁶ Dupuy talks about 'la révolution de droits de l'homme', Dupuy, *supra* Ch.2 n. 3, at 114. On the 'disruptive' effect of human rights in various areas of international affairs see also Cassese, *Human Rights, supra* Ch.1 n. 120, at 162–181.

⁷ See B. Conforti, *Diritto Internazionale*, 2002, Naples, Editoriale Scientifica, at 22; A. Cassese, *International Law in a Divided World*, 1989, Oxford, Oxford University Press, at 99; F. Francioni, 'Alternative Perspectives on International Responsibility for Human Rights Violations by Multinational Corporations', in Wolfgang Benedek et al. (eds), *supra* Ch.1 n. 71. V. Lowe, 'Corporations as International Actors and International Law Makers' (2004) 14 *Italian Yearbook of International Law* 23; G. Arangio-Ruiz, 'Dualism Revisited. International Law and Inter-individual Law' (2003) 86 *Rivista di Diritto Internazionale* 909, at 999.

full legal capacity (comprising all legal positions, rights, obligations and competences), they nonetheless recognize that new subjects are able to enjoy a limited legal personality in international law.

Cassese identifies primary subjects of international law, that is States, whose existence follows from a *de facto* process, and derivative subjects, such as international organizations and the individual, that find the source of their personality in a decision by States. Henkin rejects the assumption that States are the only subjects of international law but underlines that only States can enforce those laws that create other entities and they can even delegate their law-making authority and grant personhood to other bodies.[8] Brownlie refers to the definition of subjects of international law given by the ICJ in the *Reparation for Injury* case. According to this definition a subject of the law is an entity capable of possessing international rights and duties and having the capacity to maintain its rights by bringing international claims. Despite his warning against an easy generalization of the subject of legal personality, he recognizes the existence of a number of entities with personality 'for particular purposes'.[9]

Apart from international organizations, individuals have acquired an increasingly relevant role in international life.[10] As noted by Cassese, one of the main breakthrough effects of human rights law was the acknowledgement of new subjects on the international stage: individuals.[11] However, he immediately narrows down the scope of this affirmation by pointing out that their powers are extremely limited and they have no mechanisms by which to enforce them. In the light of the progress in international human rights law, in international dispute settlement and international adjudication in the last ten years this position can be slightly revised.[12]

---

[8]   See Cassese, *International Law supra* Ch.2 n. 7 at 100ff. Henkin, *supra* Ch.1 n. 143, at 16–17.

[9]   Brownlie distinguishes international law subjects: in established legal persons, special types of personality and controversial candidates to legal personality, and includes MNEs in the latter. I. Brownlie, *Principles of International Law*, 1998, Oxford and New York, Clarendon Press and Oxford University Press, at 57–68.

[10]   See K.J. Partsch, 'Individuals in International Law', in Bernhardt et al., *Encyclopedia of Public International Law, supra* Ch.1 n. 121, 957 at 962.

[11]   See Cassese, *Human Rights, supra* Ch.1 n. 120, at 163

[12]   For a critique to the limited individuals' access to human rights enforcement procedures see P.M. Dupuy, *Droit International Public*, 2002, Paris, Dalloz, at 234. Vicuña provides an update reconstruction of individuals access to international jurisdictions, F.O. Vicuña, *International Dispute Settlement in an Evolving Global Society: Constitutionalization, Accessibility, Privatization*, 2004, Cambridge, Cambridge University Press.

The individual as a human being, without consideration of his/her nationality is protected by universal and regional treaties on human rights and by activities of international organizations. International conventions on human rights constitute international obligations on the participating States to treat individuals and, under certain conditions, groups of individuals according to the provisions of these treaties. Furthermore, a general consensus has developed in international law that most of these rights (at least the basic provisions, if not always the detailed provisions or limitations) have to be guaranteed by virtue of general international law.[13]

The acquisition of rights by the individual has been paralleled by the acquisition of duties.[14] Nowadays it may be clearly affirmed that international law imposes obligations directly upon all individuals of the world, irrespective of the intervention of their legal systems. These obligations relate both to conflict and to peacetime (crimes against humanity, genocide, aggression, terrorism, slave trading and torture).[15]

Other cases of limited subjectivity, such as insurgents and rebel groups, seem to be less clear cut, but they still follow the rights and duties structure. Rebels acquire the status of insurgents when third States or the government against which they are fighting consider them as the *de facto* authority in the territory of their occupation.[16] As a consequence of recognition rebels acquire rights and obligations derived from treaty-making and *ius in bello*. For instance, in certain circumstances, primarily dependent on *de facto* administration of specific territories, they can enter into valid agreements. On the other hand, rules of international law regarding the conduct of war and neutrality become applicable to the relations between the recognizing State and the community recognized as the belligerent power.[17]

Contemporary international law tends to distinguish rebels from national liberation movements. Although in both cases recognition is the central element, however, it is questionable whether it is sufficient or decisive.[18] The rationale for the recognition of national liberation movements by the international community is not their effective control over a part of

---

[13]   See Cassese, *International Law*, *supra* n. 7, at 99–103; Simma, 'International Human Rights and General International Law', *supra* n. 143, at 163–236.

[14]   See Brownlie, *supra* n. 9, at 553–602.

[15]   See Cassese, *International Law*, *supra* n. 7, at 79.

[16]   See M.J. Gamboa, *Dictionary of International Law and Diplomacy*, 1973, Quezon City, Phoenix, AZ, at 146.

[17]   See Cassese, *International Law*, *supra* n. 7, at 68.

[18]   M. Noortmann, 'Non-State Actors in International Law', in B. Arts et al. (eds), *Non State Actors in International Relations*, 2001, Aldershot and Burlington, VT, Ashgate, at 59–67.

a country's territory, but the acknowledgement of their goals, such as the struggle against colonial domination, racist oppression or alien domination, which are legitimate by virtue of the principle of self determination.[19] Also, in this case, even if their recognition was carried out primarily for granting them rights, they still acquired international duties. On the one hand, national liberation movements were granted the right to be interlocutors in the international legal process. They have attended General Assembly meetings and Security Council meetings. On the other hand, national liberation movements can become parties to the First Additional Protocol to the Geneva Convention by unilateral declaration and become subject to the rights and duties enshrined therein.[20]

This brief account of historical development and leading doctrine shows that the concept of legal personality of non-state actors in international law is still controversial and not precisely defined. The modalities of acquiring legal personality, the extent, scope and the precise consequences of acquiring it are not specifically defined. It can be inferred that the concept of legal personality is flexible and subject to evolution.[21] Rosalyn Higgins and Myres S. McDougal suggest that the notion of legal personality is a legal construction that not always reflects reality. Higgins suggests instead the use of the term 'participants' to the international legal process, which would include individuals, MNEs and NGOs.[22]

Nonetheless, commentators point to the direction that there are no inherent legal obstacles to the creation of new international subjects which enjoy different degrees of personality. This argument is reinforced by the functionalist approach indicated by the ICJ in the *Reparation for Injury* case, which inferred the UN's international legal personality from the concrete powers it performed. The Court also pointed out that the scope of legal personality may vary according to the function performed by the subject. The function will also delimit the capacities enjoyed by the subject. Finally, according to the ICJ jurisprudence, a cluster of common features defining international personality can be inferred. A subject of international law is an entity which possesses international rights and duties and has the capacity to maintain its rights by bringing international claims. In addition, according to the principle of functionality these

---

[19]   See Cassese, *International Law*, *supra* n. 6, at 91.
[20]   Mosler, *supra* n. 3, at 724.
[21]   See Dupuy, *supra* n. 3, at 118.
[22]   See R. Higgins, *Problems and Processes: International Law and How We Use It*, 1999, Oxford, Oxford University Press, at 49–50; M.S. McDougal, 'Some Basic Theoretical Concepts about International Law: A Policy-Oriented Framework of Inquiry' (1960) 4 *The Journal of Conflict Resolution* 337.

capacities do not all need to be present at the same time in order to define international subjectivity.[23]

Another point worth stressing is that a common feature of the acquisition of varying degrees of personality is that all the new subjects – individuals, international organizations, insurgents and national liberation movements have acquired rights and duties under international law in a parallel manner. MNEs represent an anomaly, since their progressive acquisition of rights has not been matched by a similar acquisition of duties.[24]

2.3 MNEs IN INTERNATIONAL LAW: FROM RIGHTS TO OBLIGATIONS

In the light of the above definition of legal personality, this section will analyze whether and to what extent MNEs can be considered addressees of norms of international law.

There is little agreement among scholars about attributing international legal personality to MNEs.[25] Even when MNEs are recognized as subjects, scholars underline the limited scope of their personality.[26] Brownlie includes MNEs among the controversial candidates for international personality.[27] According to Cassese, despite the fact that MNEs can conclude transactions with States and their disputes with States can be submitted to

---

[23]   See Dupuy, *supra*, n. 3, at 111.

[24]   See G. Uriz-Hernandez, 'Human Rights as the Business of Business. The Application of Human Rights Standards to the Oil Industry' (PhD thesis on file at the European University Institute, Florence, 2005). On the same line Kamminga, 'Holding Multinational Corporations Accountable', *supra* Ch.1 n. 70, at 557.

[25]   *Contra* According to Malanczuk the fact that individuals or companies are the beneficiaries of many rules of international law does not mean that these rules create rights for the individual or companies, in much the same way as laws prohibiting cruelty to animals do not create rights for animals. Malanczuk, *supra* Ch.1 n. 7, at 100; Anzilotti contends that only States are subjects of international law, D. Anzilotti and G.C. Gidel, *Cours de Droit International*, 1999, Paris, L.G.D.J diffuseur, Editions Panthéon-Assas, at 134.

[26]   See Brownlie, *supra* n. 9, at 66; A. Clapham, 'The Question of Jurisdiction under International Criminal Law over Legal Persons: Lessons from the Rome Conference on an International Criminal Court', in Kamminga and Zia-Zarifi (eds), *supra* Ch.1 n. 21, at 142. *Contra* Cassese, *International Law, supra* n. 7, at 103. The criticism, however, is limited to the recognition of the MNEs as 'international subjects proper', that is, on the same footing as States.

[27]   See Brownlie, *supra* n. 9, at 66.

international tribunals, they have not been upgraded by States as proper international subjects. He concludes that:

> multinational corporations possess no international rights and duties: they are only subjects to municipal and transnational law.[28] Henkin, in contrast, maintains that 'in a privatized world the company may prove to be the essential unit of the world economy. It may be time for the system slowly to re-conceive the company and rethink the notion of nationality of companies. It may be time to give serious thought to establishing the multinational company as a new entity in the international system'.[29]

Dupuy underlines the limited character of MNE personality,[30] but also affirms that there is no legal obstacle to the creation of such a legal situation.

Traditional international law did not recognize companies as subjects of international law. In the *Anglo-Iranian Oil*[31] case the ICJ refused to define the agreements between a corporation and a State as an international agreement.[32] For instance, in the *Barcelona Traction*[33] case the ICJ maintained that companies are dependent on States to exercise diplomatic protection on their behalf.[34]

A historical analysis shows that MNEs have gradually acquired rights, and in particular procedural rights, and duties in specific areas of international law. Since the 1950s the capacity of MNEs to enter into contracts regulated by international law has been recognized.[35] During the 1970s the emphasis was placed on the protection of companies and in par-

---

[28]   See Cassese, *International Law, supra* n. 7, at 103.

[29]   See Henkin, *supra* Ch.1 n. 143, at 17, 24, 159.

[30]   Dupuy affirms '*On sera en présence d'une personnalité monofonctionnelle et temporaire*'; Dupuy, *supra* n. 3, at 112.

[31]   See *Anglo Iranian Oil (United Kingdom v Iran)*, Judgement, [1952] ICJ Rep 96, at 112ff. For a commentary on this case see F. Francioni, *Imprese Multinazionali, Protezione Diplomatica e Responsabilità Internazionale*, 1979, Naples, Giuffré, at 19.

[32]   Ibid., Francioni, *supra* n. 31 at 19.

[33]   See *Barcelona Traction, Light and Power Co.* Ltd (*Belgium v Spain*), Judgement [1970] ICJ Rep 3.

[34]   The Court rejected the claim of the State of nationality of the shareholder for a company to pierce the 'corporate veil'. The Court held that a State that admits a foreign company does not thereby have to accept diplomatic protection by a State whose nationals own shares in the company.

[35]   See W. Friedmann, *The Changing Structure of International Law*, 1964, London, Stevens, at 223. *Contra* G. Abi-Saab, 'The International Law of Multinational Corporations: a Critique of International Legal Doctrines' (1971) 2 *Annals of International Studies* 97.

ticular on the protection of investors' rights against expropriation and compensation. After several sensational cases of abuse by corporations,[36] the emphasis shifted towards the duties of corporations. This attempt, however, resulted in various soft law instruments, such as the 1976 OECD Declaration on International Investments and Multinational Enterprises, and the 1977 ILO Tripartite Declaration of Principles Concerning Multinational Enterprises and Social Policy.[37] On the contrary, the negotiations of the MAI, which would have granted general rights to investors in an international binding agreement, have failed.

The progressive acquisition of rights has been paralleled by the possibility of enforcing these rights before international dispute settlement bodies.[38] The most significant step towards direct access of companies to international dispute settlement procedures was provided by the International Centre for the Settlement of Investments Disputes (ICSID). The ICSID, established under the 1965 World Bank Convention on International Settlement of the Disputes,[39] was specifically designed to settle disputes between private investors and States, whereas it has no jurisdiction to settle disputes between two States or between two private entities.[40] The aim of the ICSID was to protect investors' rights in host countries by granting them remedies through arbitration without the need for diplomatic protection by their home States.[41] According to the ICSID Convention, any legal person which has the nationality of one of the contracting States can bring a complaint before the ICSID.[42] The provisions

---

[36]   See Francioni, *Imprese Multinazionali, supra* n. 31, at 166–7.

[37]   Tripartite Declaration of Principles Concerning Multinational Enterprises and Social Policy, (adopted by the Governing Body of the International Labour Office at its 204th Session (Geneva, November 1977)), OB Vol. LXI, 1978, Series A, No. 1.

[38]   As pointed out by Vicuña, the process of globalization has also prompted the participation of private entities in the international dispute settlement system. This is particularly so in the case of investments, trade and other forms of economic cooperation which involve corporations as main actors. Vicuña, *International Dispute, supra* n. 12, at 63–83.

[39]   International Centre for the Settlement of Investment Disputes (ICSID), *Convention on the Settlement of Investment Disputes between States and Nationals of Other States*, Washington, 18 March 1965 (entered into force 14 October 1966).

[40]   See Art. 25, ICSID Convention. See also Muchlinski, *Multinational Enterprises, supra* Ch.1 n. 40, at 540.

[41]   See Sornarajah, Ch.1 *supra* n. 6, at 8. Similarly Dupuy, *Droit International Public, supra* n. 12, at 685.

[42]   Pursuant to Art. 25.1 of the ICSID Convention 'the jurisdiction of the centre shall extend to any legal dispute arising directly out of an investment, between a Contracting party and . . . a national of another contracting State, which the

of the Convention and their interpretation by arbitral tribunals have further facilitated the effective exercise of investors' rights. A first problem could be that once a legal person is incorporated in the country of origin, it would no longer be considered a national of another contracting party and, hence, would not be able to benefit from ICSID Conventions rights. The solution is provided by the foreign control clause, according to which any juridical person incorporated in the host State party to the dispute and which is under foreign control may be considered a national of another contracting State if the parties have so agreed.[43]

Not only are the parties to the ICSID Convention over 140,[44] but as a result of the adoption of the Additional Facility Rules, a State which has not ratified the convention or a national of a non-party to the convention can also have access to the ICSID conciliation and arbitration services, if the parties to the dispute so agree.[45]

However, what has greatly increased the role of the ICSID in the protection of investment is that the large majority of existing Bilateral Investment Treaties (BITs),[46] contain a so called 'ICSID clause'.[47] This clause would refer disputes between the host State and the investor to arbitration by ICSID.[48] Furthermore, since the award in *Asian Agricultural Products Ltd (AAPL) v. Sri Lanka,*[49] it was admitted that a company could sue a State simply for breaches of the bilateral (and so inter-State) investment agreement, even if a violation of the contract between the State and enterprise had not occurred.[50] This interpretation amounts to a sort of 'direct invocability'[51] of the inter-State agreement to allow private investors access to arbitration without the need for a contractual consent between the State

---

parties to the dispute consent in writing to submit to the centre. When the parties have given their consent, no party may withdraw its consent unilaterally'.

[43]   Art. 25.2(b), ICSID Convention. See also *Amco Asia Corporation v Republic of Indonesia,* 1 ICSID Rep 389, [1984] 23 ILM 351.

[44]   The list of contracting States is available at: http://www.worldbank.org/ icsid/constate/c-states-en.htm (accessed 3 May 2006).

[45]   Arts 2 and 4 of the *Rules Governing Additional Facilities for the Administration of Proceedings by the Secretariat of the ICSID,* available at: http://www.worldbank.org/icsid/facility/3htm (accessed 4 September 2005).

[46]   Bilateral investment treaties are currently more than 2700 of which 300 have an ICSID clause. See http://www.worldbank.org/icsid/treaties/treaties.htm (accessed 4 September 2008).

[47]   See. Dupuy, *Droit International Public, supra* n. 12, at 684.

[48]   See Sornarajah, Ch.1 *supra* n. 6, at 68.

[49]   *Asian Agricultural Products Limited v Sri Lanka,* ICSID Case No. ARB/87/3, 4 [1991] ICSID Reports 245.

[50]   Dupuy, *Droit International Public, supra* n. 12, at 685.

[51]   Ibid.

and the investor. The general consent given in an investment treaty is, indeed, considered valid for particular cases.

As a result, the protection of private investors within the ICSID system has acquired such an extensive reach that it could be argued that what used to be an exceptional remedy to the uncertainty in the law of investment protection has now become a sort of generalized and well established system of protection of investors rights at the international level. This assumption is further supported by the consideration that more than half of the ICSID caseload has been launched over only the last seven years.[52]

A number of multilateral agreements have further strengthened the mechanisms for dispute settlement available directly to investors. Under the North American Free Trade Agreement (NAFTA) corporations have access to a panel for dispute settlement,[53] where they can bring a case against one of the participating States for a regulation or government decision which violates investor protection.[54] In addition, private parties have been authorized to participate in some NAFTA dispute settlement mechanisms or examination arrangements, such as the review and appeal of determinations of origin[55] or complaints under the Agreement on Environmental Co-operation.[56]

Another example of private parties acquiring access to arbitration is the 1981 Iran–United States Tribunal. This tribunal originally set up on an *ad hoc* basis, subsequently developed into a permanent international court. Sectoral agreements, such as the United Nations Convention on the Law of the Sea, and in particular Annex VI establishing the Statute of the International Tribunal for the Law of The Sea,[57] and the Energy Charter Treaty[58] provide companies with access to dispute settlement mechanisms.

The emphasis on MNEs rights', however, probably reached its highest point in the negotiations on the Multilateral Agreement on Investment (MAI), conducted in the context of the OECD. The underlying aim of the

---

[52]   The list of cases is available at: http://www.worldbank.org/icsid/cases/cases. htm (accessed 22 October 2010).

[53]   Ch 11, NAFTA.

[54]   Arts 904(4), 905(3), NAFTA.

[55]   Art. 510, NAFTA.

[56]   The NAFTA mechanism has already been adopted in the MERCOSUR agreement and it may provide a model for an eventual investor to State disputes within the WTO. See Uriz-Hernandez, *supra* n. 24, at 52.

[57]   Annex VI Arts 35–40 of the Law of the Sea Convention.

[58]   The Energy Charter Treaty and the Energy Charter Protocol on Energy Efficiency and Related Environmental Aspects, The Hague, 17 December 1994.

MAI was to offer legally binding guarantees to international investors.[59] It also envisaged the creation of an international tribunal – built on the ICSID model – through which investors could sue State parties over alleged breaches of the provisions of the agreement. Standing, however, would have been granted only to corporations against host States and not the other way round.[60] Negotiations on the MAI reached a deadlock in 1998[61] after strong criticism by environmental and human rights NGOs and the opposition of developing countries. Furthermore, no agreement could be reached on the provisions that made reference to environmental protection and labour standards.[62] The failure of the MAI is perceived by some commentators as a missed opportunity for the regulation of international investments.[63] Having highlighted the scant regard paid to environmental and social issues, it is to be hoped that future negotiations on multilateral investments, such as those resumed within the framework of the WTO,[64] will address these issues more thoroughly.

The recognition of MNEs' rights, however, is not limited to the international protection of investments. The European Court of Human Rights (ECrtHR), for instance, has recognized not only substantive but also procedural rights of companies.[65] Not only can companies file a complaint before the Court[66] but they can also enjoy rights such as the rights to fair trial,[67] privacy[68] and freedom of religion.[69] Nevertheless, complaints regarding human rights violations can be brought before the Court only when a State has not complied with its obligations arising from the European Convention, so corporations cannot be accused of human rights violations before the Court.

---

[59]   See P. Muchlinski, 'A Brief History of Business Regulation', in Picciotto and Mayne (eds), *supra* Ch.1 n. 21 at 55.

[60]   Kamminga, 'Holding Multinational Corporations Accountable', *supra* Ch.1 n. 70, at 557.

[61]   Joseph, 'Taming the Leviathans', *supra* Ch.1 n. 8, at 202.

[62]   See Dupuy, *Droit International Public*, *supra* n. 12, at 684.

[63]   See Kamminga, 'Holding Multinational Corporations Accountable', *supra* Ch.1 n. 70, at 558.

[64]   Sornarajah, *supra* Ch.1 n. 6, at 336.

[65]   See Addo, 'The Corporation as a Victim of Human Rights Violations', in Addo (ed.), *supra* Ch.1 n. 28, at 194.

[66]   Ibid, at 194. See e.g. *Bosphorus Hava Yollari Turizm Ve Ticaret Anonim Şirketi v Ireland* ECHR (2005), VI [n. 45036/98]; *Autronic AG v Switzerland* ECHR (1990) Series A, No. 178, 12, EHRR 485, para. 47.

[67]   *Dombo Beheer v Netherlands* ECHR (1993) Series A, 274; EHRR (1994) 213.

[68]   *Société Colas Est and others v France*, Case No. 37971/97, ECHR 2002-III.

[69]   *X and Church of Scientology v Sweden* 7805/77 [1979] ECHR 9.

European Community law provides both direct rights and duties on corporations, on the basis of the provisions of the Treaty Establishing the European Community (TEC)[70] and on the doctrine of direct effect.[71] Arts 81 and 82 TEC, for instance, create direct obligations on companies in the field of competition. The Commission is endowed with the power to investigate and impose sanctions[72] in order to ensure compliance with these provisions.[73] The European Court of Justice (ECJ) moved ahead by asking companies to comply with the principle of non-discrimination. In *Walrave and Koch*[74] and *Defrenne*,[75] the ECJ, pursuant to a teleological interpretation of the TEC, also found that private entities are required to contribute to the elimination of nationality and gender based discrimination.[76] Similarly, in *Eugen Schmindberger, Internationale Transporte und Planzüge v Austria*[77] the Court held that Community law had to be applied in a way that gave priority to the right of freedom of expression of inhabitants who protested against the crossing of trucks of the applicant company in their region.[78] Pursuant to the ECJ's case-law,

---

[70] 'A regulation . . . shall be binding in its entirety and directly applicable in all member States'. Art 249 TEC Consolidated Version of the Treaty Establishing the European Community, in European Union Consolidated Treaties, (1997) Luxembourg, Office for Official Publications of the European Communities, at 35–168.

[71] The landmark decision on direct effect is 26/62 *Van Gend en Loos v Nederlandse Administraties Der Belastingen* [1963] ECR 3, at 12. On recent developments on the direct effect of directives See T. Tridimas, 'Liability for Breach of Community Law: Growing Up and Mellowing Down?' (2001) 38 C.M.L.R. 301.

[72] Art 85 TEC and Council Regulation (EC) 1216/1999 of 10 June 1999 amending Regulation No 17: first Regulation implementing Articles 81 and 82 of the Treaty [1999] OJ L/5 148. See V. Korah, *An Introductory Guide to EC Competition Law and Practice*, 2000, Oxford and Portland, Or., Hart, at 155–91.

[73] The review of Regulation 17/62 resulted into a shift towards private enforcement and by, the same token, a reduction of Commission enforcement powers. See P. Craig and G. De Búrca, *EU Law, Text, Cases and Materials,* 2003, Oxford, Oxford University Press, at 1062–86.

[74] The ECJ referred in particular to Arts 12, 39, and 59 TEC (former Arts 7, 48 and 59 TEC), Case 36/64, *Walrave v Association Union Cycliste Internationale* [1974] ECR 1405, at 1419.

[75] The ECJ refers to Art. 119 TEC. See Case 43/75 *Defrenne v Société Anonyme Belge de Navigation Aérienne Sabena* [1976] ECR 445, at 457–463.

[76] However, it has been pointed out that the European system constitutes an exception on the international scene, since it is more similar to a State system than to an international organization: see Uriz-Hernandez, *supra* n. 24, at 48.

[77] Case C-112/00 *Eugen Schmindberger, Internationale Transporte und Planzüge v Austria* [2003] ECR I-5659.

[78] Ibid., at para. 74.

not only was it confirmed that the European Community as such has to respect human rights, but that as a consequence of this, other non-State actors, such as private businesses, can exercise their economic freedoms under Community law only to the extent that such exercise does not disproportionately interfere with the enjoyment of international human rights.[79]

As far as corporate duties are concerned, several treaties impose liability not upon States, but upon private, often corporate, actors. International law applies directly to corporations in areas other than human rights such as labour law,[80] environmental law[81] and anti-corruption conventions.[82] All of these treaties impose corporate liability for actions or omissions by

---

[79]   Ibid., at para. 76. This view is supported by Clapham, *Human Rights Obligations*, *supra* Ch.1 n. 50, at 185. However it has been pointed out that the European system constitutes an exception on the international scene since it is more similar to a State system than to an international organization; see Uriz-Hernandez, *supra* n. 24, at 48.

[80]   See the ILO Convention on Occupational Safety and Health, which enshrines obligations on the employers to attain certain standards.

[81]   See, e.g., Convention Relating to Civil Liability in the Field of Maritime Carriage of Nuclear Material, 17 December 1971, 974 UNTS 255, at 256; Convention on Civil Liability for Oil Pollution Damage Resulting from Exploration for and Exploitation of Seabed Mineral Resources, 17 December 1976, in Intergovernmental Conference on the Convention on Civil Liability for Oil Pollution Damage from Offshore Operations: Final Act and Text of Convention, opened for signature 1 May 1977 (1977) 16 *International Legal Materials* 1450, at 1452.

[82]   For example, the United Nations Convention against Transnational Organized Crime defines the crimes of participation in an organized criminal group, money laundering, corruption and obstruction of justice, all of which apply to corporations as well as natural persons. GA Res. 55/25, UN GAOR, 55th Sess., 62d plenary meeting, Annex 1 at arts 5, 6, 8 and 23, UN Doc. A/Res/55/25 (2001), available at: http://www.unodc.org/unodc/crime_cicp_signatures_convention.html (accessed 21 November 2008). Many provisions in the treaties that address bribery and corruption apply to legal as well as natural persons. See, e.g., Council of Europe: Criminal Law Convention on Corruption, opened for signature 27 January 1999, Europ. T.S. No. 173, [1999] 38 *International Legal Materials* 505, at 509 (active bribery, trading in influence and money laundering); Organization of American States: Inter-American Convention Against Corruption, 29 March 1996, [1996] 35 *International Legal Materials* 724, 730 (prohibiting offering an article of monetary value to a government official of another State); OECD Convention on Combating Bribery of Foreign Public Officials in International Business Transactions, 17 December 1997, Art 1, [1997] 37 *International Legal Materials* 1, at 4 (entered into force 15 February 1999); Basel Convention on the Control of Transboundary Movements of Hazardous Wastes and Their Disposal, 22 March 1989, [1989] 28 *International Legal Materials* 657, at 662 (entered into force 5 May 1992) applies to legal persons.

companies having potentially detrimental effects. Although these conventions do not all expressly concern human rights, they indicate that MNEs are subject to duties under international law. Furthermore, if corporations can be held liable for unintentional torts resulting from contravening the international law described above, then it would be reasonable for them to be held liable for torts resulting from intentional breaches of international law, such as human rights violations.

However, in the area of international human rights law, States have not been ready to impose legally binding international obligations upon MNEs. A strict international law analysis shows that only a limited number of human rights are covered by the OECD and ILO codes of conduct, and that they are enshrined in soft law instruments.

2.4   CONCLUSION

It was not the purpose of this chapter to examine the merits of attributing legal personality to MNEs. What is important here is the recognition that MNEs have been shown to be capable of having rights under international law and they have increasingly recognized access to international courts and international dispute settlement bodies to enforce them.

The analysis of human rights obligations relevant for MNEs will be carried out in the following Chapter. What is worth underlining here is that, although MNEs are still not unanimously recognized as subjects of international law, the above analysis shows that companies already participate in the current international legal framework as addressees, or beneficiaries, of certain rights and duties and have gained access to international courts to enforce them.

MNEs cannot be seen any longer as a sum of fragmented legal entities subject to the jurisdiction of the different States in which they operate, but must be seen rather as unitary economic entities which, although not endowed with full legal personality as a State or an international organization, must assume a share of responsibility in securing human rights in the conduct of their business abroad.

The rise of corporations as holders of international relevant legal situations has, indeed, been unbalanced. While the rise of new subjects of international law – international organizations, individuals, insurgents and national liberation movements – has followed a pattern of progressive acquisition of both rights and duties, in the case of MNEs the scales are strongly tipped in favour of rights.

As was shown in this chapter, MNEs have not hesitated to invoke international law for the protection of the rights to property, to privacy, to fair trial and even to freedom of religion, before both international arbitration bodies and regional human rights courts.[83]

The extension of the ICSID arbitration system to virtually all BITs and the adoption of similar arbitration schemes in other regional agreements, such as NAFTA, has turned the protection of foreign investment from an exceptional remedy into a sort of generalized and well-established system of the protection of MNEs against host States. As also shown by the failed proposal of an OECD Multilateral Agreement on Investment, the international law of investments has been directed to the objective of investment protection to the exclusion of other interests involved in that process.[84]

MNEs also play a role in the shaping of international principles either by themselves or in alliance with their home States, through their organized lobbying power; they affect international law by operating through non-governmental bodies of which they are members and by advocating standards of investment protection.[85] Ultimately, also international arbitration, which is itself a private, consensual method of dispute settlement, can be used as a manipulable mechanism through which the interests of MNEs can be given expression.[86]

From the above analysis, two strong arguments can be drawn in favour of the necessity of imposing international obligations upon MNEs. First, not only are MNEs increasingly the addressees of international law but their legal situation is also characterized by a marked prevalence of rights over duties. This seems to be in contrast with the concept of legal personality in itself, which entails the capacity of being the addressees of both positive and negative legally relevant situations. MNEs also appear to be an anomaly when compared to other non-State actors, which have gained both rights and duties in international law.

A second caveat of this argument requires that actors which invoke international law, and in some cases even human rights law, for the protection of their rights, should also be bound by the duties deriving from the very same body of law. Since MNEs have successfully invoked protection under international law and they are even able to influence the international law-making process to some extent, they cannot claim to be absolved from international obligations when it comes to human rights abuses.

---

[83]   See above the case law of the ECrtHR footnotes 210–13.
[84]   Sornarajah, *supra* Ch.1 n. 6, at 9.
[85]   See G. Teubner (ed.), *Global Law Without a State*, 1997, Aldershot, Brookfield, Dartmouth.
[86]   Sornarajah, *supra* Ch.1 n. 6, at 335.

These arguments point in the direction of a need to impose responsibilities and obligations in return for this broad range of rights.

There are signs, however, that attention seems to be focused again on the need to rebalance corporate rights with corporate obligations, both at international and domestic level. The risk is that of a proliferation of international soft law instruments with the ambiguity they hold. Soft law can be seen as paving the way to further development into legally binding instruments, while they are also perceived as a way of private regulation,[87] substituting and even preventing the development of hard law. So far the general solutions adopted either by the EU or other international organizations attempt to combine the two instruments in order to take the greatest benefits from each.

The merits and disadvantages of this approach will be examined in the following chapters.

[87] Supiot, *supra* Ch.1 n. 46, at 542–58.

3 MNEs and international human rights law

3.1 INTRODUCTION

The question of how human rights obligations apply to MNEs will be tackled here. The scope of MNEs' responsibility has not been defined yet in international law. Therefore, this analysis draws upon the responsibility of States and the responsibility of individuals in international law. A brief critical overview of trends in international law regarding the expansion of States' responsibility in the private sphere, the rise of individual duties and direct soft law obligations on companies will be provided. Neither category of responsibility seems to be adequately equipped to cope with MNEs' behaviour. However, the fast-moving changes in this area demonstrate that international actors (both State and non-State) acknowledge that this subject is not only one of international concern, but one in which more legal developments are desirable.

3.2 THE EXPANSION OF STATE RESPONSIBILITY IN THE PRIVATE SPHERE: THE HORIZONTAL APPLICATION OF INTERNATIONAL HUMAN RIGHTS LAW

The traditional approach to human rights law commands that human rights protect the individual against the State. Protecting human rights solely through prohibitions imposed on governments seems rather uncontroversial if States represented the only threat to human dignity, or if States could be counted on to restrain conduct within their borders effectively. However, this doctrine was developed at a time when international business was less prominent and international economic interdependence was far less important. In addition, the host States' goals have recently shifted to attracting foreign investment. Host States have adjusted domestic laws to make them more attractive to corporations or simply turned a blind eye to violations of domestic law. Therefore, a system where the

State is the only target of international legal obligations may not be sufficient to protect human rights.[1]

The historical view of international law concerning exclusively the regulation of interstate relations has begun to give way to emerging trends conferring rights and duties on non-State actors such as international organizations and other actors, including insurgent or rebel groups, individuals and corporations.[2]

This new type of non-State actor liability and responsibility under international law is emerging through stretching the current system's limits in two ways. The first entails indirect responsibility through the horizontal application of international law and the other through the application of international law directly to the non-State actors in question.

International and national laws have begun to adapt in order to regulate effectively in an increasingly dynamic world. There now exists a wealth of international regulation that reflects a move away from the traditionalist view of international law,[3] whereby actions within one State's jurisdiction are subject to domestic sovereignty only.[4]

Regulations within domestic systems have advanced as well, with the adaptation of the Alien Tort Claims Act in the US[5] and the relaxation of *forum non conveniens* rules in Great Britain, which allow for MNEs to be held liable for actions of their subsidiaries committed abroad.[6]

Since human rights law in the current international legal framework is addressed to States, one could attempt to hold the State directly

---

[1]   See R. Ratner, 'Corporations and Human Rights: A Theory of Legal Responsibility' (2001) 3 *Yale Law Journal* 443, at 461.

[2]   For one of the most recent contribution on this topic see Clapham, *Human Rights Obligations, supra* Ch.1 n. 50.

[3]   S.I. Skogly, 'Economic and Social Human Rights, Private Actors and International Obligations', in Addo (ed.), *Human Rights Standards, supra* Ch.1 n. 28, at 247.

[4]   Ibid. at 244.

[5]   The ATCA (Federal Tort Claims Act, 28 U.S.C.S. paras 1346 ff. Law. Co-op. 1978 and Supp. 2004) is a piece of US legislation which dates back to 1789. The US Courts have gradually refined the list of violations of the law of nations for which the ATCA can be invoked. At present, recent rulings have determined that genocide, slave trading, slavery, forced labour and war crimes are actionable even in the absence of any connection to a State action. The *Kadic v Kardžić* case (70 F 3d 232 2nd Cir, 1995, at 243–244) added also rape, torture, summary execution, when committed in the pursuit of genocide or war crimes. On the evolution of ATCA see Joseph, *Corporations and Transnational Human Rights Litigation supra* Ch.1 n. 55.

[6]   R. Meeran, *Access to Courts for Corporate Accountability: Recent Developments,* available at: http://www.johnpickering.co.uk (accessed 11 November 2003).

responsible for human rights violations committed by a company, so that the human rights obligations of the State would apply to private action.

This option will follow the criteria of imputation as developed by international courts[7] and now codified in the International Law Commission (ILC) Draft Articles on the Responsibility of States for Internationally Wrongful Acts.[8] Pursuant to the ILC Draft Articles on State Responsibility, the conduct of non-State actors may be attributed to the State when the private conduct is in fact directed or controlled by the State,[9] and when the individuals or groups *de facto* exercise elements of governmental authority.[10] A looser test has been applied in the *Tadic*[11] case before the International Criminal Tribunal for the Former Yugoslavia (ICTY). In the *Loizidou*[12] case before the ECrtHR, the ECHR declared Turkey responsible for the acts of the Turkish Republic of Northern Cyprus because the Turkish army exercised effective and overall control on the northern part of the island.

These principles, however, could be applied to impute to a State the behaviour of a company in those cases in which it acts as an agent of the State, or the State fails to exercise proper control over the activities of private actors that are likely to cause harm.

State responsibility for human rights violations can develop beyond the above criteria of attribution when the primary human right norms impose positive obligation upon states with regard to the protection of human rights.

States' obligation to ensure respect and protection for human rights is laid down in the most important human rights treaties, including the Covenant on Civil and Political Rights (Article 2, para. 1), the Racial Discrimination

---

[7]   See *Military and Paramilitary Activities in and Against Nicaragua,* Case *Nicaragua v USA,* judgment of 27 June 1986, ICJ Rep. 14, at 14–115. See Ratner, *supra* n. 1, at 499.

[8]   ILC Draft Articles on the Responsibility of States for Internationally Wrongful Acts, Report of the International Law Commission on the Work of its fifty-third Session, Official Records of the General Assembly, fifty-third session.

[9]   Art 8 ILC Draft Articles. 'The conduct of a person or group of persons shall be considered an act of a State under international law if the person or group of persons is in fact acting on the instructions of, or under the direction or control of that State in carrying out the conduct.'

[10]   Art 9 ILC Draft Articles 'The conduct of a person or group of persons shall be considered an act of a State under international law if the person or group of persons is in fact exercising elements of the governmental authority in the absence or default of the official authorities and in circumstances such as to call for the exercise of those elements of authority'.

[11]   Case IT 94-I-T *Prosecutor v Dusko Tadic*, judgement of the appeal chamber para. 37.

[12]   Case 40/1994/435/541 *Loizidou v Turkey*, judgement of 23 March 1995, ECHR (A) 310.

Convention (Article 2, para. 1b, d), the European Convention for the Protection of Human Rights and Fundamental Freedoms (Article 1). A broad interpretation of States' obligation to ensure human rights has been upheld in general comments by UN expert bodies and decisions of regional human rights courts in Europe and the Americas. The UN Human Rights committee, in particular, has interpreted the ICCPR as imposing upon States an obligation to prevent or stop abuses by private actors with regards to the right to equality between men and women,[13] the right to life,[14] to privacy,[15] to freedom of expression[16] and the rights of the child.[17] The ICESCR Committee has gone a step further. Not only has the ICESCR Committee interpreted the obligations of States to prevent or remedy violations by private actors, but it has also addressed the behaviour of non-state actors in its General Comments and required them to act in a manner consistent with the rights at stake. In its General Comments on the Right to adequate food[18] and the Right to health[19] the Committee expressly refers to the role of companies in the protection and fulfilment

---

[13] Human Rights Committee, General Comment 28, Equity of Rights between Men and Women (Art. 3) 29/03/ 2000, CCPR/C/21/Rev.1 Add. 10, CCPR.

[14] Human Rights Committee, The Right to Life (Art. 6) General Comment 6, (Sixteenth session, 1982), Compilation of General Comments and General Recommendations Adopted by Human Rights Treaty Bodies, U.N. Doc. HRI\ GEN\1\Rev.1 at 6 (1994).

[15] Human Rights Committee, The Right to Respect Family Privacy, Family, Home Correspondence and Protection of honour and reputation (Art. 17), General Comment 16, (Twenty-third session, 1988), Compilation of General Comments and General Recommendations Adopted by Human Rights Treaty Bodies, U.N. Doc. HRI\GEN\1\Rev.1 at 21 (1994).

[16] Human Rights Committee, General Comment 10, Art. 19 (Nineteenth session, 1983), Compilation of General Comments and General Recommendations Adopted by Human Rights Treaty Bodies, U.N. Doc. HRI/GEN/1/Rev.6 at 132 (2003).

[17] Human Rights Committee, General Comment 17, Art. 24 (Thirty-fifth session, 1989), Compilation of General Comments and General Recommendations Adopted by Human Rights Treaty Bodies, U.N. Doc. HRI/GEN/1/Rev.6 at 144 (2003).

[18] UN Committee on Economic, Social and Cultural Rights, General Comment 12, The Right to Adequate Food (Art. 11), 12 May 1999, para. 20 says that 'While only States are parties to the covenant and are thus ultimately accountable for compliance with it, all members of society – individuals, families, local organisations, civil society organisations – have responsibility in the realization of the right to adequate food . . . The private business sector – national and transnational – should pursue its activities within the framework of a code of conduct conducive to respect of the right to adequate food.'

[19] UN Committee on Economic, Social and Cultural Rights, General Comment 14, The Right to the Highest Attainable Standard of Health (Art. 12), July 2000, para. 42.

of these rights. General Comment 7 on forced eviction not only compels States to ensure that the law is applied to those who practise forced evictions (being either agents of the State or third parties), but it also recommends increasing measures to prevent and punish illegal evictions by private bodies, since in many countries there is a trend towards the reduction of government responsibilities in the housing sector.[20] Nonetheless, the UN Committees' interpretative comments, while influential upon governments and non-state actors, are not binding, although they have more than a simply aspirational value. The Inter-American Commission on Human Rights recommends that not only should the State ensure that its agents do not engage in human rights violations, but also that reasonable measures are taken to prevent discrimination within the private sector.[21]

The option of holding governments to account for the behaviour of MNEs, indeed, relies on the horizontal application of human rights law.[22] According to this doctrine a State may be held directly liable not only for the vertical infringements of human rights – that is, by the State against individuals – but also for horizontal infringements, that is by individuals or private bodies against other individuals or private bodies.[23] This theory stems from a broad interpretation of the States' obligation *to protect* human rights.[24]

The ECHR has been interpreted to lead progressively to its horizontal applicability. In a vast number of cases the Commission and the Court of Human Rights have found the States responsible in cases where the administration, the legislature and the courts failed to protect the rights

---

[20] UN Committee on Economic, Social and Cultural Rights, General Comment 7, Forced Evictions, and the right to adequate housing (Sixteenth session, 1997), UN Doc. E/1998/22, annex IV, at 113 (1998), reprinted in Compilation of General Comments and General Recommendations Adopted by Human Rights Treaty Bodies, U.N. Doc. HRI/GEN/1/Rev.6 at 45 (2003).

[21] Inter-American Commission on Human Rights, Organization of American States. Report on the Situation if Human Rights in Ecuador, 24 April 1997; OEA/Ser. L/V/II.96 Doc. 10 rev.1. (VIII–IV).

[22] See generally, A. Clapham, *Human Rights in the Private Sphere*, 1993, Oxford, Clarendon Press.

[23] See 'The Maastricht Guidelines on Violations of Economic Social and Cultural Rights' (1998) 81 *Human Rights Quarterly* 87, point 18 Acts by Non State Entities.

[24] A precedent can be found in the notion of third-party effect *Drittwirkung* developed by German courts, according to which some German constitutional rights affect private legal relationships. See Ratner, *supra* n. 1, at 471 and Clapham, *Human Rights in the Private Sphere*, *supra* n. 22 at 90.

enshrined in the Convention from violations by private actors.[25] The most undisputed examples of horizontal application of the Convention of Human Rights are provided by cases regarding the right to privacy,[26] the right to freedom of expression[27] and the right to freedom of association and private assembly.[28] The ECrtHR held that the failure by the Netherlands to take legal action against a private person who committed sexual assault against a mentally handicapped dependant was in breach of the victim's right to privacy.[29] In a number of cases relating to the nuisance caused by the airports of Gatwick and Heathrow, complaints were declared admissible and the applicability of Article 8, even between private parties, was confirmed. In *Hatton* the ECrtHR spelled out that, in the specific case of environmental protection, the mere argument of economic interest was not a sufficient justification for interference with privacy and family life.[30] The right to privacy was also violated by Italy's failure to prevent a company from releasing toxic gases.[31] Similarly, in *López Ostra v Spain*, Spanish authorities were held to be in breach of Article 8 for not preventing noise, polluting fumes and smells released by a plant from reaching the applicant's house. The Commission also found that, pursuant to Article 10, the State has a duty to protect against excessive press concentrations[32] and to create a legal duty to publish a reply or rectification and to provide for a judicial remedy.[33] The Court has also declared that the rights to freedom of peaceful assembly and association require positive measures to be protected from interference by private parties. A merely negative duty upon the State not to interfere would indeed be

---

[25]   See B. Conforti, 'Reflections on State Responsibility for the Breach of Positive Obligation: The Case of the European Court of Human Rights' (2003) 13 *Italian Yearbook of International Law* 3.

[26]   Art. 8 ECHR.

[27]   Art. 10 ECHR.

[28]   Art. 11 ECHR.

[29]   *X and Y v The Netherlands* (1985) ECHR Series A, No. 91, at 11.

[30]   However, the Grand Chamber finally held that the UK was in breach of Art. 13 and not of Art. 8, because the scope of review by domestic courts was too narrow. *Hatton and Others v United Kingdom,* ECHR Application 3602/77, available at: www.coe.fr (accessed 2 April 2007).

[31]   *Guerra v Italy* ECHR (1998) 777.

[32]   *López Ostra v Spain,* Judgment of 9 December 1994, Case No. 41/1993/436/515; *De Geïllustreerde Pers. N.V. v The Netherlands* ECHR, report of 6 July 1976, D.R. 8; and *VgT Verein gegen Tierfabriken v Switzerland* Application N. 24699/94, Judgment of 21 June 2001.

[33]   *Casado Coca v Spain* [1994] IIHRL 10 (24 February 1994), ECHR Series A, No. 285.

incompatible with the object and purpose of Article 11.[34] In addition, the case law of the ECtHR has also reached the horizontal application of the right to life[35] and right to be free from torture.[36] In the *Osman*[37] case the Court held that in certain, well defined circumstances, Article 2 may imply a positive obligation on the authorities to take preventive operational measures to protect an individual whose life is at risk from the criminal acts of another individual.

Similar development can be traced in the case law of the Inter American Court of Human Rights.[38] In the landmark case *Velàsquez Rodríguez*,[39] the Inter-American Court of Human Rights held the government of Honduras responsible for not having prevented and punished a forced disappearance committed by persons connected to the security forces. In particular, the court found that the State's responsibility was triggered by the lack of due diligence by the State to prevent the violation or to respond to it.[40] The Court also pointed out that Honduras was obliged not only to refrain from violating human rights directly through its security forces, but also to take steps in order to prevent violations by private actors.[41]

The Inter-American Court and Commission have also specifically addressed the threats to human rights on behalf of private companies. The Inter-American Commission found Guatemala in breach of the right to life, the right to humane treatment, the right to personal liberty, fair trial, assembly and freedom of association and to judicial protection with regard to human rights abuses perpetrated by the Coca Cola Guatemalan

---

[34]   *Plattform Ärtze für das Leben v Austria*, Judgment of 21 June 1988, ECHR (1991) Series A, No. 191.

[35]   Art. 2 ECHR.

[36]   Art. 3 ECHR.

[37]   *Osman v United Kingdom,* Judgment of 28 October 1998, ECHR (1998) 101.

[38]   See discussion in Clapham, *Human Rights in the Private Sphere, supra* n. 22 at 190–96.

[39]   In this case, however, there was a high possibility that the persons involved were State agents. *Velásquez Rodríguez* case, Inter-Am. C.T.H.R. 8 (ser C) No 4 (1998).

[40]   Ibid., para. 172. For a discussion on the attribution of the State's responsibility in the Inter-American Court's jurisprudence, see J.M. Pasqualucci, *The Practice and Procedure of the Inter-American Court of Human Rights*, 2003, Cambridge, Cambridge University Press, at 219–29.

[41]   This approach was upheld in following judgments such as the *Godínez Cruz* Case, Order of the Court of 10 September 1996, reprinted in 1996 *Annual Report of the Inter-American Court of Human Rights* (IACHR), [213], OEA/Ser.L/V/III.35, doc. 4 (1997).

Bottling plant.[42] The 1997 Inter-American Commission Report on the situation of human rights in Ecuador, referred to human rights violations caused by oil plants and encouraged by the Ecuadorian government against the indigenous people of Oriente.[43] In the case *Yanomami – Brazil*,[44] the Inter-American Commission first formulated the basic obligations of the State to protect individuals from harm caused by an economic activity on the part of private actors. The Commission held that the Brazilian State was responsible for not having taken timely and effective measures to protect the human rights of the Yanomami indigenous population, caused by the invasion of oil workers onto their lands. More recently, Nicaragua was held responsible for having failed to protect the rights of the Awas Tingni community.[45] In practice, Nicaragua did not demarcate Awas Tingni's ancestral territory and attempted to disregard their rights over their land and resources by granting logging concessions over the community's territory.

It is worth mentioning also that the African Commission on Human and Peoples' Rights has interpreted the obligations contained in the African Charter as requiring States to prevent human rights violations by private parties. The Decision regarding human rights violations committed by the Nigerian government in relation to oil exploitation in the Niger Delta[46] pointed out that '[t]he State is obliged to protect right holders against other subjects by the adoption of legislation and the provision of effective remedies. This obligation requires the State to take measures to protect beneficiaries of the protected rights against political, economic, social interferences'.[47] Thus, upholding a progressive interpretation of the African Charter, the African Commission calls for positive action on the part of States to fulfil their obligations under human rights instruments.

This case law demonstrates that State responsibility can go very far in addressing human rights violations in the private sphere. However, when a State is bound by an obligation *to prevent,* it does not mean that the

---

[42] Inter-American Commission on Human Rights, Resolution 38/81, Case 4425 (Guatemala) (25 June 1982); IACHR (1980-1981), OEA/ Ser. L/V/II.54; Doc. 9 rev. 1, 16 October 1981.

[43] See Inter-American Commission, Report on Ecuador, *supra* n. 21.

[44] Case 7615 *Yanomami v Brazil*, 5 March 1985, Res. No 12/85, IACHR (1985).

[45] The *Mayagna Awas Tingni Community v Nicaragua,* Judgment of 31 August 2001, IACHR Decisions and Judgements, (ser. C) N. 79 (2001).

[46] The African Commission on Human and Peoples' Rights, Decision on Communication 155/96, 30th Ordinary Session, Banjul, The Gambia, 13–17 October 2001.

[47] Ibid., at para. 46.

conduct of individuals as such will be imputable to the State.[48] The responsibility of the State arises only in combination with a failure to act by State organs (for example, failure to adopt relevant legislation).[49] According to this interpretation, apart from the case of a company directly owned or controlled by the State,[50] two cases arise in which a State may be held responsible for the behaviour of an MNE. Firstly, in the case of a corporation exercising elements of governmental authority, either as a result of formal delegation by the authorities,[51] or when such a corporation *de facto* performs governmental powers; secondly when a State, responsible under international law, fails to exercise the required degree of due diligence with regard to the conduct of MNEs.[52]

In addition, despite the fact that States' obligations to prevent, investigate and remedy human rights violations against individuals have been extensively mainstreamed, they still cover only a fraction of human rights violations.

3.3   THE DEVELOPMENT OF INDIVIDUALS' OBLIGATIONS UNDER INTERNATIONAL HUMAN RIGHTS LAW

The Preamble of the Universal Declaration of Human Rights (UDHR) states that 'every individual' and 'every organ of society' is encouraged to attempt by teaching and education to promote respect for the rights and freedoms there enshrined. Not only individuals, but also companies could

---

[48]   The notion of an obligation to prevent human rights violations was defined in Art. 23 of the Draft Articles on State Responsibility provisionally adopted by the International Law Commission on first reading (1999).

[49]   See, e.g., *A v United Kingdom*, Judgment of 23 September 1998, Reports of Judgments and Decisions 1998-VI, para. 22. See also O. De Schutter, *The Accountability of Multinationals for Human Rights Violation in European Law*, Center for Human Rights and Global Justice Working Paper, 1 (2004), at 45.

[50]   This hypothesis seems to fall within the provision of Art. 8 of the ILC Draft Articles, *supra* n. 8.

[51]   The application of Arts 5 and 7 of the ILC Draft Articles, *supra* n. 8, could be invoked in these cases. See also *infra* para. 3.6.

[52]   See Art. 9, ILC Draft Articles, *supra* n. 8. On this point see F. Francioni, 'Exporting Environmental Hazard through Multinational Enterprises: Can the State of Origin be Held Responsible?', in F. Francioni and T. Scovazzi, *International Responsibility for Environmental Harm*, 1991, London and Boston, Graham & Trotman; Norwell, Kluwer, 275 at 290.

possibly be included in the definition of an organ of society,[53] given their economic and increasingly social function in society. In addition, Article 29 of the UDHR stipulates that everyone has a duty to the community and Article 30 contains a strong warning to individuals to 'not harm'.[54] This provision, which is echoed by the ICCPR and other regional human rights treaties, says that 'Nothing in this Declaration may be interpreted as implying for any State or group or person any right to engage in any activity or to perform any act aimed at the destruction of any of the rights and freedom set forth herein'.[55] In further support of such an interpretation, the most recent international regional human rights instruments, the exhortatory Asian Human Rights Charter, clearly calls for the need of corporations to take responsibility for their actions.[56] The African Charter on Human and Peoples' Rights,[57] the African Charter on the Rights and Welfare of the Child[58] and the American Declaration of the Rights and Duties of Man[59] impose duties directly on non-State actors. These actors

---

[53]   An 'organ' in the sense used in the preamble suggests an institution or group of people or thing which performs some function.

[54]   The legal force of the UDHR is contested. It has been held that the preambular and substantive provisions in the Universal Declaration have the same indirect legal effect as an authoritative guide to the interpretation of human rights Articles in the United Nations (U.N.) Charter which themselves create legal obligations. In addition, whether or not legally binding and enforceable, the UDHR bears a widely recognized authority both in law and politics. See The Vienna Declaration and Programme of Action. U.N., World Conference on Human Rights The Vienna Declaration and Programme of action, 25 June 1993, UN Doc.A/ CONF. 157/23 (1993), available at: htpp:// http://unhcr.ch/udhr/index.htm (accessed 13 April 2004).

[55]   Preamble of the ICCPR.

[56]   See para. 2.8 'States are increasingly held hostage by financial and other corporations to implement narrow and short sighted economic policies which cause so much misery to so many people, while increasing the wealth of the few. Business corporations are responsible for numerous violations of right, particularly those of workers, women and indigenous peoples. It is necessary to strengthen the regime of rights by making corporations liable for the violations of rights'. Cited in D. Kinley, 'Human Rights as Legally Binding or Merely Relevant?', in S. Bottomley and D. Kinley (eds), *Commercial Law and Human Rights*, 2002, Aldershot, Ashgate, 25–45.

[57]   African [Banjul] Charter on Human and Peoples' Rights, 27 June 1981, preamble and Art. 28, OAU Doc. CAB/LEG/67/3 rev. 5, (1982) 21 *International Legal Materials* 58 (entered into force 21 October 1986).

[58]   African Charter on the Rights and Welfare of the Child, OAU Doc. CAB/ LEG/24.9/49 (1990) (entered into force 29 November 1999).

[59]   American Declaration of the Rights and Duties of Man, O.A.S. Res. XXX, adopted by the Ninth International Conference of American States (1948), reprinted in Basic Documents Pertaining to Human Rights in the Inter-American

specifically include individuals and communities, and some duties concern social, economic and cultural rights.[60]

The above-mentioned charters and declarations however do not hold individuals responsible for compliance with all the obligations enshrined in every human rights instrument. These statements, enshrined in international law instruments, reinforce the position of individuals as subjects of international law and possible holders of human rights duties as well as States.

In international criminal law, in particular, the responsibility of individuals is more limited.[61] International criminal responsibility is mainly the result of developments in international criminal law through State practice and decisions of international courts, such as those of the ICTY and for Rwanda. It includes a closed number of egregious violations of human rights, both during peace and war time, such as crimes against humanity, genocide, aggression, terrorism, slave trading and torture.[62]

The first recognition of a direct responsibility of individuals in international law can be found in the words of the International Military Tribunal of Nuremberg which affirmed that 'Crimes against international law are committed by men, not by abstract entities, and only by punishing individuals who commit such crimes can the provisions of international law be enforced'.[63] On this occasion the International Military Tribunal of Nuremberg declared that an organization could be held to be criminal.[64] However, this tribunal did not have jurisdiction over legal persons.

Humanitarian law has also evolved to include groups of individuals, for example Common Article 3 (common to the Four Geneva Conventions)

System, OEA/Ser.L.V/II.82 doc.6 rev.1 at 17 (1992), available at: http://www1. umn.edu/humanrts/iachr/general.html (accessed 4 November 2004).

60   D. Chirwa et al., 'Obligations of Non-State Actors in Relation to Economic, Social and Cultural Rights under the South African Constitution' (2003) 7 *Mediterranean Journal of Human Rights* 29.

61   Ratner defines it as 'the corpus of primary rules applicable to the individual', Ratner, *supra* Ch.3 n. 1, at 491.

62   Ibid., at 491–492. See also Cassese, *International Law, supra* Ch.2 n. 7, at 102.

63   Case 48, *Trial of Friedrich Flick and Five Others* (1947) 9 *Law Reports of the Trials of War Criminals* 1, at 18, reproduced in (1947) 14 International Law Rep. at 266, and also cited in Clapham, 'The Question of Jurisdiction', *supra* Ch.1 n. 71, at 166.

64   Charter of the International Military Tribunal (Annex to the 8 August 1945 London Agreement establishing an ad hoc International Military Tribunal, 28 U.N.T.S 284), Arts 9 and 10.

sets minimal rules applicable to all parties engaged in combat, including private parties.[65] Furthermore, Protocol II also applies to private parties.[66]

In conclusion, it is apparent that individuals as well as States have acquired a limited number of duties under international human rights law. A minimum standard made up of legal rights which are generally considered as essential to human life in society and to the dignity of man is gradually developing into an international duty incumbent on all members of the international legal community, which seems to be recognized as *jus cogens*. At the same time, the individual is vested with the right to have this position respected by States and by other subjects of international law.[67]

3.4 CORPORATE HUMAN RIGHTS DUTIES IN INTERNATIONAL SOFT LAW INSTRUMENTS

In examining international soft law instruments on MNEs' responsibility, it must be taken into account that the legal force of these international documents is extremely varied and piecemeal. They range from a multilaterally agreed instrument (the OECD Guidelines), to a voluntary initiative (the Global Compact). In addition, they have been adopted by different international organizations which pursue different, and in some cases specific, objectives. However, they all can be included in the grey area of international law defined as 'soft law'.[68]

---

[65] Geneva Convention Relative to the Protection of Civilian Persons in Time of War, 12 August 1949, art. 3, 6 U.S.T. 3516, 3518-20, 75 UNTS 287, 288-89; Geneva Convention Relative to the Treatment of Prisoners of War, 12 August 1949, art. 3, 6 U.S.T. 3316, 3318-21, 75 UNTS 135, 136; Geneva Convention for the Amelioration of the Condition of Wounded, Sick and Shipwrecked Members of Armed Forces at Sea, 12 August, 1949, art. 3, 6 U.S.T. 3217, 3220-22, 75 UNTS 85, 86; Geneva Convention for the Amelioration of the Condition of the Wounded and Sick in Armed Forces in the Field, 12 August, 1949, art. 3, 6 U.S.T. 3114, 3116-18, 75 UNTS 31, 32.

[66] Protocol Additional to the Geneva Conventions of 12 August 1949, and Relating to the Protection of Victims of Non-International Armed Conflicts, June 8, 1977, art. 13, 1125 UNTS 609, 611.

[67] See Mosler, *supra* Ch.2 n. 3, at 726.

[68] The expression 'soft law', as opposed to hard law, was developed to describe declarations, resolutions, guidelines, principles and other high levels statements by groups of States such as the United Nations, the International Labour Organization and the Organisation for Economic Co-operation and Development, that are neither strictly binding norms nor ephemeral political declarations. It is recognized that soft law instruments can have some anticipatory effect in shaping new binding international norms and may acquire considerable strength in shaping

Soft law is usually regarded with a certain suspicion by lawyers, who accuse it of being a tool to privatize or to set aside legally binding standards;[69] at the other end of the spectrum are those who look on soft law as a necessary step towards the development of legally binding instruments,[70] or favour the interaction between soft and hard law instruments. Three ways in which soft law may have a binding effect have been described.[71] First, codes which originate in agreements within sectoral organisations may constitute legally binding contracts. Secondly, governments and international organizations may make compliance with codes a formal condition for tendering and performance in procurement contracts, or in order to gain access to markets.[72] Finally, voluntarily adopted codes can be used by judges to give substantive content to vague normative standards: for instance, to see what constitutes 'due diligence'.[73]

Leaving aside here the terms of this thorny debate, it is necessary to acknowledge that even a strict legal approach to the issue of MNEs' responsibility cannot overlook soft law instruments. It is in this area of law that the major developments on issues of corporate responsibility have been taking place.[74] Even if these statements have not gained the legal force of customary law, they provide an indication of what the majority of States as members of international organizations believe the obligations of companies should be.[75] It has been noted that, especially in the field

---

international conduct. An exhaustive definition of soft law in international law is given by Daniel Thürer, 'Soft Law', in Bernhardt et al. (eds), *Encyclopedia of Public International Law*, *supra* Ch.1 n. 121, at 452. See also F. Francioni, 'International "Soft Law:" A Contemporary Assessment', in V. Lowe and M. Fitzmaurice (eds), *Fifty Years of the International Court of Justice: Essays in Honour of Sir Roberts Jennings*, 1996, Cambridge, Cambridge University Press, at 167.

[69] See R. Liubicic, 'Corporate Codes of Conduct and Product Labelling: the Limits and Possibilities of Promoting International Labour Rights Through Private Initiatives' (1998) 1 *Law and Policy in International Business*, 111, at 112. See also Supiot, *supra* Ch.1 n. 46, at 243.

[70] See FitzGerald, *supra* Ch.1 n. 58.

[71] An exhaustive account of the possible legal effects of codes of conduct is provided by Baade, *supra* Ch.1 n. 60.

[72] This option is explored by Hanley in the context of the EU. She suggests that access to EU public procurement may be subject to compliance with a European label. See Hanley, *supra* Ch.1 n. 10.

[73] Muchlinski, 'Human Rights Social Responsibility', *supra* Ch.1 n. 85, at 129.

[74] See M. Errol and M. Ozay, *Global Governance, Economy and Law: Waiting for Justice*, 2003, London and New York, Routledge, at 116. See Avery, *supra* Ch.1 n. 21, at 50.

[75] See Muchlinski who maintains that an apparent consensus is developing that some kind of international standards for MNES should be in place. Muchlinski, 'Human Rights Social Responsibility', *supra* Ch.1 n. 85, at 151.

of human rights at the universal level, a soft law stage is practically the rule now.[76] In addition, an analysis of the content and historical development of these codes will provide useful elements on the content, scope and implementation of corporate responsibility for human rights violations.

3.4.1 The OECD Guidelines for Multinational Enterprises

The OECD Guidelines adopted in 1976 were conceived merely as a tool for maximizing the benefits of foreign investment and for reducing the risks arising from conflicting requirements on MNEs by setting internationally agreed standards.[77] Being addressed to countries that were at a good stage of development, the original text did not take into account social concerns. Human rights and social considerations regarding the impact of MNEs in third countries were largely overlooked.[78] In addition to this, the Guidelines were perceived as the expression of the interest of the countries which were the principal sources of foreign investment flow and thus 'home States' of MNEs.[79] Their impact on MNEs' activities in developing countries was further limited by the fact that the Guidelines could be applied only in the territories of States adhering to the OECD.[80]

The revised version of the OECD Guidelines has introduced the obligation of companies to respect the human rights of those affected by their activities, consistent with the host government's international obligations and commitments.[81] In other words, companies are required to respect only human rights obligations acquired by the host country.

Even if this is probably the most restrictive reference to human rights among the international codes examined here, the relevance of this statement is threefold. First, it links corporate responsibility to the 'sphere of influence of companies' activities'; secondly, it identifies in the international law obligations of the State the standards against which MNEs

---

[76]   Simma, 'International Human Rights and General International Law,' *supra* Ch.1 n. 143, at 233.

[77]   See International Council on Human Rights Policy, *supra* Ch.1 n. 46.

[78]   See S. Tully, 'The 2000 Review of the OECD Guidelines for Multinational Enterprises' (2001) 50 I.C.L.Q. 394, at 395.

[79]   See International Council on Human Rights Policy, *supra* Ch.1 n. 46, at 67.

[80]   Members of the OECD: Australia, Austria, Belgium, Canada, Czech Republic, Denmark, Finland, France, Germany, Greece, Hungary, Iceland, Ireland, Italy, Japan, Korea, Luxembourg, Mexico, The Netherlands, New Zealand, Norway, Poland, Portugal, Spain, Slovak Republic, Sweden, Switzerland, Turkey, United Kingdom, United States.

[81]   *OECD Guidelines* , para. II 2.

should measure their conduct; thirdly, the term 'those affected by their activities' seems to include a large number of stakeholders.[82]

The recommendation to respect human rights is further supported by reference to the Universal Declaration of Human Rights, as well as to all internationally recognized core labour standards. MNEs are exhorted to contribute to the effective abolition of child labour and to the elimination of all forms of compulsory labour (paragraph II-1).[83] Social accountability is encouraged in the chapter on disclosure and transparency, which has been updated to reflect the OECD Principles on Corporate Governance.

The second relevant innovation of the Guidelines refers to their scope of application. Taking into account the changes in the global economy, and in particular the fact that MNEs increasingly operate in non-OECD Member States, the new text extends the application of the Guidelines to the world-wide activities of enterprises operating in countries adhering to the Guidelines.

Significantly, the Guidelines have been adopted by a number of countries that are not members of the OECD (so called non-adhering countries). This change can contribute to a more even application of the Guidelines across developing and developed countries.

In addition, as a result of the review, the Guidelines enforcement mechanism has been improved. The enforcement mechanism is based on National Contact Points (NCPs) endowed with the tasks of raising awareness of the Guidelines and solving disputes about their interpretation, and conducting enquiries about the behaviour of companies.

> Other organisations such as non governmental organisations, not only member States, can now ask a National Contact Point for consultation when a company has violated the Guidelines. For its part the European Commission contributed to raising awareness of the Guidelines among interested parties, in order to facilitate the use and the dissemination of the new guidelines. The Commission has organised conferences and workshops to promote Corporate Social Responsibility and the Guidelines, and is supporting a series of seminars in developing countries during 2003, organised by the Trade Unions

---

[82]   The commentary to the Guidelines clarifies that: 'while promoting and upholding human rights is primarily the responsibility of governments, where corporate conduct and human rights intersect enterprises do play a role, and thus MNEs are encouraged to respect human rights, not only in their dealings with employees, but also with respect to others affected by their activities, in a manner that is consistent with host governments' international obligations and commitments'.

[83]   Tully, *supra* n. 78, at 396.

Advisory Committee to the OECD, with the aim of raising awareness of the Guidelines.[84]

3.4.2 The ILO Tripartite Declaration on Multinational Enterprises and Social Policy

Despite its being a voluntary instrument, not being legally binding upon the Member States of the ILO, the ILO Tripartite Declaration on Multinational Enterprises and Social Policy creates a political and moral obligation on Member States to follow its recommendations. Its authority derives from the fact that the Declaration was adopted by consensus by the ILO's Governing body. The ILO tripartite declaration on multinational enterprises and social policy makes reference to the UDHR, the ICCPR and the ICESCR.

The text of the Tripartite Declaration was revised in March 2000[85] to incorporate the fundamental principles and rights at work as enshrined in the 1998 ILO Declaration. Adopted in 1998, the ILO Declaration on fundamental principles and rights at work commits Member States to respect and promote: freedom of association and the right to collective bargaining; the elimination of forced and compulsory labour; the abolition of child labour; and the elimination of discrimination in the workplace. The Declaration makes it clear that these rights are universal, and that they apply to all people in all States – regardless of the level of economic development. It particularly mentions groups with special needs, including the unemployed and migrant workers. It recognizes that economic growth alone is not enough to ensure equity, social progress and to eradicate poverty.[86]

The parties to which the Tripartite Declaration is commended (governments, workers, employers and MNEs) should contribute to the

---

[84]   Council of the European Union, *EU Annual Report on Human Rights 2003*), Office for Official Publications of the European Community Luxembourg 2003 (EU Annual Report on Human Rights) at 29.

[85]   Tripartite Declaration of Principles concerning Multinational Enterprises and Social Policy, adopted by the Governing Body of the International Labour Office at its 204th Session (Geneva, November 1977) as amended at its 279th (November 2000) and 295th Session (March 2006).

[86]   This commitment is supported by a follow-up procedure. Member States that have not ratified one or more of the core Conventions are asked each year to report on the status of the relevant rights and principles within their borders, noting impediments to ratification, and areas where assistance may be required. These reports are reviewed by the Committee of Independent Expert Advisers. In turn, their observations are considered by the ILO's Governing Body.

realization of the ILO Declaration on Fundamental Principles and Rights at Work and its Follow-up. In addition, governments are urged to ratify, along with the conventions already referenced, the minimum age and child labour conventions, Convention Numbers 138 and 182, respectively, and the corresponding Recommendations Numbers 146 and 190. A section on minimum age is added to a new paragraph 36 to commend that 'multinational enterprises, as well as national enterprises, should respect the minimum age for admission to employment or work in order to secure the effective abolition of child labour.' The text is completed by provisions on the equality of opportunity and treatment, security of employment, training, conditions of work and life benefits. Like the OECD Guidelines, the Tripartite Declaration also refers to the highest attainable standard of safety and health. Interestingly, it is the only soft law instrument that makes reference to the right to a minimum wage which has then also been included in the Norms.

The follow-up procedures have been strengthened over the course of time. Member States of the ILO are requested to fully apply the Declaration and submit reports prepared by governments in consultation with employers' and workers' organizations. In November 1980 the Governing Body established a procedure regarding the interpretation of provisions of the Declaration in the case of disputes about its application. Interpretation may be requested from the ILO by a government or, in certain cases, a representative workers' or employers' organization. The Governing Body decided that follow-up procedures regarding the Declaration must not duplicate or conflict with existing procedures, such as those already provided by the ILO supervisory machinery for Conventions and Recommendations. Requests for interpretation of the Declaration must not concern national laws and practice.

According to this follow-up procedure a request can be made by a government and, under certain conditions, by a representative workers' or employers' organization itself. If a workers' or employers' organization addresses a request for interpretation directly to the ILO, the Office will inform the government concerned. If declared admissible, the ILO will prepare a draft reply, which will have to be submitted to the Governing Body Committee on Multinational Enterprises. Finally, the reply is considered by the Governing Body.

3.4.3   The Global Compact

The Global Compact, launched in 1999 by the Secretary General of the United Nations, expressly asks businesses to support and adopt voluntarily ten core principles. The principles refer to general human rights obligations, core labour standards, the protection of the environment and avoidance of corruption.[87]

First, it is pointed out that responsibility for the respect of human rights primarily lies with States, as primary addressees of international human rights norms, but it is partially shared with individuals and organizations. Therefore, companies are required to support human rights both in the workplace and within their sphere of influence (principle 1). Principle 2 recommends companies not to be complicit in human rights violations perpetrated by States. As far as labour standards are concerned, there is a clear reference to the four core labour standards enshrined in the 1998 ILO declaration. Pursuant to the Global Compact Principles, businesses should uphold the freedom of association and collective bargaining; the elimination of all forms of forced and compulsory labour, the effective abolition of child labour, the elimination of discrimination in respect of employment and occupation. The Global Compact also calls on companies to adopt human rights, as enshrined in the UDHR, as fundamental values guiding business and integrated in management strategies.

It is regrettable, however, that human rights are poorly defined by the rather vague expression of 'internationally proclaimed human rights'. The only international human rights document quoted in the Principles is the UDHR. No express reference is made to the two UN International Covenants on Economic, Social and Cultural Rights and on Civil and Political Rights.

3.4.4 Norms on the Responsibility of Transnational Corporations and Other Business Enterprises with Regard to Human Rights

The Norms on the Responsibility of Transnational Corporations and Other Businesses Enterprises with Regard to Human Rights[88] (hereinafter 'the Norms') were hailed as the first non-voluntary initiative accepted at the international level. Even if their legal force has yet to be defined, they represent the most widely agreed set of norms addressed to companies.

---

[87] On 24 June 2004, during the Global Compact Leaders Summit, UN Secretary-General Kofi Annan announced that the Global Compact would include a tenth principle, against corruption, reflecting the recently adopted United Nations convention on that subject. The Tenth Principle states that: 'Businesses should work against corruption in all its forms, including extortion and bribery'. An exhaustive and updated study on the Global Compact can be found in U. Morth (ed.), *Soft Law in Governance and Regulation: An Interdisciplinary Analysis*, 2004, Cheltenham, Edward Elgar.

[88] See UN Norms *supra* Ch.1 n. 14 at para. 52.

The Norms derive their authority from their sources in international law and their restatement of legal principles applicable to companies. Some authority should also be attached to the fact that this document is the result of four years of consultation and drafting process, which involved a great number of scholars, representatives of NGOs, companies and unions from several UN member States. Strictly speaking, however, the Norms were adopted in the form of a Resolution by the Sub-Commission on the Protection and Promotion of Human Rights, which was transmitted to the Commission for Human Rights for eventual consideration. It is not excluded that they will acquire greater authority in the future if adopted by a higher UN body, or translated into an international treaty.[89]

Having been approved in August 2003 by the UN Sub-Commission on the Promotion and Protection of Human Rights,[90] the Norms were subsequently transmitted to the Commission on Human Rights for consideration on adoption. In the light of subsequent studies, prepared by the Office of the High Commissioner for Human Rights, the UN Human Rights Commission appointed John Ruggie Special Representative of the UN Secretary General on business and human rights. The Special Representative has recently published his first interim report,[91] which aimed to identify standards of corporate accountability for businesses; elaborate on the role of States in effectively regulating the role of business, including through international cooperation; research and clarify concepts such as 'complicity' and 'sphere of influence'; develop materials and methodologies for undertaking human rights impact assessments of business activities; and compile a compendium of best practices of States and businesses.

In the present context, it is worth examining the Norms to see what they have contributed to the initiatives already discussed. In contrast with the ILO and OECD texts, the sub-commission text defines what is meant by a transnational corporation and draws a distinction between the responsibilities of transnationals and those of other business enterprises. The term

---

[89]   Weissbrot and Kruger, 'Norms on the Responsibilities of Transnational Corporations', *supra* Ch.1 n. 47, at 913–15.
[90]   The UN Sub-Commission on the Promotion and Protection of Human Rights is a body created to act as a think thank to assist the UN Commission on Human Rights which is an intergovernmental body of 53 member States of the United Nations. The UN Sub-Commission on the Promotions and Protection of Human Rights is composed of 26 members who are elected as independent experts by the Commission on Human Rights.
[91]   E/CN.4/2006/97 Report of the Special Representative of the Secretary-General on the issue of human rights and transnational corporations and other business enterprises (John Ruggie).

'transnational corporation' refers to an economic entity operating in more than one country or a cluster of economic entities operating in two or more countries – whatever their legal form, whether in their home country or country of activity, and whether taken individually or collectively.[92]

The Norms include a more comprehensive range of human rights than the other international codes of conduct or voluntary initiatives. They reflect and restate a wide range of human rights and labour legal principles, but also incorporate best practices for corporate social responsibility. The Norms and Commentary provide for the right to equality of opportunity and treatment; the right to security of persons, the rights of workers, including a safe and healthy environment and the right to collective bargaining, respect for international national and local laws and the rule of law, respect for the right to health, as well as other economic social and cultural rights; other civil and political rights such as freedom of movement, consumer protection and environmental protection.[93] It is also clarified that:

> the phrases 'human rights' and 'international human rights' include civil, cultural, economic, political and social rights, as set forth in the International Bill of Human Rights and other human rights treaties, as well as the right to development and rights recognised by international humanitarian law, international refugee law, international labour law, and other relevant instruments adopted within the United Nations system.[94]

As far as labour rights are concerned, the norms are the only international document that goes beyond the core labour standards enshrined in the 1998 ILO Declaration by also including the right to a remuneration that would ensure an adequate standard of living for them and their families and that takes into account workers' needs for adequate living conditions, with a view towards progressive improvement.

The fundamental principle of their implementation is that the Norms do not intend to reduce the obligations of States under international law to promote and secure the fulfilment of, and ensure respect for, human rights.[95] This statement is reinforced by a saving clause providing that nothing in the Norms should be interpreted as diminishing States' obligations.

---

[92] Ibid., at para. 20.
[93] The Norms are completed by provisions on the protection of the environment, transparency and avoidance of corruption and humanitarian law.
[94] UN Norms, *supra* Ch.1 n.14, at para. 23.
[95] Ibid., at para. 19.

The Norms also clearly state that:

> Within their respective spheres of activity and influence, transnational corporations and other business enterprises have the obligation to promote, secure the fulfilment of, respect, ensure respect of and protect human rights recognized in international as well as national law, including the rights and interests of indigenous peoples and other vulnerable groups.[96]

Therefore, companies are also called upon to play a role in the implementation of human rights. Companies are expected to adopt and implement their own internal rules of operation to ensure the human rights protection set forth in the instrument. However, while the distinction between the obligations to respect, protect and secure fulfilment are well known where explained with regards to States, the problem arises as to how these obligations apply to MNEs. The most valuable contribution of the Norms is probably their attempt to identify the different dimensions of the human rights responsibilities of corporations. While many legal commentators have referred to the criteria nexus[97] or the leverage[98] that companies have with regard to abuse, the Norms use the concept of companies' sphere of influence to determine how human rights obligations apply to them. The sphere of influence of a company tends to include the individuals to whom it has a certain political, contractual, economic or geographic proximity.[99] Although this concept has not been defined authoritatively, it could be useful in clarifying the extent to which companies should support human rights and make sure that they are not complicit in human rights abuses.

A valuable contribution to the definition of the scope of corporate responsibility is also given by the fact that the Norms endorse the concept of graduation of responsibility, depending on the proximity to the victim of the human rights violations. The Norms adopt a very broad definition of the term 'stakeholder', which should include both parties directly affected by the activities of business enterprises and parties which are indirectly affected by the activities of transnational corporations or other business enterprises, such as consumer groups, customers, governments, neighbouring communities, indigenous peoples and communities, non-governmental organizations, public and private lending institutions, suppliers, trade associations, and others.

---

[96]   Ibid., at para. 1a.
[97]   Ibid., and Ratner, *supra* n. 1, at 465.
[98]   N. Jägers, *Corporate Human Rights Obligations: In Search of Accountability*, 2002, Antwerp and Oxford, Intersentia, at 79.
[99]   International Council on Human Rights Policy, *supra* Ch.1 n. 46, at 136.

The Norms also indicate that businesses will be subject to periodical monitoring that is independent and transparent and includes input from all relevant stakeholders. Furthermore, businesses are called upon to provide adequate reparation to anyone harmed by conduct that is inconsistent with the standards set in the Norms.

Moreover, there are indications that the human rights standards enshrined in the Norms go beyond a simple obligation to respect, requiring companies also to contribute (to 'support')[100] to the protection of economic, social and cultural rights as well as civil and political rights and contribute to their realization, in particular the rights to development, adequate food and drinking water, the highest attainable standard of physical and mental health, adequate housing, privacy, education, freedom of thought, conscience, and religion and freedom of opinion and expression, and shall refrain from actions which obstruct or impede the realization of those rights.

The Norms also state that companies should not only refrain from engaging in war crimes, crimes against humanity, genocide, torture, forced disappearance, forced or compulsory labour, hostage-taking, extrajudicial, summary or arbitrary executions, but they are also forbidden to benefit from these crimes. It indicates that not only can companies be held responsible under domestic international criminal law, but they can also be held responsible when they simply profit from such wrongs by conducting business in a country that tolerates or perpetrates human rights violations. In other words, it seems that the drafters of the norms have taken into account situations such as apartheid in South Africa, where companies have been held accountable for human rights violations for the mere fact of operating in the country and taking indirect advantage of apartheid, even if a clear causal link in criminal legal terms could not be established.[101]

Interestingly, not only do the Norms provide a tentative list of human rights obligations binding on MNEs, but they also indicate methods for their implementation and set out a provisional monitoring mechanism.

Far from being a simple codification of existing standards, the norms were originally conceived to encourage further evolution. Although they

---

[100] See Report of the Subcommission on the Promotion and Protection of Human Rights, Report of the United Nations High Commissioner on Human Rights, on the Responsibilities of Transnational Corporations and Related Business Enterprises with Regard to Human Rights, UN Document E/CN/.4/2005/91 at 12.

[101] See *Report of the South African Truth and Reconciliation Commission, supra* Ch.1 n. 35.

include a tentative list of human rights and labour rights obligations for corporations, the Norms are not intended to create an exhaustive list of obligations. They were actually expected to be a non-voluntary instrument open to development in terms of content, legal force, and mechanisms of implementation.[102]

The interpretation of the Norms as a possible international framework for MNEs' responsibility has, however, recently been questioned by the Mid-Term Report by John Ruggie, Special Representative of the UN Secretary General on business and human rights.

Ruggie points to the discrepancy between the claim of the Norms, on the one hand, to merely 'reflect' and 'restate' international legal principles, when on the other hand, they are said to be the first such initiative at the international level that is 'non-voluntary' and thus in some sense directly binding on corporations. Ruggie finds this problematic because, if they merely restate established international legal principles, then they cannot also directly bind business because, with the possible exception of certain war crimes and crimes against humanity, there are no generally accepted international legal principles that do so. And if the Norms were to bind business directly, then they could not merely be restating international legal principles; they would need, somehow, to discover or invent new ones.

The second concern refers to the principle by which they propose to allocate human rights responsibilities between States and firms. The report suggests that, without a principled differentiation, the allocation of responsibilities under the Norms, in actual practice, could come to hinge entirely on the respective capacities of States and corporations in certain situations. In particular, since corporations are not democratic public interest institutions, that makes them, in effect, co-equal duty bearers for 'the obligation to promote, secure the fulfilment of, respect, ensure respect and protect' human rights as the General Obligations of the Norms put it – and to make governments more responsible to their own citizens. However, through several examples, Ruggie shows some 'fluidity in the applicability of international legal principles to acts by companies', and he further reminds us that States do have tools at their disposal to enforce human rights standards more rigorously.

Ruggie's analysis of the Norms has proven especially controversial among some in the NGO community. EarthRights International calls his evaluation 'unnecessarily harsh' and further charges that Ruggie 'completely disregards the process that came before him and ultimately

---

[102]   Weissbrot and Kruger, *supra* n. 89, at 913–15.

led to his appointment.'[103] More detailed criticism is contained in a position paper by the International Federation of Human Rights,[104] which also takes issue with the interim report's criticism of the Norms, and calls for the Special Representative to use his mandate to 'build on what has already been achieved', including the Norms. NGOs' reaction to the interim report can partly be explained by the wide support the Norms received in civil society. On the contrary, the business community was opposed to the Norms because there was a perception that they were considered binding and it was unclear what enforcement would look like. Moreover, international business organizations argued that the Norms subverted voluntary efforts to promote global corporate responsibility.[105]

In his second full report released in April 2008,[106] Ruggie undertakes an interesting attempt to systematize and detail business human rights obligations on the basis of extensive industry and business surveys. He significantly embraces the thesis put forward at the outset of this book regarding an open list of human rights to be applied to companies. Recognising that, business can affect virtually all internationally recognized rights, he agrees that any limited list will almost certainly miss one or more rights that may turn out to be significant in a particular instance, thereby providing misleading guidance. At the same time, it is also clearly spelled out that, as economic actors, companies have specific responsibilities that differ from those of States. Therefore, this report pursues the more promising path of addressing the specific responsibilities of companies in relation to all rights upon which they may have an impact.[107]

The result is a sort of minimum list of human rights obligations ranged into labour rights and non-labour rights, accompanied by the generic

---

[103] L.M. Manzella, *Ominous Outlook for the UN Norms*, 22 March 2006, available at: http://www.earthrights.org/legalfeature/ominous_outlook_for_the_un_norms.html accessed on 30 April 2006.

[104] Joint NGO Response to Interim Report of UN Representative on Business and Human Rights, available at: http://www.fidh.org/article.php3?id_article=3334 (accessed 4 September 2006).

[105] S. Bertasi of the International Chamber of Commerce told the *Financial Times* (13 August 2003): 'We don't have a problem at all with efforts that seek to encourage companies to do what they can . . . to protect human rights, we have a problem with the premise and the principle that the norms are based on.'

[106] A/HRC/8/5, *Protect, Respect and Remedy: a Framework for Business and Human Rights Report of the Special Representative of the Secretary-General on the issue of human rights and transnational corporations and other business enterprises,* John Ruggie, 7 April 2008.

[107] Para. 6, 50 ff. in *Protect, Respect and Remedy*, *supra* n. 106.

appeal to due diligence and a clarification of the issue of 'sphere of influence' and of 'complicity'.

According to Ruggie, it can be understood from these reports that the state duty to protect is probably the most important tool to prevent human rights abuses. Corporations will still strive to make profit, and due to their competitive nature they may be inclined to 'bend the rules' a little bit. However as we can see more and more parts of international law are being incorporated into domestic law, and companies are getting more and more inclined to preserve human rights. In addition to this, the government should be more forceful, they should bear more of the responsibility as it is in their duty to protect their citizens. For example, they should not take part in a 'race-to-bottom' where abuses of companies would be tolerated in exchange of their capital.

The framework of 'protect, respect, and remedy' can assist all social actors – governments, companies, and civil society – to reduce the adverse human rights consequences of these misalignments.

In conclusion, it can be agreed that the concerns expressed by Ruggie over the necessity of a clearer definition of the scope of MNEs' responsibility and in particular of the notions of 'sphere of influence' and of 'complicity' are well founded and shared by most legal commentators. Although the Norms in their present form may not be sufficiently clear and detailed to impose legal obligations directly on MNEs,[108] this does not invalidate current attempts to build on the Norms in order to clarify those obligations and set up monitoring mechanisms which would ensure that they are complied with. Quite the opposite, such attempts should be encouraged, even apart from their current lack of legal status. If the Norms are to be an internationally recognized point of reference and possibly lay down the basis for an internationally binding document on MNEs and human rights, they should also provide the appropriate forum to define these key concepts.

The future of the Norms is at the moment uncertain. Before the reform of the United Nations, if approved by the Human Rights Commission, the Norms still had to be adopted by the Economic and Social Council, after which the Norms could be presented to the General Assembly, which may approve them through a resolution. After the reform, pursuant to General Assembly Resolution 60/251 of 15 March 2006, all mandates, mechanisms, functions and responsibilities of the Commission on Human Rights, including the Sub-Commission on the Promotion and Protection

---

[108]   O. De Schutter, 'The Challenge of Imposing Human Rights Norms on Corporate Actors,' in O. de Schutter, *Transnational Corporations and Human Rights, supra* Ch.1 n. 37, 1, at 21.

of Human Rights, were assumed, as of 19 June 2006, by the Human Rights Council.

The Human Rights Council decided to extend exceptionally for one year, subject to the review to be undertaken by the Council in conformity with General Assembly resolution 60/251,[109] the mandates and mandate-holders of the Sub-commission. Even if the Council, in this regard, requested the Sub-Commission to continue with the implementation of its mandate, however, the concern is whether the new Human Rights Council will retain independent special rapporteurs as the Human Rights Commission. In addition, by taking the UN human rights body out of ECOSOC and making it a subsidiary of the General Assembly, social and economic rights risk being overlooked. Such a concern is particularly true for the Norms, which have been one of the most controversial topics within the 60th Commission of Human Rights.

Given the role of guidance of the Norms, the abandonment of their process of adoption would mark an extremely disappointing impasse in the creation of an international framework for the responsibility of MNEs. On the contrary, it is desirable that, after years of discussion within the Commission on Human Rights and despite Ruggie's critical mid-term report, the Norms could be finalized under the new UN body rather than following the decline which has characterized the Corporate Social Responsibility debate within the EU. On this issue, not only should the EC and its Member States support the Norms in the realm of the UN but also the EC should also refer to the UN Norms as the guiding international instrument on the responsibility of MNEs.

3.5 CLOSING REMARKS ON SOFT LAW INSTRUMENTS

The above-examined international documents touch upon most of the controversial issues related to corporate responsibility, such as the definition of MNEs; the relationship between companies and host States; the scope of corporate responsibility; a tentative list of human rights and core labour standard obligations of companies; the characteristics of monitoring mechanisms.

The four instruments converge on underlining that the primary responsibility to respect, protect and vindicate human rights falls on States. It

---

[109]   Resolution adopted by the General Assembly (A/60/L.48) 60/251, Human Rights Council.

must be noted, however, that these documents are addressed directly to companies and expect companies to respect a minimum core of obligations: in the first instance, an obligation to comply with domestic law and policy of the host country, in the second instance a general obligation of 'respect' of human rights. The Norms, however, go beyond this minimum core of obligations and call upon companies to engage in positive human rights duties to protect and fulfil human rights within their own spheres of influence. A reference to positive obligations is also contained in the Tripartite Declaration. It requires MNEs, when appropriate, to support representative employees' organizations. In some cases this may imply actively engaging in the protection of workers.[110]

As far as specific duties are concerned, at one end of the spectrum one finds the OECD Guidelines and the Global Compact, which contain only a vague reference to 'internationally recognised human rights'. At the other end of the spectrum, the Norms contain a wide range of specific human rights duties, supported by a comprehensive reference to all main UN human rights treaties and declarations.

A wider convergence seems to have been achieved on the respect of labour rights. A particular role in the promotion of labour rights has been played by the ILO's Declaration on Fundamental Principles and Rights at Work. The Declaration has become the benchmark for the respect of labour rights at the international level. This is confirmed by the fact that all the above-examined international soft law instruments expressly refer to the Declaration or contain the rights enshrined therein. This can probably be ascribed to the fact that the respect of the 1998 ILO declaration is based on its inherent value more than on the legal value of the document in which it is contained.[111]

Another relevant point can be made regarding the definition of the scope of corporate responsibility. Similarly to legal commentators who have referred to the nexus[112] criteria or the leverage[113] that companies have with regard to abuse, these documents perceive MNEs' responsibility on a sliding scale, which takes into account the 'proximity' to and the specific relationship with the victims of corporate abuses. Such an approach seems to be endorsed by the Norms, which refer to the 'sphere of influence' and by the OECD Guidelines. The ILO Declaration contains a principle

---

[110]   *ILO Tripartite Declaration, supra* Ch.1 n. 12, paras 1417, 1419.
[111]   See P. Alston, '"Core Labour Standards" and the Transformation of the International Labour Rights Regime' (2004) 15 *European Journal of International Law* 3.
[112]   Ratner, *supra* n. 1 at 465.
[113]   Jägers, *Corporate Human Rights Obligations, supra* n. 98, at 79.

of gradation as well, since it places more stringent duties on MNEs operating in developing countries.

Finally, a historical analysis of these international documents indicates that the expectations of States on the behaviour of human rights have developed in three directions: a broader inclusion of human rights and core labour standards; a wider geographical scope of application; and the progressive strengthening of enforcement/implementation mechanisms. In addition, the UN Norms, which are the result of more than thirty years of discussion within the UN and, despite the latest developments, represent an attempt to move from voluntary to non-voluntary measure, expressly define themselves as an evolutionary step towards a legally binding instrument.

3.6 ELEMENTS FOR CORPORATE RESPONSIBILITY UNDER INTERNATIONAL HUMAN RIGHTS LAW

Some elements for the definition of MNEs' responsibility can be drawn from the above analysis of the current international legal framework. These elements are intended as a preliminary assessment of MNEs' obligations at the international level.

A formal analysis of international human rights law points to the direction of equating corporations' obligations to those of individuals. Corporations have only those obligations pertaining to all non-State actors, the minimum set of obligations directed at individuals to refrain from breaching *jus cogens.* Even if there is no formal prohibition on corporations committing international crimes, affirming that corporations do not even have this obligation to refrain from such abuses would not make sense from an international law point of view. It would mean that corporate form could be used to trump *jus cogens.*

Even if individual human rights obligations seem to be more adaptable to corporations, this option is not devoid of shortcomings. It is true that a general negative duty of being bound not to interfere with others' enjoyment of rights is imposed on all individuals. However, the breaches of human rights obligations relevant under international criminal law are codified *in numerus clausus*, so extremely limited. It would be largely insufficient, since it will not address the fact that corporate activities have the potential to affect virtually every aspect of human rights and it is not limited to international crimes and international humanitarian law. In practice, this would leave most corporate human rights violations without redress.

Secondly, most human rights abuses do not give rise to individual responsibility. In many cases, human rights violations are the result of the convergence of acts and omissions of States and other actors that lead to a human rights deprivation which eschews pinpointing a closed and determined number of violators. The deprivation of human rights, such as the right to health or to adequate food, can be the result of a combination of institutional inadequacy of the host State (i.e. lax regulations, inefficient judiciary system) together with irresponsible management choices. This was, for instance, the case of a diffuse complicity between some industry sectors and the South African government during the apartheid regime.[114]

Thirdly, the corporations act as organizations and they are not simply the sum of the individuals working for them. For instance, in the *Bhopal*[115] case, even if the individual executives of the corporation did not engage in criminal conduct, higher standards of care should be expected from a company given its collective might and resources.[116] The discourse on MNEs' responsibility is based on the assumption that, in practice, MNEs bear different capacities to harm human dignity and to avoid State control than individuals.

Finally, the assumption that corporations would have at least as many obligations under international law as individuals have to face another theoretical objection: the lack of mechanisms to make this responsibility effective. Even if we equate corporate responsibility with the international criminal responsibility of individuals, international criminal liability for legal persons has not yet been recognized. As far back as 1945, the International Military Tribunal of Nuremberg declared the principle that an organization can be criminally responsible, but it did not have jurisdiction over legal persons.[117] In the context of the Rome Conference of 1998, which would lead to the establishment of the International Criminal Court, the final proposal to grant the Court jurisdiction over legal persons such as MNEs was not adopted. The rejection of the proposal was due more to technical complexities and time constraints of the participants

---

[114]   *Report of the South African Truth and Reconciliation Commission, supra* Ch.1 n. 35.

[115]   See *Bhopal* case, *supra* Ch.1 n. 30.

[116]   B. Fisse and J. Braithwaite, 'The Allocation of Responsibility for Corporate Crime: Individualism Collectivism and Accountability' (1998) 11 *Sydney Law Review* 468.

[117]   Charter of the International Military Tribunal (Annex to the 8 August 1945 London Agreement Establishing an *ad hoc* International Military Tribunal, 28 U.N.T.S 284), Arts 9 and 10.

than on firm objections of principle.[118] The discussion, however, has the merits of having drawn attention to the importance of considering ways to cope with corporate breaches of international humanitarian law.[119] The present condition of 'impunity' of MNEs is not irreversible. Once it is accepted that companies can be addressees of norms of international law (as examined in the previous chapter), the fact that they are not yet internationally accountable does not imply that they cannot have obligations.[120]

As noted by Ratner, the option of translating international States' responsibility to corporations faces several problems. First, extending these obligations would mean ignoring the differences between the nature and functions of States and corporations. Duties on States are not simply transferable to corporations. It can be affirmed, however, that the same human rights that impose duties on States may create the same or different duties on corporations. International human rights law should develop in the sense of identifying new duty holders, such as non-State actors, that go beyond States.[121]

In conclusion, thus far, binding human rights instruments have not imposed obligations on companies. This situation is paradoxical if one looks at the rights acquired by companies at the international level. The classical categories of international States' responsibility and individual criminal responsibility have some limitations in addressing corporate human rights violations, due to the fact that corporations find themselves at the crossroads between the position of individuals and those of States in international law.

At this point, it is worth identifying and summarising three trends which point in the direction of redefining the responsibility of companies. The imbalance, or better this 'gap', between MNEs' rights and duties has so far been bridged by a creative use of existing human rights instruments, such as stretching States' obligations in order to also cover breaches between private parties and by reaffirming and expanding international criminal responsibility. In addition, even if States have not been ready to impose

---

[118]   See Clapham, *The Question of Jurisdiction, supra* Ch.1 n. 71, at 157. Seidermann adds that some domestic systems do not recognize the principle of corporate criminal responsibility. See I.D. Seidermann, *Hierarchy in International Law: The Human Rights Dimension,* 2001, Antwerp, Intersentia, at 229.

[119]   Clapham, *The Question of Jurisdiction, supra* Ch.1 n. 71, at 140.

[120]   Clapham, *Human Rights Obligations, supra* Ch.1 n. 50.

[121]   A. Reinisch, 'The Changing International Legal Framework for Dealing with Non-State Actors', in Alston, *Non-State Actors and Human Rights, supra* Ch.1 n. 81, at 37.

obligations on companies, they have increasingly set minimum standards for corporate behaviour in a broad number of areas such as labour law and general respect for human rights. They have agreed on programmatic declarations, such as international codes of conduct and international voluntary initiatives, on which corporate behaviour would be in compliance with human rights and labour rights.

As a result, even if MNEs do not yet have human rights responsibility under international law, they are increasingly 'surrounded' by them.[122] The analysis of current trends in international law shows that not only is a minimum obligation established in the sense of 'respecting' human rights, but there is also pressure for MNEs to go beyond this scope. International human rights instruments have been interpreted by regional courts and treaty body international courts. These courts have interpreted international human rights instruments broadly by expanding corporate responsibility, even to the obligations to protect and fulfil human rights in some specific cases. In particular, corporate responsibility is perceived as growing in relation to the proximity to and the relationship with the victim.

This argument is reaffirmed by the fact that both international codes and international interpretation bodies agree on the fact that the responsibility of a company cannot be limited to its workers, but it includes all those affected by the activity. Therefore, a principle of graduation of responsibility, depending on the type or right at stake, proximity and vicinity to the victim seems to be a common feature of the evolving definition of corporate responsibility at the international level.

3.6.1   Which Human Rights Obligations for MNEs?

A fundamental question that remains unanswered concerns which human rights can be the object of breaches by companies. There have been several attempts to identify a list of human rights for companies. It seems, however, that a closed list of human rights obligations would be unsatisfactory, from both a theoretical and empirical perspective.

Dubin distinguishes between a number of rights that could be imposed on MNEs in their current formulation and those which, on the other hand, need to be reformulated before being applied to companies.[123] In the first

---

[122]   Uriz-Hernandez, *supra* Ch.2 n. 24, at 413.
[123]   L. Dubin, 'The Direct Application of Human Rights Standards to, and by Transnational Corporations', 61 *The Review of the International Commission of Jurists*, (1991) 35, at 38.

category would fall those rights recognized as part of *jus cogens*, such as the right to life, the right not to be subjected to torture or to inhumane and degrading treatment or punishment, nor to be held in slavery or servitude, the elimination of forced labour and child labour, non-discrimination, the freedom of thought, conscience and religion and the freedom of association and collective bargaining. Human rights that do not need to be reformulated and could be directly applicable to MNEs are: the right to found a family, to leave a country, to education, to rest and leisure and to social security.[124]

Joseph's analysis recognizes that MNEs are bound to the respect of three broad categories of rights: labour rights, environmental rights and freedom from bodily harm, as enshrined in international conventions and declarations.[125] Jägers identifies a number of human rights that MNEs are able to breach, such as the right to food, health, life and the prohibition of slavery and forced labour. Her analysis goes a step further, by applying to each of these rights the distinction between the obligation to respect, to protect and to fulfil.[126]

These doctrinal classifications show their weaknesses when confronted with practical cases of corporate human rights breaches. For instance, the right to a fair trial, not included by the above mentioned authors, apparently seems not to be applicable to corporations but only *vis-à-vis* States. In the case *Wiwa Shell,* however, a company was alleged to have fabricated false evidence and provided false witness testimony in order to facilitate condemnation of an activist by the government.[127]

A closed list classification of corporate duties is not entirely satisfactory, for both theoretical and practical reasons. Firstly, the ever reaffirmed principles of interdependence and interrelation of all human rights imply that they all should be protected on the same footing; in addition the protection of one right can be strictly related or underpinned by another one, so that one is necessary for the implementation of the other. Focusing on a limited number of rights could lead to paradoxical situations and leave individuals deprived of human rights in practice. Secondly, a fixed number of corporate duties defeats the complexity of factual reality. It is difficult

---

124   Ibid., at 41. Rights such as the right to asylum, to take part in government and the rights to a nationality, however, cannot be reformulated so as to produce effects on MNEs.
125   Joseph, 'Taming the Leviathans', *supra* Ch.1 n. 8, at 189. However, she also warns against the fact that the imposition of duties on non-governmental organizations such as MNEs may raise liberal dilemmas.
126   Jägers, *Multinational Corporations, supra* Ch.1 n. 28.
127   *Wiva, supra* Ch.1 n. 31.

to exclude in practice the involvement of a corporation in the breach of some rights. This is evident in the case of Shell in Nigeria, which concerned preventing the right to fair trial and the use of private security forces by companies.

Ratner's theory of corporate responsibility is centred on the State/company divide. It distinguishes between rights that can be violated by a corporation and rights that can only be directly infringed by the government. In the latter case, MNEs only have a duty not to be complicit with the government. A shortcoming of this theory is its reliance on the category of compliance, which has particularly blurred boundaries.[128]

It is submitted that a more suitable approach to corporate responsibility, as mentioned above, should explore the number and variety of duty holders, so as to include companies and their contribution to the protection and fulfilment of, as well as the respect for, each human right.

Furthermore, the responsibility of corporations can be better addressed on a sliding scale.[129] The amount and intensity of the obligation would depend on the right at stake and the capacity to make an impact on the human rights situation in question.[130] The nature of the right, the exercise of governmental authority and the presence or absence of fault should all be taken into account. For instance, the holding of special powers deriving from the corporation's taking over governmental functions and the specific relationship with the victim of the violation (employees, members of the community, etc.) would determine an increased level of responsibility. In South America and Indonesia, States seem to grant foreign corporations a sort of *de jure* or *de facto* control over the areas of the concessions. In this case private companies have duties to protect the human rights of those under their control, since they exercise quasi-State authority. According to Article 5 of the ILC Draft Articles on State Responsibility, these situations may entail the international responsibility of the State. Pursuant to Article 5, the conduct of a person or entity which is empowered by the State to exercise elements of governmental authority shall be

---

[128]   See Ratner, *supra* n. 1.

[129]   Uriz-Hernandez, *supra* Ch.2 n. 174, at 416. Ratner applies the same concept, talking about 'concentric circles emanating from the enterprise, with spheres enlarging from employees to their families, to the citizens of a given locality , otherwise affected by their operations . . . and eventually an entire country', Ratner, *supra* n. 1, at 508. Similarly Jägers refers to the leverage that companies wields on the subject they deal with, Jägers, *supra* n. 98, at 79.

[130]   See also M. Jungk, 'A Practical Guide to Addressing Human Rights Concerns for Companies Operating Abroad,' in Addo, *Human Rights Standards*, *supra* Ch.1 n. 28, at 178. See also Uriz-Hernadez, *supra* Ch.2 n. 24, at 370, 377.

attributed to the State under international law, when the person or entity is acting in that capacity in the particular instance.

A study of the law in force and its comparison with the new developments that are taking place is necessary not just to grasp the loopholes of the system, but also to determine what reforms are needed more urgently and which are more feasible.

3.7   CONCLUSION

The point of departure for the definition of MNEs' responsibility is acknowledging that MNEs have acquired a limited personality in international law (see discussion in previous chapter). As seen above, the legal status of MNEs is fraught with an imbalance between rights and duties.

Current international law has attempted to reassess the balance mainly in two ways: by stretching States' human rights obligations to prevent violations by private parties; by imposing international criminal responsibility on individuals for breaches of *jus cogens*. In addition, treaty interpretation bodies have interpreted existing human rights law in the sense of imposing a number of direct duties on companies. The most notable development, however, is to be found in so-called international 'soft law instruments' addressed directly to both companies and States.

It can be drawn from the above study that a minimum core of obligations on companies can be found in the respect of host States' law and in a duty not to interfere with people's enjoyment of human rights (*obligation to respect*). A responsibility to 'respect' human rights requires business to refrain from acts that could interfere with the enjoyment of human rights. For example, a private detention centre institution should refrain from inflicting cruel, inhuman and degrading treatment on people detained. The responsibility on business entities to make sure they are not complicit in human rights abuses is also spelt out quite firmly in the international documents examined. The boundaries of the concept of complicity, however, are not always clear. For instance, questions arise as to the extent of knowledge that the business entity had or should have had in relation to the human rights abuse and the extent to which it assisted through its acts or omissions in the abuse.

It must be taken into account that this definition of corporate responsibility in negative terms is largely insufficient to take into account the variety and complexity of corporate human rights breaches. Trends have been traced in both international hard law and soft law that point in the direction of an expansion of corporate responsibility in order to include the positive duties, to *protect* and *fulfil* human rights in certain situations.

The responsibilities to 'support' human rights should be clarified by considering what business could do to protect, promote, provide and facilitate human rights.

Although it is recognized that a minimum core of fundamental human rights that MNEs are bound to respect – such as the right to life, the right not be discriminated against, the right to health, the prohibition of torture, degrading and inhumane treatment, the core labour standards as defined in relevant ILO conventions – can be identified, the definition of an exhaustive list of rights has been rejected in our approach mainly for two reasons. It would be in contrast with the principles of interrelation and interdependence of all human rights and it would risk being a fictional boundary if compared to the potential of corporate behaviour to affect (either directly or indirectly) all aspects of human rights. It has been suggested that current human rights law should develop in the sense of considering companies as duty holders, together with States and other non-state actors, for the realization of human rights. Moreover, a principle of graduation of responsibility should be applied to MNEs according to the specific human rights involved, the proximity to the victim and the element of State authority exercised by the company in a particular situation.

The above-depicted gradation of responsibility (from the obligation to respect to the obligation to promote human rights) should be matched by a gradation of corresponding implementing mechanisms. It is submitted that obligations to respect human rights, as enshrined in international human rights law, and to avoid complicity with human rights violations committed by State authorities must be addressed through legally binding measures both at the level of the host state and at the level of the home state of the MNE. As explained above, a stronger initiative at the level of home states is desirable, since they are in the best position to assess and manage the risk connected to the foreign activities that, because of their inherent danger or because of the modalities of their execution, may cause harm to people abroad.

On the contrary, the broader area of MNEs' 'support' for human rights leaves room for the use of non-binding measures. In this realm, the incentive effect of codes of conduct and of raising awareness among companies on human rights obligations can be considered. In addition, the potential of incentive measures addressed directly to MNEs in the form of linking access to public procurement to the companies which comply with human rights standards and incentive measures addressed to host states in the form of technical assistance or access to aid and to trade if complying with human rights should be further explored.

The concept of complementarity as defined above proves to be useful in this context. In our view, complementarity among different levels of intervention at the international, regional – in particular European – and national levels is required to effectively address MNEs' responsibility for human rights. From this perspective, different levels of responsibility and the multiplicity of human rights offenders should not be understood as contradictory or mutually exclusive, but rather as complementary. Similarly, different types of implementing measures such as binding, non-binding and 'mixed' should be employed in a complementary rather than exclusive way, in order to address the different degrees of responsibility of MNEs.

Another element that points in this direction is the evolutionary approach to MNEs' responsibility. The development of soft law instruments, in particular, shows a progressive enlargement of the notion of corporate responsibility and the extension of the number of human rights companies are asked to respect. The definition of MNEs' responsibility attains its maximum extension in the UN Norms, which cover all UN human rights treaties and declarations. Furthermore, OECD and ILO code-monitoring mechanisms have been slightly strengthened and their geographical scope of application has been extended. An evolution in the sense of a changing legal force has also been observed. The UN Norms present themselves as a non-voluntary document able to acquire a higher legal force. Another example is given by the universal value accorded to the international core labour standards, as enshrined in the 1998 ILO Declaration, although this Declaration is a non-binding international instrument.

The above mentioned developments point in the direction of exploring the possibility offered by the existing legal framework and of adapting existing human rights instruments to current legal situations.

The framework obtained will provide a point of reference for the analysis of the following section, which will be devoted to the human rights obligations of MNEs in the existing EU legal framework. Solutions at the EU level cannot be placed in a void, but need to be related to the international legal framework. In addition, this analysis will provide a benchmark against which it would be possible to assess similarities and divergences between the international and the EU legal framework.

As a result of this analysis it is evident that any EU instruments should take into account the development and initiatives undertaken by the other international organizations such as the UN, the OECD and the ILO. These international hard- and soft-law instruments should be used as benchmarks in creating EU human rights standards for European companies working world-wide. This would ensure greater inclusiveness and acceptance of standards.

For the purpose of this book, however, not only the similarities but also the differences between the international and the EU legal framework will be examined. The EU, indeed, displays some differences from all other international organizations, which makes the EU more similar to a State than to an international organization.

The status of MNEs within the EU is different; the relevance of human rights and labour rights have been strongly reaffirmed by the Treaty of Lisbon, which gave the Charter of Fundamental Rights the same value as the Treaties.

Part II attempts to define the characteristics of the EU that point to a more proactive role in placing responsibilities over European companies operating abroad. The main initiatives addressed directly to MNEs based in the European Union will be considered. These include initiatives both within the European Union and at the external level, ranging from binding to non-binding initiatives. At the internal level, among legally binding initiatives, particular attention will be given to the possibility of introducing social concerns in public procurement. On the side of non-binding measures, the voluntary initiatives promoted by the European Commission that go under the label of 'Corporate Social Responsibility' will be examined. At the external level, EU measures addressed to MNEs mainly take the form of codes of conduct – such as the Code of Conduct for Companies Operating in South Africa and the European Union Code of Conduct on Arms Export and the proposal for a European Code of Conduct for European Multinational Enterprises (The Howitt Resolution).[131] In this context, IFAs can be regarded as one of the most interesting recent instruments developed at the EU level to address MNEs' responsibility for labour rights and human rights. These agreements are concluded between an MNE and a global union federation.[132] While they have the form of a contract between private parties, they have a potential global reach, since IFAs protect the fundamental social rights of the employees of the company concerned in all its operations.[133] Measures addressed to the host States of MNEs, which in turn are intended to enhance MNEs' compliance with human rights, will be considered in Part III.

---

[131]   Resolution on EU Standards for European Enterprises Operating in Developing Countries, *supra* Ch.1 n. 72.

[132]   Global union Federations are the international representatives for unions organizing in specific industry sectors or occupational groups.

[133]   According to ICFTU definition: 'A framework agreement is an agreement negotiated between a multinational company and a global union federation concerning the international activities of that company. The main purpose of a framework agreement is to establish a formal ongoing relationship between the multinational company and the global union federation which can solve problems and work in the interests of both parties', http://www.icftu.org (accessed 23 July 2006).

PART II

MNEs and human rights in the European
Union

4 Multinational enterprises in the present European Union system and the emergence of corporate social responsibility

4.1 INTRODUCTION

Having examined how international law has so far addressed the issue of MNEs' responsibility for human rights, Part II brings the issue of the responsibility of MNEs for human rights into the EU context. This chapter addresses some fundamental but preliminary questions which will serve for the analysis of EU measures, both those addressed directly to MNEs, which are the object of Part II, and of EU measures addressed to the host States of MNEs, which will be dealt with in Part III.

In setting the scene, the first step is the recognition that there is a problem of a lack of MNEs responsibility for human rights violations in the EU. By focusing on the status of MNEs within the EU and the growing relevance of human rights within the EU, both at the internal and external level, a paradoxical gap of accountability becomes apparent. The capability of the EU to enact rules directly applicable to companies and its reaffirmed commitment to human rights, both at the internal and the external level, have not been matched by consistent political and legal action to increase the accountability of MNEs.

Secondly, the powers of the EU to take measures which would increase the responsibility of MNEs for human rights will be examined. Two aspects of this issue will be distinguished. On the one hand, since the EC is an organization with limited competence, it is necessary to verify the powers conferred upon it in respect of those which are retained by Member States. On a different level, the EC as an international organization is also an addressee of international human rights norms, to the extent that they have become generally recognized norms or principles of international law,[1] therefore its activities in the field of human rights should take into due account the development of international human rights law.

This chapter argues that not only does the EC have powers and, indeed, an obligation to integrate human rights in all its polices but also, that the activities in this field should be consistent with international human rights regarded as principles of international law binding on the EC itself. It is further submitted that the central role given to the protection of human rights within the European legal framework together with the particular status enjoyed by MNEs in EU law, point to a more decisive role for the EU in holding European MNEs accountable for human rights.

4.2   THE EXISTING GAP OF MNES' ACCOUNTABILITY FOR HUMAN RIGHTS

The European Union is a powerful and uniquely representative actor on the international scene. Its influence in world affairs is increasing. The process of integration, the launch of a single currency and the progressive development of a common foreign and security policy are all providing the EU with political and diplomatic status to match its economic and commercial clout. Considering that the European Union is the largest development aid donor and that European enterprises are the largest direct investors in developing countries,[2] it can play a decisive role in global sustainable development. It can therefore be argued that the European Union can influence significantly the human rights policies of other States, as well as those of international institutions. The fear that European intervention could undermine the competitiveness of Europe-based MNEs on the world market is countered by the fact that one of the European Union's major commercial partners and competitors and home State of a great number of MNEs, the United States, has already taken an active role in standard setting and monitoring corporate responsibility. In the United States 85 per cent of large companies have adopted voluntary codes of conduct. Recently, legislation covering

---

[1]   See O. de Schutter, 'Mainstreaming Human Rights in the European Union,' in P. Alston and O. de Schutter, *Monitoring Fundamental Rights in the EU: The Contribution of the Fundamental Rights Agency*, 2005, Oxford and Portland, Or., Hart, 37.

[2]   54 of the top 100 MNEs are based in an EU Member State. See The World's Top 100 Non-Financial TNCS, ranked by foreign assets, 2007, 17/09/09 (WIR/2009/TNCs), available at: http://www.unctad.org/sections/dite_dir/docs/wir2009top100_en.pdf (accessed on 17 September 2009).

corporate codes of conduct was introduced in the Congress of the United States.[3]

European multinationals have been increasingly subjected to stringent requirements from within, by EU laws that regulate the protection of workers' rights, the environment and consumers. The situation changes dramatically when the activities of MNEs' subsidiaries in third countries are concerned. A vast number of cases brought before US and British courts have accused EU multinationals of attempts on the right to health, the right to life and the exploitation of forced labour and child labour in countries such as South Africa,[4] Nigeria,[5] and Myanmar.[6] It is the impact of MNEs' activities that may have a particularly detrimental impact on third countries when the practice of delocalization and outsourcing of MNEs based in one of the EU Member States implies lowering of human rights and social standards.

Despite the fact that the potential negative impact of the expansion of multinational enterprises was already a problem for the European Community in the early 1970s, for a long time there has been sustained reluctance to thoroughly address the issue.[7] The existing gap in the accountability of European MNEs was first brought to our attention as early as the late 1970s.[8] Since then different commentators have suggested ways forward for improving the accountability of European MNEs operating in third countries.[9]

Torremans has suggested the development of extraterritorial application of human rights, building on the extraterritorial application of EC regulations in competition law.[10] Territoriality, however, is an extremely controversial principle. The discrepancy between regulation of competition and financial aspects of MNEs' conduct and the reluctance to

---

[3]   See Kinley, *supra* Ch.3 n. 56, at 36.

[4]   See *Lubbe* case, *supra* Ch.1 n. 20.

[5]   *Wiva* case, *supra* Ch.1 n. 31.

[6]   Testimony by Marco Simons for EarthRights International at the hearing of the Development and Co-Operation Committee of the European Parliament on European Oil Companies in Burma – 11 October, 2001.

[7]   See Baade, *supra* Ch.1 n. 60, at 407.

[8]   See Francioni, *Imprese Multinazionali*, *supra* Ch.2 n. 31; F. Francioni, 'International Law Aspects of the Control of MNEs in the ECC' (1983) 95 *Studi Senesi* 450.

[9]   Kamminga, 'Holding Multinational Corporations', *supra* Ch.1 n. 70, at 554–69.

[10]   P. Torremans, 'Extraterritoriality and Human Rights', in N. Neuwahl and A. Rosas (eds), *The European Union and Human Rights*, 1995, The Hague, M. Nijhoff, at 281–96.

regulate their human rights violations highlights a lack of consistency in present structures.[11] If we are well aware of the consequences of breaches of competition rules, even when they happen outside of the EC territory, to the point of invoking the extraterritorial applicability of these rules (these being fundamental to the EU), why should this not also be the case for human rights, given the importance they have gained in the EU institutional setting?[12]

Hanley thoroughly explored the option of linking the EC's public procurement law to promote the purchase of goods manufactured by those multinational companies that have verifiably demonstrated their respect for core human rights and labour rights in the developing world.[13] Considering that the possibility of participating in public procurement can operate as a powerful incentive for companies to self regulate, Hanley links a soft law instrument, such as a European social label, to binding EC legislation on public procurements.[14] She also demonstrates the compatibility of such a scheme with both EC and WTO law.[15] As will be examined later, Hanley's analysis has been partially confirmed by the recent reform of EC public procurement directives.[16]

---

[11]   Francioni, *Imprese Multinazionali,* supra n. 183, Ch.IV. More recently F. Francioni, 'Alternative Perspectives on International Responsibility for Human Rights Violations by Multinational Corporations', in Benedek et al. (eds), *Economic Globalisation and Human Rights*, 2006, Cambridge, Cambridge University Press, 245–64.

[12]   Torremans, *supra* n. 10, at 295.

[13]   See Hanley, *supra* Ch.1 n. 10., at 97. Similarly Uriz-Hernandez points out that international lending agencies, such as the World Bank, should reinforce their corporate social responsibility policies by, for instance, considering the good CSR record of the company as a prerequisite for lending and exerting an effective influence once the loan is paid, *supra* Ch.2 n. 24, at 418.

[14]   The Current EC legal framework for public procurement is given by: Council Directive 93/36 on public supply contracts; Council Directive 92/50 on public service contracts; Council Directive 93/37 on public work contracts; Council Directive 93/38 coordinating the procedures of entities operating in the water, energy transport and telecommunications sectors. See also Proposal for a Directive of the European Parliament and the Council on the co-ordination of procedures for the award of public supply contracts, public service contracts and public works contracts (2001/0115/COD) and Proposal for a Directive of the European Parliament and the Council co-ordinating the procurement procedures of entities operating in the water, energy and transport sectors (2000/0117/COD).

[15]   Hanley, *supra* Ch.1 n. 10., at 53–4. See also Uriz-Hernandez, *supra* n. 174., at 396.

[16]   See *infra* Part II, Ch.2.3.

De Schutter suggests the use of the Brussels Convention, now Regulation (EC) nr. 44/2001,[17] which is similar to the US Alien Tort Claims Act, which gives jurisdiction to federal US courts over actions lodged by aliens claiming damages for torts committed in violation of the law of the nation, wherever it occurred.[18] Article 2[19] of the Regulation already grants the courts of European Union Member States the option of hearing tort claims against MNEs registered or having their headquarters in a Member State, even when the damage has occurred in a third State. In the Howitt Resolution the Parliament requested the Member States to introduce such extraterritorial jurisdiction into their national legislation, and requests the European Commission to conduct further research as to the application of this principle by national courts of the Member States. By adopting a broad interpretation of Article 2 and Article 5[20] of the Regulation, it is suggested that, for cases of basic duty of care, legal action in respect of any third country may be taken against a company in the EU country where it has its registered office.[21]

Despite academic discussion of the need for reform, however, the European Union has been reluctant to deal with MNEs' compliance with human rights. The reasons for such reluctance have been identified respectively in a lack of consensus among the stakeholders and, in particular, in the dichotomy between industry and enterprises on the one hand and non-governmental organizations and trade unions on the other.[22] This conflict is somehow mirrored by different attitudes among different European institutions. While the European Parliament took a progressive position by calling for the imposition of legally binding sanctions on European MNEs operating abroad,[23] the Commission counterbalanced, embracing

---

[17] Council Regulation (EC) No 44/2001 of 22 December 2000 on Jurisdiction and the Recognition and Enforcement of Judgments in Civil and Commercial Matters [2001] OJ L 12/1.

[18] See Stephens, *supra* Ch.1 n. 19.

[19] Art. 2(1) Regulation 44/2001 '1. Subject to this Regulation, persons domiciled in a Member State shall, whatever their nationality, be sued in the courts of that Member State', *supra* n. 17.

[20] Ibid., Art. 5: 'A person domiciled in a Member State may, in another Member State, be sued: . . . (3) in matters relating to tort, delict or quasi-delict, in the courts for the place where the harmful event occurred or may occur. . . . (5) as regards a dispute arising out of the operations of a branch, agency or other establishment, in the courts for the place in which the branch, agency or other establishment is situated'.

[21] See *infra* Ch.5, section 5.2.

[22] Interviews with Commission's officials, Brussels, 2002.

[23] See Resolution on EU Standards, *supra* Ch.1 n. 72.

a cautious and strictly voluntary approach in particular in the field of CSR.[24]

The EU's reluctance to take a more active role in setting standards of conduct of its enterprises in developing countries has so far been justified on the grounds of three arguments. Firstly, the European Union aims to avoid undue duplication on the basis that there are already existing principles for the conduct of MNEs adopted by other international organizations.[25] The European Union prefers to limit its role to the improvement of enforcement mechanisms of existing measures and to promoting human rights issues within these organisations. Secondly, there is a fear that an initiative at the European level as opposed to a global level, may create a competitive disadvantage for European companies in the world market. Finally, it has been pointed out that initiatives exclusively at the level of the Member States can adequately address the problem.

The difficulty in tackling the problem is also due to the very cross-cutting nature of the issue, which is placed at an intersection between economic and commercial policies on the one hand and development and human rights policies on the other. While the legitimacy of the European Union's positive measures of integration[26] in fields such as competition, social and environmental policy is no longer called into question, the shift from negative measures of integration to positive ones in the field of human rights is more recent and has yet to be explored.[27]

While recognizing already in Part I that all three levels (international, regional and national) of intervention are of utmost importance in holding MNEs accountable, it can be argued that the European Union enjoys a specific and relevant *espace de manœuvre* in which it can take positive steps in standard setting and monitoring the conduct of European enterprises operating in third countries.

The first set of arguments in support of the above stem from the analysis of the enhanced role of human rights both in the internal and external dimension of the European Union. The likely evolution of the Charter of

---

[24] See *Corporate Social Responsibility: a Business Contribution, supra* Ch.1 n. 24.

[25] In particular the ILO Tripartite Declaration, *supra* Ch.1 n. 12. and the OECD Guidelines, *supra* Ch.1 n. 13.

[26] 'Whereas positive integration requires that affirmative steps be taken to expedite the achievement of specified goals, negative integration confines itself to a prohibition of violations of the principle in question'. European University Institute, *Leading by Example: A Human Rights Agenda for the European Union for the Year 2000. Agenda of the Comité de Sages and Final Project Report*, 1998, Florence, European University Institute, at 26–7.

[27] Ibid., at 26–32.

Fundamental Rights into a more significant legal instrument[28] and the relevance given to human rights in the Treaty of Lisbon[29] also supports this analysis. Secondly, at the international level the EU is not only a powerful economic actor but it is also an organization bound by international human rights law.[30] Thirdly, from a legal point of view there are many legal provisions relating to the status of MNEs in EU law that could facilitate positive measures on the part of the European Union and that can improve the human rights accountability of MNEs operating abroad. Finally, from a policy perspective, the argument for coherence and avoiding hypocrisy, and the argument concerning the need to correct European Union excessive market orientation both support the exercise by the European Union of stricter scrutiny over the activity of European MNEs operating abroad.

The first reason why EU law occupies a particularly advantageous position, which justifies arguments for EU regulation of MNEs, is its strong commitment to human rights. The protection of human rights has progressively become one of the principal characteristics of the European Union[31] and its emerging legal framework.

Even if human rights (or 'fundamental rights') were originally conceived by the ECJ as limits to the discretion of supranational institutions,[32] they have acquired a prominent role in the policies and the legal system of the European Union. Initially, in the 1970s, the Court of Justice began to formulate and define the system of respect for fundamental rights as a system which is based on the unwritten, judicially articulated source of 'general principles' of EC law. The Court has conceived fundamental rights in the constitutional traditions common to the Member States, and in international human rights instruments to which Member States are parties, paying particular reference to the ECHR. On this grounds it examines, within the limits of its jurisdiction, whether or not the acts of the EU institutions infringe fundamental rights.

---

[28]   *Charter of Fundamental Rights of the European Union* [2000] OJ C 364/1. M.P. Maduro, 'Europe and the Constitution: What if This is as Far as It Gets?', in J.H.H. Weiler and M. Wind (eds), *European Constitutionalism Beyond the State*, 2003, Cambridge, Cambridge University Press, 74.

[29]   Treaty of Lisbon amending the Treaty on European Union and the Treaty establishing the European Community, signed at Lisbon, 13 December 2007 [2007] OJ C 306.

[30]   See *infra* Ch.4, section 4.2.2.

[31]   Craig and De Búrca, *supra* Ch.2 n. 73, at 317–50.

[32]   F. Sudre, *Droit Communautaire des Droits Fondamentaux: Recueil de Décisions de la Cour de Justice des Communautés Européennes*, 1999, Bruxelles, Bruylant.

The general principle of respect for human rights was confirmed at Maastricht by what is now Article 6(2) Treaty on European Union (TEU).[33] Article 6(1) TEU, goes even further by spelling out that the Union is founded on the principles of liberty, democracy, respect for human rights and fundamental freedoms, and the rule of law.[34] Moreover, the TEU lists as one of the objectives of the EU the strengthening of '. . . the protection of the rights and interests . . . of its member States' and 'to maintain and develop a Union as an area of freedom, security and justice'.[35] The European Union's commitment to respecting fundamental rights as general principles is confirmed by the provision that serious breach of fundamental rights may lead to the suspension of the Member State in question in the European Council.[36] In recognition of this responsibility, the European Union has also insisted that countries seeking admission to the Union must satisfy strict human rights requirements. In the context of enlargement, the first criteria to be fulfilled by candidate countries (as set out in the Copenhagen summit in June 1993) is 'the existence of stable institutions guaranteeing democracy, the rule of law, human rights and the respect for and protection for minorities.'[37]

The proclamation in 2000 of a European Union Charter of Fundamental Rights (hereinafter the Charter) and its subsequent reference into the Treaty of Lisbon [38] can also be read as part of an ongoing process

---

[33]   Art. 6, in the the Treaty of Lisbon.

[34]   Art. 6, para. 2, TEU: 'The Union shall respect fundamental rights as guaranteed by the European Convention for the Protection of Human Rights and Fundamental Freedoms . . . as they result from the constitutional traditions common to the Member States, as general principles of Community law'.

[35]   Art. 2, TEU.

[36]   Art. 7, TEU.

[37]   On the relevance of human rights to become Members of the EU see B. De Witte and G.N. Toggenburg, 'Human Rights and Membership of the European Union', in S. Peers and A. Ward (eds), *The European Charter of Fundamental Rights*, 2004, Oxford, Hart, 59; W. Sadurski, 'The Role of the EU Charter of Rights in the Process of Enlargement', in G. Bermann and K. Pistor (eds), *Law and Governance in an Enlarged European Union*, 2004, Oxford, Hart, 61.

[38]   Pursuant to Art. 6 'The Union recognises the rights, freedoms and principles set out in the Charter of Fundamental Rights of the European Union of 7 December 2000, as adapted at Strasbourg, on 12 December 2007, which shall have the same legal value as the Treaties. The provisions of the Charter shall not extend in any way the competences of the Union as defined in the Treaties. The rights, freedoms and principles in the Charter shall be interpreted in accordance with the general provisions in Title VII of the Charter governing its interpretation and application and with due regard to the explanations referred to in the Charter, that set out the sources of those provisions.' Treaty of Lisbon, *supra* n. 29.

that has the potential to transform substantially the EU legal system. Although the Charter was not aimed at creating new rights, the Charter makes fundamental rights more visible to EU citizens by codifying material from various sources, such as the European Convention on Human Rights, common constitutional traditions and international instruments. Furthermore, Chapter IV, Solidarity, of the Charter of Fundamental Rights of the European Union, highlights how the Union is moving towards redressing the balance between economic interests and fundamental rights.[39] It enshrines a new set of rights aimed at drawing a balance between economic activities and individuals' rights. Among these are: access to services of general economic interest (Article 36); consumer protection (Article 38); environmental protection (Article 37); and health protection (Article 35). In order to enhance consistency and coherence, the Charter is held to play a guiding role in the activities of the EU at the level of both internal and external policies.[40] As a confirmation of this intention, the Charter has prompted renewed efforts to prevent any deterioration of standards within the Union, such as the proposal of setting up an independent Human Rights Agency with the task of monitoring fundamental rights in all the Member States in areas covered by the Charter.[41]

The promotion of human rights has been even more prominent in the external relations of the EU.[42] The constitutional roots of this policy lay in Article 177(2) of the EC Treaty, according to which one of the

---

[39]   M. P. Maduro, 'Striking the Elusive Balance Between Economic Rights and Social Rights in the EU', in P. Alston et al. (eds), *The EU and Human Rights, supra* Ch.1 n. 70, at 449–71.

[40]   Communication from the Commission to the Council and the European Parliament, *The European Union's Role in Promoting Human Rights and Democratisation in Third Countries* COM (2001) 252 final, 8 May 2001.

[41]   European Commission, *Proposal for a Council Regulation establishing a European Union Agency for Fundamental Rights and Proposal for a Council Decision, empowering the European Union Agency for Fundamental Rights to pursue its activities in areas referred to in Title VI of the Treaty on European Union*, COM (2005) 280 final, 30 June 2005. See P. Alston and O. de Schutter, *Monitoring Fundamental Rights in the EU: The Contribution of the Fundamental Rights Agency*, 2005, Oxford and Portland, Or., Hart.

[42]   Most commentators agree that external human rights policies are more meaningful than the internal one: P. Alston and J.H.H. Weiler, 'An "Ever Closer Union" in Need of a Human Rights Policy: The European Union and Human Rights', in Alston et al. (eds), *The EU and Human Rights, supra* Ch.1 n. 70, at 3–68. For a critical analysis of the reasons why human rights have developed more at the external rather than at the internal level see A. Williams, *EU Human Rights Policies: a Study on Irony*, 2004, Oxford, Oxford University Press, at 111–25.

objectives of the development and cooperation policy is to contribute
to the general objective of developing and consolidating democracy and
the rule of law, and to that of respecting human rights and fundamental
freedoms. Similarly, pursuant to Article 11 of the EU Treaty, the EU's
foreign policy shall develop and consolidate democracy and the rule of
law, along with respect for human rights and fundamental freedoms. The
importance attached to human rights in European foreign policy was
underlined by three developments in 1999. For the first time responsibility for this area was given to one Commissioner, the External Relations
Commissioner; secondly, the adoption of Council Regulations 975/1999
and 976/1999,[43] which provided the legal basis for the European Initiative
for Democratisation and Human Rights (EIDHR) activities; thirdly,
every new development, cooperation and association agreement between
the EU and third countries includes a human rights clause,[44] allowing for
trade benefits and development cooperation to be suspended if abuses are
established. With regard, in particular, to development and cooperation
programmes, the Treaty of Nice has also extended the objective of promoting the respect of human rights and fundamental freedoms from development cooperation to all forms of cooperation with third countries.[45]
Mechanisms such as the human rights special incentive in the GSP, which
is used as a lever on third countries so as to ensure or enhance compliance
with labour standards, has been recently revised in order to include the
main international human rights treaties and conventions.[46] As a result,
the European Union has been keen to present itself as the promoter of the
triptych – human rights, democracy and rule of law in its relations with
third countries.[47]

---

[43] Council Regulations 975/1999 and 976/1999 of 29 April 1999 On the consolidation of democracy and the rule of law and respect for human rights and
fundamental freedoms [1999] OJ L 120.

[44] E. Riedel and W. Martin, 'Human Rights Clauses in External Agreements
of the EC', in Alston et al. (eds), *The EU and Human Rights, supra* Ch.1 n. 70, at
723–55.

[45] Art. 181a TEC.

[46] See the GSP Regulation, *supra* Ch.1 n. 91. On the evolution of the GSP see
also B. Brandtner and A. Rosas, 'Trade Preferences and Human Rights', in Alston
et al. (eds), *The EU and Human Rights, supra* Ch.1 n. 70, at 699–722; A. Gatto 'The
Integration of Social Rights Concerns in the External Relations of the European
Union', in G. de Búrca, B. de Witte and L. Ogertschnig (eds), *Social Rights in
Europe,* 2005, Oxford, Oxford University Press.

[47] B. Simma, J.B. Aschenbrenner and C. Shulte, 'Human Rights Considerations
in the Development Co-operation Activities of the EC', Alston et al. (eds), *The EU
and Human Rights, supra* Ch.1 n. 70, at 571–626.

Finally, the central role given to human rights, both at the internal and external level, has culminated in the Treaty of Lisbon's recognition that:

> The Union is founded on the values of respect for human dignity, freedom, democracy, equality, the rule of law and respect for human rights, including the rights of persons belonging to minorities. These values are common to the Member States in a society in which pluralism, non-discrimination, tolerance, justice, solidarity and equality between women and men prevail.[48]

The same values and interests should be upheld and promoted by the EU in its 'relations with the wider world' where it states that:

> 1. The Union's action on the international scene shall be guided by the principles which have inspired its own creation, development and enlargement, and which it seeks to advance in the wider world: democracy, the rule of law, the universality and indivisibility of human rights and fundamental freedoms, respect for human dignity, the principles of equality and solidarity, and respect for the principles of the United Nations Charter and international law.
>
> The Union shall seek to develop relations and build partnerships with third countries, and international, regional or global organisations which share the principles referred to in the first subparagraph. It shall promote multilateral solutions to common problems, in particular in the framework of the United Nations.[49]

The development in the field of human rights, as outlined above, points towards a conclusion that human rights have progressively been placed at the centre of the EU polity and legal framework.[50]

4.2.1   EU Competence in the Field of Human Rights

Although the protection of human rights has progressively become one of the principal characteristics of the European Union and its emerging legal

---

[48]   Art. 1A, Treaty of Lisbon, *supra* n. 29.

[49]   Article 10 A, Treaty of Lisbon, *supra* n. 29.

[50]   See for instance Report of the three Sages on the situation in Austria, adopted in Paris on 8 September 2000, 1–5. See A. Bogdandy, 'The European Union as a Human Rights Organization? Human Rights and the Core of the European Union' (2000) 37 C.M.L.R. 1307. See O. De Schutter, 'Mainstreaming Human Rights in the European Union,' in Alston and de Schutter, *supra* n. 41, at 37–72.

framework[51] neither the European Union nor the European Community
has been given explicit competence to fulfil fundamental rights, except in
rather specific settings.[52] When addressing the issue of human rights in
the EU it is striking to note that, while it is affirmed that the EU does not
have a general competence to adopt measures in the field of human rights,
the EC has actually engaged in a variety of human rights activities both at
the internal and external levels. Similarly, in academic discourse, a broad
agreement on the absence of an express and general EC power in the field
of human rights is confronted with a variety of positions on the extent to
which the EC can adopt measures in the field of human rights.[53] In order
to address how and to what extent the EU can hold MNEs accountable
for human rights violations, the question regarding the EC's legitimacy to
act in the field of human rights should be preliminarily addressed. Since
the Community is an organization with conferred powers, it is necessary to
identify an appropriate substantive legal base for action and to constantly
check its powers *vis-à-vis* those which are retained by Member States.

This paradoxical situation has probably been generated by the often
unclear attitude of EC institutions on the issue and by the sometimes contradictory case law of the ECJ. In order to untangle the net, it is useful to
distinguish two aspects of the EC's powers in the field of human rights. On
the one hand, the question arises whether there is a general EC power to
enact rules on human rights; on the other hand, the problem of identifying
whether EC institutions have some measure of rule making power to integrate human rights into other policies of the EU should be addressed. This
distinction is necessary because the existence of an EC general competence
on human rights is clearly more precarious and disputed. The implications
of a general competence in the field of human rights would reach much
further in constitutional terms than a human rights competence in relation
to the various EC policies.[54] Transferring the power to define standards
and rules for the protection of human rights to the EU in any general way
would indeed raise Member States' concerns of a potentially limitless EC
competence.

To start with, there is no Treaty provision which confers on the
Community institutions any general power to enact rules on human rights

---

[51]   Craig and De Búrca, *supra* n. 31, at 317–50.
[52]   See generally J.H.H. Weiler and S.C. Fries, 'A Human Rights Policy for the
European Community and Union: The Question of Competences,' in Alston et al.
(eds), *The EU and Human Rights, supra* Ch.1 n. 70, at 147.
[53]   Weiler and Fries, *supra* n. 52. P. Eeckhout, 'The EU Charter of Fundamental
Rights and the Federal Question' (2002) 39 C.M.L.R. 945.
[54]   Eeckhout, *supra* n. 53.

or, at the external level, to conclude international conventions in this field, as the Court pointed out in *Opinion 2/94*.[55] In 1994 the Council lodged a request for an opinion from the Court concerning the possible accession of the European Community to the ECHR, which has long been advocated by the Commission and the European Parliament. On this occasion, the Court declared the request admissible to the extent it concerned the Community competence to conclude an agreement of the kind envisaged and finally ruled that the EC lacked competence to adhere to the ECHR.

In order to understand the impact of this ruling on the current interpretation of EC competence in the field of human rights, it is worth revisiting the Court's reasoning.

The Court starts its analysis by referring to the principle of conferred powers as described by article 5 TEC, which provides that the Community has only those powers which have been conferred upon it by the Member States. That principle must be respected in both the internal and international action of the Community. The Court then describes the principle of implied powers. It subsequently points out that 'no treaty provision confers on the Community institutions any general power to enact rules or to conclude international conventions in this field'.[56] In turning to Article now 308 TEC, which is designed to fill the gap where no provisions of the Treaty confer on the Community institutions' express or implied powers to act, the Court points out that this provision cannot serve as a basis for widening the scope of Community powers beyond the general framework created by the Treaty. In particular, this Article cannot be used as a basis for the adoption of provisions whose effect would, in substance, be to amend the Treaty.

Consistent with its previous case law, the Court also points out that respect for human rights is a condition of the lawfulness of Community acts. Accession to the ECHR, however, would entail a substantial change in the present system, in that it would involve the entry of the Community into a distinct international institutional system, as well as integration of all the ECHR provisions into the Community legal order. Such a modification, with equally fundamental institutional implications for the Community and for the Member States, would be of constitutional significance and could only be brought about by way of Treaty amendment.

It is important to point out here that it would be wrong to conclude from *Opinion 2/94* that the Community (or Union) institutions have no powers at all as regards fundamental rights protection. On the one hand,

---

[55]   *Opinion 2/94* [1994] ECR I-5267.
[56]   Ibid. para. 28.

Opinion 2/94 set a negative limit to the present discussion. The Court does indeed refer to the fact that no Treaty provision confers on the Community a general power to enact rules on human rights. However, that is not the basis for the Court's decision but, rather it is only the starting-point of the analysis. Rather, in the Court's view, the constitutional-type consequences of joining the ECHR are decisive[57]. The Court does not in fact deal with any, more limited, human rights powers which the institutions may have. On the contrary, the Opinion can be read as supporting the view that there may be some such powers. The tenor of the Opinion is clearly that accession to the ECHR is not possible under the current institutional setting, rather than affirming a lack of any human rights power whatsoever. Taking this argument a step further, as suggested by Alston and Weiler, a Community human rights policy could be based, in part, on Article 308 TEC, provided that it is interpreted consistently with the Court's reasoning in *Opinion 2/94*.[58] In other words, it is submitted that a human rights policy that does not entail the entry of the EU into a distinct international institutional system which does not modify the material content of human rights within the community legal order and does not have fundamental institutional implication would be consistent with the ECJ's *Opinion 2/94* and it would not require a Treaty amendment.

Once excluded that the EC is endowed with general powers to enact rules on human rights according to the current institutional setting, it is necessary to turn to the question of what are the specific powers of the EC in this field. In other words, the question of what is the scope of the EC's rule making power in the field of human rights needs to be tackled. EC human rights competence at the external level will be discussed later, when EC measures addressed to MNEs' host States are examined.[59]

It is worth recalling here that for decades the ECJ has interpreted the respect for fundamental rights, as guaranteed by the ECHR and as they result from the constitutional traditions common to the Member States, as a condition for the lawfulness of community acts.[60] Human rights (or 'fundamental rights') were indeed originally conceived by the ECJ as limits to the discretion of Community institutions,[61] rather than the foundation of a proactive policy towards their achievements. Human rights, however,

---

[57]　Para. 34–35.
[58]　Alston and Weiler, *supra* n. 42, at 27.
[59]　See *infra* Ch.7, section 7.2.
[60]　See B. De Witte, 'The Past and Future Role of the European Court of Justice in the Protection of Human Rights', in Alston et al. (eds), *The EU and Human Rights*, *supra* Ch.1 n. 70, at 859–98.
[61]　Sudre, *supra* n. 32.

have been regarded for some time as the bases for negative integration, to be achieved by simply prohibiting violations rather than by taking affirmative steps.[62] The move from a negative to a positive form of integration has always been hindered by the assumption that judicial protection would have been sufficient to protect individual fundamental rights in the EC legal system and by the concerns of a potentially limitless expansion of Community human rights powers in relation to Member States.[63]

On the other hand, Weiler and Fries correctly note that the ECJ had been moving beyond the mere prohibition of measures that might violate human rights and setting up a positive duty to ensure that certain rights are not compromised. They also submit that such legislative competence is inherent in each and every field of legislative competence of the Community.[64] Similarly Eeckhout notes that if human rights law is considered not autonomous, but embedded in and an organic part of legal systems generally, then it logically follows from the current system of protecting fundamental rights as general principles of EC law that the institutions must have some measure of rule-making power in this field, too.[65] Not only has the EC increasingly engaged in areas which are closely linked to the protection of human rights, such as asylum policy, cooperation in criminal matters and non-discrimination, but human rights issues can arise in areas of law which are *prima facie* not related to human rights. It is clear from the ECJ's and Court of First Instance (CFI)'s case law that the institutions, even when adopting anti-dumping measures, for instance, must respect rights of defence and the right to good administration. These fundamental rights, imply, for example, that companies involved have a right to be heard. In this case, denying the EC institutions all rule-making power in the field of human rights, would imply effectively denying them the capacity to include in the regulation provisions on the right to be heard. This would be contrary to the respect for fundamental rights as a condition for the lawfulness of Community acts, as the Court stated in *Opinion 2/94.*

Therefore, it can be concluded that the requirement of respect for fundamental rights implies that the institutions may at least provide for rules, in specific acts adopted under the powers vested in them by the Treaties, so as to ensure that fundamental rights are respected. Thus EC competence in the field of human rights can be considered not an autonomous power

---

62 Weiler and Fries, *supra* n. 53.
63 Alston and Weiler, *supra* n. 42, at 3–68.
64 Weiler and Fries, *supra* n. 53, at 156.
65 Eeckhout, 'The EU Charter of Fundamental Rights', *supra* n. 54, at 983.

to legislate on human rights, as it is strictly a function of the other, non-human-rights powers which are conferred on the institutions.

Having submitted that the EC is under an obligation to respect fundamental rights and needs to have the legal tools to ensure such respect, the question turns to what are the possible legal bases for implementing these measures. In some cases the Treaty foresees a specific legal basis for EC activity in the field of human rights and express references to human rights have increased by successive Treaty amendments. There are cases where there is a coincidence between EU legislation and a classic fundamental right such as equal pay (Article 141(1) TEC). This has also been the case for the prohibition of all forms of discrimination as enshrined in Articles 12 and 13. In the case of gender discrimination, for example, community policies have made an important contribution, having afforded a degree of protection going well beyond that of which was available at the time within Member States. This is of relevance since the right to non-discrimination and equality are at the core of all other human rights and can provide a broad platform for human rights action. In other fields, concern for human rights is specifically mentioned. While competence issues in the context of the EC external relations will be discussed in detail in Part III, where EC measures addressed to MNEs' host States are examined, it is worth recalling here that human rights are expressly mentioned as one of the objectives of the development and co-operation policy[66] (Article 177 (2) TEC). Article 181a TEC, inserted by the Treaty of Nice, introduced a new category of cooperation agreements to be concluded both with developing and developed countries.[67] The protection of human

---

[66]   See *supra* n. 42.
[67]   The Treaty of Nice added Art. 181a on economic, financial and technical cooperation with third countries, which reads:

> 1. Without prejudice to the other provisions of this Treaty, and in particular those of Title XX, the Community shall carry out, within its spheres of competence, economic, financial and technical cooperation measures with third countries. Such measures shall be complementary to those carried out by the Member States and consistent with the development policy of the Community. Community policy in this area shall contribute to the general objective of developing and consolidating democracy and the rule of law, and to the objective of respecting human rights and fundamental freedoms. 2. The Council, acting by a qualified majority on a proposal from the Commission and after consulting the European Parliament, shall adopt the measures necessary for the implementation of paragraph 1. The Council shall act unanimously for the association agreements referred to in Article 310 and for the agreements to be concluded with the States which are candidates for accession to the Union. 3. Within their respective spheres of competence, the

rights is mentioned among the objectives of the action to be undertaken by the EC under this provision. Similarly, pursuant to Article 11 TEU, the EU's foreign policy shall develop and consolidate democracy and the rule of law, along with respect for human rights and fundamental freedoms.

Apart from these express references, human rights have indeed been integrated to different extents in a number of areas of exclusive Community competence,[68] such as in the common commercial policy of the EC. Pursuant to the ECJ's ruling in *Portugal v Council*[69] human rights clauses can be inserted into commercial agreements to the extent that they do not constitute the main objective of the agreement. The right to defence of companies has been granted in proceedings relating to competition law. The possibility of introducing social clauses in public procurement has recently been endorsed by EC legislation.

It may, however, be necessary, in order to enable the Community to carry out its functions with a view to attaining one of the objectives laid down by the Treaty, to have a measure not directly connected to any specific policy. The problem would arise for instance for the adoption of an internal measure which has human rights as its main objective. In this case recourse to Article 308 TEC has been seen as the last resort.[70] Article 308 allows the Council to take measures even if the EC Treaty has not provided the necessary powers, but it can only be invoked if action by the Community should prove necessary to attain, in the course of the operation of the common market, one of the objectives of the Community. An example was given by the adoption of the human rights regulations in 1999. Regulation 975/1999 relating to development cooperation operations was adopted on the basis of current Article 179 TEC, which no doubt provided an adequate legal basis. Regulation 976/1999, relating

---

Community and the Member States shall cooperate with third countries and the competent international organisations. The arrangements for Community cooperation may be the subject of agreements between the Community and the third parties concerned, which shall be negotiated and concluded in accordance with Article 300. The first subparagraph shall be without prejudice to the Member States' competence to negotiate in international bodies and to conclude international agreements.

[68]   Article 2C4 of the Treaty of Lisbon foresees that: 'In the areas of development cooperation and humanitarian aid, the Union shall have competence to carry out activities and conduct a common policy; however, the exercise of that competence shall not result in Member States being prevented from exercising theirs' thus keeping development cooperation and humanitarian aid as areas of shared competence.

[69]   Case C-268/94, *Portugal v Council* [1996] ECR I-6177.

[70]   Weiler and Fries, *supra* n. 52, at 154.

to cooperation with developed third countries, had to be adopted on the basis of current Article 308 TEC as there were, at that time, no specific treaty provisions on cooperation with developed third countries. In the light of the limitations on the use of Article 308 set out by the Court in *Opinion 2/94*, this legal basis seemed to be precarious.[71] In the meantime, the Treaty of Nice inserted Article 181a EC enabling cooperation with developed countries, which is also to contribute to development of human rights. Regulation 2004, which amends regulation 976/1999, has indeed been adopted on the basis of Article 181a.

To sum up, despite a number of significant changes in the last decade, the position remains that the EU does not have general competence in the field of human rights, and neither the Charter on Fundamental Rights nor the Treaty of Lisbon would significantly change this formal position. In particular, it seems unlikely that the EU can have a comprehensive human rights policy, as suggested by Alston and Weiler in 1998, when there is still such a clear concern with limiting its competences[72] and sometimes a reluctant political attitude.[73]

Nevertheless, it is submitted that, since human rights constitute general principles of Community law whose observance the Court should ensure, this also implies a functional competence for the EC to take all necessary measures to ensure that human rights are respected in its policies. The fact that there is an obligation and not merely a duty of the community in pursuing human rights in its policies can be deduced from the ECJ's reasoning in *Opinion 2/94* and from its consistent interpretation of Article 6 of the Treaty, which reads 'The Union shall respect fundamental rights as guaranteed by the European Convention for the Protection of Human Rights and Fundamental Freedoms . . . as they result from the constitutional traditions common to the Member States, as general principles of Community law.'

As explained at the beginning of this book, the issue of MNEs' responsibility for respect of human rights has a distinct cross-cutting nature, including measures addressed directly to MNEs and measures addressed to host States. Within the EC, for instance, the regulation of MNEs impinges on company law, competition law and procurement law. MNEs have also been the object of a limited number of CFSP measures. At the external level, development cooperation and common commercial policy

---

[71] Eeckhout, *supra* n. 54, at 469.
[72] See G. De Búrca, *Setting Constitutional Limits to EU Competence*, Francisco Lucas Pires Working Papers Series, Universidade Nova de Lisboa, (2001), available at: http://www.fd.unl.pt/je/wpflp02a.doc (accessed 23 April 2004).
[73] Williams, *EU Human Rights Policies*, *supra* n. 42, at 111–26.

pursue the objective of raising human rights standards in host countries of MNEs. Therefore, the responsibility of MNEs for human rights in the EU's legal framework will be addressed by examining to what extent human rights have been and can be integrated into the different policies which are relevant for the conduct of MNEs.

4.2.2   The EU and International Human Rights Law

Another aspect of the relationship between the EU and human rights worth addressing is the relationship between EU activities in the field of human rights and the international human rights law framework. While a comprehensive consideration of the rules of general international law which are applicable to the EU[74] falls outside the scope of this section, attention should be directed to the question of the EU as an addressee of general international rules on human rights. The question is then to what extent the EC, as an entity possessing rights and duties deriving from general international law rules, is bound by international human rights obligations.

For some time the European Union has maintained that the obligations incumbent upon it in the area of human rights stem from its own internal legal order. Under this limited approach, the EU is merely under an obligation not to violate human rights when it acts (i.e. a negative obligation to respect human rights) and effectively only to respect those rights enumerated in the ECHR. This view seems rather limited if one looks at the relevance that human rights have gained both at the internal and external level of the EU and at the development of international law itself.

Indeed, it has been increasingly accepted that while governments bear the primary responsibility to ensure respect for human rights, international organizations are important instruments to provide policies that can contribute to (or weaken) the implementation and fulfilment of human rights.[75] The ICJ itself held that: 'International organisations are subjects of international law and as such are bound by any obligations incumbent upon them under general rules of international law, under their constitutions or under international agreements to which they are

---

[74]   See Tomuschat, 'The International Responsibility of the European Union', *supra* Ch.1 n. 96, at 177–191.

[75]   See P. Alston, *Diritti Umani e Globalizzazione. Il Ruolo dell'Europa*, 1999, Torino, Gruppo Abele, at 51; Clapham, *Human Rights Obligations, supra* Ch.1 n. 50, at 109–94.

parties'[76] and the responsibility of international organizations is currently under discussion at the International Law Commission.[77]

However, the place given to international human rights in the EU legal system is still controversial. On the one hand, over the last decade the ECJ has shown a more open attitude to using international law as a source for the interpretation of community law. The Court of Justice has stated that the Community 'must respect international law in the exercise of its powers.'[78] In the *Racke* [79] case the court affirmed that the EU is to be bound by the general rules of international law and that a violation of customary international law could be relevant to a determination that a piece of Community secondary legislation was invalid and inapplicable to an individual or a legal person.[80] Similarly, in *Opel Austria,*[81] the CFI applied the international law principles of good faith and legitimate expectations, as expressed in Article 18 of the Vienna Convention, on the Law of Treaties concerning the obligation to refrain from acts which would defeat the object and purpose of a treaty before its entry into force. The Court of Justice will regularly refer to decisions of other international courts and tribunals, including the ICJ[82] and the ECrtHR. Not only has the ECJ frequently been referred to the ECHR as a source of general principles of EC law, but it has also referred directly to the Convention and the case law of the ECtHR when controlling respect for human rights.[83]

---

[76] *Advisory Opinion of 20 December 1980 on the Question Concerning the Interpretation of the Agreement of 25 March 1951 between the World Health Organisation and Egypt* (1980) ICJ Reports 73.

[77] United Nations (UN), UN Doc. A/CN 4/532, *Third Report on Responsibility of International Organizations*, G. Gaja, A/CN 4/533, 26 March 2003.

[78] Case C-286/90 *Poulsen and Diva Navigation* [1992] ECR I-6019.

[79] Case C-162/96 *Racke GmbH & Co v Hauptzollant Mainz* [1998] ECR I-3655:

It is therefore required to comply with the rules of customary international law when adopting a regulation suspending the trade concessions granted by, or by virtue of, an agreement which it has concluded with a non-member country. It follows that the rules of customary international law concerning the termination and the suspension of treaty relations by reason of a fundamental change of circumstances are binding upon the Community institutions and form part of the Community legal order.

[80] Ibid., at para. 45–6.

[81] Case T-115/94 *Opel Austria GmbH v Council* [1997] ECR II-39.

[82] For example Case C-162/96 *Racke* [1998] ECR I-3655, at para. 50; Case T-306/01 *Yusuf & Al Barakaat International Foundation v. Council and Commission* [2005] ECR II-3533, at para. 233–4.

[83] For example Case C-249/95 *Grant v South-West Trains* [1998] ECR I-621, at para. 34.

On the other hand, a few recent cases relating to EC measures implementing the United Nations Security Council sanctions, have shown that EC courts take a contradictory approach towards the relevance of international human rights, and in particular *of jus cogens,* in the EC legal system.[84]

The issue was first addressed by the Court of Justice in the *Bosphorous* case.[85] The Court not only interpreted a sanctions Regulation taking into account the text and aims of the UN Security Council Resolution which it implemented, but also considered a claim that the Regulation should be declared invalid on grounds of proportionality and breaches of human rights. The fundamental right at stake in this case was the right to property and to exercise a commercial activity. The Court held that these rights do not have an absolute character and that:

> as compared with an objective of general interest so fundamental for the international community, which consists in putting an end to the state of war in the region and to the massive violations of human rights and humanitarian international law in the Republic of Bosnia-Herzegovina, the impounding of the aircraft in question . . . cannot be regarded as inappropriate or disproportionate.[86]

Although the Court of Justice in the *Bosphorus*[87] case declared the Regulation to be in conformity with Community law, Ireland was held to account before the European Court of Human Rights in respect of its implementation of the Regulation. In the first place, the ECtHR made clear that even where the Member States are implementing their (international and Community law) obligations without discretion they are responsible for compliance with the ECHR;[88] there is no absolution of

---

[84]   The sanctions examined in the following cases were adopted on the basis of the EC Treaty thus allowed for judicial review before the Court of Justice. On the contrary remember that where sanctions or other restrictive measures are adopted in relation under CFSP powers only, they cannot at present be reviewed by the ECJ. This gap however should be filled by the Treaty of Lisbon.

[85]   Case C-84/95 *Bosphorus* [1996] ECR I-3953. The case related to an aeroplane leased by a Turkish company but owned by the Yugoslav national airline JAT. The aircraft was impounded in Ireland under Regulation No 990/93, which implemented in the Community certain aspects of the sanctions taken against the Federal Republic of Yugoslavia by the Security Council of the United Nations.

[86]   Ibid., para. 26.

[87]   *Bosphorus Airways v Ireland* Application No. 45036/98, ECHR Grand Chamber Judgment of 30 June 2005.

[88]   This reasoning is in contrast with what the court of first instance held in *Yusuf*, where the CFI argued that because the institutions had no autonomous discretion, to review the Community Regulation would be equivalent to reviewing the

responsibility from ECHR obligations whenever a Contracting Party is implementing EC law. What is more relevant here is that the Court's assessment of Ireland's compliance then rests on its doctrine of 'equivalence' whereby:

> State action taken in compliance with such legal obligations is justified as long as the relevant organisation [the EU] is considered to protect fundamental rights, as regards both the substantive guarantees offered and the mechanisms controlling their observance, in a manner which can be considered at least equivalent to that for which the Convention provides.[89]

Moreover, after careful analysis of the system of protection of fundamental rights in the European Union, and after reviewing the treatment of the *Bosphorus* case by the judgement of the ECJ, the Strasbourg Court found that protection of fundamental rights in the EC was equivalent, or rather comparable to that of the ECHR system. The ECrtHR, further, held there was no dysfunction of the mechanism of control of the observance rights enshrined in the ECHR and concluded on that ground that there was no violation of the Convention.

In the recent *Kadi*[90] and *Yusuf* [91] cases, both based on identical legal reasoning, the Court of First Instance was asked to determine whether EC action, taken pursuant to its competence under the Treaty, should be unrestricted by EC human rights standards when that action is taken to comply with a Security Council resolutions. In essence, the CFI argued that it is legally bound by the UN Security Council Resolutions in the same way as the EC Member States, which prevents it from providing judicial review regarding their compatibility with Community law and fundamental rights as protected by EC law and the ECHR. The only exception is – according to the CFI – if *jus cogens* would be violated. The CFI first argued that not as a matter of international law (since it is not a member of the United Nations), but in terms of Community law itself, the Community 'must be considered to be bound by the obligations under the Charter of the United Nations in the same way as its Member States'. Afterwards, quite contradictory to this assumption, the Court declared itself competent to: 'check, indirectly, the lawfulness of the resolutions of

---

United Nations Security Council resolution: 'the origin of the illegality alleged by the applicant would have to be sought, not in the adoption of the contested regulation but in the resolutions of the Security Council which imposed the sanctions.' See *Yusuf, supra* n. 82 para. 266.

89 *Bosphorus Airways, supra* n. 87.
90 Case T- 315/01 *Kadi v Council and Commission* (not yet published).
91 *Yusuf, supra* n. 82.

the Security Council with regard to *jus cogens* [92] understood as a body of higher rules of public international law binding on all subjects of international law, including the bodies of the United Nations, and from which no derogation is possible.'[93] It then commenced a review on the basis of three fundamental rights – right to effective judicial review; a right to property; and a right to be heard, which, according to the Court, have the status of mandatory prescriptions under *jus cogens.*

This finding prompted the conclusion of the court that the real object of the review sought by the applicants was not so much the EC measures; rather, they desired direct review of the Security Council resolution. However, in the court's view, Security Council Resolutions could not be reviewed on the basis of EC human rights standards, and may be reviewed uniquely on the basis of the international *ius cogens*, conceived by the court as the only limit erected by international law to the power of the Security Council.

This finding is quite surprising, since the right to effective judicial review and the right to be heard are clearly enshrined in Article 6 of the ECHR which, according to Article 6 (2) TEU and to the constant case law of the ECJ, constitute general principles of EU law. Whilst the CFI's decisions met the expectations both of the EC institutions and of the Member States intervening in the proceedings, its findings are not entirely free from criticism. Many of its passages are obscure and convoluted, and appear technically questionable, to say the least. The overall impression is that the magnitude of the issue, and the unanimous political consent surrounding the determination of the Security Council, weighed heavily on the CFI's decision, and led to the abandonment of its role as a guarantor of human rights.[94]

Furthermore, the CFI seems to have attempted to substantially modify the existing hierarchy of norms within the Community legal order. This new hierarchy would place international law (*jus cogens* and obligations arising out of international treaties/decisions of international

---

[92]   Conforti argues that the question of the protection of fundamental rights regarding the UN Security Council resolution should have been addressed more correctly in terms of EC fundamental rights rather than in relation to international *jus cogens*. B. Conforti, 'Decisioni Del Consiglio Di Sicurezza e Diritti Fondamentali, in Una Bizzarra Sentenza del Tribunale Comunitario di Primo Grado' (2006), 2 *Il Diritto dell'Unione Europea* 333, at 341. On these grounds the judgment in *Yusuf* has been appealed.

[93]   See Conforti, 'Decisioni del Consiglio', *supra* n. 92, at 226.

[94]   Ibid., at 341. Similarly E. Cannizzaro, *Machiavelli, the UN Security Council and the Rule of Law*, Global Law Working Paper, New York University Law School, 11 (2005).

organizations) above primary EC law (TEC and ECHR). In addition, the Court, however, does not explain why, or how, the fundamental rights at stake acquired this status of *jus cogens*, nor does it clarify place and status given to *jus cogens* in the EC legal system.[95] Even if the CFI has taken a courageous step forward in acknowledging the primacy of the UN system over the Community legal order, the Court did not confine its assessment to *jus cogens* proper, but resorted to applying to their full extent the standards evolved in the practice of the Community's judicial bodies.[96]

The obligations imposed by an international agreement cannot have the effect of prejudicing the constitutional principles of the EC Treaty, which include the principle that all Community acts must respect fundamental rights, that respect constituting a condition of their lawfulness which it is for the Court to review in the framework of the complete system of legal remedies established by the Treaty.

While reaffirming that respect for human rights is therefore a condition of the lawfulness of Community acts, and measures incompatible with respect for human rights are not acceptable in the Community, the Court of Justice reversed the CFI's judgment on appeal.[97] The Court clarified that primacy at the level of Community law would not extend to primary law, in particular to the general principles of which fundamental rights form part. It follows that the Community judicature must, in accordance with the powers conferred on it by the EC Treaty, ensure the review of the lawfulness of all Community acts in the light of the fundamental rights forming an integral part of the general principles of Community law, including review of Community measures which, like the regulation at issue, are designed to give effect to the resolutions adopted by the Security Council under Chapter VII of the Charter of the United Nations.[98]

It is clear from the above analysis that a number of uncertainties remain concerning the hierarchy of norms as between international law and primary or fundamental principles of Community law (including the protection of human rights), and the conditions under which Community

---

[95]   M. Cremona, *External Relations of the EU and the Member States: Competence, Mixed Agreements, International Responsibility, and Effects of International Law*, EUI Working Paper Law, 22 (2006), at 34.

[96]   C. Tomuschat, 'Case law – Case T-306/01, *Ahmed Ali Yusuf and Al Barakaat International Foundation v Council and Commission*; Case T-315/01, *Yassin Abdullah Kadi v Council and Commission*' (2006) 43 C.M.L.R. 537.

[97]   *Yassin Abdullah Kadi and Al Barakaat International Foundation v Council of the European Union and Commission of the European Communities*, Joined cases C-402/05 P and C-415/05 P, [2008] ECR I-6351.

[98]   Ibid. paras 306–8, 326.

acts may be declared unlawful as a result of a breach of international law, including treaty obligations.

It is submitted here that these uncertainties should be addressed in a more consistent manner by EC courts, since this attitude risks undermining the legitimacy and credibility of the EU's activities in the field of human rights, in particular when they are addressed to third countries.

One example is given by the fact that the EU invokes international human rights law *vis-à-vis* third countries and that EC treaties with third countries include commitments to respect human rights.[99] The content of human rights as described in these clauses has been identified primarily in the human rights norms contained in the UDHR.[100] As pointed out by Cannizzaro,[101] if we accept that some rules formerly considered not to be binding, such as those contained in the UDHR, or as having a conventional character, such as those contained in the UN covenants of 1966, have assumed or are going to assume the nature of general rules of international law,[102] it must follow that the EC is also bound by them. It can be safely assumed that the Community considers the Universal Declaration of Human Rights as reflecting the principles of international law binding on the Community and the States with which it concludes such treaties.[103] There is no reason to believe that the EU is not similarly bound by the same international human rights obligations that it invokes in relations to third countries. It follows that the EC must exercise its competence in a manner consistently with general rules of international law, including human rights.[104]

---

[99]   P. Eeckhout, *External Relations of the European Union: Legal and Constitutional Foundations*, 2004, Oxford, Oxford University Press, at 465.

[100]   Brandtner and Rosas, 'Human Rights and the External Relations', *supra* Ch.1 n. 97, at 489.

[101]   E. Cannizzaro, 'The Scope of EU Foreign Power: Is the EC Competent to Include Human Rights Clauses in Agreements Concluded with Third States?', in Cannizzaro (ed), *The European Union, supra* Ch.1 n. 96, 297.

[102]   Simma and Alston, 'The Sources of Human Rights Law', *supra* Ch.1 n. 99, at 82–108; Simma, 'International Human Rights', *supra* Ch.1 n. 143, at 153–256, 213–30.

[103]   Clapham, *Human Rights Obligations, supra* Ch.1 n. 50, at 177–193. Some authors go a step further and consider the EC should accept to be bound by the main international instruments for the protection of human rights adopted either within the framework of the Council of Europe or within the United Nations when a significant number of Member States are parties to them. De Schutter, 'The Implementation of the Charter', *supra* Ch.1 n. 98.

[104]   Cannizzaro, 'The Scope of EU Foreign Power', *supra* n. 101, at 317.

Similarly other legal commentators argue[105] that the EU may be subject to more extensive human rights obligations, incumbent on it by virtue of international law. As an intergovernmental organization is an addressee of international law, and considering the provision contained in the Treaty of Lisbon to give the EU legal personality[106], it can be argued that the EU is bound by customary international law, treaties to which it is a party, and human rights treaties entered into individually by Member States through the principle of succession or substitution. This would extend the range of applicable rights far beyond those in the ECHR to other obligations in, for instance, UN human rights treaties.[107]

Aligning Union law with international law would present advantages by increasing both the legitimacy and the credibility of EU's action in the field of human rights. First, anchoring the EU's human rights activities to international human rights law will counterbalance the uncertainty that still surrounds the status of human rights in the EU legal system and the question of EU powers in this field. In particular, a clear commitment to international human rights will reinforce the credibility of EU activities *vis-à-vis* third countries. In particular, linking the promotion of human rights in third countries to the international system of human rights law, the EU can avoid the allegations of particularism and of promoting European rather than universal human rights.[108] Finally, if the EU were to present itself as an organization bound by international human rights law, it would at least partially address the issue of incoherence between human rights standards adopted at the internal level and those required by third countries, which has for long flawed EU action.[109]

---

[105]   T. Ahmed and I. Butler, 'The European Union and Human Rights: an International Law Perspective' (2006) 17/4 E.J.I.L. 771; Clapham, *Human Rights Obligations*, *supra* Ch.1 n. 50, at 350; Tomuschat, 'The International Responsibility of the European Union', *supra* Ch.1 n. 96, at 187.

[106]   Art. 1 'The Union shall replace and succeed the European Community' and Art. 46 A 'The Union shall have legal personality', Treaty of Lisbon, *supra* n. 29.

[107]   Alston and de Schutter (eds), *Monitoring Fundamental Rights*, *supra* n. 41, at 21.

[108]   P. Leino, 'European Universalism. The EU and Human Rights Conditionality', in P. Leino-Sandberg, *Particularity vs Universality: The Politics of Human Rights in the European Union*, 2005, Helsinki, Erik Castrén Institute, Hakapaino, at 239–301.

[109]   Clapham, 'Where is EU Human Right Policy?', *supra* Ch.1 n. 95.; M. Bulterman, *Human Rights in the Treaty Relations of the European Community: Real Virtues or Virtual Reality?*, 2001, Antwerpen, Intersentia, 153; Alston and Weiler, *supra* n. 42, at 27, Williams, *supra* n. 42, at 112.

The arguments for legitimacy and credibility become even more stringent if one looks at how the EU can address the activities of European based MNEs. The need for universally, rather than merely European human rights standards, is essential for all types of EU initiatives in this field. As discussed above, the central problem of the regulation of MNEs worldwide is identifying common standards that can be accepted across countries and across jurisdictions, rather than being trumped by national legislation. It is well known that these characteristics are proper of internationally recognized human rights. Secondly, as will be discussed later, EU measures addressed to MNEs or to the host States of MNEs are even more vulnerable to allegations of misguided colonialism and protectionism. Addressing MNEs' human rights violations underscores the conflict between economic interest and protection of human rights.

Therefore, it is submitted that despite existing uncertainties regarding the status of international human rights law in the EU's legal system, EU measures to address human rights abuses by MNEs should refer to international rights law and should be conducted in coordination with the activities of other international organizations.

4.2.3 Multinational Enterprises in EU Law

In addition to a firm commitment to human rights both at the internal and the external level and the role of the EU on the international scene, EU law presents some features that make it one of the potentially best equipped regional organizations in terms of regulation of the activity of its companies abroad.

First, the European Union has the capacity to enact legal rules regarding both individuals and enterprises. A distinct feature of European Community law lies in the combination of the doctrine of direct effect of EC law[110] and of the referral mechanism which, under Article 234 TEC[111], in fact obliges national jurisdictions to submit to the interpretation of the requirements of EC law by the European Court of Justice. This creates a direct channel of communication between the national courts of the Member States and the European Court of Justice. As a result, in contrast to most international treaties, the European treaties not only confer rights to private individuals and impose obligations on them, but they do so directly, without necessarily having to rely on the fidelity with which

---

[110] *Van Gend en Loos, supra* Ch.2 n. 71.
[111] Art. 234, Treaty of Lisbon.

the States (under the jurisdiction of which these individuals are situated) respect their international obligations.

Secondly, the status of MNEs within the EU does not seem to face the same uncertainty that characterizes their standing in international law. MNEs have been granted extensive substantial and procedural rights under EC law. They are the object of direct regulation and can be subjected to administrative sanctions by the European Commission for violations of competition rules.[112] As pointed out above, in the realm of competition law, in particular, the Commission can enforce compliance by autonomously imposing fines and penalties.[113] The Commission may also order a company to cease any infringement[114] and can grant interim measures in urgent cases of irreparable damage to competition. It also enjoys wide powers to commence proceedings which include a power to seek and require information, a power to conduct interviews and even to carry out inspections of the premises of companies and (in some cases) also outside of them.[115]

These powers are also balanced by the recognition of companies' rights. Under Article 27(1) of Regulation 1/2003, for instance, the Commission is required to give the parties under investigation the right of being heard. Corporations are also granted a wider direct court access to challenge legally binding legislative and administrative acts.[116] Finally, companies' *locus standi* before the European courts has been granted in broader terms. The concept of legitimate interest which is a necessary prerequisite to have *locus standi* before EC courts, has been interpreted more generously in the context of competition law and anti dumping-cases, rather than in other areas of EC law.[117]

---

[112] Korah, *An Introductory Guide*, *supra* Ch.2 n. 72.

[113] Art. 23 Council Regulation (EC) 1/2003 of 16 December 2002 on the Implementation of the Rules on Competition Laid Down in Articles 81 and 82 of the Treaty [2003] OJ L1/1, foresees fines in those cases in which a company provides misleading information to the Commission and in case of infringements of Arts 81 and 82 of the EC Treaty.

[114] Pursuant to Art. 7 of Regulation 1/2003 'it [the Commission] may impose on them [undertaking and associations of undertakings] any behavioural or structural remedies which are proportionate to the infringement committed and necessary to bring the infringement effectively to an end'.

[115] Arts 17–22 Council Regulation 1/2003, *supra* n. 113.

[116] Decisions by the Commission pursuant to competition policy may be challenged under Art. 230 of the EC Treaty and a failure to take such a decision under Art. 232. These matters are dealt with by the Court of First Instance subject to appeal on points of law to the ECJ.

[117] The express power for the Commission was introduced by Art. 8 of Regulation 1/2003, *supra* n. 113.

Not only have companies gained extensive powers within the EU, but they can also ask the EU to protect their commercial interests before an external adjudicating body such as the WTO dispute settlement body. Under the Trade Barriers Regulation,[118] any enterprise within the Community is entitled to ask the Commission to intervene on its behalf before the WTO, when the enterprise has suffered the adverse effects of barriers to trade.[119]

Another element worth considering here is the tendency in EU law to consider MNEs as a unit. In contrast with the problematic definition of multinational in international law multinationals, which are usually defined by EU law as 'groups of undertakings', have been subjects of specific rules on taxation[120] and for the establishment of procedures for the purposes of informing and consulting employees.[121] This tendency to consider a 'group of companies' as a unity is even more evident within the realm of EC competition law.[122]

The jurisprudence of the ECJ has developed the concept of 'economic unity', which is defined as comprising bodies with identical interests and

---

[118]   Council Regulation (EC) 3286/94 of 22 December 1994, laying down Community procedures in the field of the common commercial policy in order to ensure the exercise of the Community's rights under international trade rules, in particular those established under the auspices of the World Trade Organization, [1994] OJ L 349/71.

[119]   Ibid., Art. 4 reads as follows 'Any Community enterprise, or any association, having or not legal personality, acting on behalf of one or more Community enterprises, which considers that such Community enterprises have suffered adverse trade effects as a result of obstacles to trade that have an effect on the market of a third country may lodge a written complaint. Such complaint, however, shall only be admissible if the obstacle to trade alleged therein is the subject of a right of action established under international trade rules laid down in a multilateral or plurilateral trade agreement. The complaint must contain sufficient evidence of the existence of the obstacles to trade and of the adverse trade effects, resulting there from. Evidence of adverse trade effects must be given on the basis of the illustrative list of factors indicated in Article 10, where applicable'.

[120]   Council Directive 2003/123/EC of 22 December 2003 amending Directive 90/435/EEC on the Common system of taxation applicable in the case of parent companies and subsidiaries of different Member States, OJ L 7/ 41, 13 January 2004 and Council Directive 2006/98/EC of 20 November 2006 adapting certain Directives in the field of taxation, by reason of the accession of Bulgaria and Romania OJ L 363, 20 December 2006, pp.129–36; OJ L 352M , 31 December 2008, pp.757–64.

[121]   Directive 2009/38/EC of the European Parliament and of the Council of 6 May 2009 on the establishment of a European Works Council or a procedure in Community-scale undertakings and Community-scale groups of undertakings for the purposes of informing and consulting employees.

[122]   Korah, *supra* Ch.2 n. 72, at 36–9.

subject to common control. Economic considerations, rather than legal ones, seem to prevail in this definition. As a consequence, in applying Articles 81 and 82 the Commission will take into account the economic strength of other members of a group of undertakings if they are implicated in abusive behaviour.[123] In *United Brands Co.*, for instance, the Court considered the overall structure and policy of the group, and not simply its European subsidiary.[124] In *Istituto Chemioterapico Italiano Commercial Solvents Co. v Commission*[125] the ECJ held that the American parent company was responsible for the breach of Article 82 TEC,[126] which was committed by the Italian subsidiary Imperial Chemical Industry. In the case the conduct of a 51 per cent subsidiary was attributed to its parent because the subsidiary had followed the policy decided by the parent. Similarly, in *Sugar Cartel* a parent company was fined for the conduct of its subsidiary, which was acquired later, when it continued to pursue the same policy after its acquisition.[127] On the contrary, an agreement between a parent and a subsidiary will not breach Article 81(1) TEC,[128] unless the subsidiary enjoys full independence from the parent, on the grounds that in the latter case the two companies were never competing, since they were part of the same economic unit.[129]

It stems from the above that, in contrast with their status under international law, MNEs are unanimously recognized as subjects of EU law enjoying both substantive and procedural rights and duties. In addition, a conceptualization of MNEs as economic units tends to prevail over their separation into different legal units. To a certain extent the Commission has sanctioned anticompetitive conduct of MNEs taking place outside the common market to the extent that such behaviour could affect the common market. On these grounds it can be argued that there do not seem to be many obstacles to directly imposing human rights obligations upon European MNEs and to applying them extraterritorially to European companies in analogy with competition law.[130] Reality falls short of these theoretical assumptions. As will be examined in the following chapter, the

---

[123]   Case D-6/72 *Europemballage and Continental Can v Commission* [1973] ECR 215.

[124]   Francioni, *Imprese Multinazionali, supra* Ch.2 n. 31, at 161–4.

[125]   Cases 6&7/73 *Istituto Chemioterapico Italiano Commercial Solvents Co. v Commission* [1974] ECR 223, para. 41.

[126]   Art. 82, Treaty of Lisbon.

[127]   Joined cases 40–48, 50, 54–56, 111, 113 and 114–73 *Coöperative Vereniging UA and Others v Commission (The Sugar Cartel)* [1975] ECR 1663, paras 76–88.

[128]   Art. 81, Treaty of Lisbon.

[129]   Case C-73/95 *Viho Europe BV v Commission* [1996] ECR I-5457.

[130]   See Torremans, *supra* n. 12.

European Union has so far rejected an active role in setting standards of conduct of its enterprises in developing countries.

4.3   CONCLUSION

Chapter 1 brought the issue of MNEs' responsibility for human rights into the EU framework. Firstly, it described how the EU has to date displayed a reluctant attitude in fully addressing the problem. The reasons for such reluctance have been identified respectively in the lack of consensus among the stakeholders and, in particular, in the dichotomy between industry and enterprises on the one hand, and non governmental organizations and trade unions on the other.[131]

Nevertheless, it was submitted, that the European Union enjoys a specific and relevant *espace de manœuvre* in which it can take positive steps in standard setting and monitoring the conduct of European enterprises operating in third countries.

The first argument in support of the above stems from the analysis of the enhanced role of human rights both in the internal and external dimension of the European Union. As we have seen, human rights have acquired a prominent role in the policies and the legal system of the European Union. The EU, however, does not have general competence to adopt rules in the field of human rights. Nevertheless, it has been submitted that, on the basis of Article 6 and of ECJ's reasoning in *Opinion 2/94,* the EC/EU is under an obligation and not merely a duty of the community in pursuing human rights in its policies. It was submitted that, since human rights constitute general principles of Community law whose observance the Court should ensure, this implies a functional competence for the EC to take all necessary measures, including positive ones, to ensure that human rights are respected in its policies, if the EU seeks to promote human rights, both within its borders and in its relations with third countries.

Secondly, at the international level the EU is not only a powerful economic actor, but it is also an organization bound by international human rights law. The extent to which the EU has become, or is likely to become, a human rights based organization is evaluated to different degrees by scholars.[132] Many commentators have expressed the criticism that the

---

[131]   Interviews with Commission's Officials.

[132]   Many commentators have expressed criticism as to whether the discourse on human rights is matched by reality. See A. Von Bogdandy, 'The European Union as Human Rights Organization? Human Rights and the Core of the European Union' (2000) 37 C.M.L.R. 1307. Others believe that the EU should

discourse on human rights is perhaps not matched by reality.[133] In particular, it seems unlikely that the EU can have a comprehensive human rights policy when there is still such a clear concern with limiting its competences[134] and sometimes a reluctant political attitude.[135] On the other hand, the EU, as an addressee of international law, is said by the ECJ to be bound by the general rules of international law, so that a violation of customary international law could be relevant to a determination that a piece of Community secondary legislation was invalid and inapplicable to an individual or a legal person.[136] EC treaty relations include commitments to respect human rights in the context of relations with third States.[137] The assumption is that the Community considers the Universal Declaration of Human Rights as reflecting the principles of international law binding on the Community and the States with which it concludes such treaties.[138] There is no reason to believe that the EU is not similarly bound by the same international human rights obligations, also in the context of the Treaty of Lisbon that will give the EU a single legal personality.[139]

It has been argued that linking EU law with international law would increase both the legitimacy and the credibility of EU action in the field of human rights by counterbalancing the uncertainty that still surrounds EU powers in this field and by reinforcing the credibility of EU activities in relation to third countries. The arguments for legitimacy and credibility are even more relevant in the context of the activities of European based MNEs. The need for universal, rather than merely European, human rights standards is essential for the whole range of EU initiatives in this field. Thus, it was submitted that, despite existing uncertainties regarding

---

develop into an organization that place human rights at the core of its policies and its legal framework. See Weiler and Fries, *supra* n. 53, at 147–66.

[133]   The issue of whether the EU itself shows sufficient respect for human rights in its external activities came to the forefront in the context for instance of the agreement on criminal justice cooperation signed in 2003 between the EU and the USA ('Agreement on Extradition between the United States of America and the European Union, of 25 June 2003' (2004) 43 *International Legal Materials* 749).

[134]   See De Burca, *Setting Constitutional Limits, supra* n. 72.

[135]   Williams, *EU Human Rights Policies, supra* n. 42, at 111–26.

[136]   *Racke GmbH, supra* Ch 1 n. 96. According to Tomuschat 'The ECJ has become the guardian of legality not only with respect to the three Community treaties, but also with regard to international law in general': Tomuschat, 'The International Responsibility of the European Union', *supra* Ch.1 n. 96, at 187.

[137]   Brandtner and Rosas, 'Human Rights and the External Relations', *supra* Ch.1 n. 97, at 489.

[138]   See Simma and Alston, *supra* n. 103.

[139]   Art. 1(3): 'The Union shall replace and succeed the European Community', Treaty of Lisbon, *supra* n. 29.

the status of international human rights law in the EU's legal system, EU measures to address human rights abuses by MNEs should refer to international rights law and should be conducted in coordination with the activities of other international organizations.

Finally, many legal provisions relating to the status of MNEs in EU law that could facilitate positive measures on the part of the European Union and which can improve the human rights accountability of MNEs operating abroad have been examined. The status of MNEs within the EU does not seem to face the same uncertainty that characterize their standing in international law. MNEs have been granted extensive substantial and procedural rights under EC law. In addition, they are the object of direct regulation.

In conclusion, it is submitted that not only is the EC under an obligation stemming from the EC legal system to ensure that human rights are respected in all its policies, but also that it should do so in accordance with international human rights norms. If human rights are to be of guidance, both in internal and external policy,[140] it can be argued that the European Union has to come to terms with the problem of redressing the balance between economic interests and respect for fundamental values, both in its internal and external dimensions. The challenge of taking responsibility for the expansion of European MNEs in developing countries and for ensuring that this expansion will be consistent with European Union development and human rights policy, is indicative of the future of human rights within the institutional framework of the European Union and in the context of globalisation.

From a policy perspective, the argument for coherence and avoiding hypocrisy, and the argument concerning the need to correct the European Union's excessive market orientation both support the exercise by the European Union of a stricter scrutiny over the activity of European MNEs operating abroad. The argument of consistency calls for the European Union to take steps to ensure and to promote the respect for those human rights by European economic actors, such as MNEs, operating abroad.

The following chapters examine how the issue of ensuring the respect for human rights by European MNEs has been tackled by the EU. The emergence of concerns over the conduct of multinational companies has taken different shapes, ranging from legislation relating to company law and labour law within the EU to voluntary instruments, such as codes of conduct, to more recent mechanisms such as the IFAs and the inclusion

---

[140] Commission Communication on *The Charter of Fundamental Rights of the European Union*, COM (2002) 559 final, 13 September 2002.

of social clauses in public procurement, which has merged voluntary and binding elements. In Part III a distinction will be made between measures addressed to MNEs within internal and external policies, and the analysis of measures addressed to third States which are host States of MNEs will be dealt with.

5 Internal measures addressed to MNEs

5.1 INTRODUCTION

This chapter examines to what extent the EU has integrated concerns in respect of human rights obligations by MNEs into its internal policies. For a matter of simplification, these measures are defined here as 'internal', which refers more to the internal character of the EC policies examined rather than to the effect of these measures. As said at the outset of this book, when it comes to measures addressed to MNEs, the internal/external divide appears evanescent. Although adopted in the context of one of the internal policies of the EC, these measures are able to affect the behaviour of European-based MNEs operating outside of the EU's borders.

As discussed above, the EC has a power, and is indeed under an obligation, to comply with human rights in the fields of its competence. It has also been argued that the EC is endowed with stringent powers over the regulation of companies based in one of its Member States. Thus, the question arises to what extent human rights concerns have been integrated into EC policies which are strictly related to the conduct of MNEs, such as company law, competition law and public procurement. As we will see, the extent of this integration and the possibility offered by the Treaties vary greatly. While competition and company law so far have not been seen as the appropriate policy areas to address compliance with human rights, some potential has been individuated in social policy and in the introduction of social clauses into EC public procurement.

The measures addressed to MNEs taken in the areas of company law, competition and public procurement all have in common a *regulatory* character. In these fields the EC is endowed with rule making powers which in some cases – such as competition law – are matched with specific supervisory powers conferred on the Commission. Therefore, the EC has the power to impose rules which would be binding on MNEs.

However, similarly to the development occurring at the international level, in the EC MNEs' responsibility for human rights violations has been addressed more through non-regulatory measures, rather than legally binding ones. Next to the possibilities offered by company law, competition law and public procurement law, it seems appropriate to discuss here the vast array of voluntary initiatives addressed to MNEs that go under the umbrella term of 'Corporate Social Responsibility'.

5.2 THE EC's POWERS UNDER COMPETITION LAW AND COMPANY LAW

The impotent nature of the EU's response to human rights abuses by MNEs is more disappointing than that of other international organizations because under EC law corporations are subject to direct regulation. As discussed above, under Articles 81 and 82 of the TEC undertakings are prohibited from engaging in activities which prevent, restrict or distort competition within the common market and from exploiting in an improper manner a dominant position within the common market.[1] In addition, the European Commission has far-reaching powers to enforce these provisions *vis-à-vis* undertakings, including imposing fines and penalties[2] and ordering a company to cease any infringement.[3] MNEs are the object of direct regulation and can be subjected to administrative sanctions by the European Commission for violations of competition. It also enjoys wide powers to commence proceedings, which include a power to seek and require information, a power to conduct interviews and even to carry out inspections of the premises of the companies and (in some cases) also outside of them.[4] In principle, the EC is therefore better equipped to regulate the conduct of MNEs than other international organizations.

It is true that at first sight Articles 81 and 82 do not offer the necessary legal basis for regulating the external conduct of community based MNEs. After all, the scope of these provisions is restricted *ratione materiae* to the antitrust field and *ratione loci* to the common market area. However, this has not prevented the court from applying Articles 81 and 82 of the EC Treaty to any undertaking in the world as long as abusive practices take effect within the common market. This gives rise to a sort of extraterritorial application of EC competition law, which is upheld by the ECJ.[5] In

---

[1] Korah, *An Introductory Guide, supra* Ch.2 n. 72.

[2] Art. 23 Regulation 1/2003, *supra* Ch.4 n. 113.

[3] Pursuant to Art. 7 of Regulation 1/2003 'it [the Commission] may impose on them [undertaking and associations of undertakings] any behavioural or structural remedies which are proportionate to the infringement committed and necessary to bring the infringement effectively to an end', *supra* Ch.4 n. 113.

[4] Ibid., Arts 17–22.

[5] See Torremans, *supra* Ch.4 n. 12.

Wood Pulp,[6] for instance, the ECJ held that even when the agreement was made by non-EU nationals outside the common market, the Commission would be competent if the agreement was to be implemented within the common market. Similarly, the European merger regulation[7] was considered to be applicable to a merger between two companies extracting platinum in South Africa. The judgement was based on consideration of the rise of international prices of platinum worldwide, and the fact that this would have affected prices in the EC, although indirectly.

Therefore, it can be argued that there do not seem to be many obstacles to imposing human rights obligations directly upon European MNEs and to applying them extraterritorially to European companies in analogy with competition law.[8] In addition to analogical interpretation, difficulties regarding the legal basis have never prevented the Commission from proposing legislative action in the fields in which it was keen to act. In fact it seems, that no creative attempts have been made to get around the lack of legal bases by seeking to base a proposal on Article 308 when it was still possible or by proposing an extension of its powers under the EC Treaty.[9]

This argument can reinforce the fact that action at Member States' level is not sufficient. The possibilities of regulating the conduct abroad of subsidiaries of Community based MNEs are complicated by the fact that attempts to harmonize the law of corporate groups in the European Community have so far been not entirely successful. EU 'groups of undertakings', have been subjects of specific rules on taxation[10] and for the establishment of procedures for the purposes of informing and consulting employees.[11]

A partial attempt at harmonization is constituted by the Statute of the

---

[6]   Cases 89/85, 114/85, 116–117/85, 125–129/85, *A. Ahlström Osakeyhtiö v Commission (Wood Pulp)* [1988] ECR 5193.

[7]   Council Regulation (EC) 139/2004 of 20 January 2004 on the Control of concentrations between undertakings (the EC Merger Regulation), [2004] OJ L 24/1.

[8]   See Torremans, *supra* Ch.4 n. 10.

[9]   Kamminga, 'Holding Multinationals Accountable,' *supra* n. 70, at 566.

[10]   Directive 2003/123, *supra* Ch.4 n. 120.

[11]   Council Directive 94/45/EC of 22 September 1994 on the establishment of a European Works Council or a procedure in Community-scale undertakings and Community-scale groups of undertakings for the purposes of informing and consulting employees, OJ L 254, 30.9.1994, pp. 64–72. The Directive was replaced by Directive 2009/38/EC of the European Parliament and of the Council of 6 May 2009 on the establishment of a European Works Council or a procedure in Community-scale undertakings and Community-scale groups of undertakings for the purposes of informing and consulting employees.

European Company. The Council Regulation (EC) No 2157/2001[12] (hereinafter Regulation 2157/2001) on the Statute of a European Company (the so-called *Societas Europea*), which has been under discussion for several years, permits the creation and management of companies with a European character, free from obstacles arising from the disparity between, and limited territorial application of, national company laws. The recitals of Regulation 2157/2001 fix the objective of the regulation as to connect the economic unit to the legal one.[13] The harmonizing effect, however, should not be overestimated. Upon closer examination, Regulation 2157/2001 will clarify that the adoption of the definition of a '*Societas Europea*' is merely an alternative to the definition that a company has in the Member State where it is listed. Secondly, all the most relevant areas are left to be defined in national legislation. The outcome seems to be that, instead of a new European company, there will be as many legal regimes for companies as the Member States stemming from the implementation that the regulation will receive in each Member State. This can be interpreted as evidence of the fact that the perception of what a company is and what its structure should be, still differ greatly among Member States and are far from being homogeneous. This disparity between both legal regimes and corporate theories is one of the major obstacles that hinder the creation of a common framework for the responsibility of MNEs at the European Union level. Regulation 2157/2001 is supplemented by Council Directive 2001/86/EC of 8 October 2001, which regulates to the involvement of employees in the case on the creation of an European company.[14]

However, this setback has not prevented the Court and the Commission from developing their own doctrine on corporate group liability when dealing with non EC parent companies suspected of anticompetitive conduct within the common market area. According to this doctrine, the so called enterprise approach, the mere existence of a subsidiary relationship is sufficient to establish jurisdiction over the parent company.[15] The tendency to consider a 'group of companies' as a unity, is even more

---

[12] Council Regulation (EC) 2157/2001 of 8 October 2001 on the Statute for a European company (SE) [2001] OJ L 294/1.

[13] A. Malatesta, 'Il Regolamento CE 21 57/2001 sulla Società Europea', in U. Draetta and F. Pocar, *La Società Europea. Problemi di Diritto Societario Comunitario*, 2002, Milano, Egea, at 7.

[14] Council Directive 2001/86/EC of 8 October 2001 supplementing the Statute for a European company with regard to the involvement of employees [2001] OJ L 294 22–32.

[15] Muchlinski, *Multinational Enterprises*, *supra* Ch.1 n. 40., at 137–8.

evident within the realm of EC competition law.[16] As we have already pointed out in paragraph 1.2.5 above, the jurisprudence of the ECJ has developed the concept of 'economic unity', which is defined as comprising bodies with identical interests and subject to common control. Economic considerations rather that legal ones seem to prevail in this definition.

In the Howitt Resolution, the Parliament requested the Member States to introduce such extraterritorial jurisdiction in their national legislation, and requested the European Commission to conduct further research as to the application of this principle by national courts of the Member States.

It was also suggested to use Regulation (EC)44/2001 in a way similar to an European ATCA. By adopting a broad interpretation of Article 2[17] and Article 5[18] of cases of basic duty of care, legal action by any third country national, may be taken against a company in the EU Member State where its registered office is. The Regulation, however, differs fundamentally from the ATCA.[19] Unlike the ATCA, the Regulation only addresses violations by MNEs that are registered in or have their headquarters in a Member State.[20] Furthermore, the Regulation only designates the competent judge; it does not necessarily imply the application of international law. Whether this Regulation can be turned into a genuine European ATCA is questionable, as a sufficient legal basis seems to be lacking in the current TEC. Article 65 TEC provides for the EC's competence to take measures in the field of cooperation in civil matters with transnational consequences. Yet these measures should be necessary for the proper functioning of the internal market. Article 308 TEC, as well, is an article that allows the Council to take measures even if the EC Treaty has not

---

[16]   Korah, *An Introductory Guide, supra* Ch.2 n. 72, at 36–9.

[17]   Art. 2 of Regulation 44/2001: 'Persons domiciled in a Member State shall, whatever their nationality, be sued in the courts of that Member State', *supra* Ch.4 n. 17.

[18]   Ibid, Art. 5 of Regulation 44/2001: 'A person domiciled in a Member State may, in another Member State, be sued: . . . (3) in matters relating to tort, delict or quasi-delict, in the courts for the place where the harmful event occurred or may occur. . . . (5) as regards a dispute arising out of the operations of a branch, agency or other establishment, in the courts for the place in which the branch, agency or other establishment is situated'.

[19]   See for a more elaborate comparison of the ATCA and the Regulation: de Schutter, *The Accountability of Multinationals, supra* Ch.3 n. 49, at 30–47.

[20]   Article 60 of Regulation 44/2001: 'A company or other legal person or association of natural or legal persons is domiciled at the place where it has its: a) statutory seat, or b) central administration, or c) principal place of business', *supra* Ch.4 n. 17.

provided the necessary powers. It can only be invoked if action by the Community should prove necessary to attain, in the course of the operation of the common market, one of the objectives of the Community.[21]

In conclusion, despite the extensive powers conferred on the EC to regulate the anticompetitive conduct of MNEs, competition law does not seem to offer the most appropriate avenue to address MNEs' human rights abuses in third countries.

The difficulties of using Articles 81 and 82 as an appropriate legal basis, however, are certainly matched by a lack of will in this respect by EC institutions. In fact, it has been noted that no creative attempts have been made to get around it by seeking to base a proposal on Article 308 TEC[22] before the Treaty of Lisbon excluded to invoke this article for harmonisation measures. Similarly, recent developments in European company law do not suggest any move towards the creation of a common European code on corporate governance and even less so a code on corporate responsibility.[23] According to the proposals for the reform of company law[24] reform will opt for a lighter and more flexible form of regulation for companies. In order to achieve this objective, it has been suggested extending the use of secondary legislation by the Commission, in areas such as security regulations and in the adoption of model laws that can be voluntarily implemented by companies. Furthermore, it has been pointed out that the abuse of company law should be avoided. Such abuse consists of using company law rules in order to achieve objectives that fall outside company law itself, such as social or human rights concerns.

---

[21] However, this does not prevent the Member States from introducing ATCA-like legislation at the national level. Nevertheless, it has been pointed out that, in the light of its peculiarities and problems, the ATCA can hardly be considered a 'model' for other national legal systems. See J. Wouters, L. de Smet and C. Ryngaert, *Tort Claims Against Multinational Companies for Foreign Human Rights Violations Committed Abroad: Lessons from the Alien Tort Claims Act?* K.U. Leuven Faculty of Law Institute for International Law, Working Paper, 46 (2003), at 14.

[22] Kamminga, 'Holding Multinationals Accountable', *supra* Ch.1 n. 70., at 565.

[23] J. Winter, *The Future of European Company Law*, speech delivered at the Conference European Company Law Company – Law in Europe, 22 May 2002, Law Faculty, University of Maastricht, The Netherlands. See also J. Winter, 'EU Company Law on the Move' (2004) 31/2 *Legal Issues of Economic Integration* 97, at 98.

[24] Available at: http://europa.eu.int/comm/internal_market/smn/smn29/s29 mn22.htm.

5.3 EC's SOCIAL POLICY TOWARDS MNEs

Although there has been a limited use of competition law and company law for the integration of social concerns, looking at the internal measures towards the enhancement of the responsibility of European MNEs, it is possible to notice the progressive recognition of the rights of new groups of stakeholders such as workers and by enhancing transparency and accountability.

The first evidence of European concern over the conduct of MNEs can be found in an oral inquiry in 1972, where the Parliament questioned the Commission on the subject of investment, merger, competition and social policy aspects of a synthetic fibre plant closure and mass dismissal.[25] The Commission recognized very early on the potential problems related to MNEs' activities, at least within the Community ambit. Already in 1977, the Commission[26] warned that the expansion of MNEs, although beneficial and desirable, had led to an imbalance between enterprises and their political, social and economic counterparts, such as governmental agencies and trade unions. It recommended that the Council take action in order to redress this balance through the adoption of legally binding rules, with particular reference to the preservation of working places, the monitoring of tax evasion and the control of speculative capital movements.

The European Community has subsequently issued a series of directives aimed at enhancing corporate accountability within the EC by reforming the internal structures of the MNEs. The Commission called for measures equally applicable to national and to multinational enterprises, but with effects limited to the Community area.

Initially, the first objectives were focused on taking into account the interest of workers, considered as a distinct group of stakeholders in the corporation. In order to achieve this objective the EC has followed two methods. The first is exemplified by the Draft Fifth Directive on Company Law.[27] The draft directive required some structured form of worker participation. In addition it also sought to revise directors' duties and related

---

[25] Oral Question No. 3/72, Abl. C. 46/26–27.

[26] Communication from the Commission to the Council, *Multinational Undertakings and the Community*, Bulletin of the European Communities, Supplement 15/73, 8 November 1973.

[27] *Proposal for A Fifth Directive on the Coordination of Safeguards Which for the Protection of the Interests of Members and Outsiders, Are Required by Member States of Companies Within the Meaning of Article 59, Second Paragraph, with Respect to Company Structure and to the Power and Responsibilities of Company Boards*, [1972] OJ C 131/49.

enforcement, to strengthen the powers of the general meeting, making the executive directors of the company more accountable to the shareholders.

A Council Directive regarding collective redundancies was adopted in February 1975.[28] Article 2 of this directive provided that:

> 1. Where an employer is contemplating collective redundancies, he shall begin consultations with the workers' representatives with a view to reaching an agreement.
> 2. These consultations shall, at least, cover ways and means of avoiding collective redundancies or reducing the number of workers affected, and mitigating the consequences.

Similar rights appear in the Directive on the Safeguarding of Employees' Rights in the Event of Transfer of Undertakings, Businesses or Parts thereof.[29]

The second approach is contained in various proposals put forward since 1980, that seek to institute the provision of information and consultation of workers in enterprises operating in more than one Member State. After some unsuccessful proposals,[30] the European Works Council in Community Scale Undertakings Directive was finally adopted.[31] This

---

[28]   Council Directive 75/129/EEC of 17 February 1975 on the Approximation of the laws of the Member States relating to collective redundancies [1975] OJ L 48/29. This Directive has been consolidated with Directive 92/56/EC Council Directive 98/59/EC of 20 July 1998 on the Approximation of the laws of the Member States relating to collective redundancies [1998] OJ L 225/16.

[29]   Art 3 (1) of Council Directive 77/187/EEC of 14 February 1977 on the Approximation of the laws of the Member States relating to the safeguarding of employees' rights in the event of transfers of undertakings, businesses or parts of businesses [1977] OJ L 61/26, subsequently amended by Council Directive 98/50/EC of 29 June 1998 amending Directive 77/187/EEC on the Approximation of the laws of the Member States relating to the safeguarding of employees' rights in the event of transfers of undertakings, businesses or parts of businesses, [1998] OJ L 20/88, at 88–92. These Directives were finally consolidated in Council Directive 2001/23/EC of 12 March 2001 on the approximation of the laws of the Member States relating to the safeguarding of employees' rights in the event of transfers of undertakings, businesses or parts of undertakings or businesses.

[30]   Proposal for a Council Directive on Procedure for Informing and Consulting Employees of Undertakings with a Complex Structure in Particular Transnational Undertakings (so called 'Vredeling Proposal') [1989] OJ (1980) C 297/13; revised in [1983] OJ C 217/3. The first proposal and the subsequent revised version were shelved mainly due to the opposition of the UK Government.

[31]   Council Directive 94/45/EC of 22 September 1994 on the establishment of a European Works Council or a procedure in Community-scale undertakings and Community-scale groups of undertakings for the purposes of informing and consulting employees [1994] OJ L 254 64–72. The directive was replaced by Directive

directive, which made express reference to the Community Charter of Fundamental Rights of Workers,[32] aims to ensure that the rights of information, consultation and participation for workers are protected in the process of international business restructuring that would follow the completion of the single European market. It provides for information and consultation in cases where employees may be affected by a decision taken outside the Member State in which they are employed. The Directive required the Member States of the EU, with the exception of the United Kingdom,[33] to enact legislation requiring the establishment of European Works Councils by September 1996. European Works Councils are councils established by the central management or employees of a company that transmit information from management to employees, to ensure that decisions made in a company's operations in one State affecting workers in another State are communicated to those affected workers. The Council requirement applies to companies with at least 1000 employees within the participating EU States, and with at least 150 employees in each of two States. Importantly, companies in non-adopting countries, such as the United States or the United Kingdom, can still be bound by the legislation if they have divisions located in participating States. The councils shall be elected or appointed in proportion to the number of employees employed in each Member State by the Community-scale undertaking or Community-scale group of Undertakings. Employee representation on the council must be proportional to the number of employees in the company as a whole.[34]

While until the 1992 Maastricht Treaty there was the progressive inclusion of consumers, environmental concerns and workers' rights through the different branches of EC legislation, after Amsterdam it is possible to address the regulation of companies in a unitary manner.[35] The Treaty of

---

2009/38/EC of the European Parliament and of the Council of 6 May 2009 on the establishment of a European Works Council or a procedure in Community-scale undertakings and Community-scale groups of undertakings for the purposes of informing and consulting employees, *supra* Ch.4 n. 121.

[32] The preamble of the directive expressly refers to point 17 of the Charter. Directive 2009/38 now refers to the Charter of Fundamental Rights of the European Union (Preamble, recital 46).

[33] The Directive was a measure approved under the Protocol and Agreement on Social Policy, which originally did not apply to the UK. See J. Dine, 'Human Rights and Company Law', in Addo (ed.), *Human Rights Standards*, *supra* Ch.1 n. 28, 209, at 218.

[34] See Annex I, Directive 2009/38.

[35] See U. Draetta, 'La Società Europea e il Federalismo Strisciante del Diritto Comunitario', in U. Draetta and F. Pocar (eds), *La Società Europea. Problemi di*

Amsterdam incorporated the Agreement on social policy signed by eleven Member States into the Treaty establishing the European Community, thus bringing a complicated situation to an end. Between 1993 and 1999, there were two distinct legal bases for social policy: the EC Treaty itself and a separate agreement that the United Kingdom had not signed. Now, all the measures are brought together in Title XI of the EC Treaty. The social policy objectives defined in the EC Treaty were inspired by the 1961 European Social Charter and the 1989 Community Charter of the Fundamental Social Rights of Workers: promoting employment, improving working conditions, proper social protection, social dialogue, workforce training to achieve a high and sustainable level of employment and combating exclusion.

In the field of labour law the EU has acted to support and encourage the development of rules specific to transnational firms. Furthermore, there is awareness of the fact that MNEs pose specific problems with regards to the protection of social rights and in particular of workers rights. It is not fortuitous that Regulation 2157/2001 has been complemented by the Council Directive EC 2001/86 regarding the involvement of workers.[36] The directive is aimed at ensuring that the establishment of an SE does not entail the disappearance or reduction of practices of employee involvement existing within the companies participating in the establishment of a *Societas Europea.* In view of the great diversity of rules and practices in the Member States as regards the manner in which employees' representatives are involved in decision making within companies, there are no plans for a single European model. Employee information and consultation procedures at transnational level are nevertheless ensured.[37] If and when participation rights exist within one or more companies establishing an SE, they are preserved through their transfer to the SE, once established, unless the parties involved decide otherwise within the 'special negotiating body' which brings together the representatives of the employees of all the companies concerned. In addition, in order to guarantee inherent complementarities of both directives,

---

Diritto Societario Comunitario, 2002, Milan, Egea, 1.

[36] The Directive upheld the basic principle according to which 'employee involvement is to be established in any SE' (Art. 1(2)). This should cover at least information, consultation and, in many cases, also participation of employees. See Jonathan Rickford, 'The European Company', in Jonathan Rickford (ed.), *The European Company. Developing Community Law of Corporations*, 2003, Antwerp, Intersentia, 26.

[37] R. Blanpain, *European Labour Law*, 2006, The Hague and Frederick, Md., Kluwer Law International and Aspen Publishers.

the status of *Societas Europea* cannot be acquired until the directive on the involvement of workers has entered into force. It seems that EU law takes into account the originality and specific features of the MNEs by treating them as specific *fora* for negotiation and representation.[38] Examples of such a development are the creation of European work councils, the provisions regarding workers representation within *Societas Europea* or within European cooperatives. Finally, in 2002, a Directive establishing a general framework for informing and consulting employees in the European Community was enacted.[39]

Another set of initiatives concerned the enhancement of environmental and social disclosure of information. The EC has introduced regulations requiring disclosure to the public authorities of specific information relevant to the control of industrial hazards in the fields of construction and operation facilities, sale of products and health and safety in the workplace. The EC Eco-auditing Regulation[40] introduced a voluntary scheme for environmental auditing which aims at the establishment, by firms of effective environmental protection systems. It also requires the regular evaluation of the performance of such systems and the provision of information about this performance to the public. The evaluation of this system has to be carried out mainly by means of environmental auditing that would cover issues such as assessment, control and prevention of environmental impact of the activity concerned, energy management savings and choice.

It can be inferred from the above that there is specific concern over MNEs (even if not defined as such) within the ambit of the EU. Awareness that any reform of the structure of MNEs alters the condition of workers, implies that it then needs to be matched by pieces of legislation aimed at protecting them. An innovation can be found in the way the EU has faced these problems. In addition, it is in the area of multinational enterprises that the EU has experimented with new forms of decision making, making

---

[38]   Marie-Ange Moreau, 'Le territoire – Aspects Européens et Internationaux – Des Rattachements Territoriaux Nationaux a la Transnationalité des Normes du Travail', 1128 *Semaine Sociale Lamy* (June 2003) 80, at 84–85.

[39]   Directive 2002/14/EC of the European Parliament and of the Council of 11 March 2002 establishing a General framework for informing and consulting employees in the European Community – Joint declaration of the European Parliament, the Council and the Commission on employee representation, OJ L 80/29, 23 March 2002.

[40]   Regulation (EC) 761/2001 of the European Parliament and of the Council of 19 March 2001 Allowing Voluntary Participation by Organisations in a Community Eco-Management and Audit Scheme (EMAS), [2001] OJ L 114 / 1.

the EU a sort of laboratory for the regulation of MNEs.[41] These initiatives however apply only to groups of undertakings within the EU borders.

5.4   THE INTRODUCTION OF SOCIAL CONCERNS INTO PUBLIC PROCUREMENT

The possibility of introducing social considerations into public procurement was partially favoured by the CSR Multi-Stakeholder Forum Report as a viable incentive to promoting companies' compliance with social and human rights standards, both within the EU and in relation to third countries.[42] Previously, this option was advanced in the Communication of the Commission on Corporate Social Responsibility which suggested that:

> Making access to subsidies for international trade promotion, investment and export credit insurance, as well as access to public procurement, conditional on adherence to and compliance with the OECD Guidelines for Multinational Enterprises, while respecting international commitments, could be considered by EU Member States and by other States adherent to the OECD Declaration on International Investment.[43]

---

[41]   Moreau, *supra* n. 38, at 86. On the specificity of the regulation of MNEs in the EU see M.A. Moreau, G. Trudeau and G. Murray, *Peut-on déceler une dynamique spécifique de regulation de l'enterprise mondialisée dans l'Union européenne?*, Conference organized by the CRIMT, Toward a Social Regulation of a Global Firm, Montreal, Canada.

[42]   The stakeholders have very different views on CSR and public authorities. Employer organizations disagree with the establishment of these kinds of linkages. The other stakeholders think that the EU policies could develop CSR, e.g. through trade incentives and sustainable impact assessments. Some stakeholders argue that the inclusion of environmental and social clauses in certain public supply contracts, consistent with the directive on public procurement, or in the award of credit under special conditions (particularly export credit), can encourage companies' CSR practices and, in certain cases, adherence to international CSR codes. However, there was concern as to the possible distorting effects on companies, particularly in developing countries and with local companies. It was also criticized that this meant moving away from the recognition of CSR as a voluntary practice and misusing policies and instruments for aims which they were not conceived for. See European Multi-Stakeholder Forum on CSR – RT 'Improving Knowledge about CSR' at 10, and European Multi-Stakeholder Forum on CSR – RT 'Fostering CSR among SMEs' at 7, and European Multi-Stakeholder Forum on CSR – RT 'Development aspects of CSR' at 7–8.

[43]   *Corporate Social Responsibility: a Business Contribution, supra* Ch.1 n. 24 at 23.

This proposal draws on the consideration that, besides its activity as a direct regulator of the conduct of MNEs, the European Union could encourage positive developments in corporate conduct by rewarding the most deserving enterprises in the EC's public procurement and by authorizing Member States to do so under their national public procurement laws. This would provide companies with an incentive to comply with certain ethical standards. Considering that the amount of public procurement in the European Union amounts to over €1000 billion every year across the European Union (16 per cent of EU GDP),[44] if social and human rights considerations were taken into account by public authorities when reaching their decisions, this would provide a substantial incentive to MNEs to abide by voluntary human rights guarantees.

The possibility of integrating human rights considerations with public purchasing decisions, so as to influence MNEs' activities in the external field, has already been explored to a certain extent at the local and State levels in the United States in relation to South Africa, Northern Ireland and most recently Burma.[45] Social clauses in public procurements have been recently introduced at local level by the city of San Francisco and in the State of California[46] and a similar proposal was made in the city of New York.[47]

Attempts to link access to public procurement with companies' compliance with social or human rights requirements have, however, encountered some criticism. The concern from the market liberalization point of view is that the inclusion of social criteria potentially expands the area of practical discretion of the purchasing authority by permitting it to make decisions based on less than objectively formulated criteria. Liberalized public procurement markets require the decision-making criteria to be clearly formulated and also the decision-making process to be non-discriminatory and transparent. The easiest way to ensure that this is so is to make sure that the key award criteria for a public contract are the lowest price and the measurable technical performance of the product purchased.

In the EU context, the possibility of incorporating social considerations into public procurement was clarified by the Commission Communication

---

[44]   Available at: http://europa.eu/publicprocurement/index_en.htm. (accessed 3 March 2009).

[45]   See Hanley, *supra* Ch.1 n. 10.

[46]   Ordinance no 223/05 passed on 13 September 2005 and Assembly Bill 633 signed into law in September 1999.

[47]   Proposal to amend the administrative code of the city of New York, in relation to Procurement of Apparel and Textile Services by City Agencies. Proposed Int. No 693-A.

in 2001.[48] The possibility of including environmental and social requirements at different stages of the process was finally introduced by new
Directives on public procurement which merge the four existing European
directives into two legal instruments: the Directive 2004/18/EC[49] for public
works contracts, public supply contracts and public service contracts; and
Directive 2004/17/EC[50] on the 'special sectors' of water, energy, transport
and postal services.

The Directives recognize that labour and social clauses may be relevant
at three different stages of the process and in the procedures for the award
of public contracts. Firstly, certain social or labour standards may be relevant as qualification criteria. Social or labour criteria may be stipulated
as conditions or qualifications for participating in the tendering process,
so that a tender which does not fulfil these requirements is not eligible and
has to be excluded.

Secondly, social and labour standards can be included as award criteria. Article 53 of Directive 2004/18/EC states that in cases where various
criteria are given relevance, when determining the most advantageous
tender, the contracting authority shall specify in the contract notice or
in the contract documents or, in the case of a competitive dialogue, in
the descriptive document, the relative weight which it gives to each of
the criteria chosen to determine the most economically advantageous
tender. The formulation of this provision, read in combination with the
interpretative indication of the Preamble, still leaves many interpretative
questions unanswered. On the one hand it is reaffirmed that contracts
should be awarded on the basis of objective criteria such as the 'lowest
price' and 'the most economically advantageous tender', which ensure
compliance with the principles of transparency, non-discrimination and
equal treatment, and which guarantee that tenders are assessed in conditions of effective competition. As a result, it is appropriate to allow the
application of two award criteria only. On the other hand it is also specified that:

---

[48]   Commission Communication on the Community Law Applicable to Public
Procurement and the possibilities for Integrating Social Considerations into Public
Procurement, COM (2001) 566 final, 15 October 2001.
[49]   Directive 2004/18/EC of the European Parliament and of the Council
of 31 March 2004 On the coordination of procedures for the award of public
works contracts, public supply contracts and public service contracts [2004] OJ
L 134/114.
[50]   Directive 2004/17/EC of the European Parliament and of the Council of 31
March 2004 Coordinating the procurement procedures of entities operating in the
water, energy, transport and postal services sectors [2004] OJ L 134/1.

If these conditions are fulfilled, economic and qualitative criteria for the award of the contract, such as meeting environmental requirements, may enable the contracting authority to meet the needs of the public concerned, as expressed in the specifications of the contract. Under the same conditions, a contracting authority may use criteria aiming to meet social requirements, in response in particular to the needs – defined in the specifications of the contract – of particularly disadvantaged groups of people to which those receiving/using the works, supplies or services which are the object of the contract belong.[51]

A third phase in which social criteria may be relevant is during the performance of the contract. These criteria may be explicitly included in the contract after having previously operated as qualification or award criteria. They can also include elements of the mandatory public labour law in the territory where the project is to be performed. Pursuant to Article 27, requirements on employment protection and labour conditions can be integrated as part of the contract. The fulfilment of these requirements may also be followed up by certain procedures and enforced by sanctions. There is also the possibility of imposing a degree of responsibility upon the contractors for subcontractors to respect some standards. These issues, however, are to be addressed in the implementation of legislation at the national level.

With respect to environmental clauses, the extension was authorized by the Court before it was formally recognized by the European legislature in the Public Procurement Directive 2004/18/EC of 31 March 2004. In its judgment of 17 September 2002, in the case of *Concordia Bus Finland*[52] – where a Finnish municipality took into account the environmental performances which could be satisfied in the execution of the contract to be awarded – the European Court of Justice considered that:

> where the contracting authority decides to award a contract to the tenderer who submits the economically most advantageous tender, in accordance with Article 36(1)(a) of Directive 92/50, it may take criteria relating to the preservation of the environment into consideration, provided that they are linked to the subject-matter of the contract, do not confer an unrestricted freedom of choice on the authority, are expressly mentioned in the contract documents or the tender notice, and comply with all the fundamental principles of Community law, in particular the principle of nondiscrimination.

To sum up, according to Directives 18/2004 and 17/2004, relevant environmental and social requirements may be specified but must be defined sufficiently precisely to allow bidders to understand the requirement and

---

51   Preamble recital 46.
52   Case C-513/99 *Concordia Bus Finland Oy Ab (previously Stagecoach Finland) v Helsingin Kaupunki* [2002] ECR I-7213, para. 64.

to allow award of the contract. Production process standards and eco label criteria can be referenced, but alternatives which demonstrate equivalence must be considered. 'Most economically advantageous' contract award criteria may include environmental and other characteristics, provided these are linked to the subject matter of the contract and are economically advantageous from the point of view of the contracting authority.

The Commission has tended, however, to take a very restrictive interpretation of the permissibility of specific social concerns in public procurement. Economic consideration of best price or best value are considered to be the primary objectives of EC public procurement law. Therefore, social considerations inconsistent with economic objectives can be accommodated only at the margins and with great difficulty. This approach seems to begin with a flawed interpretation of the leading case law on this topic. As pointed out by Bercusson and Bruun,[53] the ECJ left open the possibility for social criteria to be integrated in public procurement, provided that they did not imply discrimination on the grounds of nationality, while the Commission interpreted the ECJ case-law in such a way to preclude this possibility. In *Beentjes*[54] it was acknowledged that social criteria could be used, given that they did not contravene the prohibition of discrimination on grounds of nationality.[55] In *Commission v. France*[56] the Court held that Article 30(1) of Directive 93/37, did not preclude all possibility for the contracting authorities to use as a criterion a condition linked to the Campaign Against Unemployment, provided that that condition is consistent with all the fundamental principles of Community law, in particular the principle of non discrimination.[57] A second concern over the introduction of social clauses in EC procurement relates to its compatibility with the WTO regime.

5.4.1 Compatibility with WTO Agreement on Government Procurement of 1994

The introduction of social clauses into EC procurement raised concerns over its compatibility with the WTO regime. The fear of incompatibility

---

[53]   B. Bercusson and N. Bruun, 'Labour Law Aspects of Public Procurement in the EU', in R. Nielsen and S. Treumer (eds), *The New Public Procurement Directives*, 2005, Copenhagen, Djøf, 97, at 106–10.

[54]   Case 31/87 *Gebroeders Beentjes BV v State of the Netherlands* [1988] ECR 4635.

[55]   Ibid. paras 29–30.

[56]   Case C-225/98 *Commission of the European Communities v French Republic* [2000] ECR I-7445.

[57]   Ibid., para. 50.

of social public procurement with the WTO are clearly spelt out in the Communication on introducing social concerns into public procurement[58] and it is even more evident by the reaction of the Commission to the Massachusetts selective purchasing law for companies operating in Burma.[59] The European Commission formally complained to the US in January 1997 regarding the Massachusetts/Burma legislation and threatened to invoke the WTO dispute settlement procedure. The WTO dispute was suspended when the law was challenged domestically in the US.

A plurilateral agreement on Government Procurement was concluded as part of the World Trade Organisation Uruguay negotiating round on 15 December 1993, entering officially into force in 1996.[60] The GPA is currently undergoing formal review with the aim of improving and simplifying the text.[61] In its current form, the majority of the GPA covers the rules of tendering, including the specific criteria that may be considered in accepting offers. The GPA is problematic because it requires that any conditions for participation in tendering procedures shall be limited to those which are essential to ensure the firm's capability to fulfil the contract in question.[62] Moreover, the GPA requires that, unless it is in the public interest not to issue a contract, a State must accept the lowest tender offer that meets economic criteria.[63] In its challenge against the Massachusetts law regarding Burma, the EC cited both these provisions.[64]

All Member States of the European Union are parties to the GPA, as is the European Community. The GPA does not have direct effect within the Union but the Community is under a legal obligation as a party to the plurilateral agreement to ensure that its policies do not infringe the agreement. Therefore, any change in Community procurement policy

---

[58] See COM (2001) 566, s.1.

[59] 'An Act Regulating Contracts with Companies Doing Business with or in Burma (Myanmar)' Chap. 130, 1996 Session Laws, Massachusetts General Laws, Chap. 7. 223 (West 1997). See McCrudden, 'A framework for discussion of the legality of selective-purchasing-laws under the WTO Government Procurement agreement' (1999) 2 *Journal of International Economic Law* 3.

[60] Government Procurement Agreement (GPA) of the World Trade Organisation, 15 April 1994. LT/UR/A-4/Pluri/2.

[61] S. Arrowsmith, 'Reviewing the GPA: The Role and Development of the Plurilateral Agreement after Doha' (2002) 5 *Journal of International Economic Law* 761.

[62] GPA, Art. VIII (2).

[63] GPA, Art. XIII (4)b.

[64] World Trade Organisation, WT/DS88/1, GPA/D2/126 June 1997, United States – Measure Affecting Government Procurement. Request for Consultations by the European Communities, at 1.

must obviously take cognisance of the GPA and the Community's commitments under it. The GPA also provides that disputes between parties under the agreement are subject, with a few modifications, to the procedures of the WTO Understanding on Rules of Procedures Governing the Settlement of Disputes (DSU).[65] However, according to Article XXII of the GPA, breach of an obligation under the GPA, 'cannot result in the suspension of concessions or obligations under any other agreement', which obviously includes the GATT.[66] Therefore, should the Community be found to have breached the GPA, retaliatory measures under the GATT by the United States, or any other party, are not permissible.

The fact that WTO GPA constitutes an obstacle to the integration of social concerns in EC public procurement has been convincingly confuted by Hanley on two grounds. First, the Community public procurement regime is more developed than the present GPA model and has been in existence for much longer (since 1971, as opposed to 1994). In fact, EC Directives served as a model for many of the GPA provisions.[67] This renders the Community's arguments as to the constraining nature of GPA commitments less convincing.

Secondly, the comparison of certain provisions, of the importance of a purely economic advantage and of the successful tender and finally the exceptions permissible under both procurement regimes reveal a stricter approach on the part of EC directives than under the GPA. As far as the award criteria is concerned, unlike the Community regime, the GPA does not limit the non-price criteria to 'most economically advantageous' tender, merely to the 'most advantageous' in terms of the criteria stated in the tender documentation.[68] This can be read in the sense that in applying, for example, environmental or social criteria, it is not necessary for a contracting body to demonstrate any economic advantage or direct benefit for itself. Kunzlik[69] argues convincingly that this is an acceptable approach, since the principles underlying the GPA, of transparency and

---

[65] GPA 1994, Art. XXII(1).

[66] General Agreement on Tariffs and Trade (GATT) 30 October 1947, 61 Stat. A3, 55 UNTS 188.

[67] S. Arrowsmith and A. Davies, *Public Procurement: Global Revolution*, 1998, London and Boston, Kluwer.

[68] Article VIII(4) of the GAP reads that: '(b) the entity shall make the award to the tenderer who has been determined to be fully capable of undertaking the contract and whose tender . . . is either the lowest tender or the tender which is determined to be the most advantageous'.

[69] P. Kunzlik, 'Environmental Issues in International Procurement', in Arrowsmith and Davies, *supra* n. 67, at 199.

non-discrimination, are not threatened by allowing contracting parties to apply published award criteria which reflect values that are objectively verifiable but cannot always be easily expressed in terms of economic benefits to the bodies concerned. This reasoning could clearly be applied to certain core social rights' considerations. It would appear, however, that the Community Directives before the latest reform[70] were interpreted and applied by the Commission as requiring an economic link to any advantage incurred by the public body itself. In addition, the exceptions under the GPA do not appear to be narrower than those available under Article 30 TEC. GPA Article XXIII lists amongst the permissible exceptions public morals, order or safety. Significantly, Article 30 TEC does not include 'public order' as an exception, rather it refers only to public morality, security and policy. The exception provision Article XXIII GPA however, has not yet been the subject of a dispute settlement, as such all speculation as to how broadly it would be interpreted is based on interpretive comparisons with GATT Article XX.

Other authors convincingly maintain that it is by no means certain that human rights conditionality in public procurement would *per se* infringe the GPA. McCrudden for instance claims that there are three different possible approaches that could be taken to a selective purchasing law such as the Massachusetts Burma legislation for it to have been found compatible with the provisions of the GPA. First, he claims that the thresholds for the contracts for which the Burma legislation applied could be lowered, so as to fall below the threshold stipulated in the GPA. Secondly, he suggests linking human rights considerations to the contract terms, rather than to the price preference.[71] Finally, he examines the possibility of applying one of the exceptions contained in Article XXIII such as 'public order' to the Burma Legislation.[72] He argues that the promotion of international human rights norms could amount to a fundamental interest of society, therefore falling within the margin of appreciation of the State to consider whether dealing with a firm, which itself engages in these practices, would

---

[70]   E.C. Directive 93/36, Article 34 established 'that: the criteria on which the contracting entities shall base the award of contracts shall be: (a) the most economically advantageous tender . . . (b) The lowest price only.

[71]   Contra S. Arrowsmith, 'Public Procurement as an Instrument of Policy and the Impact of Market Liberalization' (1995) 111 L.Q.R. 235.

[72]   Zeisel examines the possibility of allowing selective public procurement under the exceptions of protection public morals and of protection of life and health. K. Zeisel, 'The Promotion of Human Rights by Selective Public Procurement Under International Trade Law', in de Schutter, *Transnational Corporations*, *supra* Ch.1 n. 37, 361, at 387.

constitute the required 'genuinely and sufficient threat to that fundamental interest'. The Burma Legislation, however, involved a general boycott of Burma's human rights policies, rather than the human rights impact of a single contract.

In conclusion, it is submitted that a close textual comparison of certain provisions of procurement regimes in the EC and under the WTO GPA does in fact reveal a stricter approach to non-economic considerations on the part of the previous Community Directives on public procurement than under the GPA. This underscores the weakness of the Commission's arguments when it chooses to cite its WTO commitments as an obstacle to allowing the incorporation of such considerations into public procurement decisions. In addition, despite the lack of WTO jurisprudence to date on the GPA, on the basis of McCrudden's analysis it can be argued that the introduction of human rights concerns into EC public procurement would be very likely to be judged GPA-compatible. This approach however will not cover general economic sanctions for human rights breaches.

5.4.2   Conclusion on the Introduction of Social Concerns into Public Procurement

As seen above, the restrictive approach to the introduction of social concerns in EC public procurement is not justified either in terms of EC law or in terms of its compatibility with WTO commitments. On the contrary, since a number of Member States have adopted or are considering adopting social or environmental procurement laws, there is a strong argument in favour of harmonizing the rules concerning the introduction of these concerns at EC level. Since EC public procurement policy aims to guarantee effective competition and non-discrimination, it is necessary to ensure harmonization pursuant to Article 95 TEC[73] in this field.

Even if the new Directives have partially responded to the demand for integrating some social concerns into public procurement, they have failed to clearly resolve many questions. It is submitted that in order to fully exploit the potential of introducing social concerns in public procurement to ensure the responsible behaviour of MNEs, the EC should improve its public procurement directives in two ways.

On the one hand, the new Directives recognize the possibility for Member States to determine the extent to which social and labour standards may

---

[73]   Art. 94, Treaty of Lisbon.

be adopted as criteria at the different stages of the public procurement process. By allowing Member States to take account of social concerns in their national legislations the new Directive on Public Procurement has a mere permissive effect. A number of Member States including Belgium,[74] France,[75] and Italy[76] indeed introduced social considerations into public procurement well before the adoption of these Directives. However, for public procurement to be an effective tool to induce MNEs to respect social rights and human rights, these should be included as mandatory clauses rather than as simply permissive considerations.

A second development to be considered relates to the range of social considerations currently allowed by EC procurement Directives. This recognition is limited to social and environmental criteria, however; it does not extend to fundamental rights. In *Benteejes* and in *Commission v France* the Court adopted a reading of Article 36(1) of Directive 92/50 favourable to States wishing to take into account environmental criteria in the assessment of the economically most advantageous tender. Since the requirements of environmental protection are to be integrated into the definition and implementation of Community policies and activities on the grounds of Article 6 EC[77] nothing seems to stand in the way of

---

[74] In November 2001, the Belgian Government approved the introduction of a social clause for certain federal public procurement favouring the inclusion of disadvantaged groups (e.g. 5 per cent of the total share of the contract is to be used to hire long term unemployed people). Besides the price and quality of products or services, environmental criteria can also be part of the selection criteria.

[75] Since March 2001, the French law on public procurement authorizes the inclusion of social and environmental considerations among the clauses of public procurement contracts (Art 14). A new reform, which is being presently elaborated, will introduce sustainable development and high quality environment in public procurement criteria.

[76] SA8000 certification is among the awarding criteria of some public tenders of the Tuscan region (for instance, for public transport). The Umbria region, with the regional law of 12 November 2002, issued a register of enterprises which are certified SA800. Inclusion on this register implies a preferential treatment in public procurement, financial supports for training and certification, simplified administrative procedures and fiscal incentives. In February 2003, the Provincia di Chieti in the Abruzzo region presented a proposal for a regional law which grants companies that are certified SA 8000, EMAS, ISO14000, and OHSAS18001, a preferential treatment in public procurement, financial support for training and certification, simplified administrative procedures and fiscal incentives.

[77] Pursuant to Art. 6(1) TEU. the requirements of fundamental rights are ranked among the principles upon which the Union is founded, and which are considered to be common to all its Member States.

an extension of also integrating fundamental rights into public procurement. A motion for a resolution recently submitted to the European Parliament supports this view[78] and urges the Commission to link public procurement to compliance with the ILO Core Conventions and OECD Guidelines.

To take this argument a step further, once the EC has paved the way to allowing social considerations in Member States' procurement laws, the same measures should be made mandatory for EC institutions' procurement procedures. Therefore, the Commission, the European Investment Bank and the European Bank for Reconstruction and Development should apply strict social and environmental criteria to all grants and loans allocated to private sector companies, backed by clear complaint mechanisms.

In this sense, a parallelism can be drawn between internal and external measures addressed to MNEs. Making access to EC procurement subject to compliance with social criteria could be applied to grants and loans within the EU and at the external level in the framework of financial assistance to third countries. Such a solution has the advantage of targeting equally companies operating within the EU and outside its borders. In addition, by applying the same standards at the internal and at the external level, the overall coherence of the EC's approach to the promotion of human rights will be enhanced.

5.5 VOLUNTARY INTERNAL MEASURES ADDRESSED TO MNEs: THE EMERGENCE OF CORPORATE SOCIAL RESPONSIBILITY

In addition to the regulatory initiatives provided by EC internal policies, a series of voluntaries initiatives over the conduct of MNEs have recently converged with the notion of Corporate Social Responsibility. Corporate Social Responsibility is defined by the Commission as a concept whereby companies decide 'voluntarily to contribute to a better society and a cleaner environment . . . in their business operations and in their interactions with their stakeholders.'[79]

---

[78] European Parliament, A6 – Committee on Employment and Social Affairs Rapporteur: Richard Howitt 0471/2006 Final, 20 December 2006, *Report on Corporate Social Responsibility: a New Partnership*, 006/2133(INI), para. 42.

[79] Commission of the European Communities, *Green Paper – Promoting a European Framework for Corporate Social Responsibility* [the Green Paper], *supra* Ch.1 n. 102, para. 8.

The debate on Corporate Social Responsibility was launched by the Commission on 18 July 2001 with the adoption of a Green Paper entitled 'Promoting a European Framework for Corporate Social Responsibility' (the Green Paper).[80] Through this initiative a wide consultation process was launched both at national and European levels on Corporate Social Responsibility and ways for the European Union to promote it. The Green Paper defined Corporate Social Responsibility as a concept whereby companies decide 'voluntarily to contribute to a better society and a cleaner environment . . . in their business operations and in their interactions with their stakeholder.'[81] As a follow-up to the consultation, on 2 July 2002, the Commission issued a Communication entitled 'Corporate Social Responsibility: A Business Contribution to Sustainable Development'.[82] Despite the declared objective of designing an overall EU strategy for voluntary initiatives addressed to MNEs, however, it seems that the Corporate Social Responsibility debate has had only a very limited impact, so far, on the EU's concrete initiatives. With the latest Communication from the Commission 'Implementing the Partnership for Growth and Jobs: Making Europe a pole of excellence on CSR'[83] the possibility of setting up a coherent European framework, even limited to voluntary initiative seems to have reached a dead end. Rather than the evolutionary approach envisaged in the Howitt Resolution, the CSR debate seems to have designed a descending trajectory instead. It is worth remembering here the main steps of this debate, with particular reference to the relevance given to human rights in the context of CSR.

5.5.1   The Green Paper and the Consultation Process

The consultation process launched by the Commission through the Green Paper was significant in that, for the first time, European stakeholders were invited to express their views on Corporate Social Responsibility and to discuss their expectations on the role of the European Union. The consultation process was highly inclusive. Indeed, contributions to the debate were submitted by a great number of stakeholders across Europe,

---

[80]   Ibid.

[81]   Ibid., para. 8.

[82]   *Corporate Social Responsibility: a Business Contribution, supra* Ch.1 n. 24.

[83]   Communication from the Commission to the European Parliament, the Council and the European Economic and Social Committee – *Implementing the partnership for growth and jobs: Making Europe a pole of excellence on corporate social responsibility*, COM (2006) 0136 final.

including NGOs, academia, company networks, individual enterprises and trade unions.[84] The inclusiveness of the debate did not reach the extent envisaged in the Howitt Resolution, where there was a call for a dialogue with civil society not only from the European Union, but also from developing countries. However, the launch of a consultation process was perceived as a positive step towards the creation of a wider basis of consensus on Corporate Social Responsibility. Furthermore, the availability of all contributions on the internet guaranteed transparency.

It must also be noted that the Commission acted as a catalyst for dialogue, offering all the main stakeholders a long awaited platform for debate. This seemed to show the Commission's intention to take a positive role in the promotion of Corporate Social Responsibility after initial and sustained reluctance of previous years.

What emerged from the Green Paper debate was the existence of little agreement among stakeholders on the definition of corporate social responsibility, its objectives and which measures might be most appropriate to promote it. The recognition of the need for businesses to address the social, economic and environmental impact of their operations (the triple bottom line approach) was shared by a large number of actors, across different stakeholder groups. Both the business sector and NGOs agreed that Corporate Social Responsibility should be integrated into an overall business strategy instead of being simply an 'add-on' to business core activities. The voluntary nature of Corporate Social Responsibility, however, was contested mainly by NGOs submissions[85] who maintained that it could not be reduced to simply an 'add-on' or an act of philanthropy, and cannot rely exclusively on voluntarism.

On the other hand, the Commission's definition is fully endorsed and supported by the business community.[86] While recognizing the role of reg-

---

[84]   The consultation, launched on 18 July 2001, ended on 31 December 2001. Over 250 contributions were sent to the Commission. Business organizations, company networks and individual enterprises (mostly large ones) account for about half of the contributions. The others came from trade unions, NGOs, academics, individuals and from other organizations. The participation of trade unions was very limited (only 15 replies) and in terms of geographical distribution the largest number of responses came from the United Kingdom.

[85]   See for instance the responses to the Green Paper from Amnesty International, Christian Aid, Oxfam and Tradecraft Exchange, available at: http://www.europa.eu.int/comm//employment_social/soc-dial/csr (accessed 5 April 2002).

[86]   Particularly representative is the response from CSR Europe, formerly the European businesses network for social cohesion since this association includes some of the biggest European multinational corporations. Among others, Royal Dutch Shell, Danone, Volkswagen. *CSR response to the European Union's Green*

ulation in particular areas, such as safety or exploitative employment, or in particular cases (such as the UK pensions disclosure regulations of July 2000, which require pensions funds to disclose whether or not they take social, ethical and environmental issues into account),[87] the need for a flexible approach and avoidance of a prescriptive one was strongly advanced by the business community. This is justified mainly along three lines of reasoning. First, regulation would hamper the innovative and voluntary forces stemming from business itself;[88] secondly, the fact that there is no single formula for Corporate Social Responsibility that is applicable to all businesses in all sectors; thirdly, the fact that there is still a certain degree of divergence among national corporate cultures and national legislation in EU Member States.

A second point of divergence related to the objectives of Corporate Social Responsibility. These were not fully outlined in the Green Paper, but it seems that on this highly contentious topic the debate has stimulated the most divergent and groundbreaking proposals. Business understood Corporate Social Responsibility as a tool to achieve business success and enhance competitiveness. In turn, profitability was regarded as a precondition for the adoption of Corporate Social Responsibility practices. On the contrary, NGOs emphasize the *legal* and *ethical* component of Corporate Social Responsibility by underlining that Corporate Social Responsibility should contribute to the promotion of human rights and sustainable development. Therefore, NGOs maintained that Corporate Social Responsibility should not be promoted only on the instrumental grounds of economic benefit, but that it should be based on broader ethical concerns. As a consequence, measures that enhance CSR may also imply costs for companies.

Diverging conceptions of CSR were mirrored by different views as to which measures to implement Corporate Social Responsibility are most effective. The sharing of responsibility between companies and Sates was a key point. The business community, trade unions and NGOs shared the

---

Paper, available at: http://www.europa.eu.int/comm//employment_social/soc-dial/csr (accessed 15 April 2002).

[87] CSR Europe's response to the European Union's Green Paper, at 6, available at: http://www.europa.eu.int/comm//employment_social/soc-dial/csr (accessed 15 April 2002).

[88] Sometimes the argument that 'It is illogical to speak of regulating Corporate Social Responsibility activities, if they are simultaneously to be encouraged as activities that lie beyond regulation' is put forward. CSR Europe's Response to the Green Paper, at 9, available at: http://www.europa.eu.int/comm//employment_social/soc-dial/csr (accessed 15 April 2002). Although it can be considered a deliberately created confusion meant to obfuscate the real debate.

view that public authorities play a key role in assisting third counties in the promotion and enforcement of fundamental rights.

Another factor taken into account was the distinction between an EU level of implementation of Corporate Social Responsibility and a global one. Although all the parties agree that the EU should link its initiative to the main global initiative at a UN, ILO, OECD and WTO level, the link between the promotion of accountability mechanisms and the role of the EU in third countries is not always emphasized. At one end of the spectrum stand NGOs arguing for strong measures such as conditionality of aid and export credit, sanctions, foreign direct liability and inclusion of social clauses in trade agreements. Submissions from NGOs during the consultation process emphasized the link between globalization and corporate responsibility by analyzing the role of European foreign investment in third countries and called for trade and investment regimes which integrate Corporate Social Responsibility concerns.[89] On the other hand, business supported a softer approach by, for example, calling on the European Union to support training and capacity building in third countries. The human rights dimension of Corporate Social Responsibility has been recognized in particular in relation to international supply chains, the process of globalization and the EU's development policy. It can be said that a comprehensive description of what should be understood as human rights norms and a more detailed reference to the relevance of human rights for the current development of the European Union would have raised the profile of the debate.

In fact, although the Green Paper devotes one paragraph to human rights, it mainly refers to labour rights. No mention is made of the main international human rights law instruments. Reference to 'soft-law' is restricted to the ILO Declaration on Principles and Fundamental Rights at Work, and to the OECD Principles for Multinational Corporations, while more pertinent documents such as the ILO Tripartite Declaration of Principles Concerning MNEs[90] and the revised OECD Guidelines for MNEs are not referred to.

As pointed out by leading NGOs, it would have been appropriate to indicate which human rights may be relevant to companies, and to have made reference to the typology of complicity in human rights violations in which companies may be involved, and the relationship between MNEs,

---

[89]   Oxfam's response to the Green Paper, available at: http://www.europa. eu.int/comm//employment_social/soc-dial/csr (accessed 15 April 2002).

[90]   *ILO Tripartite Declaration, supra* Ch.1 n. 12.

the right to development and their responsibility regarding social economic and cultural rights.

Such a limited reference to well established principles of human rights law such as the indivisibility, interdependency and interrelationship of civil and political rights and economic, social and cultural rights, gives the impression that scarce attention has been paid to the most recent developments in the interpretation of human rights law at the international level, notably to the Draft Universal Human Rights Guidelines for Companies.[91]

Furthermore, the references made to the role of human rights within the current European legal framework are also rather incomplete. For example, a general reference to the Charter of Fundamental Rights and Freedoms in the introduction is not supported by mention of its relevant provisions, such as Articles 1–5 on Human Dignity, Articles 21 and 23, and Articles 27–38 on Solidarity.[92] Reference to Article 6 of the Treaty on European Union, according to which the EU 'is founded on the principles of liberty democracy, and the rule of law, principles which are common to the Member States,' is also omitted.

To conclude, the main shortcomings of the Commission's definition are: not having made clear the existence of human rights as a defined set of rules enshrined in international legal instruments; and simply and partially making reference to 'soft law' and existing codes of conduct. The fragmentary definition of human rights relevant for the external dimension of Corporate Social Responsibility has attracted the strongest criticism from development and human rights NGOs. Furthermore, it has allowed submissions from the business community to skirt around the issue of human rights.[93] It was hoped that the contribution to the debate by a range of different actors would have redressed the balance towards a definition of Corporate Social Responsibility, with a more central role for human rights.

---

[91]   UN Commission on Human Rights, Sub-Commission on the Promotion and Protection of Human Rights E/CN.4/Sub.2/2001/ WG.2/ WP.1/ Add.1 (2001).

[92]   The Charter of Fundamental Rights of the European Union, signed at the European Council Nice on 7 December 2000, available at: http://www.europarl. eu.int/charter (accessed 3 March 2002).

[93]   See   http://www.europa.eu.int/comm//employment_social/soc-dial/csr (accessed 15 April 2002).

5.5.2 Communication from the Commission Corporate Responsibility and Its Follow Up

The results of the debate on CSR were partially acknowledged in the Commission's Communication on Corporate Social Responsibility: A Business Contribution to Sustainable Development.[94] Starting from the consideration that businesses are confronted with the challenge of working through the voluntary initiatives and national frameworks that can enhance and sustain the positive benefits of business activity, the Commission urged the creation of a common European strategy for the promotion of Corporate Social Responsibility.

Consistent with the Green Paper, but in contrast with the views expressed during the consultation, the Commission maintained its definition of Corporate Social Responsibility as merely voluntary in the Communication. In this document reference to human rights is very limited and then presented in broad terms rather than linked to relevant international human rights treaties and conventions. The Commission proposes a holistic approach to Corporate Social Responsibility, intended not as a collection of corporate activities, but rather as a new business strategy. The definition adopted in the Green Paper on Corporate Social

---

[94]   Sustainable development was defined by the Brundtland report (UN Doc. A/42/427) in 1987 as 'development that meets the needs of the present without compromising the ability of future generations to meet their own needs'. It is development based on consumption and production patterns that do not degrade natural resources, that protect the environment, promote equitable sharing of well-being to all and alleviate poverty. Although a large number of international binding and non-binding instruments refer to the term sustainable development, the term remains an uncertain notion in both its definition and status under international law, it can be argued that it has made some progress to the status of principle of international law. D. McGoldrick, 'Sustainable Development and Human Rights an Integrated Conception,' (1996) 45 I.C.L.Q. 796, at 802. In the EU context, sustainable development was introduced as a fundamental objective of the European Union since 1997. It was enshrined as Article 2 of the Treaty. It is supposed to underpin all EU policies and actions as an over-arching principle. As a complement to the broad EU strategy for socio-economic reforms, defined at the Lisbon European Council in 2000 (the 'Lisbon agenda'), the EU adopted an equally ambitious Strategy for Sustainable Development (SDS) at the Gothenburg Summit one year later and added an external dimension to the strategy in Barcelona in 2002. The EC's approach to sustainable development was redefined by the Council in June 2006. See Council of the European Union, Brussels, Renewed EU Sustainable Development Strategy 10117/06, 9 June 2006. See W. Douma, 'Evolution of Sustainable Development in the European Union', in F. Weiss et al. (eds), *International Economic Law With a Human Face*, 1998, The Hague and Cambridge, Mass., Kluwer Law International, 271.

Responsibility identifies four main areas of impact for Corporate Social Responsibility, which represent the interests of different groups of stakeholders: the community in which MNEs operate, employees, consumers and shareholders.

The contributions to the Green Paper consultation process by NGOs and trade unions, that stressed the need for mandatory measures were clearly not followed. This is counterbalanced to some extent by the definition of Corporate Social Responsibility as not an optional 'add-on' to core business activities, but as 'about the way in which businesses are managed.'[95]

The Commission agreed to the suggestion of introducing, or indeed *mainstreaming,* Corporate Social Responsibility in all relevant European Union policies. Although, the degree to which Corporate Social Responsibility will be integrated into different European Union policies varies greatly. For example, the paragraph regarding enterprise policy is particularly cautious. It is stated that '[o]nly competitive and profitable enterprises are able to make a long term contribution to sustainable development by generating wealth and jobs without compromising the social and environmental needs of society.'[96]

By defining the scope of Corporate Social Responsibility merely in terms of 'not compromising' the needs of the community in which a company operates, the Commission seems to have paid little regard to the expansion of the scope of Corporate Social Responsibility, which was at the heart of the Green Paper and its adoption. In other words, restricting corporate responsibility to the core obligation of 'not to harm' (not to prevent someone from the enjoyment of a right) means not taking account of the converging pressures for the expansion of such scope, which emerged during the debate following the Green Paper. Furthermore, the paragraph on enterprise policy emphasizes competitiveness and profitability as a precondition to the adoption of corporate social responsible practice, whereas the contribution of Corporate Social Responsibility to the enhancement of profitability and competitiveness is not clearly delineated. This is probably due to the lack of solid evidence of the business case for Corporate Social Responsibility. Indeed, one of the most frequent criticisms put forward by industries during the debate over the Green Paper was that the Commission did not provide sufficient evidence for the contention that by integrating Corporate Social

---

[95] *Corporate Social Responsibility: A Business Contribution, supra* Ch.1 n. 24., para. 3.

[96] Ibid., para. 7.2.

Responsibility into their activities, enterprises would enhance their performance and competitiveness. In response, the Communication resolved to focus on research on the impact of Corporate Social Responsibility on business practice.

Most of the measures to promote Corporate Social Responsibility envisaged in the Communication, such as management standards, measurement, reporting and assurance,[97] are addressed directly to enterprises and are to be introduced into management practice. In this context, it would have been opportune to highlight the link between Corporate Social Responsibility and European company law, which, on the contrary, has been overlooked.

In the Communication on CSR the paragraph regarding external relations policy[98] and the subsequent Report from the Multi-stakeholder Forum the approach to CSR seems to have slightly shifted. First, a specific role for the European Union in the promotion of Corporate Social Responsibility at the international level is recognized. The European Union can improve Corporate Social Responsibility by pooling together its external policy tools such as agreements with third countries and the European Union's GSP.

Secondly, it must be underlined that great emphasis has been placed on dialogue within civil society in developing countries and on capacity building in order to promote convergence. It is recognized that civil society, NGOs and trade unions can play an important role in raising awareness of fundamental rights and in promoting compliance with Corporate Social Responsibility principles by monitoring corporate practices on the ground.

According to the Communication, the European Union's role in improving Corporate Social Responsibility in developing countries seems to rely mainly on international 'soft law' instruments (such as the OECD Guidelines for Multinational Enterprises[99] and the OECD Declaration on International Investment),[100] rather than on international human rights declarations and conventions. Despite the fact that the revised version of the OECD Guidelines for Multinational Enterprises introduced a general statement that said that multinational enterprises should respect human

---

[97] Ibid., paras. 5.2, 5.3.
[98] Ibid., para. 7.5.
[99] The *OECD Guidelines, supra* Ch.1 n. 13.
[100] OECD, *Declaration on International Investment and Multinational Enterprise,* 1976, Paris, OECD, available at: http://www.oecd.org/daf/investment/guidelines/mnetext.htm (accessed 5 April 2002).

rights, the document expressly says that it is a non-legal recommendation that companies are invited to follow voluntarily.[101]

The focus does not seem to have changed in the context of the Multi-stakeholder Forum. Rather than the drafting of a single code for MNEs, the Forum has encouraged compliance with already existing codes and, in particular support for the OECD Guidelines for Multinational Enterprises. As seen above, not only do the revised Guidelines encourage companies to respect the human rights of those affected by their activities, but they are also applicable to States that are not members of the OECD. As a result, the OECD Guidelines would be a standard applicable to both European companies and to those of their main competitors from other industrialized countries (including Canada, Japan, Korea, New Zealand, Turkey and the United States).

5.5.3 The European Multi-stakeholder Forum and the Second Communication on CSR

One of the most tangible results of the first Communication on CSR has been the setting up of a Multi-stakeholder Forum, which was given by the Commission the task of identifying common guidelines on CSR. The Multi-stakeholder forum on the CSR was composed of representatives of enterprises, trade unions, civil society and consumer associations. Representatives of European regions and of other international organizations concerned with MNEs, such as the ILO were also invited to take part in the round tables. Most notably, in accordance with the recommendations of the Howitt Resolution members from third countries have also participated in the Forum. The Forum, chaired by the Commission, presented their Final Report on 29 June 2004. The Report has not brought about substantial modifications to the definition of CSR contained in the previous Communication of the Commission.

The Final Report of the Multi-Stakeholder Forum essentially addresses the necessity of improving understanding and awareness of CSR and the creation of suitable conditions for its development. According to the Final Report, cooperation and exchange of information between enterprises and other stakeholders should be furthered to this end. Co-operation between the entrepreneurial and the academic worlds should also be encouraged. The round table on 'Diversity, Convergence and Transparency', in

---

[101] Highly debatable is the question whether the guideline provisions have become part of customary law through consistent State practice since 1976. On this point International Council on Human Rights Policy, *supra* Ch.1 n. 46.

particular, has pointed to the importance of giving thorough and credible information to all the stakeholders. Another suggestion has been to involve external observers in order to guarantee the transparency and credibility the of CSR practices. However, there was no agreement about the instruments needed to improve transparency. Trade unions and NGOs supported moves to make the publication of information compulsory and to encourage the elaboration of social relations to assess the social and environmental impact of the company. The business world, on the other hand, disagrees with the compulsory character of these proposals claiming that it would reduce the innovative features and the flexibility of CSR.

A similar disagreement emerged in terms of the process of ensuring converging standards on CSR. NGOs and trade unions maintained that the core of CSR should be found in international human rights, international environmental law and international agreements. Contrasting with this view, enterprises maintain that the process of convergence, which is already taking place in a few sectors on a voluntary basis, should not be driven by binding rules. This would contradict the voluntary character of CSR. Despite these divergences, the Final Report acknowledges that the EU could develop a certification or a regulatory system at the European level which combines a level playing field with incentives for companies.

The Forum sees the EU as the appropriate institution to guarantee uniform conditions for the development of CSR. It therefore calls on the EU to promote a more consistent use of its common commercial policy and to develop external relations in accordance with the principles of sustainable development. According to the Forum, EU institutions should collaborate with the relevant stakeholders to promote knowledge about and the spread of CSR. One of the most interesting recommendations of the Final Report is that of taking into consideration the possibility of using public funding in a more responsible manner. One of the options would be to link a company's social and environmental performance to its access to public procurement opportunities.

In addition, a stronger link between CSR and development cooperation policy was underlined. It was suggested exploring the possibility of including social and environmental criteria with EU funds that support private investment in developing countries, such as funds that contribute to the promotion of the private sector under the Cotonou Agreement, and criteria to ensure that publicly funded instruments, such as public procurement and export credits, are consistent with public policies on CSR.[102] The need

---

[102]   European Multistakeholder Forum on CSR – RT 'Development aspects of CSR', at 8.

to evaluate the effectiveness of OECD guidelines and to explore the level of efficiency of national policies supporting CSR was also highlighted.[103]

Only two years after the final report of the CSR Multi-stakeholder Forum there was a second communication on Corporate social responsibility Communication from the Commission 'Implementing the Partnership for Growth and Jobs: Making Europe a pole of excellence on CSR',[104] presented by the Commission on 22 March 2006. This delay and the fact that the publication of the Communication was initially announced for the spring of 2005, illustrate the intensity of the internal debates within the Commission on the issue. With this communication, the Commission announces backing for a European Alliance for CSR. This is an open alliance of European enterprises to further promote and encourage CSR. The alliance is a political umbrella for CSR initiatives by large companies, small and medium-sized enterprises, and their stakeholders, which duplicate the model of the UN Global Compact. It is not a legal instrument to be signed by enterprises, but rather a vehicle for mobilizing the resources and capacities of European enterprises and their stakeholders in the interests of sustainable development, economic growth and job creation.

The Communication acknowledges that enterprises are the primary actors in CSR, but also stresses the important contribution of non-business stakeholders. In the text, the Commission states that 'it continues to attach utmost importance to dialogue with and between all stakeholders', and recognizes that 'without the active support and constructive criticism of non-business stakeholders, CSR will not flourish.' The document also underlines the potential of CSR to contribute to sustainable development and to the European Growth and Jobs Strategy.[105] The Commission suggests that CSR practices, while not a substitute for public policy, can nevertheless contribute to a number of public policy objectives, such as: skill development, more rational use of natural resources, better innovation performance, poverty reduction, and greater respect for

---

[103] Ibid., at 9.

[104] Communication from the Commission to the European Parliament, the Council and the European Economic and Social Committee – *Implementing the partnership for growth and jobs: making Europe a pole of excellence on corporate social responsibility* COM (2006) 0136 final.

[105] On 2 February 2005 the European Commission launched the European Growth and Jobs Strategy which aims to revitalize the so-called Lisbon Agenda – the EU's economic reform agenda from 2000. The actions proposed today by the European Commission could boost GDP by 3 per cent by 2010 and create over six million jobs. See Communication from the Commission 2006.

human rights. Eight areas which the Commission will emphasize in further promoting CSR: awareness-raising and best practice exchange; support to multi-stakeholder initiatives; cooperation with Member States; consumer information and transparency; research; education; small and medium-sized enterprises; and the international dimension of CSR.

The Commission has decided that it can best achieve its objectives by working more closely with European business, and therefore announces backing for the launch of a European Alliance on CSR, a concept drawn up on the basis of contributions from businesses active in the promotion of CSR. The Alliance is an open alliance of European enterprises, for which enterprises of all sizes are invited to express their support. It is a political umbrella for new or existing CSR initiatives by large companies, small and medium enterprises and their stakeholders. It is not a legal instrument and is not to be signed by enterprises, the Commission or any public authority. It is a political process to increase the uptake of CSR amongst European enterprises.

According to the Commission backing for the new alliance should be understood as a key component of a wider partnership that the Commission wishes to pursue with all stakeholders involved in CSR. The Commission continues to affirm that it attaches utmost importance to dialogue with and between all stakeholders, and proposes to re-convene meetings of the Multi-stakeholder Forum at regular intervals with a view to continually reviewing progress on CSR in the EU.

The impression, however, is that in presenting this Communication, the Commission has not taken into account several years of public debate and consultation with all stakeholders, most particularly in the context of the European Multi-stakeholder Forum. The political message is particularly damaging. Firstly, establishing an alliance on CSR, the Commission was perceived as expressing a clear preference for one category of stakeholders over the others – unions and NGOs, thus disregarding the equality of standing between these parties, which has been maintained throughout the CSR Multi-stakeholder forum process.[106] Secondly, the CSR was effectively presented as being driven purely by market mechanisms, without there being any need for a regulatory framework to ensure its adequate functioning. On a number of issues, ranging from promoting knowledge and awareness about CSR to promoting OECD Guidelines on MNEs, the

---

[106] O. de Schutter, *Corporate Social Responsibility European Style*, Paper presented at the conference 'Corporate Social Responsibility in the EU-10: Expectations v. Reality', organized in Prague as part of the GARDE programme of EPS, available at: http://www.responsibility.cz/ with the Czech League of Human Rights on 15 September 2006.

Commission had made no progress since the launch of the Green Paper in 2001.

In conclusion, it seems the CSR debate within the EU has followed the same descending trajectory that characterized the MNEs' responsibility debate within the UN.[107] The Green Paper on CSR seemed to mark the Commission's willingness to include CSR in all relevant EC policies – ranging from public procurement, to enterprize policy, development and cooperation – had increased. Although a shift towards business's approach to CSR was clearly marked in the following Communication on 'business' contribution to sustainable development, the expectations of the NGOs and other stakeholders were raised again by the setting up of the Multi-stakeholder Forum, which aimed to provide inputs for an EC overall strategy on CSR. Similarly, the uncertainties that surround the Norms at the UN level, the outcome of the forum and the latest communication on CSR, signal a stalemate in the process of the establishment of a framework for CSR at the EU level. By purporting an alliance with the business sector the Commission seems to envisage a sort of Global Compact at the EU level rather than promoting an EU framework for CSR.

5.6 CONCLUSION

This chapter examined to what extent the EU has integrated concerns over the responsibility of MNEs for human rights in its internal policies. We have seen that the extent to which human rights concerns have been integrated into EC policies strictly related to the conduct of MNEs varies greatly. Despite the extensive powers conferred on the EC to regulate the anticompetitive conduct of MNEs, competition law does not seem to offer the most appropriate avenue to address MNEs' human rights abuses in third countries. The difficulties of using Articles 81 and 82 as an appropriate legal basis, however, seems to be matched by a lack of will in this respect by EC institutions. In fact, it has been noted that the use of Article 308 TEC [108] as a possible legal basis has not been explored. Similarly, recent developments in European company law do not suggest any move

---

[107] D. Lucchetti, *Il Buco Nero Della Rsi. Un commento alla Comunicazione della Commissione EU sulla Responsabilità Sociale d'Impresa e sul rapporto del Rappresentate Speciale dell'ONU John Ruggie sulle Norme per le imprese*, available at: http://www.faircoop.it/PDF/Il_buco_nero_della_Rsi.pdf (accessed 13 September 2006).

[108] Kamminga, 'Holding Multinational Corporations Accountable', *supra* Ch.1 n. 70., at 565.

toward the creation of a common European code on corporate governance and even less so a code on corporate responsibility.[109] The option of
using Regulation (EC) 44/2001 to sue European MNEs in a court of the
Member State for human rights violations in the hypothesis of breach of
basic duty of care should be further investigated. Although, the legal basis
allowing the transformation of Regulation (EC) 44/2001 into a sort of
European ACTA seems to be lacking.

One normative argument can be drawn from this analysis. The EC has
extensive regulatory powers over MNEs in several fields and it cannot turn
a blind eye when it comes to addressing human rights violations by MNEs
based in one of its Member States. This argument has been convincingly
developed by Francioni in relation to the responsibility of home States
for human rights violations committed by their MNEs abroad.[110] Similar
considerations can be applied to the EC, considering that in the areas of
law examined above it has reached extensive if not exclusive regulatory
powers. The EC has a vast practice of regulatory powers over foreign
activities of corporations, when the exercise of such powers is considered
to be necessary to fulfil certain societal interests or policy objectives, such
as antirust enforcement. Thus, if capital-exporting countries, especially
European countries, are willing to assert extra-territorial regulatory
powers over foreign corporate activities through the effective control they
have over the parent companies in the above-mentioned contexts, it is
hard to understand what would prevent them from exercising the same
powers and the same degree of extraterritorial interest with regard to the
internationally shared objective of securing and promoting human rights.

On the contrary, social policy provided for a progressive recognition of
the rights of new groups of stakeholders within European MNEs and in
particular of workers. Thus, a specific concern over multinational companies (even if not defined as such) within the ambit of the EU has been
matched by specific initiatives, such as the Directive on the Safeguarding
of Employees' Rights in the Event of Transfer of Undertakings, Businesses
or Parts thereof.[111] The EU has experimented with new forms of decision-
making in the area of multinational enterprises, such as the European
work councils. These initiatives however, have a close internal reach, since
they apply to activities of MNEs across the borders of Member States
rather than outside the EU's borders. In this context, including social

---

[109]   Winter, *The Future of European Company Law*, *supra* n. 23. See also
Winter, 'EU Company Law on the Move', *supra* n. 23, at 98.
[110]   Francioni, 'Alternative Perspectives', *supra* Ch.1 n. 71.
[111]   Directive 2001/23, *supra* n. 29.

clauses in public procurement, both at Member States and at EC level, seems to be the most effective proposal for encouraging positive developments in corporate conduct, by rewarding the most deserving enterprises in the EC's public procurement and by authorizing Member States to do so under their national public procurement laws.

In addition, it seems that, since social clauses have been introduced in the latest EC directives on public procurement, no major obstacles arise either from EC law or from the EC's commitments under the WTO regime to include fully fledged human rights clauses in public procurement. Indeed, compliance with social and human rights concerns should not simply be permitted but mandatory. Furthermore, similar considerations should be introduced into grants and loans of EC institutions.

The limited use of regulatory initiatives in the context of EC internal policies seemed to be for some time counterbalanced by the attention given to voluntary initiatives. In the EU context, the debate over Corporate Social Responsibility gained momentum in 2001. As seen above, the number of responses to the Commission's Green Paper, which launched the debate, showed that a coordinating initiative had been long awaited. In particular, NGOs and civil society organizations perceived the CSR initiative as the appropriate occasion to bring to the attention of the Commission the human rights implications of CSR and its relationship with the development policies of the EU. Although these aspects were finally introduced into the Multi-stakeholder Forum Report, they have been overlooked in the latest Commission Communication. Despite the declared objective of designing an overall EU strategy for voluntary initiatives addressed to MNEs, however, it seems that the CSR debate has only had a very limited impact, so far, on the EU's concrete initiatives. With the latest Communication from the Commission 'Implementing the Partnership for Growth and Jobs: Making Europe a pole of excellence on CSR'[112] the Commission showed a preference for businesses, rather than the other stakeholders. In addition, thus, after five years of debate, not only has CSR had a limited impact on the EU's concrete initiatives, but even the possibility of creating a common European Framework on CSR seems to have been removed from the Commission's agenda.

---

[112] *Implementing the Partnership for Growth and Jobs, supra* Ch.1 n. 25.

6 External measures addressed to MNEs

6.1 INTRODUCTION

Increased interest in the adverse effects of the activities of companies within the EC has been matched by a series of initiatives which have targeted the conduct of European MNEs in relation to third countries. This chapter focuses on the external measures addressed to European MNEs. The definition of external measure captures what, at first sight, seems to be a heterogeneous set of initiatives, ranging from the Code of Conduct on Arms Export and the Code of Conduct for companies operating in South Africa, adopted under political cooperation, to the proposed Code of Conduct for European Companies Operating in Developing Countries, contained in a Resolution of the European Parliament, and the International Framework Agreement, which are agreements signed by the International trade union associations and an MNE. Although contained in different types of legal texts, these measures are all characterized by the fact that they directly address MNEs and, in particular, they target their activities in third countries.

We saw in the previous chapter that the internal measures addressed to MNEs have, to some extent, progressively translated stakeholders' needs, and in particular workers participation, into legislation. In addition, at the internal level a variety of regulatory and voluntary measures have been adopted or are currently under discussion. A similar development cannot be traced in relation to the European Union's monitoring of European MNEs' activities in developing countries. As shown by the examples of the Code of Conduct on Arms Export and the Code of Conduct for companies operating in South Africa, the European Union has acted in response to crises rather than more proactively, taking action in order to overcome specific problems. This may be related to the absence of an overall European strategy to deal with the present deficit of responsibility of MNEs.

Regarding the tension between the regulatory versus voluntary approach, the examples below suggest that at the external level, the use of codes of conduct, adopted in the form of political declarations, has been preferred to legislation. In this context, the most original contribution seems to be provided by the IFAs, which are commitments undertaken by international trade unions associations and MNEs. The agreements, although not leally binding, lay down standards which are valid across borders since they should be respected by the different components of MNEs and by their suppliers.

6.2 CODE OF CONDUCT FOR COMPANIES OPERATING IN SOUTH AFRICA AND THE EUROPEAN UNION CODE OF CONDUCT ON ARMS EXPORT

The interest in the responsibility of MNEs within the European Union was matched by two isolated initiatives which had an external impact. The Code of Conduct for Companies Operating in South Africa and the European Union Code of Conduct on Arms Export were both adopted under political cooperation and they were addressed to European companies operating outside the EC borders.

In September 1977, a Code of Conduct for Community Companies with Subsidiaries, Branches or Representation in South Africa[1] was approved by the Foreign Ministers of the European Community. From a legal perspective, one of the interesting features of this Code is that it was not strictly speaking a European Community instrument. It was not adopted by the Ministers of Member States in their capacity as members of the Council and of the Communities, since the Code was created as an instrument of European Political Co-operation.[2] The Code had greater value as a policy declaration rather than as a legal instrument and the European Commission played no active role. On the other hand the legal effect of this code within individual Member States relied entirely on their national laws.

---

[1] 'Code of Conduct for Community Companies with Subsidiaries, Branches or Representation in South Africa of 16 November 1985' (1985) 24 *International Legal Materials* 1477.

[2] European political cooperation was introduced informally in 1970 (in response to the Davignon report) and formalized by the Single European Act with effect from 1987. The object is consultations between the Member States in foreign policy matters. The Member States have regard to the views of the European Parliament and wherever possible take common positions in international organizations. European political cooperation was superseded by the common foreign and security policy. (Title V TEU European political cooperation).

The Code was strengthened in 1985[3] and it was kept in force until 1993, when South Africa entered a democratic transition process. The Code was addressed to MNEs with headquarters in any of the Member States. It called on these enterprises to comply with certain specified industrial relations, employment and social policies in relation to their Black African employees, designed to mitigate the effect of Apartheid and segregation policies in effect locally.

Although the Code did not create legal obligations for companies, it required companies to publish detailed and fully documented annual reports on the progress made in applying this Code and to submit a copy to their national governments. Member States then agreed to review annually progress made in implementation of the Code.

The main problem that emerged from the adoption of this Code was the inefficient monitoring mechanism. In the absence of a common reporting format the information supplied varied greatly and did not allow effective comparison. Moreover, the merely voluntary character of the code and the absence of a supervisory mechanism at the European Community level and of sanctions, further watered down the Code's impact.

Although it cannot be excluded that the European Code of Conduct had some positive impact on human rights in South Africa, the inefficiency of measures taken at the European Union level are documented in the *Report of the South African Truth and Reconciliation Commission.*[4] Despite United Nations sanctions, MNEs attempted to circumvent and break the ban by flooding South Africa with foreign investment, which undermined the effectiveness of international sanctions. Although the number of British companies operating in South Africa decreased from the 1970s to the mid-1980s, the withdrawals were far from complete. In crucial sectors such as arms supplies, British companies were replaced by French ones.[5]

Despite its many weaknesses, this Code sets a precedent and could be of significance for the Common Foreign and Security Policy, which has been strengthened and which has acquired a new role in European Union external policy. The creation of a Code of Conduct under the title of Common Foreign and Security Policy may have the advantage of circumventing any obstacle arising from the lack of a legal basis for the Commission's initiatives in this respect.

---

[3] 'Comprehensive Anti Apartheid Act of 1986' (1987) 26 *International Legal Materials* 79.

[4] *Report of the South African Truth and Reconciliation Commission, supra* Ch.1 n. 35, at 50–51.

[5] Ibid., at 50.

6.3 CODE OF CONDUCT ON ARMS EXPORT

Another relevant initiative at European Union level is the Code of Conduct on Arms Export. The Code presents an interesting precedent in view of the possible adoption of a code for European MNEs operating abroad. As with the issue of corporate responsibility, the issue of arms export raises contradictory political and economic concerns. The arms industry called for a 'level playing field', but preferred a situation where controls were established at the lowest level, thus allowing the market to regulate itself. On the contrary, with political pressures emphasizing the relevance of human rights, international security and sustainable development, national governments were forced to moderate exports of arms. A compromise agreement on the Code was achieved only after a long-term debate both at a grass-root, governmental and inter-governmental level.[6] The reluctance to adopt unilateral controls on arms exports was based on the argument that 'if we do not sell arms, someone else will'. This argument sounds similar to that frequently put forward by MNEs investing in countries with serious records of human rights abuses 'if we do not invest there, others will'.

Also in the case of the Code of Conduct on Arms Export, there was a legal obstacle to be found in Article 296 (*ex* Article 223) TEU, under which all the matters related to arms come under the exclusive control of Member States. This obstacle was overcome by adopting the Code under the Common Foreign and Security Policy, so that it is politically rather than legally binding.

In May 1998, the European Union Member States finally agreed on the adoption of this Code, which consists of three parts. The first defines the aims and objectives of the Code; the second sets out export guidelines which further develop each of the eight criteria previously agreed by the Member States,[7] specifying the circumstances that should be taken into account when licensing the export of arms; the third foresees the 'operative provisions' that are the basic system for exchanging information on

---

[6] A. McLean, 'The European Union Code of Conduct on Arms Exports', in Addo (ed.), *supra* Ch.1 n. 27, 115.
206. See Art. 223 (now Art. 296) TEC.

[7] In 1991 and 1992 European Union Member States agreed eight criteria governing arms exports, such as the human rights record of the recipient, whether there is a situation of tension in the region of the recipient, or whether there is a situation of armed conflict. These criteria were extremely vague and subject to different interpretation by Member States and have not prevented the flows of arms from European Union Member States to countries with egregious human rights violation records.

the denial of exports, and on the annual review of the developments of the Code.

One of the central aims of the Code is to avoid situations where a denial by one partner is undercut by another. In order to avoid such undercutting practice, a consultation mechanism should have been established to ensure that all Member States are swiftly informed of approvals or denials of export licences, and that any Member State intending to undercut a decision by another would be obliged to inform and consult with all other Member States. Despite the fact that the European Parliament[8] called for such a multilateral consultation mechanism, the final draft adopted a merely bilateral mechanism. This is one of the weakest points of the Code. Preventing a Member State from knowing exactly how the Code is being carried out in the other Member States will lead to inconsistency in its implementation.

The Code also foresees a system of annual reports at the State level, which will then be integrated into a consolidated report to be presented to the European Union Council of Ministers. However, the fact that all these reports are confidential, shield them both from the scrutiny of national parliaments and from the supervision of civil society at large.

Although the Code presents lacunae both in its substantial part and shows serious limits regarding its monitoring and enforcement mechanism, some positive aspects must also be acknowledged. The establishment of a minimum level of agreement on such highly controversial issues, among governments and among the main actors involved, represents a first step towards harmonization and control of arms export at the EU level. It sets benchmarks against which Member States' behaviour can be judged. The annual reports procedure, although a disappointing monitoring mechanism, may prove to be an opportunity to progressively strengthen the Code.

Some suggestions can be drawn by the examples of the Code of Conduct on Arms Export and the Code of Conduct for Companies Operating in South Africa. Two conditions should be met for a Code of Conduct to be effectively implemented. In the first place, the Code of Conduct should impose clearly verifiable obligations on the enterprises who decide to adopt them, and violations of the Code should be sanctioned. Secondly, uniform standards should be set in order to ensure comparability between the companies, although the concrete significance these standards will take may differ from sector to sector or from context to context.[9]

---

8   European Parliament, Resolution on a code of conduct for arms exports (B4-0502, 0505, 0520, 0522, 0529 and 0546/98) at point C. [1998] OJ C 167/226.

9   de Schutter, *The Accountability of Multinationals, supra* Ch.3 n. 49.

6.4 EUROPEAN CODE OF CONDUCT FOR EUROPEAN MULTINATIONAL ENTERPRISES: THE HOWITT RESOLUTION

A proposal for the creation of a Europe-wide code of conduct for European MNEs was advanced by the European Parliament in 1999 with a Resolution proposed by MEP Richard Howitt.[10] The European Union attempt to Draft a European Code of Conduct for European Enterprises Operating in Developing Countries (the Howitt Resolution) represented a breakthrough and aimed at setting the key tenets of the European approach to standard setting for European enterprises.

First, the European Parliament clearly puts forward an 'evolutionary approach' to MNEs' responsibility. According to this approach regulation and legally binding rules at the national and the international level should not be intended as both mutually exclusive, but complementary. In this light, voluntary initiatives are meant to promote best practice in order to qualitatively upgrade corporate actions. Once a wider base of consensus has been achieved, voluntary measures can more easily be translated into mandatory regulation.[11] It is pointed out, however, that although self-regulation has the potential to promote best practice, it is not able to address the worst offences, which can be prevented only by means of binding rules. In this view, the Resolution calls on the European Union to establish legally binding requirements on European MNEs, to ensure that they comply with international law relating to the protection of human rights and the environment when operating in developing countries.

Secondly, in the context of the Resolution, the European Commission was instructed to draw up a model code based on existing minimum standards for MNEs. The proposed code of conduct will not be legally binding. Similarly, as with the UN Norms, the Code does not aim at creating new standards, but brings together a wide range of existing international documents, starting with the Universal Declaration of Human Rights and including standards on labour rights, minority and indigenous rights, protection of the environment, protection of civilians in armed conflict, corruption and behaviour of the police.

---

[10] The *Howitt Resolution, supra* Ch.1 n. 72.
[11] Explanatory statement appended to the Motion for Resolution adopted by the committee on development and cooperation of the European Parliament on EU Standards for European Enterprises operating in developing countries: towards a European Code of Conduct (Rapporteur: R. Howitt), 17 December 1998 (A 4-0508/98).

The European Commission was also urged to ensure that at least MNEs acting on behalf of, or financed by the European Union, act in accordance with basic standards for human rights. This position has been upheld in a recent motion for a Parliament Resolution on corporate social responsibility.[12] Companies failing to meet these requirements should not be entitled to receive further funding from the European Union. This option has been partially endorsed by the EU in the latest Directive on Public Procurement, which foresees the possibility of introducing social and environmental clauses in pubic procurement procedures.[13]

Furthermore, the Resolution promoted the creation of a new monitoring mechanism called the European Monitoring Platform. This new monitoring mechanism, was designed not only to monitor how multinationals implement the proposed Code, but also to monitor implementation of other existing international standards and MNEs' own codes of conduct. The Platform is to be composed of a panel of independent experts and representatives from European business, international trade unions, environmental NGOs and representatives from civil society in developing countries. The encouragement of the participation of the developing world in the process is particularly valuable and the most innovative feature of the Resolution. First of all, participation of civil society actors from countries potentially most affected by MNEs' misdeeds, in both standard setting and monitoring systems, is essential in order to avoid frequent allegations of abuse of human rights standards for protectionist purposes and of a new colonialism by imposing European values on third countries. Secondly, awareness raising and capacity building in third countries where MNEs operate, by encouraging scrutiny by civil society, will in turn improve enforcement mechanism directly at the level of host States.

As the legal basis for both a binding code and monitoring system has not yet been found,[14] the Parliament decided to set up itself, as a matter of urgency, a temporary European Monitoring Platform. The European Parliament Committee on Development and Cooperation decided to hold public hearings at least once a year where victims of abuses by MNEs could complain publicly before Members of the European Parliament, in the presence of representatives of the company, who have the opportunity to reply. The press and media are also invited. These meetings have been shown to be useful both in terms of assuring public accountability of

---

[12]   *Report on Corporate Social Responsibility: a New Partnership, supra* Ch.5 n. 78.

[13]   See EU Multi-Stakeholder forum – Final Report, July 2004.

[14]   See European University Institute, *Leading by Example, supra* Ch.4 n. 26, at 102.

companies by turning the spotlight on major cases of corporate violations of human rights, and also highlighting MNEs' compliance with their own internal ethical policies in developing countries.

The hearing of 11th October 2001, for instance, concerned allegations of complicity by the British MNE Premier Oil and the French TotalFinaElf in human rights violations committed by the Burmese militia. These breaches had been committed not only through violations of international law, but also in the breach of the companies' own internal standards since both Total's and Premier's human rights policies indicate that they respect the Universal Declaration of Human Rights.[15] In particular, Premier indicated that it would withdraw from relationships with business partners not showing progress towards the prohibition of human rights abuses.

This system presents a number of shortcomings. This forum relies on the effectiveness of subjecting companies to the glare of publicity and has only a semi-judicial setting. Firstly, much lobbying is required to obtain a hearing before the Parliament, as it is necessary that a committee endorses it, before the presidency decides on it. So far, only the Committee on Development and Cooperation has agreed to hold a hearing on MNEs. Secondly, its limited impact is due to its semi-judicial setting. Nonetheless, some advantages are apparent: hearings are forums where companies are confronted with complaints, exposed to the glare of publicity and often facts speak for themselves.

Yet some merits should be recognized to this initiative. The Howitt Resolution envisioned an ambitious and far-reaching project for the regulation of European enterprises operating in developing countries. Years after its adoption, this project, for the reasons listed above, is facing an impasse. There has been a shift in the EU's attitude to codes of conduct. Rather than promoting an EU wide code of conduct, the Commission has preferred to rely on an existing and internationally recognized code, the OECD Guidelines on Multinational Enterprises.

Even though the Commission has not as yet fully followed the Parliament's suggestions,[16] it has however, stated it would insist on the inclusion in EU external relations agreements of the phrase: 'the Parties (or the European Community and its Member States) remind their multinational enterprises of their recommendations to observe the

---

[15] Testimony by Marco Simons for EarthRights International at the hearing of the Development and Co-Operation Committee of the European Parliament on European Oil Companies in Burma, 11 October 2001.

[16] To date the Commission has financed seminars (organized by DG Trade) to raise awareness of the OECD Guidelines in developing countries.

OECD Guidelines for Multinational enterprises, wherever they operate'.[17] This will be examined in greater detail later. A similar wording has been included in the EU-Chile Free Trade Agreement.[18] The European Union intends to contribute to the improvement of the implementation procedures of the OECD Guidelines and to introduce compliance with OECD Guidelines for MNEs as a condition for the MNEs to gain the benefit of public support and public procurement.

Leaving aside the consideration of whether the OECD Guidelines represent the most appropriate international instrument among those available – such as the ILO Tripartite Declaration on Multinational Enterprises or the UN Norms for Transnational Businesses – it is important to note that the problem of ensuring an efficient monitoring system has been overlooked. As emerged from the analysis of the main codes of conduct existing at the international level in the first part of the book, the weakest point of voluntary measures is their limited implementation, which is largely due to an inefficient monitoring system. By encouraging reliance on the OECD Guidelines, the EU does not seem to have tackled this issue. Nor has the EU suggested an alternative way to improve the impact and operation of existing codes.

6.5   INTERNATIONAL FRAMEWORK AGREEMENTS

Even if they have not yet attracted much attention in the context of the debate on CSR, International Framework Agreements (IFAs) can be regarded as one of the most interesting recent instruments developed at the EU level to address MNEs' responsibility for labour rights and human rights. Such agreements are concluded between a MNE and a global union federation[19] in order to protect fundamental social rights of the employees of the company concerned in all its operations.[20] Framework agreements

---

[17]   See *Corporate Social Responsibility: A Business Contribution, supra* Ch.1 n. 24, at 26.

[18]   EU–Chile Agreement, *supra* Ch.1 n. 93.

[19]   Global Union Federations are the international representatives for unions organizing in specific industry sectors or occupational groups.

[20]   IFAs are defined by the International Confederation of Free Trade Unions (ICFTU) as: 'A framework agreement is an agreement negotiated between a multinational company and a global union federation concerning the international activities of that company. The main purpose of a framework agreement is to establish a formal ongoing relationship between the multinational company and the global union federation which can solve problems and work in the interests of both parties', available at: http://www.icftu.org.

aim to establish a formal ongoing relationship between a multinational enterprise and the global union federation.

According to the definition provided by the International Federation of Trade Unions, International Framework Agreements must have a global scope and must be referenced to the ILO. They must be signed by a Global Union Federation, which has to be involved in the implementation of the agreement. Most notably, the agreement must require the MNE to influence suppliers and a right to bring complaints must be provided for.[21]

All framework agreements operate on the principle of respecting minimum labour and human rights standards, as well as domestic regulations and industry codes of conduct. Framework agreements normally commit MNEs to the core labour standards found in the 1998 ILO Declaration on Fundamental Principles and Rights at Work, (that is, ILO Conventions 87, 98, 100, 105, 111, 138, whereas Convention 182 was only added in 1999).[22]

Next to a reference to the labour rights of the ILO, agreements very often declare respect for the UN Universal Declaration of Human Rights, the UN Global Compact, the ILO Tripartite Declaration on the Fundamental Rights of Workers, the OECD Guidelines for Multinational Enterprises and, again in a vaguer version, affirmations to support 'fundamental human rights in the community and in the place of work' (Statoil IFA) or 'corporate social responsibility' and 'social justice' (Freudenberg IFA).

Still, a closer analysis of the agreements reveals a number of differences of degree. Whereas the emphasis of some IFAs is on establishing fundamental rights, there are others that come much closer to bargaining agreements, in that they contain detailed provisions about regular meetings, deal with a range of issues beyond core labour rights and define the regularity of meetings. What International Framework Agreements do, then, is to really transform global unions into bargaining parties *vis-à-vis* MNEs and to make them part of a voluntary enforcement mechanism.

As far as the legal nature and effectiveness of IFAs are concerned, let us make clear that IFAs are not foreseen by international law nor do they

---

[21] N. Hammer, *International Framework Agreements: Overview and Key Issues*, Presented at the Industrial Relations in Europe Conference, Utrecht (August 2004).

[22] Hammer argues that since only 35 countries have ratified all seven core conventions in 1998 there is the potential for IFAs to raise minimum standards in MNEs foreign operations. This mechanism, however, is mainly valid for the core conventions dealing with fundamental rights, that is non-discretionary freedoms or protection. See N. Hammer, *International Framework Agreements: Global Union Federations and Value Chains*, Paper Presented at the International CRIMT Colloquium, 'Union Renewal: Assessing Innovations for Union Power in a Globalised Economy', HEC Montréal, 18–20 November 2004, at 15.

refer to the law applicable to the agreement or the competent jurisdiction in case litigation arises. In addition, their legal nature as unilateral commitments, contracts, contracts *sui generis,* or collective agreements has not been determined and could vary according to different domestic legal regimes. In order for an IFA to acquire legal force it should therefore be incorporated either into a collective agreement at the national level or into individual job contracts.[23] This option, which builds on the similarities between IFAs and domestic framework agreements, however, is not satisfactory, since it plays against the purpose of IFAs themselves, which is to create an agreement which is equally applicable in all the countries affected by the activities, rather than substituting national legislation.

Another issue to be addressed is to what extent the IFA can be opposed to third parties, in particular to suppliers of the company who signed it. Since there is no international law applicable to IFAs, recourse should be made to the classical instruments of private law. For instance, an express reference to the IFA in the contracts signed between the MNE and its suppliers would render the IFA applicable also in relation to the suppliers. According to this option, there will be a transmission of the obligation to respect the IFA from the parent company to its suppliers.[24] The majority of IFAs, however, do not envisage such a solution. They either exhort suppliers to respect the ILO Conventions mentioned in the IFA[25] or they simply refer to the respect of labour rights as a criteria of selecting among suppliers.[26]

It is important to make clear, however, that no enforcement mechanisms exist at the global level for IFAs. Thus, any enforcement of the provisions of an IFA relies almost exclusively on the capacity and strength of unions to compel companies to resolve complaints. To date, there have been relatively few examples where complaints have been raised under an IFA, and even fewer where they have been resolved. Without doubt, the most experience with handling complaints under an IFA has been in Daimler-Chrysler. Ten concrete cases of violations have been identified, seven of them relating to suppliers and three to dealers. Most of the complaints relate to breaches of the IFA provisions on freedom of association and the right to collectively bargain.[27]

---

[23]   I. Daugareilh, 'La Negoziazione Collettiva Internazionale' (2005) 19 *Lavoro e Diritto*, 599, at 628.

[24]   Ibid., at 626.

[25]   See Chiquita–UITA Framework Agreement.

[26]   Renault–FIOM, Framework Agreement.

[27]   J. Holdcroft, 'International Framework Agreements: A Progress' (2006) 3 *Metal World* 18.

They are meant to be discussed, renegotiated or prolonged after certain intervals. The distinct advance made by framework agreements is further highlighted when we consider the specific status of the ILO conventions mentioned in the agreements.[28] The International Labour Conference has come to define these principles as so fundamental that it considers all ILO members as bound by them, (as opposed to only those who ratified the Conventions in question).

In conclusion, while IFAs fall into the category of voluntary initiatives they represent an interesting alternative to codes of conduct. IFAs clearly moved beyond codes of conduct in that they are not mere unilateral declarations. The agreement (as opposed to unilateral codes of conduct) character of IFAs not only commits MNEs, but also the trade union side. Both parties find themselves in a process of social dialogue with their own formal or informal rules and/or constraints. This is reflected, for example, in the signature of the IKEA agreement being made by the company's procurement officer. In fact, these efforts do not have to be limited to the MNE's own operations, but can extend to the supply chain. The signature of the IKEA agreement has integrated the IFA into a code of conduct which is part of its contractual relations with suppliers and it has also established a separate compliance organization.[29]

Secondly, such agreements are of particular interest because, despite their global reach, they can be considered mainly as a European phenomenon. All but three[30] of the IFAs, thus far, have been signed with European based companies and often with a global union federation (formerly known as international trade secretariats) as signatory or co-signatory from the labour side, and initiated in the context of existing European Works Councils (European Works Councils).[31] The fact that, the formation of these councils is legally required, rather than merely voluntary,

---

28   Daugareilh, *supra* n. 23, at 629.
29   E. de Haan and J. Oldenziel, *Labour Conditions in IKEA's Supply Chain. Case Studies in India Bulgaria and Vietnam*, 2003, Amsterdam, SOMO, available at: http://www.somo.nl/html/paginas/pdf/IKEA_eindrapport_2003_NL.pdf (accessed 13 March 2007).
30   The exceptions are the IUF agreement with Chiquita (headquartered in the United States); the IUF agreement with Fonterra (headquartered in New Zealand); and the ICEM agreement with AngloGold (headquartered in South Africa). See. V. Devillechabrolle, 'Ces groupes qui jouent la carte du dialogue social au niveau mondial' (Avril 2005) *Liaisons Sociales*, 52, at 53.
31   R. Blanpain, *European Works Councils in Multinational Enterprises: Background, Working and Experience*, ILO Working Paper, Annex, 83 (1999); L. Riisgaard, *The IUF/COLSIBA – CHIQUITA Framework Agreement: a Case Study*, ILO Working Paper, 94 (2004).

suggests that strong theoretical underpinnings for the development of IFAs in the EU existed before the agreements themselves. The councils have arguably established in the EU a background of collaborative partnership building and information sharing that provided the foundation upon which IFAs were first concluded.

Finally, despite their non binding character, IFAs offers two advantages as compared to codes of conduct. First, an IFA can oblige or at least encourage suppliers to follow certain principles. Second, they also provide a key role for trade unions in the implementation and monitoring process. Trade unions can bring to the attention of the company any breach of the agreement. IFAs further deal with government failure by setting global minimum standards and by getting MNEs to accept some responsibility for the labour rights situation up the supply chain. Moreover, the IFAs binds MNEs to respect certain rights and principles in all their activities worldwide, even in those countries that have not ratified the ILO conventions mentioned in the agreement. Finally, IFAs actively involve employees in the implementation of the agreement, as well as in a regular monitoring process. International Framework Agreements therefore have been regarded not as better codes of conduct, that is with trade union involvement, but as qualitatively different and as a platform for international industrial relations. In fact, the overview below shows that IFAs are heterogeneous as to their substance and form. Others locate them on a continuum between labour rights agreements and collective bargaining agreements.[32]

Even if it is still too early to assess thoroughly the success of their implementation, case studies conducted to date[33] illustrate that IFAs, when implemented, have had a mixed record in terms of their impact on the rights of workers employed by transnational corporations. The first problem is that IFAs are less successful where labour relations between the local union and the MNE are not already well established. If unions are not accustomed to working with management and engaging in a process of negotiation over fundamental needs, it is difficult for them to insist on significant changes under an IFA. A second problem, closely related to the first, is that the success of an IFA is largely dependent on the quality of organization of the local unions affected by the agreement. These problems are evident in both the negotiation and implementation phases.

These problems highlight IFAs' limitations when it comes to improving the labour rights of workers in the developing world, where labour

---

[32]   Hammer, *supra* n. 21.
[33]   Accor, Chiquita, Statoil and DaimlerChrysler.

legislation or existing collective agreements are either under-enforced, or nonexistent. The IFA concluded between IUF and Chiquita, similarly to that negotiated with Accor, has operated to the advantage of workers in workplaces that are already well organized, but has worked less well in locales where workers lack the opportunity, or lack the structures, that make unionization possible.[34]

Through their combination of voluntary global bargaining based on international legislated standards that are mandatory for States, framework agreements present an interesting alternative to the voluntary/binding divide in regulating the conduct of MNEs. The EU example also shows that the creation of an appropriate institutional structure, such as the European Works Councils, can facilitate the adoption of IFAs.

6.6 CONCLUSION

This chapter focused on EU measures addressed directly to MNEs and, in particular, to their activities in third countries. While at the internal level a certain variety of binding and non-binding measures has been noted, external measures addressed to MNEs largely rely on non-binding measures. The Code of Conduct on Arms Export and the Code of Conduct for companies operating in South Africa, which were the first examples of EC measures specifically addressed to the external activities of MNEs, were adopted under political cooperation. These codes showed many deficiencies in their implementation and in particular with reference to monitoring and enforcement mechanisms. It was submitted, however, that on the bases of these experiences, any proposal for an effective code of conduct for European MNEs should impose clearly verifiable obligations on the enterprises who decide to adopt them, and violations of the Code should be sanctioned. In addition, uniform standards should be set in order to ensure comparability between companies.

These suggestions were taken into consideration in the European Parliament Resolution for a European Code of Conduct for European Multinational Enterprises. Not only does the proposed code refer to international human rights standards but it also foresees the setting up of a monitoring mechanism.

The weak results of the debate on Corporate Social Responsibility examined in the previous chapter, as compared with the proposals of the Howitt Resolution, suggest that the reasons for its limited implementation

---

[34] Riisgaard, *supra* n. 31.

are to be identified in the gap between the ambition of the reform project on one hand and the absence of a sound basis for consensus among the stakeholders on the other. The idea of creating a European Code for MNEs seems to have been finally set aside by the EC in favour of supporting the existing OECD Guidelines for MNEs.

As mentioned above, the exclusive reliance on the OECD Guidelines as the appropriate instrument to promote MNEs' compliance with human rights while operating in third countries does not seem to be entirely convincing. Not only do the OECD Guidelines have only a very limited reference to human rights, but their implementation mechanism is also very weak. It is submitted that, coherently with EC commitment to human rights both at the internal and at the international level, the UN Norms would provide a more comprehensive international instrument of reference to address MNEs' responsibility for human rights.

In conclusion, the voluntary character of Codes of Conduct makes them necessarily useless or harmless to companies, of no help to their workers or the communities they affect by their activities. Codes of Conduct standards which companies proclaim to adopt and abide by, which implies that trade unions will be able to rely on these standards in the course of negotiating collective agreements or that the content of the code of conduct may serve the purpose of identifying what constitutes a 'fault' in the context of civil liability proceedings against the company. Moreover, Codes of Conduct could – once they are voluntarily adopted or accepted by companies – impose on these certain obligations, also by the institution of independent monitoring mechanisms.

As compared with codes of conducts, IFAs present the advantage of setting voluntary standards which are binding across borders, since they are binding on the different components of MNEs and on their suppliers. The main shortcomings are also in this case related to the difficulty in monitoring a company's compliance with such standards. On the other hand, by making access to public procurement conditional upon compliance with social and human rights standards, the EU and the Member States could encourage positive developments in corporate conduct by encouraging rewards for the most deserving enterprises. Such a mechanism constitutes a strong economic incentive for companies to behave consistently with human rights and social rights. In addition, it can be used to combine a binding legal instrument, such as the rules on public procurement, with compliance with voluntary measures, such as an international codes of conduct, with the result of enhancing the leverage of voluntary measures.

PART III

MNEs and human rights in the external relations of the European Union

7 The external relations of the European Union, MNEs and human rights

7.1 INTRODUCTION

Having examined the EU measures addressed directly to MNEs in Part II, Part III focuses on measures addressed to host States. It suggests that a possible option to promote MNEs' respect for human rights in developing countries is to raise MNEs' human rights standards in recipient countries. Governments in developing countries will in turn be encouraged to enforce human rights obligations on MNEs operating in their countries. In addition, the scrutiny of MNEs in developing countries could be enhanced by strengthening local NGOs and increasing awareness about the conduct of MNEs directly at the host State level. Great potential in both respects is offered by the instruments available to the external relations of the European Union.

First, the EU counts on a well established network of diplomatic relations with a vast majority of developing countries in different geographical areas. The past five years have seen the evolution of relationships between the EU and developing countries in all regions of the world, many of them former colonies of the Member States. At the centre of these relationships has been a multifaceted and highly institutionalized system of developing cooperation with African Caribbean and Pacific States, the Mediterranean countries and the Asian and Latin American (ALA) countries, which include 92 of the world's least developed countries.[1] The EC maintains 127 overseas delegations and in return 164 states have established permanent diplomatic missions to the Community. Their main task is the management of trade and aid relations.[2] A co-ordination role among the initiatives originating in the ILO, OECD and domestic context could be

---

[1] Relationships with former colonies in North Africa, other Mediterranean non EU members and members of the former eastern bloc have evolved differently and they are now included in the neighbourhood policy.

[2] See http://ec.europa.eu/comm/external_relations/delegations/intro/web. htm. See also C. Bretherthon and J. Vogler, *The European Union as a Global Actor*, 1999, London and New York, Routledge.

given to the EU delegation in developing countries. The de-concentration process, which started in 2001, has led to a gradual transfer of resources and responsibilities to the EC Delegations. It is believed that this process will help to improve the quality of the participatory approach in EC development policy.[3] In turn, this should enable a more efficient and prompt intervention capacity. The proposed reform of the EU external relations service in the context of the Treaty of Lisbon [4] also militates in this respect. In fact, it is foreseen that the role of EU delegations should be extended and improved, with EU delegations acting as coordination points.

As seen in Part II, the promotion of human rights has occupied a central role in the external relations of the EU.[5] According to Article 177(2)[6] one of the objectives of the development and cooperation policy is to contribute to the general objective of developing and consolidating democracy and the rule of law, and to that of respecting human rights and fundamental freedoms. Similarly, pursuant to Article 11 of the TEU[7] Treaty, the EU's foreign policy shall develop and consolidate democracy and the rule of law, along with respect for human rights and fundamental freedoms. Every new development, cooperation and association agreement between the EU and third countries includes a human rights clause,[8] allowing for trade benefits and development cooperation to be suspended if abuses are established. With regard, in particular, to development and

---

[3] Communication from the Commission to the Council, the European Parliament and the Economic and Social Committee of 7 November 2002, *Participation of Non-State Actors in EC Development Policy*, COM (2002) 598 final.

[4] Article 13a: 'In fulfilling his mandate, the High Representative shall be assisted by a European External Action Service. This service shall work in cooperation with the diplomatic services of the Member States and shall comprise officials from relevant departments of the General Secretariat of the Council and of the Commission as well as staff seconded from national diplomatic services of the Member States. The organisation and functioning of the European External Action Service shall be established by a decision of the Council. The Council shall act on a proposal from the High Representative after consulting the European Parliament and after obtaining the consent of the Commission': Treaty of Lisbon, *supra* Ch.4 n. 29.

[5] Most commentators agree that external human rights policies are more meaningful than the internal one: Alston and Weiler, 'An "Ever Closer Union" in Need of a Human Rights Policy', *supra* Ch.4 n. 42, 3. For a critical analysis of the reasons why human rights have developed more at the external rather than at the internal level see Williams, *EU Human Rights Policies*, *supra* Ch.4 n. 42, at 120.

[6] Art. 188D, Treaty of Lisbon.

[7] Art. 11, Treaty of Lisbon.

[8] Riedel and Martin, 'Human Rights Clauses in External Agreements of the EC', *supra* Ch.4 n. 44.

cooperation programmes, the Treaty of Nice has also extended the objective of promoting the respect of human rights and fundamental freedoms from development cooperation to all forms of cooperation with third countries.[9] Mechanisms such as the human rights scheme in the GSP, which is used as a lever on third countries so as to ensure or enhance compliance with human rights standards, have recently been revised in order to include all main human rights international conventions.[10] As a result, the European Union has been keen to present itself as the promoter of the triptych – human rights, democracy and rule of law in its relations with third countries.[11] Human rights clauses and human rights special incentives are designed to raise the level of democracy and respect of human rights records in developing countries. These countries, in turn, often host the subsidiaries of EU Member State MNEs. It is argued that, through raising the human rights obligations of host states indirectly, human rights obligations on MNEs will be strengthened.

Finally, not only does the EU use its trade and economic power to encourage governments to improve their human rights standards, but it also acts as a development and humanitarian actor, through its development and assistance policy. The EU provides technical assistance on trade and funds cooperation programmes aimed at the reinforcement of civil society and NGOs in developing countries, and at creating partnerships with the private sector in the EU and in developing countries. The Cotonou Agreement of 23 June 2000 expressly calls on private actors, including companies, to participate to the implementation of the partnership. An increasing part of the European Initiative for Democracy and Human Rights[12] projects aimed at strengthening the role of trade unions and combating discrimination in developing countries, while technical assistance of cooperation programmes is devoted to the promotion of the private sector and assistance for economic development. The involvement of non-state actors, such as NGOs and businesses in the definition of objectives of cooperation and in its implementation can be seen as complementary to incentives posed on government. The involvement and

---

[9] Art. 181a TEC.
[10] Brandtner and Rosas, 'Trade Preferences and Human Rights', *supra* Ch.4 n. 46, at 699; Gatto, 'The Integration of Social Rights Concerns', *supra* Ch.4 n. 46.
[11] Simma et al., 'Human Rights Considerations', *supra* Ch.4 n. 47, 571.
[12] Regulation (EC) 1889/2006 of the European Parliament and of the Council of 20 December 2006 on *Establishing a Financing Instrument for the Promotion of Democracy and Human Rights Worldwide*, [2006] OJ L 386/1.

strengthening of civil society is considered, indeed, the first step towards a closer scrutiny and early warning against human rights abuses by MNEs.[13]

Part III argues that, in addition to the internal measures examined in Part II, the European Union could use and improve existing external relations tools in order to encourage developing countries to raise their scrutiny over MNEs' compliance with human rights.

Two levels at which the EU can operate can be distinguished. On the one hand, the EU can encourage governments in developing countries to raise their human rights standards by subjecting access to assistance and to trade to the respect of human rights (so called *conditionality*).[14] In turn, governments which are the direct addressees of human rights obligations can impose compliance with such standards on MNEs operating in their countries (*indirect obligations on MNEs*). To this end, the impact of instruments such as human rights clauses in development and assistance programmes, in the Cotonou Agreement and the human rights arrangement of the GSP will be examined.

On the other hand, the EU could use its incentive measures such as technical assistance and EIDHR projects to empower local NGOs sensitive to human rights matters and to extending knowledge about the responsibility of MNEs in developing countries. From the standpoint of the regulatory versus voluntary debate delineated in Part I, it can be put forward that the EU's external relations have for some time experienced regulatory mechanisms (such as conditionality) for the promotion of human rights and placed the burden of compliance with these rights on States. Only recently has the EU drawn attention to the potential of non-binding mechanisms for the promotion of human rights. By the same token, the influence of non-state actors and in particular NGOs and MNEs, on the respect and fulfilment of these rights has been progressively recognized.

It must be pointed out from the outset that the use of external relations to raise human rights standards in third countries and, in turn, imposing indirect obligations on MNEs raises a number of objections. The first question relates to the competence of the EC/EU to adopt measures in the field of human rights. As examined already with reference to the EC's internal policies, even if there is a widespread practice on the promotion of human rights, it is still questionable to what extent the Treaties and case-law of the ECJ provides an appropriate legal basis for the EU to take

---

[13]   T. Fox and H. Ward 'Moving the Corporate Citizenship Agenda to the South', in *Words into Action,* International Institute for Environment and Development (IIED), (2002), at 59, available at: www.iied.org (accessed 5 April 2003).
[14]   Fierro, *supra* Ch.1 n. 107, at 100–102.

action in this respect. Having provided the overall framework of EC/EU's powers in the field of human rights in Part II, the question as to what is the margin left to the jurisdiction of the EU, as opposed to the Member States, in the field of human rights in the context of external relations will be addressed here. The second objection refers to the overall effectiveness of the EU's external relations policies to promote human rights in third countries. The use of conditionality as a mechanism to link aid or trade to the respect of human rights has been seriously questioned in recent years.[15] In addition, the set of human rights that the EC/EU has decided to promote may give rise to allegations of promoting European rather than universal human rights.[16]

In the following paragraphs the question of legitimacy of the EC's and EU's competence in external relations is examined. An overview of the instruments available to the external relations of the EU for the promotion of human rights and their implications for the effectiveness of EC/EU action will also be provided. A more detailed assessment of the effectiveness of the different EC external relations measures in relation to MNEs' responsibility for human rights will be the object in the following chapters. In examining these instruments a distinction will be made between regulatory measures, such as human rights clauses and GSP special arrangements on human rights, and non regulatory measures, such as incentive measures included in assistance programmes, strengthening civil society in developing countries and raising awareness of MNEs' responsibility.

7.2 THE EU's EXTERNAL COMPETENCE ON HUMAN RIGHTS

In Part II it was submitted that although a general EC competence to adopt acts in the field of human rights does not exist at the moment, such rights must be integrated into all the EC's policies which may have an impact on them. Similarly to what we have already noted for the internal polices of the EC, despite the fact that the external action of the EC and the EU is largely focused on the promotion of human rights, it is still questionable as to the extent to which the existing Treaties and case law of the ECJ provide an appropriate legal basis for the EU to take action in this field.

The question of competence in the external action of the EU is further complicated by the horizontal, transversal and inter-pillar character of

---

15   Williams, *EU Human Rights Policies*, *supra* Ch.4 n. 42.
16   Leino, 'European Universalism', *supra* Ch.4 n. 108, at 239.

human rights policy. The integration of human rights in the external relations of the EU, indeed, finds itself at the cross-roads of the external relations of the EC and the CSFP. Therefore, far from being a merely formalistic question, the problem of identifying the appropriate legal basis for each EC act entails the questions of identifying the appropriate European institutions, law making procedures and jurisprudential control over the act. Further, it is necessary to constantly check the powers conferred upon the EC/EU *vis-à-vis* those which are retained by Member States.

Human rights can no longer be considered as an ancillary objective of EC external relations.[17] The practice of incorporating human rights clauses into the terms of commercial, development and cooperation agreements has progressively increased in the last decade and it is now firmly established in the external relations with third states.[18] Autonomous trade measures such as the GSP have been designed to promote respect for human rights. Two internal measures, the Council Regulations 975/1999 and 976/1999[19] (as amended by Council Regulation 1889/2006)[20] provide funding for projects aiming at the promotion and protection of human rights in developing countries.

A second element worth noting is that the protection of human rights in development co-operation and cooperation is expressly enshrined in the EC Treaty. The constitutional foundations of the EC's external human rights policy can be found in the Treaty of Maastricht, where EC development cooperation policy was defined, with emphasis on the general objective of developing and consolidating democracy and 'the rule of law and .of respecting human rights and fundamental freedoms' (Article 177(2) EC). Beyond Article 177(2), there were no other provisions of the EC treaty that confer on the EC the power to act in international relations for the protection of human rights. This lacuna was filled to some extent by the new article

---

17 Eeckhout, *supra* Ch.4 n. 54, at 466.

18 *Promoting Human Rights*, *supra* Ch.4 n. 40.

19 Council Regulation (EC) 975/1999 of 29 April 1999 laying down the requirements for the Implementation of development cooperation operations which contribute to the general objective of developing and consolidating democracy and the rule of law and to that of respecting human rights and fundamental freedoms and the rule [1999] OJ L 120/1. Council Regulation (EC) 976/1999 of 29 April 1999 laying down the requirements for the Implementation of Community operations, other than those of development cooperation, which, within the framework of Community cooperation policy, contribute to the general objective of developing and consolidating democracy and the rule of law and to that of respecting human rights and fundamental freedoms in third countries [1999] OJ L 120/8.

20 See *supra* n. 12.

181a inserted by the Treaty of Nice[21], which introduces a new category of co-operation agreements to be concluded with developed third countries.[22] The protection of human rights is mentioned among the objectives of the action to be undertaken by the EC under this provision. Developing and consolidating democracy and the rule of law, and the respect for human rights and fundamental freedoms is also one of the objectives of the CFSP, according to Article 11 TEU. Finally, Article 6 TEU,[23] despite originally being intended to have mainly an internal dimension, has been interpreted to cover the whole range of Union competence and activities.

The question of competence on human rights, however, is not exhausted by the textual references in the Treaties, as much as EU's external action is not confined to the adoption of measures in the field of development cooperation and cooperation. It is useful to distinguish three aspects related to the question of the EC's external competence on human rights. The first question relates to the EC's power to conclude agreements which have human rights as their main objective, in the sense of laying down rules and standards of human rights protection for all contracting parties. The second question deals with the EC's power to conclude agreements

---

[21] Now Art. 188G, Treaty of Lisbon.

[22] The Treaty of Nice added Art. 181a on economic, financial and technical cooperation with third countries, which reads:

1. Without prejudice to the other provisions of this Treaty, and in particular those of Title XX, the Community shall carry out, within its spheres of competence, economic, financial and technical cooperation measures with third countries. Such measures shall be complementary to those carried out by the Member States and consistent with the development policy of the Community. Community policy in this area shall contribute to the general objective of developing and consolidating democracy and the rule of law, and to the objective of respecting human rights and fundamental freedoms. 2. The Council, acting by a qualified majority on a proposal from the Commission and after consulting the European Parliament, shall adopt the measures necessary for the implementation of paragraph 1. The Council shall act unanimously for the association agreements referred to in Article 310 and for the agreements to be concluded with the States which are candidates for accession to the Union. 3. Within their respective spheres of competence, the Community and the Member States shall cooperate with third countries and the competent international organisations. The arrangements for Community cooperation may be the subject of agreements between the Community and the third parties concerned, which shall be negotiated and concluded in accordance with Article 300. The first subparagraph shall be without prejudice to the Member States' competence to negotiate in international bodies and to conclude international agreements.

[23] Art. 6, Treaty of Lisbon.

which are predicated on respect for human rights, or contain provisions on cooperation in this field. This category may cover all bilateral cooperation, partnership and association agreements between the EC and third countries. The third aspect to be examined relates to the interface between human rights competence falling under the first pillar (EC) and those falling under the third pillar (CFSP). As will be explained in the next section, the latter question is of lesser relevance in the context of this book, since the analysis will focus on EC measures addressed to host states, rather than CFSP measures.

As far as the former question is concerned, the analysis necessarily leads us back to *Opinion 2/94*. The content of the Opinion was discussed in Part II, paragraph 2.1.4. It is necessary to recall here that on this occasion the ECJ stated that no Treaty provision conferred on the Community institutions any general power to enact rules on human rights or to conclude international conventions in this field.[24] As seen above, this statement cannot be interpreted as excluding any competence of the EC in the field of human rights. The Court did not rule out EU participation in the negotiations and conclusions of human rights agreements. The decision focused on the constitutional and institutional consequences of EC participation in the ECHR system. This seems to indicate that the Court did not wish to peremptorily exclude the participation of the EC to any human rights treaty. A confirmation of this can be seen in the fact that the Treaty of Lisbon states that the EU shall accede to the ECHR.[25]

As noted by many authors,[26] the Court does not provide an exhaustive analysis of EC powers from the standpoint of the doctrine of implied powers.[27] The Court firstly refers to the principle of conferred powers laid down in (current) Article 5 EC, which provides that the Community has only those powers which have been conferred upon it by the Member States. In the field of external relations, however, it is settled case law[28]

---

24   *Opinion 1/94* [1994] ECR I-5267, para. 28.
25   Art. 6(2), Treaty of Lisbon, *supra* Ch.4 n. 29.
26   A. Arnull, 'Left to Its Own Devices? Opinion 2/94 and the Protection of Fundamental Rights in the European Union', in A. Dashwood and C. Illion (eds), *The General Law of EC External Relations*, 2000, London, Sweet & Maxwell, 61 at 71. M. Cremona, 'The EU and the External Dimension of Human Rights Policy', in S.V. Konstantinidis (ed.), *A People's Europe Turning a Concept into a Content (EC/International Law Forum III)* 1998, Ashgate and Dartmouth, 155.
27   See Eeckhout, *supra* Ch.4 n. 54, at 85; Weiler and Fries, *supra* Ch.4 n. 53; Cannizzaro, 'The Scope of EU Foreign Power', *supra* Ch.4 n. 101.
28   The doctrine of implied powers was firstly formulated by the ECJ in Case C-22/70 *Commission of the European Communities v Council of the European Communities – European Agreement on Road Transport (ERTA)* [1971] ECR 263.

that the competence of the Community to enter into international commitments not only flowed from express provisions of the Treaty but could also be implied from those provisions.[29]

It can be argued that in this case the Court could have applied the doctrine of implied powers, according to which whenever Community law had created for the institutions of the Community powers within its internal system for the purpose of attaining a specific objective, the Community was empowered to enter into the international commitments necessary for the attainment of that objective, even in the absence of an express provision to that effect.[30] Instead, after having pointed out that no Treaty provision expressly conferred on the Community institutions any general powers to enact rules or to conclude international conventions in the field of human rights, the Court turned to consider whether Article 308[31] could constitute an appropriate legal basis, without addressing the issue of possible implied powers.

Eeckhout suggests that the doctrine of implied powers could be applied to *Opinion 2/94*. As the EC has increasingly engaged in areas which are closely linked to the protection of human rights – such as asylum policy, cooperation in criminal matters and non-discrimination, it can be argued that there is some measure of community competence to conclude international agreements which lay down specific rules on human rights. Eeckhout draws a parallel between the doctrine of implied powers, as in the *ERTA* case, and the exercise of EC competence in antidiscrimination policy based on Article 13. Once the EC has exercized its powers in this field by enacting two directives on antidiscrimination,[32] it could be endowed with the exclusive competence to conclude Protocol 12 to the ECHR, which deals with non discrimination, in so far as the provisions of that protocol affect Community legislation.

Even if one does not want to fully uphold this position, it can be safely argued that, since respect of human rights constitutes a condition of the lawfulness of community acts, institutions are bound to ensure the

---

[29]   Eeckhout points out that the most innovative aspect of the judgement is in its recognition of the EC's power to conclude an international agreement in the absence of an express recognition of such power. See Eeckhout, *External Relations, supra* Ch.4 n. 99, at 63.

[30]   Paras 23–26, *Opinion 2/94*.

[31]   Art. 308 and 308 A, Treaty of Lisbon.

[32]   Council Directive 2000/43/EC of 29 June 2000 Implementing the Principle of Equal Treatment between Persons Irrespective of Racial or Ethnic Origin [2000] OJ L 180/22 and Council Directive 2000/78/EC of 27 November 2000 Establishing a General Framework for Equal Treatment in Employment and Occupation [2000] OJ L 303/16.

respect of human rights in all their acts, both in their internal and external policies.[33] In other words, if EU institutions need to respect human rights because those provisions are general principles of EC law which the court upholds, they also need to have the legal tools to ensure such respect. This may include committing itself at the international level by concluding international human rights agreements,[34] if the limits defined by the court in *Opinion 2/94* are met.[35]

EC powers to conclude agreements which are predicted on respect for human rights, or contain provisions on cooperation in this field is less contentious. As mentioned above, the EC Treaty expressly confirms that development cooperation and other cooperation policies must contribute to the general objective of developing and consolidating democracy and the rule of law and, thus, that of respecting human rights and fundamental freedoms. With the introduction of Art 181a EC by the Treaty of Nice all co-operation agreements with third countries, be they developing countries or not, should contribute to that objective, including associa-tion agreements, which are also mentioned in Art 181a. The Treaty bases therefore may cover all bilateral cooperation, partnership and association agreements between the EC and third countries.

The problem of powers may arise in relation to the introduction of human rights clauses into pure trade agreements concluded under Article 133 TEC on common commercial policy. The question would be whether human rights can be introduced into such an agreement, even though Article 133 does not mention respect for human rights. A positive answer to this question is supported by the consideration that human rights can be regarded as a general objective of all EC external policies.[36] Both Articles 177 and 181a(1) EC refer to the general objective of respect for human rights, to which both policies should contribute. This general objective, which transcends each policy, should be read in the light of article 11(1) of the TEU: which provided that 'The Union shall define and implement a common foreign and security policy covering all areas of foreign and

---

[33]   Eeckhout, *External Relations, supra* Ch.4 n. 99, at 86.
[34]   Signs of a changing approach are provided in *Matthews v United Kingdom*, App. No. 24833/94, Judgment of 18 February 1999 (1999) 28 EHRR 361.
[35]   See Weiler and Fries, *supra* Ch.4 n. 53 and Alston and Weiler, *supra* Ch.4 n. 42.
[36]   Eeckhout, *External Relations, supra* Ch.4 n. 99, at 472; G. Gaja, 'Casenote: Accession by the Community to the European Convention for the Protection of Human Rights and Fundamental Freedoms – Opinion 2/94' (1996) 33 C.M.L.R 973, at 984. E. Riedel and M. Will, 'Human Rights Clauses in the External Agreements of the EC', in Alston et al., *supra* Ch.1 n. 70 at 736.

security policy, the objectives of which shall be: . . . to develop and consolidate democracy and the rule of law, and respect for human rights and fundamental freedoms.' If one adds Article 6, requiring that '1. The Union is founded on the principles of liberty, democracy, respect for human rights and fundamental freedoms, and the rule of law, principles which are common to the Member States' and that 'the Union shall provide itself with the means necessary to attain its objectives and carry through its policies', it can be deduced that the general objective of respect for human rights transcends the realm of Articles 177(1)[37] and 181a TEC.[38] In the light of Article 6 TEU, all EC external policies, be they First or Second or Third Pillar, should contribute to the general objective of developing and consolidating democracy and the rule of law, and respect for human rights and fundamental freedoms.

This will be clearer in the context of the Treaty of Lisbon, which talks about one EU external action which will encompass all components of the current external relations, including the common commercial policy. Article 10 A states that:

The Union shall define and pursue common policies and actions, and shall work for a high degree of cooperation in all fields of international relations, in order to:

(a) safeguard its values, fundamental interests, security, independence and integrity;

(b) consolidate and support democracy, the rule of law, human rights and the principles of international law;

(c) preserve peace, prevent conflicts and strengthen international security, in accordance with the purposes and principles of the United Nations Charter, with the principles of the Helsinki Final Act and with the aims of the Charter of Paris, including those relating to external borders;

(d) foster the sustainable economic, social and environmental development of developing countries, with the primary aim of eradicating poverty;

(e) encourage the integration of all countries into the world economy, including through the progressive abolition of restrictions on international trade;

(f) help develop international measures to preserve and improve the quality of the environment and the sustainable management of global natural resources, in order to ensure sustainable development;

(g) assist populations, countries and regions confronting natural or man-made disasters; and

(h) promote an international system based on stronger multilateral cooperation and good global governance.[39]

---

[37] Art. 188D, Treaty of Lisbon.
[38] Art. 188H, Treaty of Lisbon.
[39] Article 10A, Treaty of Lisbon, *supra* Ch.4 n. 29.

Further, indent 3 of the same article specifies that:

> The Union shall respect the principles and pursue the objectives set out in paragraphs 1 and 2 in the development and implementation of the different areas of the Union's external action covered by this Title and by Part Five of the Treaty on the Functioning of the European Union, and of the external aspects of its other policies. The Union shall ensure consistency between the different areas of its external action and between these and its other policies. The Council and the Commission, assisted by the High Representative of the Union for Foreign Affairs and Security Policy, shall ensure that consistency and shall cooperate to that effect.

The scope of this objective and the corresponding limits to the relevant EC powers remain to be examined. The ECJ addressed this question in *Portugal v Council*.[40] In this case, the Portuguese Government challenged the validity of the legal basis of Community competence and the corresponding procedure by which the Community concluded a cooperation agreement with India. The discussion will be limited here to the Portuguese argument that the legal basis of the contested Council decision did not confer on the Community the necessary powers to conclude the Agreement, as regards, firstly, the provision therein relating to human rights. It considers that recourse should also have been had to Article 308 of the Treaty and to participation of all the Member States in the conclusion of the Agreement. The Court held that by declaring that 'Community policy . . . shall contribute to the general objective of developing and consolidating democracy and the rule of law, and to that of respecting human rights and fundamental freedoms', Article 177(2) requires the Community to take account of the objective of respect for human rights when it adopts measures in the field of development cooperation. The mere fact that Article 1(1) of the Agreement provides that respect for human rights and democratic principles 'constitutes an essential element' of the Agreement does not justify the conclusion that that provision goes beyond the objective of Article 177(2) of the Treaty. The very wording of this provision demonstrates the importance to be attached to respect for human rights and democratic principles, so that, amongst other things, development cooperation policy must be adapted to the requirement of respect for those rights and principles. With regard, more particularly, to the argument of the Portuguese Government that the characterization of respect for human rights as an essential element in cooperation presupposes specific means of

---

[40] Case C-268/94 *Portuguese Republic v Council of the European Union – Cooperation Agreement between the European Community and the Republic of India* [1996] ECR I-6177.

action, the court stated that to adapt cooperation policy to respect for human rights necessarily entails establishing a certain connection between those matters whereby one of them is made subordinate to the other. In particular while development policy is subordinate to human rights, an agreement may need to be suspended under the essential element clause.

As part of the common commercial policy, trade relations with third countries fall into the exclusive competence the European Community (Article 133 TEC).[41] In the *GSP* case[42] the European Court of Justice acknowledged that the existence of a link with development problems does not cause a measure to be excluded from the sphere of the common commercial policy, as defined by the treaty. It considered that it would no longer be possible to carry on any worthwhile common commercial policy if the Community were not in a position to avail itself also of means of action going beyond instruments intended to have an effect only on the traditional aspects of external trade. A 'commercial policy,' understood in that sense, would be destined to become nugatory in the course of time.[43] It follows that the EC is competent to introduce social considerations into measures adopted on the basis of Article 133, such as the GSP Regulation, as long as these measures do not have the promotion of human rights as their general and principal objective.

To sum up, the majority of the measures addressed to host States of MNEs, which will be examined in Part III, are covered by existing legal basis of TEC Articles 177–181a (in development cooperation policy and in cooperation agreements). The possibility of introducing non-trade considerations (in particular development) on the basis of Article 133 common commercial policy has been upheld by the ECJ, as long as trade remains the general and principal objective of these measures. Additionally, Article 308 TEC,[44] which provided for a general competence on the EC to take action, if this is necessary to attain one of the Community's general objectives listed in Article 6 TEC, could provide a basis for Community external action in the field of human rights considered as one of the Community's general objectives. Even if Article 308 did not confer an unlimited power on the EC, as the Court made clear in *Opinion 2/94.*[45] As seen above, the use of Article 308 to adopt Council Regulation 976/1999 concerning

---

41   Art. 188C, Treaty of Lisbon.
42   Case C-45/86 *Commission of the European Communities v Council of the European Communities (GSP)* [1987] ECR 1493.
43   *Opinion 1/78* [1979] ECR 2871.
44   Arts 308 and 308a, Treaty of Lisbon.
45   *Opinion 2/94 (European Convention on Human Rights)* [1996] ECR I-1061, para. 26.

community founding of human rights, relating to action in developed third countries, although it may not be considered the most appropriate legal basis in that case, was not challenged. The legislator subsequently intervened by adding article 181a which provides the adequate legal basis. The adoption of Council Regulation 976/1999 on the basis of article 308 seems, however, to confirm that the Court applied a certain flexibility to the use of Article 308 for the adoption of human rights measures where no other legal basis is available.

7.3   THE EC's AND EU's INSTRUMENTS TO ENGAGE IN HUMAN RIGHTS ACTIVITIES

Another aspect of EC/EU powers in the field of human rights refers to the delimitation of competences between the EC pillar and the CFSP one. External relations measures in the field of human rights often generate a contrast between the pillars. This has been the object of a number of disputes among Member States and EC institutions and it has been broadly addressed in the academic debate.[46] Overlaps are particularly evident in the case of sanctions against third countries. In this case a Common Position, which is an CFSP measure, adopted under Article 15 of the TEU,[47] is implemented at Community level by Article 301,[48] and, where financial restrictions are concerned, Article 60 of the TEC.[49] In these cases, the Commission is required to make a proposal for a Council Regulation, which the Council can adopt by a qualified majority. While in the case of economic sanctions there is an explicit *passerelle* provided by Articles 301 and 60 TEC, in other areas, such as that of conclusion of external agreements or for the suspension of agreements which are predicted to the respect of human rights, such as the Cotonou agreement, the relationship between the EC and the CFSP pillar is more difficult to address.

The inter-pillar question of competence is of minor relevance in the context of the present book, since it focuses on EC measures, while CFSP measures are only marginally examined in the context of EU measures addressed to MNEs. Thus, the issue of distribution of EC/EU powers will

---

[46]   Cremona, *External Relations of the EU, supra* Ch.4 n. 95, R. Baratta, 'Overlaps between European Community Competence and European Union Foreign Policy Activity', in Cannizzaro (ed.), *The European Union, supra* Ch.1 n. 96, 51.

[47]   Art. 15, Treaty of Lisbon.

[48]   Art. 188K, Treaty of Lisbon.

[49]   Art. 61H, Treaty of Lisbon.

not be dealt with in this context. Suffice it to mention here that, with the integration of the pillars in the Treaty of Lisbon, the issue of delimitation of competences will not disappear. On the contrary there are likely to be an increasing number of issues, as the CSFP effectively develops and grows.

The common foreign and security policy (CFSP) was established and is governed by Title V of the Treaty on European Union (EU). It replaced European Political Cooperation (EPC) and provides for the eventual framing of a common defence policy, which might in time lead to a common defence. The objectives of this second pillar of the Union are set out in Article 11 of the EU Treaty and are to be attained through specific legal instruments (joint action, common position), which have to be adopted unanimously in the Council. With the entry into force of the Treaty of Amsterdam (1999), the European Union also has a new instrument at its disposal – the common strategy. The Treaty of Amsterdam also provided for qualified majority voting under certain conditions and, since it was signed, the CFSP field has been developing in practice at every European Council. The Treaty of Nice (2001) introduced the possibility, under certain conditions, of establishing closer cooperation in the CFSP field for the implementation of joint actions and common positions. This closer coop-eration may not be used for matters with military or defence implications.

The instruments provided for in the framework of the CSFP, such as common strategies, joint actions and common positions (Article 12 TEU),[50] can and have been used to carry out actions with human rights implications. Common strategies lay down the objectives of the European policy towards third countries. In concrete terms, a common strategy sets out the aims and length of time covered and the means to be made available by the Union and the Member States. Common strategies are implemented by the Council, in particular by adopting joint actions and common positions. The Council can recommend common strategies to the European Council. Common positions set out the approach of the EU on particular themes designed to make cooperation more systematic and improve its coordination. The Member States are required to comply with and uphold such positions, which have been adopted unanimously at the Council. Joint actions lays the basis of the EU's operational action coordinated by the Member States, whereby all kinds of resources (human resources, know-how, financing, equipment, etc.) are mobilized in order to attain specific objectives set by the Council, on the basis of general guide-lines from the European Council.

CFSP measures are usually addressed at fostering a better climate for

---

[50]   Art. 12, Treaty of Lisbon.

human rights and democracy, such as support for the elections in Russia[51] and of the peace agreement in Indonesia[52] and providing humanitarian aid to Sudan,[53] strengthening democratic principles and democratic institutions, and respect for human and minority rights. CFSP activities have included the promotion of regional political stability and the prevention and settlement of conflicts. One example can be found in the fight against the illicit traffic in diamonds, as a contribution to prevention and settlement of conflicts[54] which are centred on countries such as Liberia, Sierra Leone and Angola. It also includes the fight against arms proliferation, terrorism and traffic in illicit drugs. One example is the support for the Palestinian Authority in its efforts to counter terrorist activities emanating from its territories.[55]

Even if a number of CFSP measures can certainly contribute to create a more democratic climate in third countries, these measures affect only in a very indirect way the conduct of MNEs in third countries. Furthermore, the impact of these measures on the activities of MNEs in third countries is extremely difficult to assess. For instance, one can assume that monitoring and observing the elections in one country is a precondition for the setting up and correct functioning of democratic institutions in that country. In turn, it can be inferred that if democratic institutions are established and well functioning, MNEs are prevented from taking any, even indirect, advantage from conducting their operations in an authoritarian regime. This would amount in some cases to preventing a form of incidental or silent complicity which is given by MNEs' mere presence in a country where human rights abuses are widespread. Leaving aside the theoretical difficulties to define this type of

---

[51] Common Strategy of the European Union of 4 June 1999 on Russia (1999/414/CFSP) [1999] OJ L 157/1.

[52] Council Joint Action 2005/643/CFSP of 9 September 2005 on the European Union Monitoring Mission in Aceh (Indonesia) (Aceh Monitoring Mission) [2005] OJ L 234/13.

[53] Council Joint Action 2005/557/CFSP of 18 July 2005 on the European Union civilian–military supporting action to the African Union mission in the Darfur region of Sudan [2005] OJ L 188/46.

[54] Council Common Position 2001/758/CFSP of 29 October 2001 on Combating the illicit traffic in conflict diamonds, as a contribution to prevention and settlement of conflicts [2001] OJ L 286/2.

[55] Council Joint Action 2000/298/CSFP of 13 April 2000 on a European Union assistance programme to support the Palestinian Authority in its efforts to counter terrorist activities emanating from the territories under its control [2000] OJ L 097/4.

corporate complicity,[56] it seems that the impact of these types of CFSP measures seems to rest at a very general level, rather than addressing MNEs' compliance with human rights. The only exception is probably represented by the two codes of conduct for companies operating in South Africa and for arms exports, adopted under political cooperation and discussed in Part II.

In contrast with the mainly political character of the CSFP instruments, EC instruments address human rights in a more specific manner, for instance through the inclusion of human rights clauses. Human rights clauses have been included in external agreements, as well as in unilateral measures of the EC, providing assistance to third countries such as the MEDA Regulation,[57] the TACIS Regulation[58] and the ALA Regulation;[59] the new EIDHR Regulation, which provides additional budget to human rights projects, and the Regulation establishing a scheme of generalized tariff preferences (the GSP Regulation).[60]

For the purpose of this book, the analysis will be limited to the EC's external measures, which are able to have a more targeted impact on MNEs' responsibility for human rights. Among these instruments a distinction will be made between measures adopted in the realm of EC development policy, which will be dealt with in Chapter 8, and measures which fall within the EC common commercial policy, which are the object

---

[56] Clapham and Jerbi, 'Categories of Corporate Complicity', *supra* Ch.1 n. 32. See also I. Tófalo, 'Overt and Hidden Accomplices. Transnational Corporations' Range of Complicity for Human Rights Violations', in de Schutter (ed.), *Transnational Corporations*, *supra* Ch.1 n. 37, at 338.

[57] Council Regulation (EC) 1488/96 of 23 July 1996 on Financial measures to accompany (MEDA) the reform of economic and social structures in the framework of the Euro-Mediterranean partnership [1996] OJ L 189/1. Modified by Council Regulation (EC) 2698/2000 of the November 2000 amending regulation (EC) No. 1488/96 of 23 July 1996 on Financial measures to accompany (MEDA) the reform of economic and social structures in the framework of the Euro-Mediterranean partnership [2000] OJ L 311/1.

[58] Council Regulation (EC, EURATOM) 99/2000 of 29 December 1999 Concerning the Provision of Assistance to the Partner States in Eastern Europe and Central Asia [2000] OJ L 12/1. It provides assistance to Armenia, Azerbaijan, Belarus, Georgia, Kazakhstan, Kyrgyz Republic, Moldova, Russian Federation, Tajikistan, Turkmenistan, Ukraine and Uzbekistan.

[59] Council Regulation (EEC) 443/92 of 25 February 1992 on Financial technical assistance to and cooperation with developing countries in Asia and Latin America (the ALA Regulation) [1992] OJ L 52/1.

[60] Council Regulation 2501/2001 of 10 December, 2001 applying A Scheme of Generalised Tariff Preferences for the Period from 1 January 2002 to 31 December 2004 [2001] OJ L 346 /1.

of Chapter 9. Within each of these chapters a distinction is made between regulatory instruments, such as human rights and the GSP human rights arrangement, and non-regulatory, incentive measures, such as technical assistance provided by regional programmes and projects.

7.4   REGULATORY INSTRUMENTS: THE HUMAN RIGHTS CLAUSE

The inclusion of a clause calling for the respect of human rights in external agreements is one of the instruments most widely used by the EC for the promotion of human rights in third countries. An explicit reference to human rights was included for the first time in the preamble of the Third Lomé Convention (1984). However, only in the Fourth Lomé Convention (1989) was a human rights clause included in the text of the Agreement. In its first formulation the clause was merely exhortatory, since its breach did not constitute grounds for the suspension of the agreement.

Two years later in the Declaration on Human Rights of the Luxembourg European Council, the inclusion of human rights clauses in agreements with third countries was suggested, as an element of an active human rights policy. The Declaration was followed up by the 1991 Resolution on human rights, democracy and development, which lays down the basic tenets of EC human rights and development policy. Given the expansion of the EC's treaty relations and the increasing references to human rights in the agreements, the Commission adopted a communication which proposed the adoption of social clauses in all economic and cooperation agreements with third countries, which was then approved by the Council in 1995. As a result the essential element human rights clause was introduced. According to the standard wording of this clause 'respect for the democratic principles and human rights inspires the domestic and external policies of the Community and of third country and constitute an essential element of the agreement.'[61] This clause is usually supplemented by a non-execution clause, which applies in case of failure by one of the contracting parties to fulfil an obligation pursuant to the agreement.[62]

---

[61]   In Bulterman, *supra* Ch.4 n. 109.

[62]   Other typologies of human rights clause are also present in agreements concluded before 1995. For an extensive analysis see Bulterman, *supra* Ch.4 n. 109, at 156ff. and Fierro *supra* Ch.1 n. 107.

In addition to external agreements, human rights clauses have also been introduced into unilateral EC measures. These will be examined in detail in Chapter 8. Suffice to point out that these unilateral instruments cannot create rights or obligations on third parties. The EC can still invoke the human rights clauses in these instruments as a basis for withdrawing the assistance or preference as a response to human right violations.

The positive and negative dimensions of the human rights clause are usually distinguished. On the one hand the human rights clause expresses the common interest of the contracting parties in human rights. Human rights constitute a relevant issue during consultations and positive measures can be taken to improve the human rights situation of the country. On the other hand, the relations between the parties being conditional upon respect of human rights, it can be broken in case of a human rights violation (sanction based approach). The Commission has placed emphasis on the use of positive measures.[63] There is a gradual scale of measures that a country may adopt. The most serious measure is considered to be a trade embargo. Negative conditionality largely involves relations amongst governments, even though, once the negative measure has been applied, the main victim is often the population. Negative conditionality has turned out to be seriously limited in its application.[64] The EU will consider the taking of restrictive measures only when the EU's efforts to further respect for human rights through positive measures are unsuccessful, due to the lack of commitment on the part of the third country concerned,[65] such as the temporary withdrawal of access to the GSP from the Republic of Belarus.[66]

As stated above, the wording of human rights clauses usually makes a generic reference to respect for human rights. Some for the clauses also refer to the Universal Declaration of Human Rights. This brings up the problem of the identification of the human rights contained in the clause. According to Brandtner and Rosas the clause does not seek to establish new standards in the international protection of human rights. It simply

---

[63] *Promoting Human Rights, supra* Ch.4 n. 40, at 9.

[64] For a discussion of the application of negative conditionality see Fierro, *supra* Ch.1 n. 107.

[65] Resolution of The Council and of the Member States Meeting in the Council on Human Rights, Democracy and Development, 28 November 1991, *Bulletin of the European Communities* 1991, 122.

[66] Council Regulation (EC) 1933/2006 of 21 December 2006 Temporarily Withdrawing Access to the Generalised Tariff Preferences from the Republic of Belarus [2006] OJ L 405/35.

reaffirms existing commitments which, as general rules of customary international law, already bind all States and have a basic term of reference in the Universal Declaration of Human Rights.[67]

The repeated call for the principles of indivisibility and interdependence of all human rights points in the direction of the inclusion of economic and cultural rights on the same footing as civil political rights. This hypothesis is confirmed by the fact that, referring to the human rights clause, the Commission said that this clause also encompasses core labour standards,[68] as set out in the eight core ILO Conventions.[69]

The efficiency of human rights clauses in fostering human rights is not completely convincing. The first reason behind the limited success of human rights clauses is due to the technical specifications that in practice constrain the use of conditionality. The effectiveness of conditionality depends on the feasibility of the objectives, the proportionality of the envisaged measures, and the existence of credible indicators and supervisory mechanisms.[70] Another restriction weighing upon the use of conditionality is the identification of human rights themselves. For instance, when human rights are explicitly and concretely identified, they can be more easily implemented. On the other hand, in the case of broadly defined human rights, one may risk applying a minimum standard and overlooking many human rights violations.[71]

Secondly, the respect for more social oriented conditionality is less immediately acceptable for recipient countries.[72] Developing countries tended to

---

[67] Brandtner and Rosas, 'Human Rights and the External Relations', *supra* Ch.1 n. 97 at 472.

[68] Communication from the Commission to the Council, the European Parliament and the Economic and Social Committee, *Promoting Core Labour Standards and Improving Social Governance in the Context of Globalisation*, COM (2001) 416 final, 18 July 2001; Communication from the Commission, *The Trading System and Internationally Recognized Labour Standards*, COM (1996) 402 final, 24 July 1996.

[69] The same concept was expressed on occasion of the communication from the Commission to the Council on the trading System and Internationally recognised labour standards and the Opinion of the committee on Foreign Affairs, security and defence policy and in the *Report on the proposal for a Council Decision concerning the conclusion of the Framework Agreement for trade between the European Community and its member States, of the one part and the republic of South Korea on the other part*, COM (96) 0141- C4-0073/ 97 – 96/ 0098 (CNS), A4- 0445/ 98.

[70] See Fierro, *supra* Ch.1 n. 107, at 365.

[71] Ibid., at 370.

[72] D. Schmid, *The Use of Conditionality in Support of Political Economic and Social Rights: Unveiling the Euro-Mediterrean Partnership's True Hierarchy of Objectives?*, paper presented at the Fifth Mediterranean Social and Political Research Meeting of the Mediterranean Programme of the Robert Schuman Centre for Advanced Studies

regard social clauses with suspicion in the past, as they were used for protectionist purposes.[73] Even worse, the application of sanctions can have a detrimental effect on the population of third countries whose governments do not comply with social and human rights standards. Finally, political considerations can justify occasional or repeatedly refraining from using the sanctions as a response to the violation of a human rights clause. [74]

Having identified some of the potential risks of using human rights clauses to foster human rights in developing countries and in turn encouraging them to enforce human rights obligations on MNEs, however, two further observations should be made.

In the first place, the proposed use of human rights clauses is not envisaged as a substitute or replacement for measures addressed directly to MNEs (examined in Part II) or for enforcement through courts at the level of the host State. From the standpoint of international human rights law, it is less controversial to encourage governments to raise their human rights standards and ensure that MNEs comply with them. The classical scheme of States as primary addressees of international obligations will then be followed. Under customary international law, States have the sovereign right to grant access to their territory to foreign companies. The legality of the conduct of foreign companies operating within the national territory depends upon domestic laws and can be enforced by the host State. In this sense, the host State has the 'responsibility' to enforce human rights both in terms of 'primary rules', i.e. the obligation to ensure respect for human rights on its territory, and of 'secondary obligations' to provide remedies and reparation to the victims.[75] Therefore, it is argued that EU measures have the potential to encourage developing countries to put their legislation in line with international human rights standards and to strengthen the political and judicial institutions necessary for their enforcement.

In the second place, it should be pointed out that the criticisms on human rights clauses converge upon their lax monitoring system or their politically distorted implementation, rather than on their effectiveness.[76]

---

at the European University Institute, Florence and Montecatini Terme, 24–28 March 2004. Workshop No. 14 'Economic and Social Rights in the Euro-Mediterranean Area and the Impact of the Euro-Mediterranean Free Trade Areas', jointly organized with the Euro-Mediterranean Human Rights Network (EMHRN), at 29.

[73]   P. Alston, 'Linking Trade and Human Rights' (1980) 23 *German Yearbook of International Law* 127, at 131.

[74]   Fierro, *supra* Ch.1 n. 107, at 109.

[75]   Francioni, 'Alternative Perspectives', *supra* Ch.1 n. 71.

[76]   Fierro, *supra* Ch.1 n. 107, at 325ff. For an extensive overview of the concept of conditionality, see O. Stokke (ed.), *Aid and Political Conditionality,* 1995, London, Frank Cass.

It can be concluded that promoting MNEs compliance with human rights in developing countries through the use of human rights clauses is partially hampered by the shortcomings inherent to conditionality. In particular, the effectiveness of conditionality could be improved by setting credible indicators and supervisory mechanisms. Another way forward is a move beyond the human rights clauses debate and finding and exploring new approaches to pursue a more systematic approach to the promotion of human rights.[77]

7.5 NON-REGULATORY INSTRUMENTS: INCENTIVE MEASURES AND THE INVOLVEMENT OF NGOs IN DEVELOPMENT AND COOPERATION

The EU has recently taken up the suggestion of both enhancing traditional instruments for the promotion of human rights, such as linking compliance with human rights to trade access and development aid, together with developing new approaches, such as the involvement of private and local actors in promoting the respect for human rights. Consideration of these mechanisms is in line with other recent initiatives, such as the UN Global Compact and the UN Norms for Transnational Corporations; the revision of the OECD Guidelines and the ILO Tripartite Declaration of Principles Concerning Multinational Enterprises and Social Policy.

The positive interrelation between development and the promotion of human rights in third countries in the context of EU trade and development cooperation policies was recognized for the first time in the Communication on the promotion of human rights and democratisation.[78] This document contains an express reference to the role of companies, since European MNEs were called upon to use their influence within developing countries 'to support rather than undermine that country's own effort to achieve sustainable development'.[79]

This approach was further spelt out in the Communication 'Promoting Core Labour Standards and Improving Social Governance in the Context of Globalisation.'[80] The use of bilateral dialogue with developing coun-

---

[77]   European University Institute, *supra* Ch.4 n. 26, at 60.

[78]   See *Promoting Human Rights, supra* Ch.4 n. 40.

[79]   Ibid., at 9.

[80]   *Promoting Core Labour Standards, supra* n. 68 in particular, the basic tenets of the EU approach are set out in para. 3 and further action at the European Union and international level at para. 5.

tries, of development assistance to build capacity, and of additional trade incentives under the GSP where countries comply with minimum social standards were envisaged.

More recently, it has been recognized that the private sector and Multinational Enterprises, in particular, can play a key role in poverty reduction, which currently constitutes the central aim of EU development policy, fully in line with the UN Millennium Declaration. In September 2002 the Commission issued a communication on trade and development,[81] which defined the importance of the relationship between trade, development and the integration of developing countries in the world economy. The communication conceives several measures aimed at improving the delivery of trade related assistance in key areas and at enhancing coordination and coherence within the EU and with international organizations. The overall objective is to help developing countries to acquire the expertise necessary to deal with the challenges of global trade and, by the same token, to improve their institutional regulatory capacity. In this context, the importance for developing countries to improve the investment climate for the business sector has been underlined. Technical assistance and sharing of 'best practices' are seen as key tools to achieve the objective set out in the communication.[82]

Probably the most innovative contribution to this debate is to be found in the Communication on Participation of Non-state actors in EC Development Policy.[83] The definition of Non-state actors includes: 'Non-Governmental Organisations/Community Based Organisations and their representative platforms in different sectors, social partners (trade unions, employers associations), private sector associations and business organisations, associations of churches and confessional movements, universities, cultural associations, media.'[84] The relevance of this communication lies in the fact that not only does it reiterate[85] the relevance of all the

---

[81] Communication from the Commission to the Council and the European Parliament, Trade and Development Assisting Developing Countries to Benefit from Trade of 18 September 2002 com (2002) 513 final.

[82] *Roundtable on the Development Aspects of Corporate Social Responsibility*, available at: http://forum.europa.eu.int/irc/empl/csr_eu_multi_stakeholder_ forum/info/data/en/CSR Forum roundtables meetings.htm (accessed 23 March 2006).

[83] *Participation of Non State Actors*, supra n. 3.

[84] Ibid.

[85] Communication from the Commission to the Council, the European Parliament and the Economic and Social Committee, *Towards a Global Partnership for Sustainable Development*, COM (2002) 82 final, 13 February 2002.

components of civil society to contribute to development, but it also sets out the basic components of its involvement in practice.

Finally, it is recognized that civil society, NGOs and trade unions can play an essential role in raising awareness on respect of fundamental rights and promoting compliance with Corporate Social Responsibility principles by monitoring corporate practice on the ground.[86] In many developing countries, however, 'civil society' is not yet fully-fledged, and constraints on workers' rights and freedom of association often undermine, or indeed impede, the functioning of trade unions.[87]

Recent EC documents show that a renewed attention is paid to the co-responsibility of host States in implementation of development policy. Great emphasis has been placed on dialogue with civil society in developing countries and capacity building by providing technical assistance. The development of partnerships with private sector and civil society has become a key feature of the EU energy initiative, as has the improvement of partnerships both between the public and private sectors in developing countries and between the private sectors of developing countries and EU countries. While the first type of partnership will strengthen the role of developing country governments, the second can contribute to sharing of best practice and the involvement of the local private sector in development. Nonetheless, the potential of partnerships between the public sector and private sector has not been fully explored to date. There are only limited examples of the involvement of the private sector in the development of national strategies for sustainable development and poverty reduction[88] especially in developing countries.[89]

In addition to this, both NGOs and companies in developing countries lack information on the responsibility of MNEs, more in particular on their detrimental effects on the enjoyment of human rights, such as fundamental social rights, the right to health and the right to life. This is partially due to the fact that a connection between MNEs and human rights has not been sufficiently addressed and clarified. Another problem arises in relation to the methods of monitoring compliance with human

---

[86]   Fox and Ward, *supra* n. 13, at 59.

[87]   Ibid., at 24.

[88]   T. Fox et al., *Public Sector Roles in Strengthening Corporate Social Responsibility: a Baseline Study*, The World Bank (October 2002), at 22.

[89]   Ibid., at 34: a brief account of the United Nations Industrial Development Organisation (UNIDO) Partnership Programme. The Programme aims at enhancing quality, competitiveness and efficiency of small and medium enterprises in developing countries, through the creation of multi-party partnerships and cooperation between public and private sector actors.

rights. By raising awareness on the human rights obligations of MNEs in developing countries, a closer scrutiny directly at the level of host States can be ensured. In turn, the measures aimed at raising the level of compliance with human rights in developing countries could count on a more receptive and better informed civil society.

The use of incentive measures such as technical assistance, institution building, strengthening of civil society and partnerships, however, could be particularly effective in addressing challenges specific to enhancing the scrutiny of MNEs in developing countries.

One of the most frequent objections in relation to MNEs' responsibility for human rights is that stakeholders in developing countries have perceived their role as the objects more than the active participants of these initiatives.[90] Developing countries, indeed, are rarely involved in defining both the policies and human rights standards, which are drawn up by international bodies such at the European Union.[91]

In conclusion, a strategy of bilateral dialogue with governments of developing countries, combined with the support of an active role of civil society in awareness raising and scrutiny of MNEs' misdeeds, as well as promoting compliance with human rights standards directly at the level of the host State of an MNE, can also contribute to avoiding allegations of abuse of human rights standards for protectionist purposes or of new colonialism by imposing European values on third countries.

7.6 CONCLUSIONS

This chapter argued that there are different ways in which external relations instruments can be used with a view to encouraging the raising of human rights standards in third countries by imposing indirect obligations on MNEs.

The main objections relating to the use of the EU's external instruments to promote human rights in third countries have been addressed. As far as the EC/EU's powers in the field of human rights are concerned, it was submitted that if EU institutions need to respect human rights because those provisions are general principles of EC law which the court upholds, they also need to have the legal tools to ensure such respect within its policies. While the introduction of human rights concerns into development cooperation and cooperation agreements is expressly foreseen by the TEC, the

---

[90]   Ibid., at 58.
[91]   Ibid., at 32.

introduction of development considerations in trade agreements has been upheld, under certain conditions, by the ECJ. On the other hand, despite the Court's negative opinion on the EC's accession to the ECHR, the possibility for the EC/EU to become party to international agreements which have human rights as their main objectives cannot be entirely ruled out, in view of increasing EC/EU powers in fields related to human rights such as non-discrimination.

An overview of the instruments available to the external relations of the EC/EU for the promotion of human rights in third countries was provided. In examining these instruments, preference has been given to EC measures over CFSP ones. It was submitted that CFSP measures have a more political character in this field and remain at policy consideration, rather than addressing MNEs' compliance with human rights.

Among EC measures, a distinction was made between regulatory measures, such as human rights clauses and GSP special arrangements on human rights, and non-regulatory measures, such as incentive measures included in assistance programmes, strengthening civil society in developing countries and raising awareness on MNEs' responsibility.

The linkage between compliance with human rights to trade access and development aid has been one of the underlying principles of the EU's human rights policy. The main tool for the promotion of human rights in the external relations of the European Union has been the use of conditionality, both in its negative and positive aspects. Human rights clauses have been included in EC external agreements, as well as in EC unilateral instruments. Nonetheless, it was pointed out that promoting MNEs' compliance with human rights in developing countries through the use of human rights clauses is partially hindered by the weaknesses inherent to conditionality. In particular, it was submitted that credible indicators and supervisory mechanisms can improve the effective use of conditionality. In addition, the arguments in favour of a closer linkage between the EC's external human rights activities and international human rights law, developed in Part II, should be recalled here. In the context of the use of conditionality, anchoring the EU's human rights activities to international human rights law, can contribute to overcoming the allegations of particularism and of promoting European rather than universal human rights.[92] Finally, the possibility of moving beyond the human rights clause debate and finding new approaches, while improving the existing human rights clauses in EU agreements with a view to pursue a more systematic approach to the promotion of human rights, should be explored.

---

[92]   Leino, 'European Universalism', *supra* Ch.4 n. 108, 239–301.

Non-regulatory instruments for the promotion of MNEs' compliance with human rights have a shorter history in the EC's external relations. From the standpoint of the regulatory versus non-regulatory debate, delineated in Part I, it can be concluded that the EU's external relations have for some time experienced regulatory mechanisms (such as conditionality) for the promotion of human rights and placed the burden of compliance with these rights on States. Only recently has the EU drawn attention to the potential of voluntary mechanisms for the promotion of human rights. By the same token, the influence of non-state actors, and in particular MNEs, on the respect and fulfilment of these rights has been progressively recognized. The most recent Commission communications suggest the positive involvement of non-state actors, such as MNEs, in development cooperation. In addition, the EU's strategy for the promotion of Corporate Social Responsibility emphasizes the role of non regulatory initiatives and it suggests reliance on 'international soft law' instruments at the external level.

In summary, despite their deficiencies, there are different ways in which external relations instruments can be used with a view to encouraging the raising of human rights standards in third countries by imposing indirect obligations on MNEs. The following chapters provide a closer examination on the effectiveness of examining how and to what extent regulatory and non-regulatory instruments available to the EC's external relations for the promotion of human rights could be used with a view to enhancing the scrutiny of MNEs in host States. A distinction will be made between development and cooperation programmes – such as MEDA, TACIS, ALA the Cotonou Agreement and the EIDHR – and trade-related measures, such as the GSP Regulation. The analysis will focus on three aspects: the relevance given to human rights and social rights in the legal texts; the effectiveness of assistance and trade conditionality to raise human rights standards; and the strengthening of NGOs and civil society in developing countries.

8 Measures addressed to host States in the development and cooperation of the European Union

8.1 INTRODUCTION

One of the main objectives of the EC/EU's development and cooperation is raising the human rights records of countries which are generally host States of European MNEs. As explained in Chapter 7, raising the human rights obligations of *host States* can encourage them to indirectly enforce human rights obligations on MNEs. In addition, through technical assistance and targeted projects, the EU can help developing countries in creating a civil society which can be more critical to the behaviour of MNEs on their territories.

Chapter 8 attempts to identify the ways in which both human rights conditionality and incentive measures are used to encourage scrutiny of MNEs by developing countries' governments and civil society, with particular reference to the main development assistance programmes between the European Union and Mediterranean countries, Asian and Latin American countries (ALA), Eastern European countries, ACP countries. The analysis also includes the projects funded through the EIDHR,[1] as they complement the funding of cooperation assistance of the regional programmes examined. In this perspective, three parameters will be taken into account: the relevance given to human rights and social rights in the Regulations and the Agreements that provide the legal basis of the assistance programmes; the distribution of funding; and the measures aimed at strengthening the role of NGOs and civil society in developing countries.

As mentioned in the previous chapter, the current development policy of the European Union is based on Articles 11 of the EU Treaty and 177 of the EC Treaty. Article 11 demands that the common foreign and

---

[1] Regulation (EC) 1889/2006 of the European Parliament and of the Council of 20 December 2006 on Establishing a Financing Instrument for the Promotion of Democracy and Human Rights Worldwide [2006] OJ L 386/129.

security policy aim to develop and consolidate democracy and the rule of law, and respect for human rights and fundamental freedoms. Article 177 clearly sets out the objectives of development cooperation as the sustainable economic and social development of developing countries and, in particular, the most disadvantaged among them; the smooth and gradual integration of developing countries' development and consolidation of democracy and the rule of law, respect for human rights and fundamental freedoms. Moreover, pursuant to Article 178,[2] the Community must take these objectives into account in all policies which are likely to affect developing countries. Concrete programmes found their legal basis in EC legislation, unilateral regulations, association and other agreements and related financial protocols. It must be added that Article 181a, inserted by the Treaty of Nice, introduces a new category of cooperation agreements to be concluded both with developing and developed countries.

At present Community assistance and cooperation is delivered through a range of regional instruments, for example TACIS, MEDA, ALA and a substantial number of thematic instruments, such as the European Initiative for Democracy and Human Rights. Although for the purpose of this chapter these programs will be examined, it is worth mentioning that a reform has recently been undertaken by the European Commission with a view to streamlining the financial instruments for the delivery of external assistance.[3] According to this reform four new instruments, namely an instrument for Pre-Accession Assistance,[4] a European Neighbourhood and Partnership Instrument,[5] a Development Cooperation and Economic Cooperation Instrument,[6] and an Instrument for Stability,[7] have been added to the existing instruments for Humanitarian Aid and for Macro

---

[2]   Replaced, in substance, by the second sentence of the second subparagraph of para. 1 of Art. 188D, Treaty of Lisbon.

[3]   Communication from the Commission to the Council and the European Parliament on the Instruments for External Assistance under the Future Financial Perspective, 2007-2013, COM (2004) 626 final, Brussels, 29 September 2004.

[4]   Council Regulation (EC) 1085/2006 establishing an Instrument for Pre-Accession Assistance (IPA) for Community assistance to candidate and potential candidate countries OJ L 210/82, 31 July 2006.

[5]   Regulation (EC) 1638/2006 establishing a European Neighbourhood and Partnership Instrument (ENPI) providing direct support for the EU's European Neighbourhood Policy OJ L 310/1, 9 November 2006.

[6]   Regulation (EC) No 1905/2006 of the European Parliament and of the Council of 18 December 2006 establishing a financing instrument for development cooperation OJ L 378, 27 December 2006, 41–71.

[7]   Regulation (EC) 1717/2006 establishing a Financing Instrument for Stability OJ L 327/1, 24 November 2006.

Financial Assistance, which are not in need of modification.[8] As it will be analyzed below, reference to human rights as a general objective as well as a funding priority have generally been reinforced in these new instruments.

8.2   THE MEDA PROGRAMME

The respect for human rights and fundamental freedoms constitutes an essential element of the MEDA Regulation,[9] the violation of which will justify the adoption of appropriate measures. As noted,[10] this human rights clause contains a general reference to human rights as such, but it is not reinforced by an express reference to specific human rights instruments such as the ICESCR.

The relevance of the economic and social dimension is repeatedly stressed throughout the Regulation. As noted by Schmid,[11] between MEDA I and MEDA II the attention to social issues has been expanded.[12] The development of economic and social cooperation, taking due account of the human and cultural dimension and of achieving 'long-term stability and prosperity, in particular in the fields of economic transition, sustainable economic and social development and regional and cross-border cooperation'[13] is listed among the objectives of the Regulation. Practical

---

[8]   The Humanitarian Aid instrument and Macro Financial Assistance will remain unchanged except that all Food Aid of a humanitarian nature will be included under Humanitarian Aid instead of being dealt with under a separate Regulation.

[9]   Council Regulation (EC) 1488/96 of 23 July 1996 on Financial measures to accompany (MEDA) the reform of economic and social structures in the framework of the Euro-Mediterranean partnership OJ L 189/1, 30 July 1996. Modified by Council Regulation (EC) 2698/2000 of the November 2000 amending regulation (EC) 1488/96 of 23 July 1996 on Financial measures to accompany (MEDA) the reform of economic and social structures in the framework of the Euro-Mediterranean partnership OJ L 311/1, 12 December 2000.

[10]   Fierro, *supra* Ch.1 n. 107, at 357.

[11]   See Schmid, *supra* Ch.7 n. 72.

[12]   Art. 1, as amended in 2000, reads as follows:

1. The Community shall implement measures in the framework of the principles and priorities of the Euro-Mediterranean partnership to support the efforts that Mediterranean non-member countries and territories listed in Annex I (hereinafter referred to as 'Mediterranean partner') will undertake to reform their economic and social structures, improve conditions for the underprivileged and mitigate any social or environmental consequences which may result from economic development.

[13]   Art. 2 MEDA Regulation, *supra* n. 9.

measures for the enhancement of social conditions, such as the improvement of social services, especially in the area of health, the fight against poverty, the strengthening of democracy and respect for human rights are described in detail in Annex II of the MEDA Regulation. These interventions take the form of an adjustment mechanism covering various sectors such as health and education.

Aid is also targeted at the most vulnerable social groups through specific actions to encourage social and economic stability and cohesion. Social rights concerns, in particular, are enshrined by means of interventions in all fields of the social sector. Development projects which support the rights to education, to health, the environment and rural development are currently financed by 41 per cent of the total budget of MEDA.[14] Support for economic transition and the development of the private sector amounts to 30 per cent.[15]

It has been pointed out,[16] however, that the social dimension plays an ancillary role *vis-à-vis* political and economic stability, rather that operating on its own merits. Although the support for social and economic equilibrium in Mediterranean countries is included among the main areas of intervention of the MEDA programme under bilateral cooperation,[17] these interventions are indeed aimed at reducing the adverse effect of economic transition and strengthening political stability.

Even if it is premature to assess the impact of many of the current projects, some general conclusion can be drawn from previous evaluations of EU development aid in the Mediterranean region. According to an evaluation carried out by the Commission in 1998, over the first three years of the MEDA programme a distinct lack of human rights focus was observed. Similarly, the MEDA contribution to economic and social

---

[14] For 2000–06, the MEDA programme was endowed with €5350 million in the Community budget accompanied by substantial lending from the European Investment Bank which amounted to €6.400 million for the period 2002–07.

[15] Sources available at http://europa.eu.int/comm/ (accessed 14 April 2004).

[16] I. Byrne, *Placing Economic Social and Cultural Rights at the Heart of the Euro Mediterranean Partnership*, Paper presented at the Fifth Mediterranean Social and Political Research Meeting of the Mediterranean Programme of the Robert Schuman Centre for Advanced Studies at the European University Institute, Florence and Montecatini Terme, 24–28 March 2004, Workshop No. 14 'Economic and Social Rights in the Euro-Mediterranean Area and the Impact of the Euro-Mediterranean Free Trade Areas', jointly organized with the Euro–Mediterranean Human Rights Network (EMHRN), at 15.

[17] European Commission, *Report from the Commission to the Council and the European Parliament, Parliament Annual Report of the MEDA programme 2000*, Brussels, COM (2001).

development and stability has been rather modest.[18] Moreover, further coordination among poverty, gender, environment and trade and structural adjustment policy should be attained.

The participation of NGOs in the partnership and strengthening of civil society in the region is expressly mentioned only with reference to increased environmental awareness and initiatives at a national level.[19] The importance accorded to NGOs, both in the identification of projects and in their implementation, has been strengthened in the context of the Commission Communication of 2003 on *Reinvigorating European Actions on Human Rights and Democratisation with Mediterranean Partners*[20] which aims at maximizing the effectiveness of the instruments at the disposal of the EU and its Mediterranean partners in the field of human rights and democracy. Reference is also made to a better use of the institutions for dialogue such as the association councils and the EC delegations.

It seems that the integration of the MEDA programme in the European Neighbourhood and Partnership Instrument[21] will correct a number of the shortcomings related to the prominence given to human rights and democratic principles and to the implementation of the programmes.[22] Human rights are referred to in the preamble of the Regulation[23] in its Article 1(3) as the values on which the EU is founded. Failure to observe these values may

---

[18]   T. Schumacher, *Survival of the Fittest: the First Five Years of the Euro-Mediterranean Economic Relations*, EUI Working Paper RSCAS (2004), at 13.

[19]   Euro–Med Partnership, *Regional Strategy Paper 2002–06 & Regional Indicative Programme 2002–2004*, at 29–30.

[20]   Communication from the Commission to the Council and the European Parliament Reinvigorating *EU Actions on Human Rights and Democratisation with Mediterranean Partners, Strategic Guidelines*, COM (2003) 294 final, Brussels, 21 May 2003. The communication sets out working guidelines to promote Human Rights and fundamental freedoms in co-operation with the Mediterranean partners. It proposes 10 concrete recommendations to improve the political dialogue between the EU and its Mediterranean partners, as well as EU financial cooperation on Human Rights issues. Their implementation will be enhanced by three levels of complementarity: between the political dialogue and financial assistance, between the MEDA programme and assistance under the European Initiative for Democracy and Human Rights (EIDHR), and finally between the national and regional dimensions.

[21]   Regulation (EC) 1638/2006 of the European Parliament and of the Council of 24 October 2006 Laying Down General Provisions Establishing a European Neighbourhood and Partnership Instrument [2006] OJ L 310/1.

[22]   K.E. Smith, 'The Outsiders: The European Neighbourhood Policy' (2005) 81/4 *International Affairs*, 757, at 765.

[23]   Regulation (EC) 1638/2006, Indent (4), *supra* n. 21.

lead to the suspension of EU's assistance.[24] Social rights and human rights are expressly mentioned as the objectives of EU assistance.[25] In the context of the Communication and of the Strategy Paper on Neighbourhood Policy, human rights are referred to as 'shared values' whose effective implementation of such commitments is an essential element in the EU's relations with partners. Strengthening democracy and the rule of law, the reform of the judiciary and respect of human rights and fundamental freedoms, gender equality, trade union rights and other core labour standards; support for the development of civil society; and co-operation are set as priorities intended to strengthen commitment to human rights.[26]

Although the emphasis on human rights, the promotion of gender equality and NGOs can contribute to raising human rights and social rights in the Mediterranean countries, a distinct lack of measures addressed to MNEs' behaviour can be noted. Despite the fact that the encouragement of trade and investment is one of the priorities of the EU's cooperation with Mediterranean countries, the issue of MNEs' compliance with human rights in their activities has not been introduced in the context of the MEDA Regulation, nor in the Regional Strategy Paper. It is regrettable, for instance, that no mention is made of raising awareness on MNEs' compliance with international human rights instruments, neither in the context of political dialogue with governments, nor within the so called 'people to people' projects which aim at an exchange of knowledge between individuals and companies from the EU and Mediterranean countries.

8.3   THE TACIS PROGRAMME

The TACIS programme[27] (which will be replaced by the European Neighbourhood and Partnership instrument) had the objectives of promoting the transition to a market economy and reinforcing democracy and the rule of law in partner States. The 1996 TACIS Regulation[28]

---

24   Ibid. Art. 28.

25   Ibid., Art. 2(2) i and k.

26   Communication from the Commission, *European Neighbourhood Policy. Strategy Paper* COM (2004) 373 final, at 13.

27   Created in 1991, it provides assistance to Armenia, Azerbaijan, Belarus, Georgia, Kazakhstan, Kyrgyz Republic, Moldova, Russian Federation, Tajikistan, Turkmenistan, Ukraine and Uzbekistan.

28   Council Regulation (EC, EURATOM) 99/2000 of 29 December 1999 Concerning the Provision of Assistance to the Partner States in Eastern Europe and Central Asia, [2000] OJ L 12/1. It provides assistance to Armenia, Azerbaijan,

contained a suspension human rights clause.[29] Thus, when an essential element for the continuation of cooperation is missing, the Council may, on a proposal from the Commission and acting by qualified majority, decide upon appropriate measures.[30] The 2000 Regulation subsequently introduced positive measures in support of human rights and democracy.[31] In addition to a general reference to respect for human rights, minority rights and the rights of indigenous people,[32] the preamble also explicitly refers to social rights concerns by stating that 'The long-term sustainability of reform will require due emphasis on the social aspects of reform and the development of the civil society'. Article 2(6) recognizes that the programme should be implemented through 'Measures which take into account the following criteria: the need for sustainable economic development, the social impact of reform measures, the promotion of equal opportunities for women, the sustainable use of natural resources and respect for the environment'.[33]

Similarly to the MEDA programme, assistance to the efforts of moving from centrally planned to market economies was understood as a reinforcing factor for democracy. However, Article 3(3) acknowledges that special attention should be paid to the social aspects of transition.

It has been recognized that across the board there has been little real progress towards democratization and respect for human rights in the region. On the contrary, a tendency toward increased authoritarianism,

---

Belarus, Georgia, Kazakhstan, Kyrgyz Republic, Moldova, Russian Federation, Tajikistan, Turkmenistan, Ukraine and Uzbekistan.

[29]   Article 3 (11) stated as follows 'When an essential element for the continuation of co-operation though assistance is missing, in particular in cases of violation of democratic principles and human rights, the Council may on a proposal from the Commission, acting by qualified majority, decide upon appropriate measures concerning assistance to a partner State'.

[30]   The clause was implemented in the case of Belarus. See E. Fierro, *supra* n. 107, at 369.

[31]   See Arts 1 and 2 of Regulation 99/2000.

[32]   Preamble at recital 5.

[33]   These measures are spelled out in Annex II as support for the reform of the health, pension, social protection and insurance system; assistance to alleviate the social impact of industrial restructuring by the development of employment services and retraining. Other measures relate to the reform of the institutional legal and administrative systems. They include, *inter alia*, support for the implementation of international commitments, the strengthening of civil society, education and training. The financial reference amount for the six years considered was €3138 billion. Each year the budgetary authority decides on the annual appropriations within the limits of the Union's financial perspective. EU assistance is generally provided in the form of grants.

with administrative and judicial systems which can be arbitrary and corrupt had been noted.[34] Civil society remains weak, and the marginalisation of women has increased in the region. It is also true that TACIS projects contributed to a certain extent to promoting the democratisation of the partner countries by encouraging a pluralistic society through exchange programmes and support to NGOs.

TACIS had a distinct focus on support of investment in the region.[35] In addition to technical assistance, two programmes targeted on companies operating in New Independent States were foreseen: the Managers Training Programme and the Small and Medium-sized Enterprises Investment Support Programme. The former provided training in EU companies, together with seminars on management issues and practices, EU Business and industrial policies and EU integration, in order to develop a business management capacity and a management training capacity in the Newely Indipendent States. The Small and Medium-sized Enterprises Investment Support Programme offered advice and assistance to Small and Medium-sized Enterprises in relation to the development of business and financing plans, effective implementation of sound management rules, as well as providing local and financial intermediaries with training on risk evaluation for Small and Medium-sized Enterprises, monitoring and portfolio management.[36]

As in the case of the MEDA programme, the linkage between the promotion of economic activities, in particular of investment, and the promotion of human rights in the context of development and cooperation was largely overlooked. From the standpoint of the recently proclaimed commitment to fostering human rights in developing countries and (more recently) mainstreaming CSR in all EC policies, it would have been desirable for investment programmes to include the issue of the responsibility of MNEs for the respect of human rights.

In the context of the European Neighbourhood Policy,[37] the role of human rights and the rule of law has been emphasized also in relation

---

[34] This web-based consultation is in addition to the informal consultation of EU Member/acceding States, key MEPs and partner States during the first quarter of 2004, available at: http://ec.europa.eu/comm/external_relations/consultations/cswp_tacis.htm (accessed 9 September 2006).

[35] Technical assistance and investment related assistance amounted to €23.1 millions for the period 2000–02. See *Tacis Regional Cooperation: Strategy Paper and Indicative Programme 2004–2006*, adopted by the European Commission on 11 April 2003, at 11.

[36] Ibid.

[37] General Provisions Establishing a European Neighbourhood and Partnership Instrument, *supra* n. 21.

towards the Eastern neighbours.[38] The priority cooperation sectors in this area, however, will remain cooperation on business employment and social policy.[39] The new European Neighbourhood Policy, however, seems to provide a margin for the improvement of the role of NGOs and civil society, which is extremely relevant to improving scrutiny over MNEs' respect for fundamental rights.

Taking into account the limited impact of TACIS on raising human rights in recipient countries, cooperation with Eastern neighbours should be reshaped with a view to further strengthening the relevance of human rights in the context of the European Neighbourhood and Partnership Instrument.[40] In particular, attention should be rebalanced in favour of social rights and labour rights. It is also suggested that future assistance programmes are reshaped in such a way that the MNEs' responsibilities for human rights are specifically addressed. For instance, since one of the priorities indicated in the strategy papers of 2006[41] is the promotion of trade and investment flows, technical assistance in this sector should be used to channel awareness on the human rights obligations of MNEs.

8.4   THE ALA PROGRAMME

The ALA Regulation[42] emphasized human rights by including a political commitment to their protection, a human rights clause comprising both positive and negative measures and the possibility of granting funds for the promotion of human rights and democratic principles.

The Regulation emphasized the important role that positive initiatives in relation to human rights and fundamental freedoms can play as preconditions for real and lasting economic and social development.[43] The priorities of financial and technical assistance, listed in Article 5, included

---

[38]   See M. Cremona, 'The European Neighbourhood Policy: Partnership, Security and the Rule of Law', in N. Copsey and A. Mayhew (eds), *Ukraine and the European Neighbourhood Policy*, 2006, Brighton, Sussex European Institute.

[39]   Communication from the Commission European Neighbourhood Policy. *Strategy Paper,* COM (2004) 373 final, at 21.

[40]   General Provisions Establishing a European Neighbourhood and Partnership Instrument, *supra* n. 21.

[41]   Communication from the Commission to the Council and the European Parliament on *Strengthening the European Neighbourhood Policy* COM (2006) 726 final, 4 December 2006.

[42]   The ALA Regulation, *supra* Ch.7 n. 59.

[43]   See Arts 1 and 2, ALA Regulation.

food, security and the environment. It was also stated that all cooperation projects should take into account the human and cultural dimension of development. The protection of special groups, such as women, children and ethnic minorities is given autonomous relevance.

The Latin America Regional Strategy Document for 2002–06[44] confirmed strengthening the partnership of civil society networks and the fight against social inequality as the top two priorities of cooperation in the region which will amount to respectively 60–70 per cent and 15–20 per cent of the budget. The support of civil society has been fostered through horizontal programmes and through the creation of networks which enable the actors in Latin America and in EU Member States to transfer know-how in economic and commercial fields, as well as in other fields, such as culture and education.

Similarly to TACIS, ALA foresaw programmes addressed directly to companies operating both in the EU and Latin America. For instance, €43 million was allocated in 1999 to the program AL-INVEST II, which was intended to encourage relations between companies in the EU and in Latin America.[45] Similarly, ATLAS (duration 2001–03), a project with an allocation of €2.4 million, supports relations between Chambers of Commerce in both regions and was designed to facilitate the transfer of know-how between the 200 chambers of commerce concerned.

As far as cooperation with Asia is concerned, the Commission reaffirmed its intention to strengthen the role of human rights in its cooperation with this region.[46] This priority was not mirrored by the distribution of assistance. According to the Regional Strategy Paper, cooperation with Asia focuses on financial and technical assistance and economic cooperation, which amounts to €380 million altogether.[47] This allocation of resources, however, was counterbalanced by a number of projects targeted on the promotion of human rights in this region, which were funded directly by the EIDHR. In addition, the latest Regional Strategy Paper devotes particular attention to the least developed countries in the region, with programs designed to reduce poverty.

---

[44] *Latin America Regional Strategy Document for 2002-2006*, adopted by the European Commission in April 2002.

[45] Ibid., at 14.

[46] In the Communication *A New Partnership with South East Asia* COM (2003) 399 final, Brussels, 9 July 2003, the Commission suggests to include a human rights 'essential element clause' in all future cooperation agreements with Asian countries and to launch human rights specific dialogues, at 15–16.

[47] *Strategy Paper and Indicative Programme for Multi-Country Programmes in Asia 2005–2006*, at 13.

In conclusion, while ALA placed attention on antidiscrimination initiatives, social rights, whose enforcement should go hand in hand with the opening to foreign investment, are overlooked. Moreover, ALA, similarly to MEDA and TACIS, did not show any specific recognition of the linkage between the activities of MNEs and the necessity of ensuring respect for human rights. The programmes aimed at enhancing ALA countries' capacity to attract foreign investment did not take into due account the possible risks related to the inflow of foreign companies into the regions concerned. Such an approach is in contrast with the EC's recent step in favour of promoting the OECD Guidelines for Multinational Enterprises in Latin America and in developing countries in other regions, in the context of bilateral agreements. In the EC Association Agreement with Chile, for instance, the Community and Chile jointly reminded their multinational enterprises to observe the OECD Guidelines for Multinational Enterprises. According to the Commission a similar clause will be included in all future association agreements with developing countries.[48]

It was noted that in view of enhancing the scrutiny over MNEs, the human rights dimension of development and cooperation with Latin America and Asia should have been reinforced, with particular reference to social rights. In addition, the development and cooperation instruments in these regions should include MNEs' compliance with human rights as one of the essential aspects of social and economic development. Therefore, not only should this issue be more strongly recognized in the context of bilateral agreements, but awareness on this issue should have been fostered through existing investment programmes in these regions.

Regulation (EC) No 1905/2006 takes into account some of these concerns. The Regulation reinforced its references to human rights that are mentioned in the preamble[49] as well as among the objectives[50] and the general principles.[51] Promotion of human rights and support for civil society are indicates as specific areas of intervention of the thematic programmes.[52] What is of greatest relevance here is that here CSR has been included among the priorities of the programmes supporting trade and regional integration. Article 5(2)m includes support for measures: 'sup-

---

[48] *EU Annual Report on Human Rights 2003*, at 28.
[49] Intents 1, 6, 11 of the Preamble of Regulation (EC) No 1905/2006, *supra* n. 6.
[50] Ibid. Art. 2(1).
[51] Ibid. Art 3(1), (3).
[52] Ibid. Art 5(2) e, f, g.

porting economic and trade cooperation and strengthening investment relations between the Community and partner countries and regions, including by actions to promote and ensure that private actors, including local and European businesses contribute to socially responsible and sustainable economic development, including respect for the core labour standards of the International Labour Organization (ILO) and by actions to promote local capacity building',[53]

8.5   THE COTONOU AGREEMENT

The Cotonou Agreement of 23 June 2000,[54] which replaced the Lomé Conventions,[55] provides the legal basis for the relations between the European Union and developing countries in Africa, the Caribbean and Pacific.[56] The Cotonou Agreement aims to improve the economic, social and cultural development of ACP countries and to contribute to peace, security and a stable democratic environment.[57]

The Cotonou Agreement introduced significant changes as a response to the disappointing outcome of the Lomé Conventions[58] and led to the incorporation in the EC Treaty of a new set of Articles on development.[59]

---

[53]   Ibid. Art 5(2) m.

[54]   *Supra* Ch.1 n. 108

[55]   The cooperation with the ACP countries started with the signing of the Treaty of Rome in 1957 which made provision for the association of the Overseas Countries and Territories with the EC as it was then. In 1963, the first cooperation agreement was signed under the name of Yaoundé, which was renewed in 1969. Following the accession of the UK in 1973, a new agreement, the Lomé Convention was signed in 1975 (which included certain Commonwealth countries). It was renewed in 1979, 1984 and 1990.

[56]   The Cotonou Agreement was signed by 77 States: 48 countries of Sub-Sahara Africa; 15 countries of the Caribbean; and 14 Countries of the Pacific which includes the 6 new Pacific members of Palau, The Federated States of Micronesia, The Republic of the Marshall Islands, Nauru, Niue and the Cook Islands Council Decision of 21 June 2005 concerning the signing, on behalf of the European Community, of the Agreement amending the Partnership Agreement between the members of the African, Caribbean and Pacific Group of States (ACP), of the one part, and the European Community and its Member States, of the other part, signed in Cotonou on 23 June 2000 (The Cotonou Agreement) OJ L 209/1, 11 August 2005.

[57]   Ibid., Art. 1.

[58]   C. Cosgrove, 'Has the Lomé Convention Failed ACP Trade?' (1994) 48 *Journal of International Affairs* 223.

[59]   Title XX on development and in particular Art. 177 TEC.

A human rights clause was introduced for the first time into the body of the text in the Fourth Lomé Convention[60]of 1989. This provision was replaced by an essential element clause as a result of the 'Mid term review'[61] of the Fourth Lomè Convention. In both the Conventions, social rights were placed on the same footing as civil and political rights[62] and both preambles referred to the ICCPR and to the ICESCR as the main instruments of international human rights law.[63] The Convention went on to list a variety of social rights in areas such as environmental protection, rural promotion,[64] cultural development,[65] education and training,[66] advancement of women[67] and access to health care.[68]

The recognition of human rights is slightly enhanced in the Cotonou Agreement. In line with the Fourth Lomé Convention, respect for human rights, democratic principles and the rule of law are essential elements of the partnership.[69] Article 96 allows for the suspension of cooperation as the result of serious violations of the essential elements by the State parties. Article 9(1) further states that respect for fundamental social rights, democracy based on the rule of law and transparent and account-able governance are an integral part of sustainable development. The indi-visibility of all human rights, encompassing civil political and economic, social and cultural rights, as enshrined in international instruments, is recognized in Article 9(2).

In Cotonou, priority was placed on the reduction of poverty.[70] Gender, environment, institutional development and capacity building were intro-duced as thematic and crosscutting issues, in line with the other above-examined cooperation programmes. These themes are supposed to be taken into account in all areas and at all levels and phases of EC–ACP partnership as a whole, as laid down by the Council Regulation on the integration of equality between men and women of 1995. The mainstream-

---

[60]   Art. 5 ACP-EEC Convention [1991] OJ L 229/3, 17 August 1991.
[61]   The mid-term review, as provided by Art. 336 of the Lomé Convention, was concluded in Mauritius on 4 November 1995.
[62]   Article 5 (2) IV Lomé Convention
[63]   Singularly reference is made also to regional human rights instruments such as the ECHR, the African Charter on Human and People Rights and the American Convention on Human Rights.
[64]   Art. 49 Lomé Convention.
[65]   Ibid., Arts 139–40.
[66]   Ibid., Art. 151.
[67]   Ibid., Art. 153.
[68]   Ibid., Art. 154.
[69]   Art. 9 of the Cotonou Agreement.
[70]   Art. 1 Cotonou Agreement.

ing of gender equality is also an integral part of the 2001–06 Action Plan in the field of development cooperation.[71]

Measures for the promotion of health, education and food are enshrined in Article 25 of the Cotonou Agreement, which deals with general and sectoral policies of EC–ACP cooperation. The aim of cooperation is to improve access to basic infrastructures and services and, in particular to reduce the inequality of access to these resources. Article 25(1) states that:

> cooperation shall aim at: (a) improving education and training, and building technical capacity and skills; (b) improving health systems and nutrition, eliminating hunger and malnutrition, ensuring adequate food supply and security; (c) integrating population issues into development strategies . . .; (f) improving the availability of affordable and adequate shelter for all . . .; and (g) encouraging the promotion of participatory methods of social dialogue as well as respects for basic social rights.[72]

Even if reference is made to the respect of basic social rights, the terminology of rights is rather vague in this Article and reference is not made to the ICESCR as referred to in the preamble of the Cotonou Agreement.

On the other hand, recognition of the relevance of labour rights is clear and accompanied by the reference to a respect for ILO Conventions relating to specific labour rights.[73]

It can be inferred that the Cotonou Agreement pursues the promotion of human rights in ACP countries as one of the principle objectives of the agreement. In contrast with MEDA, TACIS, and ALA, Cotonou places emphasis on the respect of labour rights and includes a specific reference to ILO Conventions. If effectively implemented, this aspect of the Agreement could contribute to reinforcing the implementation of the four basic labour rights conventions in the EU partners' countries, which could in turn enforce them on companies operating in their territories.

Another feature of Cotonou which is of particular relevance for the purpose of this book is the inclusion of non-State actors in the ACP–EU Partnership. According to the broad definition adopted in the Agreement,[74] non-State actors include the private sector, economic and social partners, trade union organizations and civil society in all its forms, according to national characteristics. According to Article 2, while central

---

[71] See *EU Guidelines on Human Rights Dialogues,* Annex 15 of Council of the European Union, *EU Annual Report on Human Rights 2002*, at 259.

[72] Art. 25 (1) (a)–(g), Cotonou Agreement.

[73] See Art. 50 (1), (3), Cotonou Agreement.

[74] Art. 6, Cotonou Agreement.

governments remain the main partners of cooperation, other actors, including the private sector, should participate. Moreover, non-State actors shall, where appropriate:

> be informed and involved in consultation on cooperation policies and strate-
> gies, on priorities for cooperation especially in areas that concern or directly
> affect them, and on the political dialogue; be provided with financial resources,
> under the conditions laid down in this Agreement in order to support local
> development processes; be involved in the implementation of cooperation
> project and programmes in areas that concern them or where these actors
> have a comparative advantage; be provided with capacity-building support in
> critical areas in order to reinforce the capabilities of these actors, particularly
> as regards organisation and representation, and the establishment of consulta-
> tion mechanisms including channels of communication and dialogue, and to
> promote strategic alliances.[75]

Even if the Cotonou Agreement offers a broader ground for the protection of human rights and labour rights and it strengthens civil society as compared to previously examined assistance programmes, its implementation seems to be restrained in practice.

While there is a wide scope for the promotion of human rights by virtue of the broad definition of human rights contained within Article 9(2), the direct financing of positive measures is considered predominantly within general programmes to improve governance, strengthen civil society, the process of institution building and the rule of law, therefore, a complete investigation of the human rights programmes is difficult to carry out. According to the most recent external report[76] on the evaluation of positive measures in ACP, there is nothing to indicate the translation of legal norms into the operational activities of development cooperation with the ACP countries.[77]

Despite the declared objective of involving non-State actors both in the definition and implementation of strategies and priorities which were previously under the exclusive jurisdiction of governments, the lack of provision for non-State actors' access to funding and the lack of clarity

---

[75]   Art. 4 Cotonou Agreement.

[76]   *Evaluation of Community Aid Concerning Positive Measures in the Field of Human Rights and Democracy in the ACP Countries, 1995–1999*, Synthesis Report Phase 3, 28 August 2000, SCR Evaluation, 951518.

[77]   O. Sheehy, *The Positive Application of Human Rights within EU-ACP Development Co-operation*, Conference Proceedings, 'The Relationship between Africa and the European Union', organized by ECSA of South Africa, University of the Western Cape, 22-23 January 2004, available at: http://www.uwc.ac.za/ ECSA-SA/conf2004_prog.htm (accessed 3 March 2005).

about procedures may render their participation difficult in practice.[78] In addition, human rights funding[79] is not automatically included in the indicative programmes of the ACP country support strategies, but instead depends on the availability of resources.[80] Finally, similarly to the previously examined assistance programmes, the emphasis on inward investment and the recognition of the role of business in development has not been accompanied by a call upon their specific responsibilities for the enjoyment of human rights in the countries where they operate.

8.6   THE EUROPEAN INSTRUMENT FOR DEMOCRACY AND HUMAN RIGHTS

By contrast with TACIS, ALA, MEDA, projects funded by the EIDHR[81] could be implemented with non governmental partners, particularly NGOs and international organizations, and the funding can be used without host governments' consent or when other EU programmes have been suspended.

Council Regulation (EC) 1889/2006[82] (which amended the so called Human Rights Regulations[83] and Council Regulations 2242/2004).[84]

---

[78]   K. Arts, 'ACP-EU Relations in a New Era: The Cotonou Agreement' (2003) 40 C.M.L.R. 95, at 101.

[79]   Most of the funding for development co-operation with the ACP States is provided by the European Development Fund (EDF). The main purpose of the EDF is to financially assist the development of ACP countries, on the basis of long-term concerted programmes, particularly for: rural development; industrialisation; and Economic Infrastructure. The EDF provides funding for any project or programmes which contribute to the economic, social or cultural development of countries.

[80]   Sheehy, *supra* n. 77, at 19.

[81]   The EIDHR, created in 1994 on the initiative of the European Parliament, rationalized the different human rights budgets by grouping together the budget headings for the promotion of human rights, democratization and conflict prevention policies and provides complementary founding to EU programmes carried out with governments.

[82]   Council Regulation (EC) 1889/2006 of the European Parliament and of the Council, of 20 December 2006 on establishing a financing instrument for the promotion of democracy and human rights worldwide [2006] OJ L 386 1–11.

[83]   Council Regulation (EC) 975/1999 and Council Regulation (EC) 976/1999, *supra* Ch.7 n. 19.

[84]   Regulation (EC) 2240/2004 of the European Parliament and of the Council of 15 December 2004 amending Council Regulation (EC) 975/1999 laying down the requirements for the Implementation of development cooperation operations which contribute to the general objective of developing and consolidating

The text of EIDHR Regulation attaches the same relevance to economic, social and cultural rights as to social and political ones. The preamble acknowledges the principles of indivisibility and of the interdependence of all human rights. The mutually supportive relationship between economic and social development and the achievement of civil and political rights is emphasized.[85] In the Regulation, the ICESCR – together with the UDHR and the ICPSR – is defined as one of the main sources for the European Community's action to promote human rights and democratic principles. Moreover, the promotion and protection of both civil and political rights and economic, social and cultural rights[86] is regarded as one of the objectives of the EC's technical and financial assistance. The Commission, however, retains the power to define the priorities, as well as planning and administering the operations undertaken.[87]

8.6.1 The Projects Funded by the EIDHR

From the outset, the principal areas of action of the EIDHR have included: the strengthening of democratization, good governance and the rule of law; electoral activities; strengthening of the legal system and institutions; conflict prevention and resolution; support for civil society; initiatives for the abolition of the death penalty, support for measures to combat xenophobia, racism and discrimination against indigenous people; human rights education and raising awareness in civil society; freedom of expression and independence of the media.[88] More recently, priorities have expanded to include activities for the protection of children, the fight

---

democracy and the rule of law and to that of respecting human rights and fundamental freedoms [2004] OJ L 390/3; Council Regulation (EC) 2242/2004 of 22 December 2004 amending Regulation (EC) No 976/1999 laying down the requirements for the Implementation of Community operations, other than those of development cooperation, which, within the framework of Community cooperation policy, contribute to the general objective of developing and consolidating democracy and the rule of law and to that of respecting human rights and fundamental freedoms in third countries [2004] OJ L 390/21.

[85]   See Preamble, at recitals 3, 7–9.

[86]   Art. 2, 1 of Regulation 1889/2006 (previously at Art. 2 of Regulation 975/1999 and Art. 3 of Regulation 976/1999)

[87]   European Instrument for Democracy and Human Rights (EIDHR) Strategy Paper 2007–2010, available at: http://ec.europa.eu/europeaid/what/human-rights/documents/eidhr_strategy_paper_2007-2010_en.pdf, accessed 7 March 2008 and *Commission Staff Working Document*, European Initiative for Democracy and Human Rights Programming Document 2002–2004, Brussels, 20 December 2001 REV 1, Final, at 6–11.

[88]   *EU Annual Reports on Human Rights* from 1998/99 to 2003.

against torture, impunity and the death penalty and in support of the setting up of international tribunals and international criminal courts.[89] Only in 2000 were economic, social and cultural rights mentioned as a separate priority, while they usually go under the general heading of support for human rights. This sporadic textual recognition, however, has not changed the overall balance, which remains in favour of support for civil and political rights, as proved by the realm of activities linked to electoral observation and monitoring. Finally, Regulation 1889/2006 has introduced CSR as one of the fields of EC assistance.[90]

The emphasis still placed on civil and political rights is partially coun-terbalanced, however, by the inclusion of cross-cutting issues such as gender equality, women's rights and the fight against poverty. Even if these themes are listed as one of the priority areas, they are considered as overarching objectives of the EU's development policy which need to be taken into account in the implementation of the budget.

The distribution of funding mirrors the preference toward civil and political rights, as laid down in the themes defined by the Commission on an annual basis. An analysis of the projects funded reveals only a very limited number of projects aimed at improving workers' conditions within firms or at fostering of trade unions rights. Tangible examples of this type of intervention are: a project for the strengthening of the trade union movement in Tunisia,[91] a project for the training of trade union leaders in Burundi[92] and a project in Ethiopia and Eritrea designed to develop capacity in the labour sector.[93]

An indirect contribution to fostering the respect for human rights by MNEs has also been provided by a number of projects which aim at or include the promotion and protection of targeted groups. Projects addressed to the empowerment of women[94] and ethnic minorities have a

---

[89]   See *Commission Staff Working Document, supra* n. 87.

[90]   EIDHR Regulation Art. 2(b) viii.

[91]   F. Ebert-Stiftung – Tunisian Office, 'Strengthening Trade Union Movement in Tunisia', *EU Annual Report on Human Rights 2002.*

[92]   343 Burundi ISCOS *Soutien au syndicat libre du Burundi à travers la for-mation de cadres et la formation de formateurs 326.642 million euros. EU Annual Report on Human Rights 2004.*

[93]   ILO – Strengthening Dialogue and Networking in the Civil Society/Capacity Development in the Labour Sector in Eritrea & Ethiopia Ethiopia/Eritrea, 979.000 million euros. *EU Annual Report on Human Rights 2004.*

[94]   See Heinrich Boëll Foundation, 'The Promotion of Women's Rights Through Empowerment, Awareness and Legal and Political Reform Regional/ Mediterranean: Egypt, Jordan, Lebanon, West Bank & Gaza'. *EU Annual Report on Human Rights 2002.*

particular impact on reducing discrimination. It can be argued that these projects indirectly favour the enjoyment of human rights by vulnerable groups, by providing access to services or by reducing disparities in the enjoyment of fundamental rights by these groups.

Although the analysis of the projects that indirectly improve labour conditions or antidiscrimination within MNEs is disappointing, both in terms of the number of projects and in terms of budget, a positive aspect of the EIDHR is the role attributed to NGOs and to civil society. Not only are projects mainly managed directly by NGOs, but they are also the target of the activities funded by the EIDHR. Strengthening the role of NGOs and civil society at large in developing countries appears, indeed, among the thematic priorities set by the Commission. Several projects seek to enhance the human rights monitoring capacity of civil society.[95] A project in Pakistan, for instance, endeavours to strengthen the participation of civil society to promote and defend workers' rights.[96] As explained in the previous chapter, the strengthening of civil society and raising awareness on MNEs' human rights responsibility is to be regarded as one important component in increasing scrutiny over MNEs at the level of host countries.

The above depiction of EIDHR measures shows that for quite some time, while the linkage between human rights and business has been increasingly recognized in a variety of EC/EU documents, the topic is still largely overlooked in the main legal and financial instruments for the promotion of human rights at the external level. This lacuna was particularly worrying in the context of the EIDHR for a number of reasons.

First, the Human Rights Regulations which created the EIDHR played a particular role in the promotion of human rights in the external relations. Not only do they provide a considerable amount of financial resources, but they were also the first legal instrument having the promotion of human rights at the external level as their main objective. Adopted

---

[95] Sudan Justice Africa Building the capacity of civil society and human rights monitoring in Sudan with a focus on non-governmental held €300.385 million and Sierra Leone IEP Bordeaux Capacity building for Human Rights Civil society organisations in Sierra Leone €309.862 million *Guatemala Movimiento por la Paz, el Desarme y la Libertad Promoción y defensa de los derechos humanos y fortalecimiento y articulación de la sociedad civil a través de las radios locales de comunicación comunitaria, para mejorar les políticas públicas especialmente en derechos humanos, desde el ámbito local*, €800.000 million EU Annual Report on Human Rights 2004.

[96] Pakistan ISCOS–CISL Strengthening civil society participation to promote and defend workers' rights, €793.010 million EU Annual Report on Human Rights 2004.

shortly after *Opinion 2/94,* the Human Rights Regulations were a tangible example of the EC's willingness to take action in the field of human rights policy and to overcome all the uncertainty relating to the most appropriate legal basis when necessary. Therefore, it is surprising that the relevance of MNEs' activities to the enjoyment of human rights has not until recently been recognized in the context of the EIDHR.

Secondly, the thematic priorities of the EIDHR were revised annually. It is striking that after more than 10 years of operation the thematic priorities remained virtually unchanged. A predominance of civil and political rights over social rights has been noted. Despite its supposed flexibility, the EIDHR has not mirrored for some time the evolution of human rights priorities over the course of the years, nor the new emphasis on CSR promoted by the Commission itself. In this sense, it is to be welcomed that, after five years from the launch of the CSR debate, the EIDHR Regulation has finally included CSR as one of the fields of activities to be funded.[97] Although it is too early to assess the impact of these new thematic priorities in the actual distribution of funding among future projects, it can be seen as a positive sign of the integration of CSR concerns in the development cooperation of the EC.

8.7 CONCLUSIONS

In the previous chapter it was suggested that a possible option to promote MNEs' respect for human rights in developing countries is to raise MNEs' human rights standards in developing countries. Governments in developing countries will in turn be encouraged to enforce human rights obligations on MNEs operating in their countries. In addition, the scrutiny of MNEs in developing countries could be enhanced by strengthening local NGOs and increasing awareness about the conduct of MNEs directly at the host State level. Great potential in both respects is offered by the instruments available to the external relations of the EU.

Two levels at which the EU can operate at the external level were distinguished: regulatory instruments, such as human rights clauses, and non-regulatory measures, such as assistance and the strengthening of civil society in developing countries.

Chapter 8 examined how and to what extent the EU's development and co-operation programs take into account the human rights obligations of MNEs and promote their compliance, by increasing governments' and civil

---

[97] Art. 2, Para. 1 viii.

society control over MNEs activities. This chapter, in particular, sought to identify the ways in which both human rights conditionality and incentive measures are used to encourage scrutiny of MNEs by governments and the civil society of developing countries. In this perspective, three parameters have been taken into account: the relevance given to human rights and social rights in the legal texts; the distribution of funding to projects related to MNEs' compliance with human rights; the measures aimed at strengthening the role of NGOs and civil society in developing countries.

Against this benchmark, assistance programmes between the European Union and Mediterranean countries, ALA, Eastern European countries, ACP countries have been examined. The analysis also included the EIDHR Regulation, as it provides complementary funding of co-operation assistance programmes examined in the area of human rights.

The relevance of human rights is recognized to varying degrees in all the above-mentioned EU aid programmes, through the inclusion of human rights clauses. The interdependence of human rights and the relationship between the promotion of human rights and development are clearly spelled out in the above-examined regulations. Express reference to the protection of economic, social and cultural rights, is rarely present. Social concerns – broadly defined – constitute a key component of technical and financial assistance. In particular, measures aiming at the improvement of education, health food security and the protection of vulnerable groups are expressly foreseen.

However, an emphasis in favour of the promotion of civil and political rights was observed. This was partially due to the above-mentioned normative deficiencies of Regulations 975/1999 and No 976/1999,[98] which made a limited reference to social rights. Only recently have these deficiencies been amended by the inclusion of the promotion of labour rights and CSR within the scope of Regulations 1889/2006 and 1905/2006 and a stronger reference to social and labour rights in all the regulations establishing new financial instruments for EU assistance.

Economic, social and cultural rights were scarcely represented in the projects funded by the MEDA, TACIS, ALA. One exception is the assistance to ACP countries. The Cotonou Agreement expressly exhorts parties to respect core labour standards, as enshrined in the 1998 ILO's Declaration.[99]

On the other hand, although projects did not include the promotion of social rights within their objectives, many of them have an indirect benefi-

---

[98]   Council Regulations 975/1999 and 976 /1999, *supra* Ch.4 n. 43.
[99]   Gatto, *supra* Ch.4 n. 46.

cial impact on the promotion and enjoyment of social rights. In addition, by involving local NGOs in the managing and implementation of the project, the EIDHR also contributes to the strengthening of civil society in the countries in which it operates.

As far as the mechanisms of implementation are concerned, emphasis is still placed on the use of human rights clauses. In addition to traditional instruments for the promotion of social rights, the EU's development cooperation also emphasizes the role of technical assistance and encourages cooperation and awareness-building at local level. This may encourage a major involvement of companies in the promotion of civil and political rights. In the MEDA programme, for instance, the TÜSIAD, one of the main Turkish business organisations, was actively involved in favour of the promotion of civil and political rights in Turkey.[100] On the contrary, the TÜSIAD paid less attention to income redistribution and the provision of social safety nets.[101] In line with principles underlying the EC development policy, the Cotonou Agreement also purports the participation of non-State actors, including companies, in development programmes.

It is worth noting that it is difficult to carry out an assessment of the impact of assistance programmes on the implementation of human rights. Therefore, the analysis is hindered by restricted assess to projects. With the exception of the MEDA and ACP cooperation, comprehensive and regular evaluations are not available. Moreover, external evaluations are rare.[102] As a result, it is difficult to determine to what extent the commitment to human rights was translated into normative reforms in recipient countries.

The overall impression is that both in legal texts and in the implementation of programmes, showed for some time a reluctance to draw a link between human rights and the activities of MNEs. Concerns related to an increase of FDI MNE activities and the enjoyment of human rights was not apparent in any of the above examined assistance programmes – MEDA, TACIS, ALA – nor in the context of the EC–ACP partnership agreement. Even more surprisingly, none of the projects funded by the EIDHR, which is the main human rights financial instrument, expressly addresses this issue.

---

[100] Assistance to Turkey, as a candidate country Turkey is currently provided under the Instrument for Pre-accession.

[101] Schmid, *supra* Ch.7 n. 72, at 32.

[102] See e.g., German Development Institute, *Evaluation on EC Positive Measures in Favour of Human Rights and Democracy (1991-1993)*, Berlin, May 1995.

Only recently has the Commission shown increased willingness to incorporate references to economic, social and cultural rights, in connection with labour rights and sexual health in developing countries. It is also argued that the necessity of ensuring equal footing to civil and political rights and social and economic rights cannot be exhausted by textual references, but should be mirrored in the implementation of cooperation programmes. As seen above, while the Regulations laying down the legal basis of current EU assistance programmes recognize equal relevance to the two sets of rights, and in some cases expressly recognize CSR as a priority. The elaboration of the normative criteria of economic, social and cultural rights would assist in the integration of these rights into the country support strategies, and provide an impetus for funding the activities of NGOs and civil society groups which operate in this domain and contribute to the enhanced definition of economic, social and cultural rights in future EC legislation relating to developing countries.

Taking this argument a step further, if human rights, as enshrined in the human rights clauses, refer to existing obligations of international law, they should also mirror the development that has occurred at the international level. In international law, for instance, there is a growing consensus and an emerging practice in international courts of recognising human rights obligations of non-state actors, and in particular MNEs. Therefore, the human rights clauses in the external agreements and in the regulations of the EC should be interpreted as taking into account the evolution of the international human rights law they refer to. Such an interpretation should be translated into the implementation of the clauses both in positive and negative terms.

Finally, as a development and humanitarian actor, through its development and assistance policy, the EU should devote part of its funding to projects aimed at, for instance, monitoring the respect of social rights and non discrimination in local subsidiaries of MNEs. EU assistance to States could be focused in sectors which are particularly sensitive to the activities of MNEs, for instance by strengthening labour codes and safety at work regulations in recipient countries.

9 Measures addressed to host States in the common commercial policy of the European Union

9.1 INTRODUCTION

Having considered, in Chapter 8, the integration of human rights in EU development cooperation and cooperation policies, the analysis now turns to the integration of human rights into the common commercial policy (CCP) of the EC, with particular reference to the GSP scheme and the EC–Association Agreement with Chile. The analysis of the CCP is relevant in the context of this book, since the EC uses unilateral trade measures to encourage compliance with human rights in developing countries. In this respect, the GSP scheme also falls within the category of EC measures directed at third countries that can be used with a view to introduce compliance by MNEs with human rights standards.

In addition to a widespread system of cooperation agreements with countries all over the world, the European Union grants preferential trade relations and other forms of preferential assistance to developing countries. Article 133 TEC[1] confers on the European Community the exclusive competence to trade with third countries.[2] In the *GSP* case[3] the European Court of Justice acknowledged that the existence of a link with development issues does not cause a measure to be excluded from the sphere of the common commercial policy, as defined by the Treaty. It considered that it would no longer be possible to carry on any worthwhile common commercial policy if the community were not in a

---

[1] Art. 188C, Treaty of Lisbon.
[2] The Treaty of Lisbon confirmed the exclusive character of the common commercial policy. Pursuant to Article 2B: 'The Union shall have exclusive competence in the following areas: . . . c) common commercial policy. 2 The Union shall also have exclusive competence for the conclusion of an international agreement when its conclusion is provided for in a legislative act of the Union or is necessary to enable the Union to exercise its internal competence, or insofar as its conclusion may affect common rules or alter their scope.' Treaty of Lisbon *supra* Ch.4 n. 29.
[3] Case 45/86 *Commission v Council* (*GSP case*) [1987] ECR 1493.

position to avail itself also of means of action going beyond instruments intended to have an effect only on the traditional aspects of external trade. A 'commercial policy,' understood in that sense, would be destined to become nugatory in the course of time.[4] It follows that, the EC is competent to introduce development considerations into measures adopted on the basis of Article 133, such as the GSP Regulation, as long as these measures do not have development as their general and principal objective.

The objectives of the CCP may end up being broadened by the Treaty of Lisbon; one of the most significant changes in the CCP field appears in Article 188a, according to which: 'The Union's action on the international scene, pursuant to this Part, shall be guided by the principles, pursue the objectives and be conducted in accordance with the general provisions laid down in Chapter 1 of Title V of the Treaty on European Union.' As seen in Part II, these principles and objectives include not only the trade liberalization objectives already enshrined in the current Article 131[5] TEC but also be guided by:

> the principles which have inspired its own creation, development and enlargement, and which it seeks to advance in the wider world: democracy, the rule of law, the universality and indivisibility of human rights and fundamental freedoms, respect for human dignity, the principles of equality and solidarity, and respect for the principles of the United Nations Charter and international law.[6]

Put together with the requirement that international commercial policy agreements must be compatible with internal policies and rules,[7] and the repeated call for 'consistency'[8] this provision will place human rights as fundamental values of both the internal and external action of the EU. By doing so, greater coherence will be encouraged not only across the Union's external policy, but also between external and internal policies.[9]

---

[4]   *Opinion 1/78* of 4 October 1979 [1979] ECR 2871.

[5]   Art. 188B, Treaty of Lisbon.

[6]   Art. 10A, Treaty of Lisbon, *supra* Ch.4 n. 29.

[7]   M. Cremona, 'A Policy of Bits and Pieces? The Common Commercial Policy After Nice' (2002) *Cambridge Yearbook of European Legal Studies* 61, at 75–6.

[8]   Arts 9, 9E4, 10A(3), Treaty of Lisbon, *supra* Ch.4 n. 29.

[9]   A similar reasoning was developed by Cremona with reference to the Treaty Establishing a Constitution for Europe: M. Cremona, 'The Draft Constitutional Treaty: External Relations and External Action' (2003) 40 C.M.L.R 1347.

9.2   TRADE AND HUMAN RIGHTS

Before considering the EC's GSP system and how it can be used in the perspective of enhancing the level of human rights protection in third countries which host MNEs, it is worth providing an overview of how different approaches to trade conditionality may affect its effectiveness on human rights.

The issue of whether and in what circumstances, trade conditionality is an appropriate response to failure to adhere to international human rights standards is the object of a vast debate.[10] There is great disagreement as to the effectiveness of trade conditionality in promoting compliance with human rights and labour rights. At one end of the spectrum there are those who believe that trade liberalization is itself able to improve working conditions. According to this approach, attempts to raise standards through rights-based interventions are doomed to fail, or even to be counterproductive. According to Alan Skyes, for instance, evidence suggests that the growth of the trading system itself generally tends to promote rather than undermine human rights.[11] Therefore, the promotion of human rights may be the consequence of rising real incomes and of greater openness to trade, without other normative intervention required. At the other end of the spectrum, some human rights lawyers and labour lawyers uphold the necessity of linking international trade law with human rights and labour law.[12] Others point out that developing countries' access to international trade, their search for foreign direct investment and the improvement of their labour standards can be pursued hand in hand.[13]

---

[10]   C.M. Vazquez, 'Trade Sanctions and Human Rights – Past, Present And Future' [2003] 6 *Journal of International Economic Law* 797, at 803ff, 817; C. Dommen, 'Raising Human Rights Concerns in the World Trade Organization: Actors, Processes And Possible Strategies' (2002) 24 *Human Rights Quarterly* 1. From an economic perspective see A.V. Brown, D.K. Deardoff, and R.M. Stern, *Pros and Cons of Linking Trade and Labor Standards*, Research Seminar in Economics, School of Public Policy, The University of Michigan, Discussion Paper, 477 (6 May 2002).

[11]   A.O. Sykes, 'International Trade and Human Rights: an Economic Prospective', in F.M. Abbott et al. (eds), *International Trade and Human Rights. Foundations and Conceptual Issues*, 2006, Ann Arbor, The University of Michigan Press, 69.

[12]   For a comprehensive analysis see S.H. Cleveland, 'Human Rights Sanctions and International Trade: A Theory of Compatibility' (2002) 5 *Journal of International Economic Law* 133; M.J. Trebilcock and R. Howse, 'Trade Policy and Labor Standards' (2005) 14 *Minnesota Journal of Global Trade* 261.

[13]   R. Sarna, *The Impact of Core Labour Standards on Foreign Direct Investment in East Asia*, 2005, Tokyo, The Japan Institute for Labour Policy and Training.

As noted by Harrison,[14] the complexity of the discussion is further increased by the fact that no difference is made among the different instruments by which trade can be linked to human rights. In addition, empirical research on the linkage between trade and labour rights or human rights has not reached conclusive results about a positive or negative correlation between the two. For instance, one of the most widely quoted economic studies on this issue, the OECD report on Trade Employment and Labour Standards of 1996, reaches contradictory results.[15] On the one hand, it suggests that it is impossible to prove the existence of an empirical link between these standards and global trade performance (or foreign investment). On the other hand, it also points out that failure to observe labour standards can hamper the economic efficiency of a country and the growth of its exports. The exploitation of child labour, discrimination in employment, slavery and exploitation of labour in general are liable to perpetuate arrangements that are economically inefficient. The exploitation of child labour, for example, hinders the development of human capital and thus retards improvements in productivity; discrimination in employment results in situations in which some workers are not employed in the positions where they would be most productive; the lack of freedom of association undoubtedly makes it more difficult to introduce modern methods of human-resource management and generates an unstable social climate, which does not encourage productive investment. Other studies based on empirical evidence argue that enforcement of labour standards would actually promote trade.[16]

Despite the difficulty of clarifying the terms of the debate, there is a broad agreement on the assumption that labour standards and workers' conditions are likely to improve by themselves through economic growth and that foreign direct investment brings this growth. It is also true that these improvements cannot be taken for granted. It is argued here that in the absence of enforcement of standards, however, benefits coming from economic growth risk remaining restricted to only a small section of privileged workers, failing to improve the conditions of a majority of workers. In particular, lax enforcement of human rights standards can leave workers vulnerable to exploitation from the ever growing powers

---

[14] J. Harrison, 'Incentives For Development: The EC's Generalized System of Preferences, India's WTO Challenge And Reform' (2009) 42 C.M.L.R 1663, at 1683.

[15] OECD, *Trade, Employment and Labour Standards: a Study of Core Workers' Rights and International Trade*, 1996, Paris, OECD Publications.

[16] P. Morici and E. Shultz, *Labour Standards in the Global Trading System*, 2001, Washington, Washington Economic Strategy Institute, at 7–11.

of MNEs. With increasing globalization and multinational operations, the need to have some global and basic labour standards in order to protect workers becomes more important than ever. By complying with these basic and minimum human rights and labour standards, developing countries will not only improve conditions of their workers but also gain legitimacy against the protectionist concerns (under the guise of labour standards) raised by the developed countries.

For the purpose of this book, the question is limited to whether the EC's GSP system would facilitate the growth of developing countries and promote their compliance with human rights by MNEs involved in investment or trade operations with beneficiary countries. It can be pointed out from the outset that two features of the EC–GSP system can, to a certain extent, positively distinguish it from other forms of trade conditionality. A first positive aspect of the EC–GSP scheme is that the EC operates a system of incentives rather than sanctions. It is characterized as utilizing 'positive' conditionality to enhance labour rights (and in the future broader human rights), by offering incentives to those countries that comply with its standards. This differentiates it from the 'negative' conditionality of schemes such as the US GSP system, which withdraws preferences from developing countries that have failed to meet required labour standards in their exports to the US. Secondly, the EC–GSP scheme, in its current formulation, seems to partially answer the usual allegations of disguised protectionism raised by developing countries. Since the EC's GSP scheme only provides preferential levels of tariffs for goods from developing countries, it will not affect the competitiveness of developed country products.[17]

The following paragraphs will examine how the EC–GSP system has developed and how these developments can be used in the perspective of enhancing the level of human rights in third countries, which are generally the host countries of MNEs. After that, the analysis will focus on three aspects of the GSP. The first characteristic is the broadening of the human rights standards whose respect entitles to preferential treatment. Another element worth examining is the review of the mechanisms for grant or withdrawal of preferential treatment. Finally, the problem of monitoring compliance with the GSP system will be tackled.

---

[17] It is also true that this scheme may generate competition amongst developing countries. Bartels lists a number of occasions where developing countries have expressed concern with the EC's scheme 'both within the political organs of the WTO, and also by way of initiating formal consultations with the EC.' See L. Bartels, 'The WTO Enabling Clause and Positive Conditionality in the European Community's GSP Program' (2003) 6/2 *Journal of International Economic Law* 507, at 508.

9.3 THE EVOLUTION OF THE GENERALIZED SYSTEM OF PREFERENCES AND THE *INDIA V EC* CASE

The GSP scheme is one of the best examples of EC commercial measures aimed at promoting human rights in developing countries. The European Community established a GSP in July 1971[18] with the aim of fostering economic development in developing countries through trade. The GSP was first allowed under the Decision on the Generalized System of Preferences of 25 June 1971[19] and later under the 'enabling clause'[20] adopted by the GATT's contracting parties, which provides for an exemption from the Most Favoured Nation clause[21] in favour of developing countries, as well as for preferential arrangements amongst developing countries. By granting a preferential tariff system, the GSP attempted to revitalize exports from developing countries and, by the same token, to favour the accumulation of capital necessary to improve the process of industrialisation in these countries.[22]

The EC–GSP system has undergone a series of revisions over the years. Under the EC's GSP Regulation,[23] applied between 2002 and 2005, five different arrangements were available to beneficiary countries. All ben-

---

[18]   The GSP scheme was initially promoted by the UNCTAD after its creation in 1964 to permit industrialized countries to grant autonomous and non-reciprocal trade preferences to all developing countries. The GSP represents an exception to the principle of the Most Favoured Nation clause and facilitates a form of positive discrimination in favour of developing countries.

[19]   GATT document 2/3545, 185/24.

[20]   *Decision on Differential and More Favourable Treatment Reciprocity and Fuller Participation of Developing Countries*, GATT document L/4903, 28 November 1979, BISD 26S/203.

[21]   The Most Favoured Nation clause is enshrined in Art. 1 of the GATT which provides that, with respect to a number of trade measures, including customs duties and other charges 'any advantage, favour, privilege or immunity granted by any Contracting Party to any product originating in or destined for any other country shall be accorded immediately and unconditionally to the like product originating or destined for the territories of all other contracting countries'.

[22]   G. Tsogas, 'Labour Standards in the General System of Preferences of the European Union and The United States' (2000) 6 *European Journal of Industrial Relations* 349, at 352; G. Tsogas, 'Labour Standards in International Trade Agreements: an Assessment of the Arguments' (1999) 2 *International Journal of Human Resource Management* 351.

[23]   Council Regulation (EC) 2211/2003 of 15 December 2003 amending Regulation (EC) 2501/2001 Applying a Scheme of Generalised Tariff Preferences for the Period from 1 January 2002 to 31 December 2004 and Extending It to 31 December 2005 [2003] OJ L 332/1.

eficiary countries enjoyed the benefit of the general arrangements, which consists of a tariff reduction. In the case of least developed countries, duty-free access was granted under the special 'everything but arms clause' to all products of such countries, except arms and munitions. In addition, three special incentive arrangements were included in the scheme: the special arrangements to combat drug production and trafficking; the special incentive arrangements for the protection of the environment were available on request to countries implementing certain standards for the sustainable management of tropical forests; and the special incentive arrangements for the protection of labour rights were available on request to countries implementing some labour standards. These incentives provided additional reductions of up to half of the already reduced GSP tariff rate.[24]

As a result of the latest amendment introduced by Regulation 980/2005[25] and largely reconfirmed by Regulation No 732/2008,[26] the previous five arrangements have been streamlined into three. The basic GSP, which consists of Preferential Tariff Treatment which the EC grants to listed products originating from all least developed countries, remained unvaried, apart from a slight improvement in terms of product coverage. However, one single arrangement, known as 'GSP Plus', which promotes sustainable development and good governance, replaced the three different sets of special incentives on labour rights, environment and drug trafficking.

In order to ensure continuity in implementation of the guiding principles for the GSP during the 10-year period 2005–15, the Regulation 732/2008 ensures that the substance of the scheme remains unchanged from that established under Regulation 980/2005. At the same time, while maintaining substantive continuity, the new Regulation implements a number of technical changes in the scheme, either to simplify the language or to take account of evolutions in relevant trade data over the most recent period.

In this context, the most interesting development is that the human rights promoted by the GSP, originally limited to labour rights, have been progressively extended to include a broad range of internationally

---

[24] For details see User's Guide to the European Union's Scheme of Generalised Tariff Preferences P5 (2003), available at: http://europa.eu.int/comm/trade/gsp/gspguide.htm (accessed 4 May 2004).

[25] Council Regulation (EC) 980/2005 of 27 June 2005, applying a *Scheme of Generalized Tariff Preferences*, [2005] OJ L 169/1.

[26] Council Regulation (EC) No 732/2008 of 22 July 2008 applying a scheme of generalised tariff preferences for the period from 1 January 2009 to 31 December 2011 and amending Regulations (EC) 552/97, (EC) 1933/2006 and Commission Regulations (EC) 1100/2006 and (EC) 964/2007 [2008] OJ L 211 1–39.

recognized human rights.[27] The single system of additional concessions for all developing countries' special development needs, indeed, accepts the main international conventions relating, for the first time, to human rights in addition to social rights, environmental protection, and the fight against drugs. The Community will withdraw entitlement to such additional preferences whenever the evaluation mechanisms of the relevant international organizations reveal serious systemic failings on the part of the beneficiary countries. In addition, the new GSP Regulation provides for a more stable, predictable, objective and simple system of concessions and it is intended to target the countries that most need it.

The main revisions to the GSP system introduced in 2005, however, were not prompted by the need to strengthen special arrangements to promote internationally recognized human rights; nor were they exclusively motivated by a wish to streamline the GSP system.[28] On the contrary, the main reasons for reforming the EC–GSP could be found outside the EC legal system. They have been prompted by an important development in the jurisprudence of the WTO: India's complaint on the legitimacy of EC–GSP special incentives. In particular, the EC's special arrangement to combat drug production and trafficking[29] was challenged.[30] Although this case did not question the labour rights preferences,[31] which are the main object of this chapter, the opinion of the WTO Dispute Settlement Body on this issue provided detailed guidelines on the compatibility of all types of special incentive schemes with WTO law. A brief account of the India case is necessary to understand the reform of the EC–GSP system and its implications for the use of preferential trade concessions as an instrument to indirectly improve MNEs' human rights records in developing countries.

On March 2002, India requested consultations with the EC about its GSP scheme.[32] India asserted that the EU's GSP special arrangement

---

[27]   Ibid., Annex III.

[28]   See *Explanatory Memorandum to the Proposal for a Council Regulation*, European Commission, COM (2004) 699 final, 20 October 2004, s. 4.

[29]   Regulation 2501/2001, Art. 10.

[30]   Ibid., Art. 25.

[31]   Initially, India challenged the special incentives for the protection of labour rights, the environment and for combating drug production. Subsequently, India decided to limit the complaint to the special incentives against dugs production and trafficking. See *European Communities – Conditions for the Granting of Tariff Preferences to Developing Countries* WT/DS246/AB/R, 7 April 2004, point 4.

[32]   For a detailed analysis of the special working group report see S. de la Rosa, 'Observations après le rapport du groupe spécial "communautés européennes – conditions d'octroi de préférences tarifaires aux pays en développement." Vers

was not compatible with Article 1 of the GATT and not justified by the 'enabling clause'.[33] Preferences are only permitted under the enabling clause 'in order to increase export earnings, to promote industrialization and to accelerate the rates of economic growth of developing countries'.[34] However, a differentiation among developing countries would have constituted a discrimination not allowed by the enabling clause. India's argument, however, was rejected by the Appellate Body (AB)'s report, published on 7th April 2004, which reversed the conclusions of the WTO panel issued in December 2003.[35] The panel had interpreted the term '*non discriminatory*' in the enabling clause[36] to mean that identical tariff preferences under GSP schemes should be provided to all developing countries, without differentiation. Yet, two exceptions were considered admissible: firstly, in favour of least developed countries and secondly, in case of *a priori* import limitations for products originating in particularly competitive developing countries.[37] Consequently, the EC's drugs arrangement was found to be discriminatory because its scheme did not provide identical tariff preferences to all developing countries and it did not fall into one of the above mentioned exceptions.[38]

Following the EC's appeal in January 2004,[39] the AB[40] overturned the strict interpretation of the term '*non-discriminatory*' of the enabling clause. The AB read the enabling clause as authorizing preference granting countries to respond positively to needs that are not necessarily common or shared by all developing countries. In rejecting the panel's interpretation of the enabling clause, the AB has taken a broader approach to its interpretation, which potentially allows developed country members far greater scope to utilize differential treatment, which distinguishes between

---

une remise en couse du SPG communautaire a la carte?' (2003) 15 *Revue de l'association Française pour les Nations Unies – Section Aix en Provence, Dossiers Spécial – l' Asie, redécouverte d' un continent* 2, at 16.

[33] *Decision on Differential and More Favourable Treatment Reciprocity and Fuller Participation of Developing Countries*, GATT document L/4903, 28 November 1979, BISD 26S/203.

[34] *Request for Consultations by India*, WT/DS246/1, 12 March 2002.

[35] *European Communities – Conditions for the Granting of Tariff Preferences to Developing Countries*, WT/ DS246/R, adopted by the special group on 28 October 2003. Made public on 1 December 2003.

[36] Para. 2(a) fn. 3 of the enabling clause.

[37] Panel report, *supra* n. 35, para. 7.116.

[38] Ibid., para. 7.177.

[39] *Notification of an appeal by the European Communities*, WT/DS246/7, 8 January 2004.

[40] *European Communities – Conditions for the Granting of Tariff Preferences to Developing Countries*, WT/DS246/AB/R, 7 April 2004.

different developing country members.[41] Nonetheless, the criteria according to which a differential treatment is provided should be transparent and objective.

According to the AB, the EC's special drugs arrangement, as set out in Regulation 2501/2001, did not provide for mechanisms or objective criteria that would allow for other developing countries that are similarly affected by the drug problem to be included amongst the beneficiary countries. In addition, the Regulation in question does not specify the criteria according to which a country would be removed from the group of beneficiary countries. Pursuant to the AB's reasoning, the EC's special incentive arrangements on the protection of labour rights and of the environment, in contrast with the drugs arrangement, included detailed provisions describing the procedure and criteria that apply to a request by a country to become a beneficiary.[42] By contrast, the EC was invited to revise its drugs arrangement, in order to comply with this interpretation of WTO law.

The importance of this decision partially transcends the object of this chapter. The AB decision encroaches upon some of the most widely debated issues relating to the compatibility of GSP systems with WTO law. The points made by the AB in the India case, however, have important implications for the use of preferential trade concessions as an instrument to indirectly improve MNEs human rights records in developing countries in at least two ways.

In the first place, the India case contributed to dispelling some of the concerns raised about an instrumental or protectionist use of trade concessions in the arrangements provided by developed countries' GSP schemes.[43] Adherence to a GSP system by a developing country would be more easily accepted if these concerns are dispelled by the use of criteria which objectively apply to all developing countries. The AB pointed out that, while it is at the discretion of developed countries whether or not to institute GSP schemes, once they have done so, these schemes have to comply with objective criteria. First, identical treatment must be available to all GSP beneficiaries who are similarly situated in terms of their

---

[41]   Ibid., para. 7.162.

[42]   Ibid., para. 7.167.

[43]   See R. Howse, 'India's WTO Challenge to Drug Enforcement Conditions in the European Community Generalized System of Preferences: A Little Known Case with Major Repercussions for "Political" Conditionality in US Trade Policy', available at: http://faculty.law.umich.edu/rhowse/Drafts_and_Publications/Howse3.pdf (accessed 19 May 2004).

development, financial and trade needs.[44] Secondly, the existence of a development, financial or trade need must be assessed according to objective standards. Thirdly, the conditions for preferential treatment should not be so onerous that they place 'unjustifiable burdens' on any developing country that wishes to take advantage of them. Finally, the tariff preferences accorded under the scheme must effectively address the need at issue, that is the development needs of developing countries. As a result, the criteria set out by the WTO AB can clearly contribute to improving the effectiveness of all GSP systems, promoting development and dispelling doubts about their protectionist or political use.[45]

The second important indication provided by the AB is a corollary of the first. The AB seems to have embraced a more comprehensive concept of development not solely based on economic factors. As shown by the reform of the GSP operated by the EC following the AB panel, it seems that this interpretation of development needs may have international human rights as an essential component. Therefore, even if the range of rights included in each regional GSP system may vary,[46] concessionary countries are obliged to show that the special arrangements set in place are genuinely aimed at promoting human rights and development in beneficiary countries. It is also interesting to note that the AB did not expressly suggest including international human rights as objective criteria. The EC, however, could not avoid referring to a number of international human rights conventions as one of the most widely accepted and objectively verifiable benchmarks for development.

To sum up, the AB decision in the India case provided a clear indication on the conditions that any GSP system should meet to be in compliance with WTO law. Not only has the AB dismissed the uncertainty about the legally binding nature of the Enabling Clause – which lays down the legal basis for GSP systems – but is has also pointed out that it requires

---

[44] According to the fundamental principle of non-discrimination, under WTO law, like countries (or products or services, depending on the context) must receive like treatment. It is rather more contentious whether this leads to a legal obligation to treat dissimilar countries in a dissimilar manner.

[45] The inclusion of Pakistan on a closed list of beneficiaries (and the exclusion of India) highlighted the fact that when such special arrangements are not subject to any kind of legal discipline, they may be utilized to fulfil the stated policy aims (e.g. rewarding countries with good anti-drug policies), but rather they may be utilized as a mechanism for achieving totally unrelated policy objectives (e.g. co-operation in combating terrorism). See Harrison, *supra* n. 14, at 1678.

[46] A comparison between the labour rights included in the US and EC GSP systems is provided by Alston, '"Core Labour Standards" and the Transformation', *supra* Ch.3 n. 111, at 492, 497ff.

developed countries to comply with specific legal obligations. After these clarifications over widely debated issues on the effect of trade on human rights and on development, GSP schemes can be seen as a more reliable instrument for the promotion not simply of labour rights, but also international human rights, whose contribution to development is no longer contested.[47]

9.4 HUMAN RIGHTS IN THE EU'S GENERALISED SYSTEM OF PREFERENCES

As noted above one of the most interesting effects of the India case on the EC's GSP has been the expansion of the human rights promoted in the context of the special arrangement defined as GSP Plus.

The mechanism for social conditionality, which was introduced within the GSP in 1998,[48] was originally limited to the protection of certain labour rights. The range of labour rights included as a condition for the concession of special arrangements and as a cause of temporary withdrawal from these arrangements was progressively expanded through this revision process.[49]

When the labour rights incentive was introduced, the countries concerned had to demonstrate that they had adopted and implemented in their national legislation the ILO's Conventions on the freedom of association (Convention n. 87), on the rights to organize and to bargain collectively (Convention n. 98), and on the minimum age for admission to employment (Convention n. 138).[50] On the other hand, withdrawal from the same labour incentives scheme was foreseen where any form of forced labour or export of goods made by prison labour were possible.[51]

---

[47] Harrison, *supra* n. 14, at 1679.

[48] The regime had already been set out in Regulations 3281/94 and 1256/96, which contained the previous regulation of GSP. See Regulation 3281/94 [1994] OJ L 348; Regulation 1256/96 [1996] OJ L 169. However, the provisions relating to the incentive arrangement needed a complementary Regulation to enable it to be put into practice. This was not approved until 1998 (referring to Regulation 1154/98 of 25 May 1998 [1998] OJ L 109). For a commentary on the Community GSP, see B. Atkinson, 'Trade Policy and Preferences', in C. Cosgrove-Sacks (ed.), *The European Union and Developing Countries,* 1999, Bruges, College of Europe, 305.

[49] On the early developments of the GSP see Brandtner and Rosas, 'Trade Preferences and Human Rights', *supra* Ch.4 n. 46, at 713ff.

[50] Art. 11, Council Regulation 2820/98.

[51] Ibid., Art. 22(1) a, b.

In line with what was suggested by the Commission in its Communication on Promoting Core Labour Standards,[52] the amended EC GSP Regulation of 2001[53] strengthened the social incentive scheme by providing for further improved market access opportunities, by making the scheme more transparent and by extending the basis to all of the four core labour standards in the 1998 ILO Declaration. The provision for temporary withdrawal was extended by broadening the basis to severe and systematic violations of any of the core labour standards.

By adding the ILO Conventions on forced labour and on non discrimination in respect of employment and occupation, Regulation No 2501/2001 brought the special incentive clause into line with the definition of 'core labour' standards adopted by the ILO,[54] Temporary withdrawal is foreseen in case of serious and systematic violation of the freedom of association, the right to collective bargaining, or the principle of non-discrimination in respect of employment and occupation or use of child labour, in addition to the already mentioned use of slavery, forced labour and prison labour.[55] The only difference left between these two provisions relates only to the use of prison labour.

The development and definition of core labour standards in the ILO's 1998 'Declaration on Fundamental Principles and Rights at Work and its Follow-up' was a factor which contributed to a broader recognition of labour rights in the GSP. Express reference to the Declaration is made in recital 18 of the Preamble and, as evidence of the EU's reliance on the ILO's work, the assessments, decisions and conclusions by the ILO's supervisory body should serve as the point of departure for considerations on the eligibility for special incentives and for investigations as to whether withdrawal from GSP would be justified.

As a result of the latest revision the GSP labour rights arrangement has finally developed into a comprehensive human rights arrangement (the

---

[52]   Communication from the Commission to the Council, the European Parliament and the Economic and Social Committee, *Promoting Core Labour Standards, supra* Ch.7 n. 68.

[53]   Council Regulation (EC) 2501/2001 of 10 December, 2001 applying a Scheme of generalised tariff preferences for the period from 1 January 2002 to 31 December 2004 [2001] OJ L 346/1. Entered into force on 1 January 2002 (See Art. 14).

[54]   See Proposal for a Council Regulation Applying a Scheme of Generalised Tariff Preferences for the Period 1 January 2002 to 31 December 2004 COM (2001) 293 final, Brussels, 12 June 2001, para. 32 of the Explanatory Memorandum. See also the position of the Commission as expressed in *Promoting Core Labour Standards, supra* Ch.7 n. 68, at 22.

[55]   Art. 26(1) a, b, c Regulation 1501/2001.

GSP Plus). Regulation 732/2008,[56] brought to 26 the number of the conventions which developing countries will need to 'ratify and effectively implement' in order to qualify for the special incentives: all sixteen core human and labour rights UN/ILO Conventions[57] which cover human rights, labour rights, and all ten conventions and protocols on environmental protection, corruption and combating illegal drug production and trafficking.[58] Moreover, the new Regulation specifies that 'the monitoring and review mechanism envisaged in the relevant conventions and related instruments' (for instance the ILO on labour issues, appropriate UN agencies on human rights issues) will be utilized in order to make decisions about eligibility for GSP Plus, and will be the point of departure for investigations into subsequent withdrawal of the benefits of the arrangements,

---

[56]   Art. 8 Regulation (EC) 732/2008 and Annex III, *supra* n. 26.

[57]   1. International Covenant on Civil and Political Rights; 2. International Covenant on Economic, Social and Cultural Rights; 3. International Convention on the Elimination of All Forms of Racial Discrimination; 4. Convention on the Elimination of All Forms of Discrimination Against Women; 5. Convention Against Torture and other Cruel, Inhuman or Degrading Treatment or Punishment; 6. Convention on the Rights of the Child; 7. Convention on the Prevention and Punishment of the Crime of Genocide; 8. Convention concerning Minimum Age for Admission to Employment (No 138); 9. Convention concerning the Prohibition and Immediate Action for the Elimination of the Worst Forms of Child Labour (No 182); 10. Convention concerning the Abolition of Forced Labour (No 105); 11. Convention concerning Forced or Compulsory Labour (No 29); 12. Convention concerning Equal Remuneration for Men and Women Workers for Work of Equal Value (No 100); 13. Convention concerning Discrimination in Respect of Employment and Occupation (No 111); 14. Convention concerning Freedom of Association and Protection of the Right to Organise (No 87); 15. Convention concerning the Application of the Principles of the Right to Organise and to Bargain Collectively (No 98) Annex III, Pt A, Regulation (EC) No. 732/2008, *supra* n. 26; 16. International Convention on the Suppression and Punishment of the Crime of Apartheid.

[58]   17. Montreal Protocol on Substances that Deplete the Ozone Layer; 18. Basel Convention on the Control of Transboundary Movements of Hazardous Wastes and Their Disposal; 19. Stockholm Convention on Persistent Organic Pollutants; 20. Convention on International Trade in Endangered Species of Wild Fauna and Flora; 21. Convention on Biological Diversity; 22. Cartagena Protocol on Biosafety; L 211/38 EN Official Journal of the European Union 6.8.2008; 23. Kyoto Protocol to the United Nations Framework Convention on Climate Change; 24. United Nations Single Convention on Narcotic Drugs (1961); 25. United Nations Convention on Psychotropic Substances (1971); 26. United Nations Convention against Illicit Traffic in Narcotic Drugs and Psychotropic Substances (1988); 27. United Nations Convention against Corruption (Mexico). See Annex III Part B, Regulation No. 732/2008 *supra* n. 26.

if there are serious and systematic violations of the principles laid down in the conventions.[59]

By listing all relevant UN human rights, environmental and anticorruption conventions the EC responded to the need for objective criteria and response to developmental needs highlighted by the AB in the India case. The impact of such amendment has further implications on the use of the GSP for the promotion of human rights in developing countries.

In the first place, reference to all main international human rights instruments reinforces the principles of indivisibility and interdependence of civil and political rights and economic social and cultural rights, which has been increasingly reaffirmed both at the international level and in the external relations of the EC.

Secondly, thanks to this development, the protection afforded to human rights in the GSP scheme seems to have been brought into line with the other external relations instruments of the EC which promote human rights. As examined in Chapter 2, human rights clauses in the EC's external agreements, as well as those enshrined in unilateral instruments, usually refer to human rights *tout court*, thus including both civil and political and economic, social and cultural rights. The principle of indivisibility and interdependence of human rights is reaffirmed in the text of relevant regulations and agreements[60] and in various Commission programmatic documents.[61] In this context, the so called 'social clause' in the GSP represented an exception. As a result, the new GSP Plus arrangement has prompted more coherence within the EC's external action[62] and between the latter and the international human rights legal framework.

Apart from having enhanced coherence, the recognition of a broader range of rights makes the GSP more suitable for the improvement of human rights records in developing countries. A particular claim can be made that holistic measures that tackle human rights standards in countries as a whole are better directed than those that simply target export sectors.[63] While the previous regime could have the shortcoming of affecting only export sectors from industries in developing countries, the new GSP

---

[59]   Arts 8(3) and 15(1), Council Regulation 732/2008 *supra*, n. 26.

[60]   See Pt III Ch.8.

[61]   See *Promoting Human Rights, supra* Ch.4 n. 40.

[62]   The need for enhanced coherence in EU's external action is also spelled out in the Treaty Establishing a Constitution for Europe (Art. I-3(4)).

[63]   See J. Harrison, 'The Impact of the World Trade Organisation on the Protection and Promotion of Human Rights' (EUI Thesis, 2005) at 96. Alston, 'Linking Trade and Development', *supra* Ch.7 n. 73.

scheme pursues an overall increase of human rights records. The new GSP scheme may encourage a broader range of industries in developing countries to respect human rights, and in turn the MNE subsidiaries working there. As a consequence, the improvement in human rights may result less uneven, also including the informal sector and women.[64]

To date, Burma/Myanmar[65] and Belarus[66] are the only countries to have had preferences withdrawn on grounds of breach of fundamental labour rights.

9.4.1 Concession and Withdrawal of Special Arrangements under the GSP

Under the previous GSP regime[67] for a country to be granted preferential treatment, it had to present a request to the Commission of the European Union which demonstrated that not only did it incorporate the substance of the relevant ILO core labour standards in domestic legislation, but it also had to prove that effective implementing and monitoring mechanisms were in place.

This approach was criticized by Alston who maintained that a widespread use of the concept of core labour standards has undermined the promotion of labour issues, by separating core labour standards from the relevant ILO Conventions and the rights based approach contained

---

[64]   One author concludes her detailed examination of the advantages for women of working in the export oriented garment industries by arguing that international labour standards on imported goods are ineffective because they fail to affect wages and conditions that prevail in alternative forms of employment: N. Kabeer, 'Globalisation Labour Standards and Women's Rights: Dilemmas Of Collective Inaction in an Interdependent World' (2004) 10 *Feminist Economics* 3, at 25.

[65]   Council Regulation (EC) 552/97 of 24 March 1997 temporarily withdrawing access to generalized tariff preferences from the Union of Myanmar [1997] OJ L 85 8–9. Moldova was already removed from the beneficiary list of the current GSP Regulation at the same time as the EC granted it more far-reaching autonomous preferences under a separate legal instrument in March 2008. This removal is confirmed in the listing of beneficiary countries of the new Regulation.

[66]   *Access to the Generalised Tariff Preferences from the Republic of Belarus*, *supra* Ch.7 n.66.

[67]   In Council Regulation (EC) 2501/2001, *supra* Ch.7 n. 60, they appeared under Title III (Arts 14–20 (labour standards) and 21–24 (environmental standards). Previously the provisions relating to these incentives appeared under Title II (Arts 8–21) of Council Regulation (EC) 2820/98 of 21 December 1998, which entered into force on 1 July 1999, [1998] OJ 1998 L 357/1, amended by Regulation No 416/2001 [2001] OJ L 60/43.

within them. The 1998 ILO Declaration encouraged monitoring systems alternative to the ILO's and the widespread use of the concept of 'core labour standards'. Notwithstanding the enthusiasm that has greeted these innovations, Alston argued that the resulting regime has major potential flaws, including: an excessive reliance on principles rather than rights; a system which invokes principles that are disconnected from the corresponding standards and are thus effectively undefined; an ethos of voluntarism in relation to implementation and enforcement; an unstructured and unaccountable decentralization of responsibility; and a willingness to accept soft 'promotionalism' as the end result. The risk is the development selection of standards almost entirely detached from any international treaty moorings, a purely national system of evaluation of other countries records, such as in the US GSP scheme.[68]

The new GSP scheme seems to be, in principle, less vulnerable to this type of criticism than the previous EC–GSP system. The EC–GSP Plus now requires countries not simply to comply with international human rights and labour rights conventions, but it also calls for countries to actually have signed and ratified the Conventions from which the standards are drawn. In doing so the EC actually goes even further then the ILO's own approach, which in recent years has favoured compliance with core labour standards as laid down in the 1998 ILO Declaration, rather than ratification.[69]

Not only have Regulation 980/2005 and Regulation 732/2008 expanded the range of labour and human rights which may lead to the temporary withdrawal of preferential arrangements provided for in the GSP Community scheme, but it has introduced an important qualitative change in the conditions for eligibility to the GSP arrangement.

The assessment of eligibility to the GSP Plus arrangement on the basis of a number of international conventions, and utilizing the expertise of relevant international organizations and agencies, also points in the

---

[68]   Alston, '"Core Labour Standards" and the Transformation', *supra* Ch.3 n. 111, at 457. B. Langille confuted Alston's arguments pointing out that this view is available only on a very narrow and conventional understanding of the purpose of international labour law. He suggests that a better understanding is available which enables us to see core labour rights as conceptually coherent (and not politically arbitrary), morally salient (and not merely part of an empty neo-liberal conspiracy) and pragmatically vital to the achievement of our true goals, including the 'enforceability' of the 'non-core' (and not an undermining of the whole regime from within). See B. Langille, 'Core Labour Rights – The True Story (Reply to Alston)' (2005) 16 E.J.I.L. 409.

[69]   For a critique of this approach see Alston, '"Core Labour Standards" and the Transformation', *supra* Ch.3 n. 111, at 476ff.

direction of a fairer evaluation of applicant countries against objective standards. The relevant conventions, indeed, are those with mechanisms that the relevant international organizations can use to regularly evaluate how effectively they have been implemented. The Commission will take account of the evaluations by the international organizations responsible for each international agreement concerned before deciding which of the applicant countries will be selected to benefit from the GSP Plus. This means that clear discriminatory treatments are less likely to occur. From a legal perspective, the coherence and transparency of the system are enhanced, since preferences are granted fairly and on the grounds of the stated policy objectives.

The relevance accorded to human rights is reinforced by the provision of temporary withdrawal from the preferential arrangements (which may affect some or all of the products from the country in question), in case of serious and systematic violations of eight selected international conventions on human rights and labour rights.[70] Withdrawal follows an enquiry and investigation procedure, and measures, and is decided by the Council. If information on alleged practices in violation of the above labour rights is received by the Commission, or by a Member State, the Commission may begin an official investigation. The investigation is carried out by the Commission in liaison with the Generalised Preferences Committee, which assists the Commission in implementing the Regulation, the beneficiary country, and international organizations and agencies which monitor the relevant conventions.[71]

In addition, for countries which do not yet meet the GSP Plus qualifying criteria, Regulation 732/2008 provides an additional opportunity for applications in mid-2010, half-way through the life of the Regulation. This is a change from Regulation 980/2005, where unsuccessful applicants were obliged to wait three years before being able to re-apply. GSP Plus applicants which are successful later this year will not be affected by this new mid-term window: their GSP Plus status should normally be maintained throughout the three year duration of the new Regulation.

In conclusion, the arrangements in the GSP have evolved in the light of an incentive scheme for the improvement of human rights records of the

---

[70]   Listed in Pt A of Annex III.

[71]   The Burma case remains the only one so far in which the negative aspects of the labour rights clause has been applied. See Council Regulation 552/97 of 27 March 1997 on temporarily withdrawing Access to generalised system of preferences from the Union of Myanmar/Burma [1997] OJ L 85/8. This decision remained confirmed by Regulation 732/2008 (Preamble, indent 23) *supra* n. 26. For a detailed account on the Burma case see Fierro, *supra* Ch.1 n. 107, at 371–6.

applicant country as such, rather than being confined to labour rights. By requiring effective ratification of a list or relevant international conventions, including ILO Conventions on which core labour standards are based, goes even further than the ILO itself requires of its member States. Since the 1998 declaration, the ILO has indeed advocated an approach of compliance with core labour standards independently of actual ratification of the relevant conventions. This reform of the GSP system seems to have embraced a holistic approach to sustainable development, which recognizes the interrelation between economic development, the protection of the environment and the respect and promotion of human rights, including labour rights and their protection.[72]

9.5   CONCLUSIONS ON THE GSP

The latest GSP regulations have expanded the types of human rights violations which may lead to the temporary withdrawal of preferential arrangements provided for in the GSP Community scheme.[73] Before the latest reform they were limited to the 'core labour standards'.[74] The new GSP Plus arrangement includes not only all social, economic and cultural rights, but also civil political rights, as enshrined in the main UN and ILO conventions. The expansion of the range of human rights is matched by a reinforcement of application requirements. Applicant countries are no longer asked merely to comply with the content of relevant conventions, but they are also required to ratify and effectively implement them.

It follows that the GSP has evolved from an instrument targeting respect for labour rights to a comprehensive instrument aimed at promoting sustainable development, with human rights as an essential component. Human rights have acquired autonomous relevance in the context of the GSP Regulation, to the point that serious breaches of eight fundamental human rights conventions may lead to the suspension of preferential arrangements.

The importance of the reform of the GSP for the overarching question of this book is twofold. To begin with, the new GSP, in line with the other human rights instruments examined in previous chapters, can exercise a

---

[72]   Recital 22 of Regulation 732/2008, *supra* n. 26.
[73]   See Art. 15(1), (2) and Art. 27 Regulation 723/2008; Art. 26, Regulation 2501/2001; Art. 22, Regulation 2820/98, and Arts 8–11 Regulation 980/2005.
[74]   See Tsogas, 'Labour Standards in the General System of Preferences International,' *supra* n. 22 at 363.

pressure on developing countries to comply with universally recognized human rights. As argued at the outset of this chapter, a higher level of compliance with human rights in developing countries can in turn improve the human rights record of MNEs operating in these countries by imposing indirect obligations on MNEs.

Having included a broader range of human rights, the GSP has the potential to involve larger sectors of industries in the improvement of workers' rights and respect for human rights. It has been pointed out that trade measures which affect only export only improve the conditions of those who are involved in the export industries of developing countries.[75] On the contrary, the new GSP scheme pursues an overall increase of human rights compliance in developing countries. As a consequence, the improvement of human rights may turn out to be less uneven, also including the informal sector and women.[76]

The second feature of the new GSP scheme that can improve its effectiveness is its reliance on the other UN and ILO mechanisms. On the one hand, relying on international monitoring systems reinforces the GSP, anchoring it to the international regime of protection of human rights and in its actual application. It represents a contribution to the unity of the system for the international protection of human rights and countervails the tendency of an increasingly fragmented approach to the protection of human rights, including unilateral conditionality.[77] On the other hand, the UN human rights monitoring system itself presents a lot of shortcomings. The fact that it has reached such a level of specialization makes coordination among different human rights monitoring systems difficult.[78] As a result, the new system may prove to be more complex than it appears at first sight. Such complexity may lead to the imposition of a real burden for the applicant country, which is required to have signed and ratified a number of conventions which are monitored by different bodies (i.e. CEDAW), against the conclusions of the panel in the *India v EC* case.

Despite the latest amendments, some critiques of the GSP scheme remain valid. Regulation No 2501/2001 had introduced some changes to the review and consultation process which improved, in part, the degree

---

[75]   Alston, 'Linking Trade and Human Rights', *supra* Ch.7 n. 73, at 127.
[76]   Ibid., at 129.
[77]   Alston, '"Core Labour Standards" and the Transformation', *supra* Ch.3 n. 111.
[78]   It is among the proposals for the reform of the UN to create a unique human rights monitoring body for the UN: F. Francioni, 'The Role of the EU in Promoting Reform of the UN in the Field of Human Rights and Enviromental Protection' (2005) 78 *Chaillot Paper* 31 at 35ff.

of transparency and participation in the procedure.[79] However, a previous suggestion put forward by the Commission, according to which unilateral suspension of GSP benefits should take place only after an ILO complaints procedure relating to breach of core labour standards has been followed,[80] has not been upheld in the new GSP Regulation.

It has to be welcomed, however, the fact that in the implementation of the GSP regulation, the Commission has retained a coordination with the ILO's monitoring system. The Council Regulation (EC) No 1933/2006,[81] which temporarily withdraws access to the GSP from Belarus, is based on negative findings of ILO reports on freedom of association.

As far as the other human rights in the regulation are concerned, however, coordination with the relevant UN agencies or monitoring committee can prove to be difficult, given the multiplication of human rights monitoring bodies within the UN system.[82] This situation may improve when the reform of the UN human rights monitoring system, which foresees a streamlining of existing committees, is fully implemented.[83]

Secondly, the overall effectiveness of GSP schemes for the improvement of human rights records in the applicant countries, and for the human rights records of MNEs in particular, is still to be proved. Some concerns have been raised by the fact that the Commission, in a decision of 9 December 2008 lists 16 beneficiary countries on one page.[84] Before the reform, the successful applications were accompanied by a notice and a reasoned opinion by the Commission. This raises the question as to the effectiveness of the new GSP scheme. The worry is that despite a broader more detailed inclusion of international human rights instruments as a condition for access to preferential treatment, control by the Commission will be more formalistic than substantial. In addition, the new GSP still suffers from the lack of a monitoring system which could evaluate compliance with international human rights standards, not only

---

[79]   Art. 16(3) Regulation 1501/2001.

[80]   *Promoting Core Labour Standards, supra* Ch.7 n. 68, at 14.

[81]   *Access to the Generalised Tariff Preferences from the Republic of Belarus, supra* Ch.7 n. 66.

[82]   J. Crawford, 'The UN Human Rights Treaty System: A system in crisis?', in P. Alston and J. Crawford (eds), *The Future of UN Human Rights Treaty Monitoring*, 2000, Cambridge, Cambridge University Press, 1.

[83]   See Francioni, 'The Role of the EU in Promoting Reform', *supra* n. 78.

[84]   Commission Decision of 9 December 2008 on the list of the beneficiary countries which qualify for the special incentive arrangement for sustainable development and good governance, provided for in Council Regulation (EC) No 732/2008 applying a scheme of generalised tariff preferences for the period from 1 January 2009 to 31 December 2011.

at the time of concession of preferential treatment, but also throughout its application.

Finally, related to the previous argument, even if the new GSP scheme may encourage a broader range of industries in developing countries to respect human rights, the reform did not fully exploit its potential in addressing human rights violations by MNEs. Had the reform also had MNEs as a target, this should probably have been reflected in the choice of products (i.e. agricultural products) and the range of conventions, in order to include broader sectors of suppliers, informal economy etc.[85]

9.6   IMPROVING THE MONITORING SYSTEM: THE US–CAMBODIA AGREEMENT

The above reflections on the development of GSP system, suggest that the GSP has moved from a mere labour rights conditionality to a more comprehensive human rights conditionality. This development seems to contribute to the overall improvement of human rights conditions in MNEs' host countries. Critiques have been addressed to the Commission's capacity to effectively control an applicant country's compliance with the large number of human rights conventions now recognized under the GSP Plus arrangement. The progressive involvement of the ILO and the UN in providing information on the countries' compliance with labour rights and human rights before entering the GSP system is welcome. It is also true that the large number of conventions covered by the new Regulation poses the question of coordination between the ILO, the UN human rights monitoring bodies and the EC. On the whole, while the new GSP regulation has defined more clearly the standards to be met, it has left open the question as to how compliance with these standards should be ensured.

The analysis carried out so far has looked at the GSP system as a measure addressed to host States of MNEs. If addressing the responsibility of MNEs for human rights has become a priority in the EC's external relations, it can be argued that the GSP system could have been revised, also taking this instance into account.

In this context, a comparison can be made between the EC's GSP and the US–Cambodia Bilateral Textile Agreement[86] (hereinafter the

---

[85]   Alston, 'Linking Trade and Human Rights', *supra* Ch.7 n. 73.

[86]   Agreement Relating to Trade in Cotton, Wool, Man-made Fiber, Non-Cotton Vegetable Fiber and Silk Blend Textiles and Textile Products Between the Government of the United States of America and the Royal Government of Cambodia, signed on 20 January 1999, and renewed in December 2001, available

Cambodia Agreement). The Cambodia Agreement may provide a useful example for the EC's GSP for two reasons. First of all, the Cambodia Agreement combines a trade measure (quota system) with a factory monitoring system to improve working conditions and core labour rights along the supply chain. In return for substantial compliance with international labour standards in its apparel sector, Cambodia was promised a 14 per cent annual increase on each textile and apparel item under US quota. Secondly, the Cambodia agreement foresees that the ILO conducts the factory monitoring.

The ILO monitoring project in Cambodia is an example of an important confluence of two different methods of protecting social rights: linking trade with labour rights, and factory monitoring. While the linkage of trade with labour rights is typically directed towards improving labour rights enforcement at the State level through better public regulation, monitoring concentrates on the factory level. In the Cambodia Agreement the trade provision was designed so that performance of the garment sector, not the government, was used as a basis for granting extra trade benefits.[87] Factory owners, therefore, have a collective incentive to improve their labour conditions because of the quota incentive created in the Agreement. The monitoring also serves a second function: factory owners have individual incentives to respect workers' rights because of pressure that is exerted by purchasers who require positive ILO reports.

The monitoring system was the result of an accord among the US, the Cambodian Government and the Garment Manufacturers Association of Cambodia, who also share the financing of the project.[88] It provides that four teams of two monitors will each inspect participating Cambodian apparel factories. Each factory will be monitored on average six times per year. The effectiveness of the monitoring system relies on exposure to public publicity in ILO reports of manufacturers which did not comply

---

at: http://www.tcc.mac.doc.gov/cgi-bin/doit.cgi?204:64:189233445:25 (accessed 10 November 2005).

[87] On the question of whether or not monitoring programs hamper or complement public regulatory systems see A. Blackett, 'Global Governance, Legal Pluralism and the Decentered State: A Labor Law Critique of Codes of Corporate Conduct?' (2001) 8 *Indian Journal of Global Legal Studies* 401.

[88] The cost of the program was budgeted at $2.2 million: $200,000 was to come from the Cambodian government, an equal amount from the Garment Manufacturers Association of Cambodia (GMAC), and the remaining $1.8 million from the US government. K. Kolben, 'Trade, Monitoring, and the ILO: Working to Improve Conditions in Cambodia's Garment Factories' (2004) 7 *Yale Human Rights & Development Law Journal* 79, at 91.

with Cambodia's Labour Code.[89] The ILO monitoring system proved to be a mechanism for changing attitudes and behaviour of at least firms in the textile industry.[90] In addition, a number of garment manufacturers used favourable ILO reports to attract international buyers in Cambodia. After being involved in a scandal relating to the use of child labour, the American MNE Nike returned to Cambodia, considering the ILO monitoring system as an important factor in its decision.[91]

Despite its positive impact on labour rights in Cambodia, the monitoring system could have been improved by wider participation of Cambodian civil society and by endowing the monitoring body with more stringent powers. For instance, the American textile garment workers Union (UNITE) suggested the establishment of a monitoring body composed equally of Cambodian government officials, independent Cambodian labour rights experts, and ILO representatives. This monitoring body would also have had the power to conduct unannounced investigations of factories. It would also have had remedial powers, such as the exclusive authority to implement the functions of dispute resolution and mediation as provided for in the law[92] It was also suggested that evaluation should have been based on individual factory performance rather than on the overall industry performance.[93]

It should be emphasized that the Cambodia Agreement represents a peculiar experiment in progress. Firstly, it is a bilateral agreement and it relates only to a small sector of imports to the US. Secondly, the existence of the agreement itself depends on pending entry of Cambodia to the WTO. As a member of the WTO, Cambodia would be part of the Agreement on Textile and clothing, thus no longer subject to export quota restrictions.[94] WTO rules on GSP would apply as well, ensuring that there

---

[89]   See ILO, Eighth Synthesis Report on the Working Conditions Situation in Cambodia's Garment Sector, available at: http:// www.ilo.org/public/english/dialogue/ifpdial/publ/cambodia8.htm (accessed 18 April 2004).

[90]   R. Abrami, *Worker Rights and Global Trade: The US-Cambodia Bilateral Textile Trade Agreement*, 2003, Boston, Harvard Business School Publishing, at 11.

[91]   Ibid., at 15.

[92]   See UNITE, Memorandum on Proposals for Bilateral Trade Agreement by/from UNITE (19 November 1998).

[93]   Interview with Prof. Mark Barenberg, Columbia University Law School, in New York, NY (November 2005).

[94]   According to Art. 19 of the Cambodia Agreement, in the event that Cambodia becomes a member of the World Trade Organization (WTO), and the United States applies the WTO Agreement) to Cambodia, the provisions set out in paras 2, 3, 4, 5, 6, 7, 8, 9, 10, 11, 12, 13, 14, 15, and 20 will be necessary in rela-

is no discrimination among developing countries, thus making it more difficult to target a specific country. Secondly, the signing of the agreement was possible only thanks to a conjunction of favourable economic and political factors.[95] Therefore, it seems that the Cambodia agreement represents an exception in the context of US bilateral trade relationships, rather than having set a trend.[96]

In drawing a comparison between the Cambodia Agreement and the EC's GSP instruments two crucial differences should be borne in mind: while the first is based on a quota system, the latter envisages a tariff system; in addition, they affect different types of products. Despite the limits of such a comparison, some elements of the Cambodia Agreement should be instructive for designers of a prospective monitoring program linked to the EC–GSP system.

The Cambodia Agreement seeks to address two of the problems that still affect the EC's GSP, such as the lack of an efficient monitoring system and the failure to directly address MNEs' compliance with the human rights standards referred to in the special arrangements. It does so by involving the relevant international monitoring agency (the ILO). A further involvement of civil society in the monitoring activities would also have been desirable. As it stands, however, it provides one of the most innovative attempts to link trade and labour rights and in setting up a transparent monitoring system. For that reason, even if it cannot be considered a flawless model, it is an example of a trade agreement that couples labour rights incentives addressed to a State with a firm level monitoring system.

In conclusion, despite its specific features, the Cambodia Agreement can provide some interesting suggestions for the prospective evolution of the EC–GSP scheme. In particular the possibility of setting up a firm monitoring system in the countries which are beneficiaries of the GSP plus special arrangement should be further explored in the European context. Not only would this contribute to ensuring States' compliance with human

---

tionship to the implementation of Agreement on Textiles and Clothing. Therefore, upon membership of Cambodia in the WTO and application of the WTO agreement by the United States to Cambodia, those provisions will remain in force and will be notified to the Textile Monitoring Body.

[95]   Abrami indicates the growing total value of Cambodia garment export. See Abrami, *supra* n. 90 at 2. Kolben underlines the role of American trade unions in the US in making pressure on Clinton's administration's for the inclusion of labour rights in the agreement. See Kolben, *supra* n. 88.

[96]   D. Kinley and J. Tadaki, 'From Talk to Walk: the Emergence of Human Rights Responsibilities for Corporations at International Law', 44 *Virginia Journal of International Law Association*, (2004) 931, at 1016.

rights and labour rights, but it would also provide an incentive for companies to comply with them.

9.7   THE EC ASSOCIATION AGREEMENT WITH CHILE

The Association Agreement between the EU and Chile is the first Agreement in which the Parties, in accordance with the Communication 'Corporate Social Responsibility: A Business Contribution to Sustainable Development', called on Multinational Enterprises to respect the OECD Guidelines for Multinational Enterprises. After the successful conclusion of the negotiations, the EU-Chile Association Agreement was initialled on 10 June 2002 in Brussels, subsequently approved by the Commission and finally signed on 18 November, hence allowing the Chilean Congress to start its own adoption procedure.[97]

The Association Agreement consists of three main chapters: trade, co-operation and political dialogue.[98] By strengthening the economic ties between the EU and Chile, the trade related provisions of the Association Agreement are expected to contribute to significant economic and commercial benefits.[99] The Agreement rules on competition, intellectual property and an effective dispute settlement mechanism were also included in

---

[97]   The adoption procedure was completed by the Chilean Parliament on 14 January 2003. Some provisions of the Agreement, (i.e. mainly provisions to the trade in goods, to government procurement, to competition and to the dispute settlement mechanism and the chapter on cooperation) have been provisionally applied since 1 February 2003. The provisions on: political dialogue, current payments and capital movements, intellectual property rights, titles of the trade part such as services and the core of the co-operation part, will enter into force after the assent of the European Parliament has been obtained and once the national Parliaments of the EU Member States have ratified the Agreement. While the European Parliament gave its assent at its plenary session of 12 February, National Parliaments must still ratify the Agreement.

[98]   Art. 2 of the EU–Chile Association Agreement, *supra* Ch.1 n. 93

[99]   '[W]e reaffirm our conviction that the trade chapter will promote economic growth and support sustainable development, to the benefit of both the European Union and Chile. Negotiations have delivered the most ambitious and innovative results ever for a bilateral Agreement of this kind by the European Union as well as Chile'. Joint Declaration signed by the President of the European Council M. José María Aznar, the President of Chile, M. Ricardo Lagos, and the President of the European Commission, M. Romano Prodi, Madrid, 17 May 2002, available at: http://europa.eu.int/comm/external_relations/chile/assoc_agr/ma05_02.htm (accessed 4 April 2006).

the Agreement. An intensified cooperation is foreseen also in several other areas, with a view to favouring a sustainable economic, social and environmental model.

The political chapter of the Association Agreement aims at strengthening the political dialogue between the EU and Chile. It is permeated by the common commitment to the promotion of democratic values. The European Union and Chile agreed to put the respect for human rights, the freedom of the individual and the rule of law at the core of their political cooperation, which will entail coordination of positions and joint initiatives in international *fora*. Political cooperation will be fostered by an increased participation and consultation of civil society in cooperation matters. Consultation with parliaments and representatives of civil society is seen as a guarantee of accountability and transparency and, the exchange of views on cooperation strategies and their implementation is encouraged.

As regards co-operation, the parties declared they would pursue the promotion of sustainable economic, social and environmental development. It is in this chapter that the most innovative aspects have been introduced. The Agreement refers to fields such as, co-operation on technical regulations, customs procedures, and intellectual property rights, which were not included in the 1996 Framework Co-operation Agreement between the EU and Chile.

The commitment of the parties to agreement to the integration of Corporate Social Responsibility principles was apparent since the negotiations[100] by affirming that: 'The Community and its Member States and Chile jointly remind their multinational enterprises of their recommendation to observe the OECD Guidelines for Multinational Enterprises, wherever they operate.'

---

[100] The intention of establishing a political and economic Association Agreement between the EU and Chile was initially drawn up in the Framework Co-operation Agreement of 1996. On the basis of this Agreement, the Commission presented directives for negotiations to the Council in July 1998, which were subsequently formally approved at the General Affairs Council of 13 September 1999. The objective of establishing a political and economic Association Agreement between Mercosur, Chile and the European Union was then strongly reaffirmed on the occasion of the first EU and Latin America and Caribbean Summit, which took place in Rio de Janeiro on 28–29 June 1999. See Meeting of Heads of State and Government from Mercosur and Chile & from the EU Joint Communiqué of Rio de Janeiro – 28 June 1999–9410/99 (Press 207), available at: http://europa.eu.int/comm/external_relations/chile/assoc_agr/pol.htm (accessed 3 April 2006). Since May 2004, negotiations are carried out on the basis of informal technical meetings between MERCOSUR and the EU.

The OECD Guidelines for Multinational Enterprises, respect for democratic principles, human rights and the rule of law are defined as essential elements of the agreement. The promotion of sustainable economic and social development and the equitable distribution of the benefits of the Association Agreement are held as guiding principles for its implementation.

In order to understand the reasons that led to the inclusion of Corporate Social Responsibility principles in the agreement, is it important to emphasize that the issue of environmental and social sustainability issues had been addressed in Chile for quite some time.[101] Environmental quality and sustainability had been promoted at a national level, by setting up structures which in some cases took the form of fully effective regulatory bodies. Given this background, the EU can play a double role in mitigating the negative sustainability consequences of the EU–Chile Agreement. The EU can act as a participant in initiatives which are already under way and as a supporter where new resources are required for research. Moreover, dialogue between stakeholders, at national and local levels, is to be facilitated where a consensus is still to be reached within Chile.

The Sustainable Impact Assessment (SIA),[102] which preceded the negotiations, strongly recommended that Corporate Social Responsibility issues were held to be included as an essential part of the Agreement and its implementation.[103] The commitment from foreign and domestic companies to high levels of environmental and social behaviour was seen as contributing 'to the efforts of governments and maximise the benefits of the Agreement, while minimising its negative impacts.'[104] Corporate Social Responsibility initiatives were held to play a major role in supporting the efforts of stakeholders and flanking measures of the Parties. The

---

[101] 'The sectors where the sustainability impacts have been most noted are those where there is competition for non-marketed resources: fishing and agriculture'. Sustainable Impact Assessment (SIA) of the trade aspects of negotiations for an Association Agreement between the European Communities and Chile (Specific agreement No. 11) Final Report October 2002, at 217, available at: http://www.planistat.com/sia/report/SA%20nbr1%20final%20Oct%202002.pdf (accessed 3 April 2003).

[102] A SIA is a process undertaken before and during a trade negotiation which seeks to identify economic, social and environmental impacts of the trade agreement, and should help to integrate sustainability into trade policy by informing negotiators of the possible social, environmental and economic consequences of a trade agreement.

[103] 'CSR issues should therefore constitute an integral part of the implementation of the Agreement' Sustainable Impact Assessment, *supra*, Ch.9 n. 101, at 217.

[104] Ibid., at 13.

EU–Chile Association Agreement aims at reinforcing the existing growth trends of Chile.

However, in order to maximize the benefit of the agreement for Chile, pre-existing social and environmental issues should be taken into account and eventual additional mitigating measures should be adopted to address underlying situations. To this aim, Corporate Social Responsibility initiatives can play a major role in supporting the efforts of stakeholders and mitigating measures of the Parties. By committing themselves to reach high levels of environmental and social behaviours, the companies, foreign and domestic, will help to support the efforts of governments, and thus maximize the benefits of the Agreement, while minimizing its negative impacts. Moreover, dialogue between stakeholders, at national and local levels, will help to reach better understandings on their respective concerns and objectives.

The commitment to comply with the OECD guidelines was not transposed into the operative part of agreement, in the form of a 'social clause', but it is contained in a Joint Declaration. It seems however, that further developments are not precluded. On the contrary, the proposal of introducing similar considerations into future EU agreements with ACP countries and Latin American countries has been put forward within the Commission.[105] To date, however, the EU–Chile represents an isolated case, since no follow up has been given to the introduction of similar clauses in other EC agreements.

Although it is early to see what the development of the inclusion of this OECD clause would be, a parallelism can be traced with the introduction of human rights concerns into the external agreements of the European Union.[106] In the context of EU relationships with the ACP States, a reference to fundamental rights was initially contained in the preamble of the Third Lomé Convention.[107] Human rights were subsequently included in

---

[105] See European Commission Directorate-General for Trade Directorate F – WTO: sustainable development, investment, standards, intellectual property, new technologies. Bilateral trade relations IV Investments, standards & certification, TBT, Note To 133 Committee, Corporate Social Responsibility and Trade policy – Implementing CSR practices and the OECD Guidelines for Multinational Enterprises in developing countries Brussels, 7 June 2004.

[106] On this development See K. Arts, *Integrating Human Rights into Development Cooperation : the Case of the Lomé Convention,* 2000, The Hague, London and Boston, Kluwer Law International, at 167; M. Bulterman, *supra* Ch.4 n. 109, at 151.

[107] Third ACP–EEC Convention signed at Lomé on 8 December 1984 [1986] OJ L 86/3.

the operative part of the Fourth Convention[108] and finally considered as an essential element of the agreement in Cotonou.[109]

9.8   CONCLUSIONS

This chapter sought to explore to what extent the EC's common commercial policy can be used to enhance respect for human rights in connection with the activities of MNEs. In particular, the GSP scheme and the EC Association Agreement with Chile have been examined.

Despite the difficulty surrounding the linkage between trade and human rights, the use of GSP systems to respond to the developmental need of developing countries has recently received a legitimization by the AB panel on the India case. Not only has the AB laid down stringent conditions under which the use of trade preferences can be allowed, but it has also opened considerations to include human rights as a core component of development. As a consequence, the EC has amended its GSP regime by subordinating trade concessions to respect and ratification of a comprehensive list of human rights clause. It is submitted that this development can contribute to a more even promotion of human rights in developing countries. In addition, the new GSP Plus is likely to involve larger sectors of industries in developing countries in respect of human rights. However, it has been pointed out that the new GSP did not fully exploit its potential in addressing human rights violations by MNEs. In conclusion, it was suggested that future development of the GSP scheme should refer to the experience of the Cambodia Agreement. In particular, the possibility of setting up a firm monitoring system in the countries that are beneficiaries of the GSP Plus special arrangement should be considered by the EC. A company monitoring system which involves both the ILO and civil society at the host country level would constitute a lever to encourage companies to comply directly with human rights and labour rights.

However, the most prominent example for the promotion of Corporate Social Responsibility in the EU's common commercial policy is given by the new Association Agreement between the EU and Chile. Not only was the agreement preceded by an SIA, which identified economic, social and environmental impacts of the trade agreement, but in a Joint Declaration

---

[108]   Art. 5 Decision of the Council and the Commission of 25 February 1991 on the conclusion of the Fourth ACP–EEC Convention [1991] OJ L 229/1.
[109]   Art. 5(1) Fourth ACP–EEC Convention as reviewed in 1995; now Art. 9 in combination with Art. 96 of the Cotonou Agreement, *supra* Ch.8 n. 56.

the parties to the agreement called upon Multinational Enterprises to respect the OECD Guidelines for Multinational Enterprises. Although, in the specific case of Chile, the introduction to this commitment has been facilitated by previous experience in the protection of the environment, the Commission expressed its willingness to include similar commitments in future external agreements. Even if to date the example of the EU–Chile agreement has not been followed up and it is too early to assess what impact this clause may have on the Parties and on other agreements currently under negotiation, it can be argued that, by strengthening the inclusion of third countries in defining CSR, the allegations of privatized neo-colonialism, which often accompany EU conditionality, are likely to be avoided. In addition, as argued in Part II, Paragraph 9.4, it would be desirable that reference to a more comprehensive international instrument, such as for instance to the UN Norms rather than the OECD Guidelines, will be included in all future EC's trade agreements.

In summary, within its trade relationships the EU, in particular through the GSP, is not only able to promote the respect of human rights in developing countries, but also to monitor their implementation within factories in developing countries. In its bilateral trade relationships the EU could call upon European and domestic companies to respect international principles of responsibility for MNEs by referring to the UN Norms on Transnational Corporations.

PART IV

General conclusions

10 Conclusions

This book addressed the question of how the European Union can ensure that EU-based MNEs respect human rights when operating in third countries. First, it identified primary obligations on MNEs as developed by international law in order to tackle the above question. Secondly, on the basis of this theoretical framework, it investigated how the European Union has acted to promote respect for human rights obligations by MNEs which are based on the territory of one of its Member States. Thirdly, the gap between the EU's commitment to the respect and promotion of human rights, the potential to regulate the conduct of MNEs, and the EU's reluctance to impose human rights obligations on MNEs was explored.

Defining the scope of MNEs' responsibility for human rights constituted an unavoidable step, in order to identify the most appropriate strategies in holding corporations accountable for human rights under EU law. In examining the scope of the human rights responsibility of MNEs, a tension has been identified between the current definition of MNE responsibility in merely negative terms (obligation to respect), which requires business to refrain from acts that could interfere with the enjoyment of human rights, and emerging ethical concerns, which call upon MNEs to participate actively in society by endorsing positive obligations to *promote*, *protect* and *fulfil*, human rights in certain situations. These obligations are already in place on an *ethical* and *moral* basis, although they still lack an appropriate legal framework and enforcement mechanisms.

It has been suggested that current human rights law should develop in the sense of considering companies as duty-holders, together with States and other non-State actors, for the realization of human rights. Moreover, a principle of gradation of responsibility should be applied to MNEs, according to the specific human right involved, the proximity to the victim and the element of State authority exercised by the company in a particular situation. The above-depicted gradation of responsibility (from the obligation to *respect*, to the obligation to *promote* human rights) should be matched by a gradation of corresponding implementing mechanisms.

It was submitted that obligations to respect human rights, as enshrined in international human rights law, and to avoid complicity with human rights violations committed by State authorities must be addressed through legally binding measures, both at the level of the host state and at the level of home state of the MNE. As explained above, a stronger initiative at the level of home states is desirable, since they are in the best position to assess and manage the risk connected to the foreign activities that, because their inherent danger or because of the modalities of their execution, may cause harm to people abroad. Similar considerations can be made in relation with the EU in those areas in which it exercises almost exclusive regulatory powers over MNEs.

On the contrary, the broader area of MNEs' 'support' for human rights leaves room for the use of non-binding measures. In this realm, the incentive effect of codes of conduct and of raising awareness among companies on human rights obligations can be considered. In addition, the potential of incentive measures addressed directly to MNEs, in the form of linking access to public procurement to the companies which comply with human rights standards and incentive measures addressed to host states in the form of technical assistance or access to aid and to trade if complying with human rights, should be further explored.

In the shift from a *violation approach* to a *responsibility approach*, two revision options are currently being debated both at global and European Union level. The first reform option implies an amendment of existing legislation, both at a national and international level, in order to create new obligations binding on companies, together with the improvement of weak enforcement and redress mechanisms. The second relies on the self-regulatory power of business by rejecting legally binding obligations. Despite a growing consensus in international law, international organizations such as the ILO, OECD and the UN have to date failed to create a legal framework for human rights obligations addressed to MNEs. Their efforts have resulted mainly in the creation of voluntary codes, with the exception of the UN Norms, which aspire to evolve into a legally binding document.

In the author's view, complementarity among different levels of intervention at the international, regional – in particular European – and national levels is required to effectively address MNEs' responsibility for human rights. From this perspective, different levels of responsibility and the multiplicity of human rights offenders should not be understood as contradictory or mutually exclusive, but rather as complementary. Similarly, different types of implementation measures, such as binding, non-binding and incentive ones, should be employed in a complementary, rather than exclusive, way to address the different degrees of responsibility of MNEs.

On the basis of this theoretical framework, the position of the EU *vis-à-vis* the human rights obligations of MNEs operating in third countries has been examined. The normative paradigm adopted by the author is that not only is the EU, as an international organization, bound to respect international human rights norms, but, by virtue of its legal order, the EU can adopt positive measures to ensure that human rights are respected in the policies within its sphere of competence. Furthermore, the EU enjoys a unique position in relation to MNEs: contrary to other international organizations, the EU can enact and enforce rules directly binding on MNEs based in one of its Member States.

Based on this premise, the extent to which the European Union has promoted the respect for human rights obligations by European MNEs within the EU and at the external level was examined. Given the complexity of MNEs' responsibility and the complementarity of different levels of responsibility (international, EU/EC, and home state and host state levels), it was necessary to make a distinction between EU measures addressed directly to MNEs at the internal and at the external level, and measures addressed to host states. Within this framework, a further graduation of measures was made with reference to their legal force. Therefore, a distinction between binding and non-binding, or 'mixed' measures was adopted. As pointed out above, these different levels of responsibility were not understood as contradictory or mutually exclusive, but rather as complementary. Similarly, it was pointed out that complementarity is required among different types of implementation measures: binding, voluntary and incentive measures should be understood as complementary rather than mutually exclusive.

As a result of this analysis, the gap between the EU's commitment for the respect and promotion of human rights, its powers to directly regulate the conduct of MNEs and the reluctance in taking steps in this respect becomes apparent.

The extent to which the human rights obligations of MNEs have been integrated into internal and external EC policies varies greatly. Even more surprisingly, the degree to which the EC takes action is not always proportional to the powers it enjoys in a certain policy area.

Notably, if one looks at competition policy, the extensive powers conferred on the EC under Articles 81 and 82 did not provide the EC's preferred avenue to address the human rights obligations of MNEs. Although recognizing that the objective of competition law is to ensure the even functioning of the internal market, however, no creative attempts have been made to get around a hypothetical lack of legal basis by seeking to base proposals on Article 308 TEC or to seek for an appropriate legal basis. This reluctant attitude seems to be related to a lack of political willingness, rather than to the lack of necessary powers to act. Similarly, the use of Regulation (EC) 44/2001 to bring civil suits against European MNEs purported by the European Parliament has not been taken up by the legislator. Finally, developments in European company law do not suggest any move toward the creation of a common European code on corporate governance and even less so a code on corporate responsibility.

Considering that, in the above-examined areas of law, the EC has obtained extensive, at times exclusive, regulatory powers, the EC has a vast practice of regulatory powers over the foreign activities of corporations, when the exercise of such powers is considered to be necessary to fulfil certain societal interests or policy objectives, such as anti-trust enforcement. Thus, if capital-exporting countries, especially European countries, are willing to assert extra-territorial regulatory powers over foreign corporate activities through the effective control they have over the parent companies in the above-mentioned contexts, it is hard to understand what would prevent them from exercising the same powers and the same degree of extraterritorial interest with regard to the internationally shared objective of securing and promoting human rights.

It must be noted, however, that the Treaty of Lisbon makes self-conferral of competence under Article 308 much more difficult:

> If action by the Union should prove necessary, within the framework of the policies defined in the Treaties, to attain one of the objectives set out in the Treaties, and the Treaties have not provided the necessary powers, the Council, acting unanimously on a proposal from the Commission and after obtaining the consent of the European Parliament, shall adopt the appropriate measures. Where the measures in question are adopted by the Council in accordance with a special legislative procedure, it shall also act unanimously on a proposal from the Commission and after obtaining the consent of the European Parliament. . . . Using the procedure for monitoring the subsidiarity principle . . . the Commission shall draw national Parliaments' attention to proposals based on this Article. . . . Measures based on this Article shall not entail harmonization of Member States' laws or regulations in cases where the Treaties exclude such harmonization. . . . This Article cannot serve as a basis for attaining objectives pertaining to the common foreign and security policy . . ..

These provisions are supplemented by two declarations. Moreover, according to the Declaration No. 41 on Article 308 of the Treaty of Lisbon, the reference to objectives of the Union does not refer exclusively to promoting peace, EU values and the well-being of EU people with respect to external action. In this connection it is recalled that legislative acts may not be adopted in the CFSP area. In the Declaration No. 42 on Article 308 of the Treaty of Lisbon, it is underlined that, in accordance with the settled case law of the Court of Justice, Article 308:

> being an integral part of an institutional system based on the principle of conferred powers, cannot serve as a basis for widening the scope of Union powers

beyond the general framework created by the provisions of the treaties as a whole and, in particular, by those that define the tasks and the activities of the Union. In any event, this Article cannot be used as a basis for the adoption of provisions whose effect would, in substance, be to amend the Treaties without following the procedure which they provide for that purpose.

On the contrary, social policy, a field in which the EC enjoys a more limited competence *vis-à-vis* Member States, offered the avenue for a more stringent control over MNEs' activities, at least within EU borders, by progressive recognition of the rights of new groups of stakeholders within European MNEs and in particular of workers. Thus, a specific concern over MNEs within the ambit of the EU has been matched by specific initiatives, such as the Directive on the Safeguarding of Employees' Rights in the Event of Transfer of Undertakings, Businesses or Parts thereof. In addition, the EU has experimented with new forms of decision making in the area of multinational enterprises, such as the European Work Councils. Work councils in turn prompted the creation of one of the most innovative instruments to address social and human rights obligations of MNEs, namely IFAs.

Turning to examine the use of non-binding measures at the EC internal level, the limited use made by the EC of its regulatory powers in the field of competition law and company law has been for some time counterbalanced by the attention given to voluntary initiatives and the launch of the Corporate Social Responsibility debate. The enthusiasm which hailed the inception of the CSR debate, however, was soon replaced by disappointment. While at the beginning the Commission's initiative seems to provide a harmonized framework for the multiplicity of voluntary initiatives – codes of conduct, social label, ethical investment – that spurred in the Member States, the latest communication suggests that this project is no longer on the Commission's agenda. After having gained through the Green Paper and the Multi-stakeholder forum, the CSR debate converged on the disappointing proposal of the Commission–business alliance, on the model of the UN Global Compact contained in the latest Communication.

The CSR debate, indeed, designed a descending trajectory, rather than the 'evolutionary approach' depicted in the Howitt Resolution. The progressive disaffection for the theme of CSR within the EU has been paralleled by the impasse that is facing the adoption of the UN Norms within the UN. The difficulties faced by both initiatives are the signal of a widespread resistance to the adoption of an international or European framework on MNEs' human rights obligations. It must be pointed out, however, that the functioning and regulatory powers of the EU and the

UN differ greatly. While the resistance for the adoption of an international treaty on MNEs is somehow inherent to the intergovernmental structure of the UN, it is more surprising that, after six years of discussion, CSR remained a project with an unclear future, enshrined in a 'soft-law' Commission document (a communication), given the EU's direct regulatory and sanctioning powers over MNEs.

Against the disappointing use of EC powers over MNEs in its internal policies, the introduction of social concerns in the amended EC directives on public procurement raises some optimism. After a long term resistance, EC public procurement directives, adopted on the basis of Article 95, finally allow Member States to introduce social considerations at different stages of procurement procedures. In my view, public procurement provides one of the most appropriate avenues to encourage MNEs to comply with social and human rights standards among EC internal policies. From a political point of view, this option has the advantage of offering a point of convergence between public demand for responsible business conduct and business resistance to the creation of a legal or even voluntary framework on MNEs' human rights obligations. At a normative level, however, it would be desirable for the EU to make full use of the possibilities opened up by the recent amendment of public procurement directives. While currently EC law allows the inclusion of social considerations by Member State contracting authorities, it is argued that compliance with social and human rights standards should be made a mandatory condition for the adjudication of public contracts. Secondly, the notion of 'social concerns' should be replaced by express reference to fundamental rights. Finally, as a matter of coherence and consistency, the introduction of the same concerns should be applied to grants and loans awarded by EC institutions, both at the internal and at the external level.

At the external level, the balance between binding and non-binding measures is partially reversed. In the realm of development-cooperation and common commercial policies, the EC has a longer tradition of exercising its regulatory powers for the promotion of human rights. Thanks to the inclusion of the promotion of fundamental rights as one of the objectives of development-cooperation (Article 177) and by a case law favourable to the inclusion of limited development concerns in the context of common commercial policy (Article 133), the EC has made access to development assistance and to trade conditional upon compliance with human rights clauses. The question, however, was whether this classical (and contested) approach to the promotion of human rights in third countries could be applied to the promotion of human rights obligations of European MNEs operating in third countries. While human rights clauses can indirectly affect the conduct of MNEs, by encouraging host states to implement human rights standards on all companies operating in their territories, their effectiveness to impose indirect obligations on MNEs is nonetheless undermined by a series of shortcomings.

First, human rights clauses in EC Regulations and agreements, which lay down the legal basis for EC development-cooperation and assistance programmes, privilege the promotion of civil and political rights, rather than economic, social and cultural rights, which are more directly affected by the activities of MNEs. This normative deficiency is mirrored in the distribution of funding for development and assistance programmes, which largely focus on the promotion of civil and political rights. In addition to the limited effectiveness of human rights clauses, the debate on CSR, which also purported the mainstreaming of CSR in development and cooperation, has not been integrated into this policy area. Finally, the possibility of moving beyond the human rights clause debate and finding new approaches, while improving the existing human rights clauses in EU agreements with a view to pursuing a more systematic approach to the promotion of human rights, should be explored. In addition, to amend the content of human rights clauses, two other components of development and cooperation should be used more effectively to enhance MNEs' compliance with human rights. First, incentive measures such as technical assistance and civil society dialogue should be used to raise awareness on MNE's obligations and on existing international monitoring systems (ILO, OECD) in developing countries. Secondly, a greater involvement of civil society in the programming and implementation of EC development cooperation programmes – as enshrined in the Cotonou Agreement – can enhance scrutiny over the conduct of MNEs at the grass-root level. The overall impression is that the link between promotion of human rights in third countries and compliance with human rights obligations by MNEs has not been drawn in the context of EC development cooperation. While the absence of this item from the EC agenda could be more easily understood in policies such as competition or company law, which are subordinated to the functioning of the internal market, it is more striking in the realm of development cooperation, which sets the promotion of human rights as one of it objectives.

This approach seems to be the result of a progressive detachment of EC promotion of human rights in development and cooperation from development occurring at the international level, where not only have social rights gained broader support, but also human rights obligations on MNEs are surrounded by a growing consensus. Indeed, since EC human rights clauses refer to internationally recognized human rights law, they should also mirror the evolution that is taking place at the international level of a progressive recognition of MNEs as addressees of human rights obligations. Furthermore, anchoring the EU's development-cooperation to international human rights law may contribute to overcoming the allegations of particularism and of promoting European, rather than universal, human rights.

Nonetheless, the use of human rights clauses followed a different pattern in the realm of the common commercial policy. Despite the fact that development can be introduced only as an ancillary consideration to a common commercial policy objective, a fully fledged human rights incentive scheme has been included by the latest amendment of the GSP. According to this new incentive scheme, preferential access to the EU market is granted only to those countries that comply with eight international human rights and labour rights conventions. Notwithstanding the absence of a specific reference to the promotion of human rights as an objective of the common commercial policy, the EC showed some readiness to conform its common commercial policy to international (WTO) law. As a result, the conditionality foreseen by the GSP Plus may prove to be more effective in encouraging indirect human rights obligations on MNEs operating in GSP beneficiary countries, and it involves larger sectors of industries in respect of human rights. Yet, similarly to the human rights clauses in development-cooperation programmes, the new GSP human rights scheme has a number shortcomings when applied to human rights obligations on MNEs. Above all, it lacks an effective monitoring system. The EC should consider the possibility of setting up a firm monitoring system in the countries that are beneficiaries of the GSP Plus special arrangement. A company monitoring system similar to the one developed in the context of the US–Cambodia Agreement would constitute a lever to encourage companies to comply directly with human rights and labour rights. The setting up of a firm monitoring system in the countries that are beneficiaries of the GSP Plus special arrangement should be considered by the EC.

The use of non-binding measures, at the external level, has been limited to a few isolated examples, such as the Code of Conduct on Arms Export and the Code of Conduct for companies operating in South Africa, which specifically addressed the external activities of MNEs and were adopted under political cooperation. Subsequent attempts to establish a code of conduct for European enterprises, either within the framework of the Howitt Resolution or as a result of the CSR debate, have been abandoned in favour of the promotion of the OECD Guidelines as an internationally recognized code of conduct.

It is submitted, however, that drawing on this experience the EC should make more effective use of voluntary measures at the external level. First, voluntary measures can be used as an instrument for raising awareness on MNEs and human rights in developing countries, and as an instrument for involving civil society in the host countries; and finally, voluntary measures could be linked to mandatory ones in order to increase their effectiveness. One of the most frequent objections in relation to MNEs' responsibility for human rights is that stakeholders in developing countries have perceived their role as the objects more than the active participants of these initiatives. CSR should be included among the possible activities conducted in the context of all the EU programs that bring together businesses and investors from the EU, developing and third countries. Secondly, the use of incentive measures such as technical assistance, institution building, strengthening of civil society and partnerships, however, could be particularly effective in addressing challenges specific to enhancing the scrutiny of MNEs in developing countries. Recourse to voluntary measures, such as exchange of best practices and awareness, should be used to raise awareness on the human rights obligations of MNEs in developing countries. Finally, a linkage between a code of conduct and an international agreement, over and above the exclusive reliance on the OECD Guidelines, is not entirely convincing as the appropriate instrument to promote MNEs' compliance with human rights while operating in third countries. Not only do the OECD Guidelines have only a very limited reference to human rights, but their implementation mechanism is also very weak. It is submitted that, coherently with EC commitment to human rights both at the internal and at the international level, the UN Norms would provide a more comprehensive international instrument of reference to address MNEs' responsibility for human rights.

Therefore, in addition to traditional instruments for the promotion of human rights, the EU's development cooperation policy should also emphasize the role of technical assistance and encourage awareness-building. At a local level, a strategy of bilateral dialogue with governments of developing countries, combined with the support of an active role of civil society in the scrutiny of MNEs' misdeeds, is not only able to promote compliance with human rights standards but can also contribute to avoiding allegations of abuse of human rights standards for protectionist purposes or of new colonialism by imposing European values on third countries. This may encourage a major involvement of companies in the promotion of civil and political rights. In line with principles underlying the EC development policy, the Cotonou Agreement also purports the participation of non-State actors, including companies, in development programmes.

On the basis of this analysis and at the conclusion of this work, three main recommendations can be formulated. First, the EU should more firmly link the promotion of MNEs' human rights obligations to international human rights law and support the constitution of an international law framework within the UN. Secondly, the EU should promote MNEs' human rights obligations within the limits of its competence, both at the international and at an external level. It has been argued that a proactive attitude in this respect would not require the acquisition of new powers, but simply the recognition of a functional competence on the basis of Article 6 TEU in taking positive (and not merely negative) steps for the promotion of human rights in the areas of its competence occurring in international law and the international framework for MNEs' responsibility. Finally, the EU should not abandon the option of exploring non-binding and incentive measures, both at the international and external levels, to be encouraged as a viable complement to binding measures.

10.1   THE INTERNATIONAL / EUROPEAN LAW DIVIDE

As pointed out from the outset, the problem of imposing human rights obligation on non-State actors requires solutions at a global level. Since a characteristic of MNEs is that they defy traditional boundaries, their regulation would require measures applicable across borders. The risk of altering global competition is also inherent in imposing stricter standards on MNEs only at the regional or State level. In addition, it can encourage companies to establish their headquarters in countries which impose less stringent requirements.

An ideal solution would imply the creation of an international treaty which defines the human rights obligations of MNEs.

In this context, the UN Norms represent the most advanced codification of human rights obligations for MNEs. If translated into an international treaty adopted in the context of the UN, they would also represent the most widely accepted international document on MNEs' obligations. A solution at the global level would have the advantage of guaranteeing a level playing field for companies operating worldwide. At the same time, an international treaty would provide a point of reference for legislation adopted at European or state level.

On the other hand, the EU as an international organization is bound by international human rights law. Notwithstanding the uncertainties still surrounding the relationship between the EU and international human rights law, the EU should take into account the growing consensus in international law and practice on considering MNEs as addressees of human rights obligations. In turn, the EU as a subject of international law should contribute to the creation or reinforcement of general principles of international law through its practice. Therefore, it is submitted that the EU and its Member States should promote the development of a coherent regime for the harmonization and enforcement of more effective mechanisms of accountability at the international level, such as the UN Norms on Transnational Corporations.

As explained above, however, it is doubtful that the UN Norms would develop into a fully fledged international treaty. Nonetheless, the potential of using the UN Norms, even in the form of a non-binding international code adopted under the auspices of the UN, should not be underestimated. Not only do the UN Norms represent the most comprehensive codification of the human rights obligations of MNEs, but also their effectiveness can be enhanced by linking them with binding or incentive measures. The EU for instance should make reference to the UN Norms in the context of its development cooperation and trade instruments. Compliance with the UN Norms should be added as a condition to access EC development cooperation programmes and to the GSP human rights arrangement. A new form of conditionality which refers to the UN Norms and specifically addressed to MNEs can be envisaged, on the model of the EC–Chile Agreement. Furthermore, the UN Norms could be included as a condition for access to EU and Member States' public procurement.

The creation of a clear framework at the international level on the responsibility of MNEs and the alignment of the EU to international law would present several advantages. First, relying on international rather than exclusively on EU human rights instruments would limit the risk of allegations of imposing a European model on third countries, or even accusations of using human rights for protectionist purposes. Secondly, it would reduce the risk of altering competition among companies at the international level. Finally, it would avoid the risk of duplication of similar initiatives. The EU business alliance recently suggested by the Commission, for instance, seems to reproduce in its structure and content the existing UN Global Contact voluntary initiative.

10.2 REGULATORY MEASURES: THE EU SHOULD USE ITS EXISTING POWERS IN THE LIGHT OF ARTICLE 6 TEU

In addition to coordination with and support for an international framework on human rights obligations, the EC should make full use of its existing powers and draw a clearer link between the protection of the economic activities of European private actors and the protection of human rights. The EU has extensive regulatory powers over MNEs in several fields and it cannot turn a blind eye when it comes to addressing human rights violations by MNEs based in one of its Member States.

On the basis of its regulatory powers the EU could adopt new legislation defining the human rights obligations of MNEs based in the EU Member States. This might be the most desirable but most difficult option. It would allow better-tailored and more effective solutions in order to improve MNE accountability, but encounters major obstacles in finding the necessary political consensus, as demonstrated by the weak results of the CSR initiative.

From the standpoint of the above-depicted 'evolutionary approach', it can be suggested that a progressive improvement of the accountability of MNEs operating abroad could follow the same development as the one that occurred at an internal EU level in the area of social policy or in the area of environmental law. The progressive recognition of the rights of groups of stakeholders has been progressively integrated into labour law or created new branches of European Union law, such as consumer protection and environmental law.

The introduction of environmental and social concerns in a highly harmonized field of EC law, such as public procurement, proves that, if supported by political will, human rights considerations can be integrated into several fields of EC law. Not only public procurement constitutes a strong economic incentive for companies to behave consistently with human rights and social rights, but it can also be used to combine a binding legal instrument, such as the rules on public procurement, with compliance with voluntary measures, such as an international or EU-wide code of conduct, with the result of enhancing the leverage of voluntary measures.

Such an innovation in public procurement may suggest that a similar development can be envisaged for the human rights obligations of MNEs operating abroad: a progressive improvement of MNEs' responsibility through an issue-based approach. This would imply a progressive convergence on single issues such as social labelling and social auditing, preceded by practice on a voluntary basis. Furthermore, human rights considerations can be progressively introduced in the areas of EU law relevant to the activity of MNEs.

This approach, rather than a full comprehensive law binding instrument for MNEs operating abroad, seems to offer a more realistic option for improving European MNEs' human rights obligations. The adoption of these measures would not require a Treaty amendment but simply a different reading of EU powers in the light of Article 6 TEU. From Article 6 TEU we can infer a functional competence of the EU to adopt not only negative but also positive measures to ensure that human rights are respected in all the policies of EC competence. Therefore, the EU should make use of its powers to address the negative impact that MNEs' activities may have on the enjoyment of human rights.

In the field of development cooperation and cooperation, where the EU enjoys an express competence for the promotion of human rights, the EU should revise the instrument of human rights clauses, which was designed to encourage human rights obligations on third states, to impose human rights obligations also on MNEs. The first step in this respect would be the inclusion of a stronger reference to economic, social and cultural rights in the relevant regulations and external agreements. In addition, conditionality should develop with a view to directly addressing MNEs. Taking the EU–Chile Agreement as a model, a call for the respect of the UN Norms should be introduced into future EC trade agreements and development-cooperation programmes.

A similar reference should be included in the GSP human rights arrangement. In this case the stronger emphasis on human rights in the GSP would probably require a change in the legal basis of the GSP Regulation. Adopting the GSP regulation on the basis of Article 177 (development policy), rather than under Article 133, would allow the introduction of broader human rights consideration, due to the express reference to human rights in Article 177(2). Finally, an effective firm monitoring system should be set up in order to ensure effective compliance with human rights by MNEs in the countries that are beneficiaries of the GSP human rights scheme.

10.3 NON-BINDING MEASURES: THE NEED FOR A COMMON EUROPEAN FRAMEWORK

Finally, in view of the above depicted principle of complementarity, the EU should not overlook the potential of voluntary measures, in addition to making full use of its regulatory powers.

Although the weak results of the debate on CSR turned a gloomy light on the future of voluntary initiatives within the EU, coordination of voluntary initiatives at the EU level is still needed. During the six years of debate on CSR both the business community and the public have asked for more transparency and coordination within the EU *vis-à-vis* the variety of voluntary initiative mushrooming at Member State, company and industry levels. In view of the objective of ensuring the smooth functioning of the internal market, the EU should consider setting up a common framework for initiatives at the European level. On the basis of previous experience of European codes of conduct, any proposal for an effective framework for European MNEs should indicate, on the model of the UN Norms, fundamental human rights treaties and ILO conventions as the minimum essential content of codes. In addition, clearly verifiable obligations on the enterprises which decide to adopt them should be indicated. Furthermore, the possibility of linking codes with binding or incentive measures should be explored. Codes of conduct complying with the European framework can be referred to in all IFAs, thus creating common grounds for negotiation between international trade union associations and MNEs. This implies that trade unions would be able to rely on these standards in the course of negotiating collective agreements. The content of the code can also serve the purpose of identifying what constitutes a 'fault' in the context of civil liability proceedings against the company. Moreover, codes of conduct could – once they are voluntarily adopted or accepted by companies – impose on these certain obligations, by the institution of independent monitoring mechanisms.

In the realm of the EC's external relations, voluntary initiatives can be a viable vehicle for spreading the knowledge of and building consensus on the human rights obligations of MNEs among companies and civil society in developing countries. Exchange of best practices and awareness raising activities should be encouraged in the context of technical assistance and civil society dialogue programmes.

10.4   CLOSING REMARKS

On a final note, considering the EU's unique legal order and its economic power on the global scene, it is hoped the EU finally takes all necessary steps to encourage the imposition of human rights obligations on MNEs. The solution for a more effective monitoring of MNEs' human rights obligations both at the EU and at the international level does not ultimately depend on human rights law but on the mainstreaming of those concerns in other branches of law. The furtherance of this objective would imply reforms across all the areas of the regulation of economic activities: corporate and securities law, international investment law, consumer law, and public procurement to name a few. An effective accountability regime would require a better articulation of norms across different areas of the law, to ensure the notion of parallelism of rights and obligations.

Finally, there are reasons to doubt the ultimate effectiveness of legal reforms if certain issues beyond the domain of the law are not addressed. MNEs' human rights violations are allowed and fostered by patterns of economic growth. Without a real internalization of social and human rights concerns in the definition of economic performance, reforms of human rights law and of the law in general will establish minimum protections of a number of concrete wrongs, but will not be able to correct the source of the problems.

Bibliography

I. ARTICLES, BOOKS, CHAPTERS IN BOOKS, CONFERENCE PAPERS AND WORKING PAPERS

Abi-Saab, G., 'The International Law of Multinational Corporations: a Critique of International Legal Doctrines' (1971) 2 *Annals of International Studies* 97–122.

Abrami, R., *Worker Rights and Global Trade: The US-Cambodia Bilateral Textile Trade Agreement*, 2003, Boston, Harvard Business School Publishing.

Addo, M., 'The Corporation as a Victim of Human Rights Violations', in M. Addo, *Human Rights Standards and the Responsibility of Transnational Corporations*, 1999, The Hague, Kluwer Law International, 187–96.

Aguirre, D., 'Multinational Corporations and the Realisation of Economic, Social and Cultural Rights' (2004) 35 *California Western International Law Journal* 53–82

Ahmed, T. and I. Butler, 'The European Union and Human Rights: an International Law Perspective' (2006) 17/4 *European Journal of International Law* 771–801.

Alston, P. and O. de Schutter, *Monitoring Fundamental Rights in the EU: The Contribution of the Fundamental Rights Agency*, 2005, Oxford and Portland, Or., Hart.

Alston, P. '"Core Labour Standards" and the Transformation of the International Labour Rights Regime' (2004) 15 *European Journal of International Law* 457–521.

Alston, P. and J.H.H. Weiler, 'An "Ever Closer Union" in Need of a Human Rights Policy: The European Union and Human Rights', in P. Alston et al. (eds), *The EU and Human Rights*, 1999, Oxford, Oxford University Press, 3–66.

Alston, P., *Diritti Umani e Globalizzazione. Il Ruolo dell'Europa*, 1999, Torino, Gruppo Abele.

Alston, P., 'Linking Trade and Human Rights' (1980) 23 *German Yearbook of International Law* 126–158.

Anzilotti, D. and G.C. Gidel, *Cours de Droit International*, 1999, Paris, L.G.D.J diffuseur, Editions Panthéon-Assas.

Arangio-Ruiz, G., 'Dualism Revisited. International Law and Inter-individual Law' (2003) 86 *Rivista di Diritto Internazionale* 909–99.

Arnull, A., 'Left To Its Own Devices? Opinion 2/94 and the Protection of Fundamental Rights in the European Union', in A. Dashwood and C. Illion (eds), *The General Law of EC External Relations*, 2000, London, Sweet and Maxwell, 61–78.

Arrowsmith, S., 'Reviewing the GPA: The Role and Development of the Plurilateral Agreement after Doha' (2002) 5 *Journal of International Economic Law* 761–90.

Arrowsmith, S. and A. Davies, *Public Procurement: Global Revolution*, 1998, London and Boston, Kluwer.

Arrowsmith, S., 'Public Procurement as an Instrument of Policy and the Impact of Market Liberalisation', (1995) 111 L.Q.R. 235–84.

Arts, K., 'ACP–EU Relations in a New Era: The Cotonou Agreement' (2003) 40 C.M.L.R. 95–116.

Arts, K., *Integrating Human Rights into Development Cooperation: the Case of the Lomé Convention,* 2000, The Hague, London and Boston, Kluwer Law International.

Atkinson, B., 'Trade Policy and Preferences', in C. Cosgrove-Sacks (ed), *The European Union and Developing Countries,* 1999, Bruges, College of Europe, 305–21.

Avant, D., *The Market for Force: The Consequences of Privatizing Security*, 2005, Cambridge, Cambridge University Press.

Avery, C., 'Business and Human Rights in a Time of Change', in M.T. Kamminga and S. Zia Zafiri, *Liability of Multinational Corporations under International Law*, 2000, The Hague, Kluwer Law International, 17–73.

Baade, H. W., 'Codes of Conduct for Multinational Enterprises', in N. Horn (ed), *Legal Problems of Codes of Conduct for Multinational Enterprises,* 1980, Deventer, Kluwer, 407–41.

Baratta, R., 'Overlaps between European Community Competence and European Union Foreign Policy Activity', in E. Cannizzaro (ed), *The European Union as an Actor in International Relations*, 2002, The Hague and London, Kluwer Law International, 51–75.

Bartels, L., 'The WTO Enabling Clause and Positive Conditionality in the European Community's GSP Program' (2003) 6 *Journal of International Economic Law* 507–32.

Bercusson, B. and N. Bruun, 'Labour Law Aspects of Public Procurement in the EU', in R. Nielsen and S. Treumer (eds), *The New Public Procurement Directives*, 2005, Copenhagen, Djøf, 97–116.

Bielefeldt, H., 'Western Versus Islamic Human Rights Conceptions? A Critique of Cultural Essentialism in the Discussion of Human Rights' (2000) 1 *Political Theory* 90–121.

Blackett, A. 'Global Governance, Legal Pluralism and the Decentered State: A Labor Law Critique of Codes of Corporate Conduct?' (2001) 8 *Indian Journal of Global Legal Studies* 401–47.

Blanpain, R., *European Labour Law*, 2006, The Hague and Frederick, Md., Kluwer Law International and Aspen Publishers.

Blanpain, R., *European Works Councils in Multinational Enterprises: Background, Working and Experience*, ILO Working Paper, 83 (1999).

Blumberg, P.I., *The Multinational Challenge to Corporation Law. The Search for a New Corporate Personality*, 1993, Oxford, Oxford University Press.

Bobbio, N., *The Age of Rights*, 1996, Cambridge, UK: Polity Press.

Bottomley, S., *Corporations and Human Rights*, in S. Bottomley and D. Kinley (eds), *Commercial Law and Human Rights*, 2002, Aldershot, Ashgate, 47–68.

Brandtner, B. and A. Rosas, 'Human Rights and the External Relations of the European Union: an Analysis of Doctrine and Practice' (1998) 9 *European Journal of International Law* 469–90.

Brandtner, B. and A. Rosas, 'Trade Preferences and Human Rights', in P. Alston et al. (eds), *The EU and Human Rights*, 1999, Oxford, Oxford University Press, 699–722.

Bretherthon, C. and J. Vogler, *The European Union as a Global Actor*, 2002, London and New York, Routledge.

Brown, A.V., D.K. Deardoff, and R.M. Stern, *Pros and Cons of Linking Trade and Labor Standards*, Research Seminar in Economics, School of Public Policy, The University of Michigan, Discussion Paper, 477 (6 May 2002).

Brown, C., 'Universal Human Rights: A Critique' (1997) 1 *The International Journal of Human Rights* 41–65.

Brownlie, I., *Principles of International Law*, 1998, Oxford and New York, Clarendon Press and Oxford University Press.

Bulterman, M., *Human Rights in the Treaty Relations of the European Community: Real Virtues or Virtual Reality?*, 2001, Antwerp, Intersentia.

Byrne, I., *Placing Economic Social and Cultural Rights at the Heart of the Euro Mediterranean Partnership*, Paper presented at the Fifth Mediterranean Social and Political Research Meeting of the Mediterranean Programme of the Robert Schuman Centre for Advanced Studies at the European University Institute, Florence and Montecatini Terme, 24–28 March 2004, Workshop No. 14 'Economic and Social Rights in the Euro-Mediterranean Area and the Impact of the Euro-Mediterranean Free Trade Areas', jointly organised with the Euro-Mediterranean Human Rights Network (EMHRN).

Cannizzaro, E., *Machiavelli, the UN Security Council and the Rule of Law*, Global Law Working Paper, New York University Law School, 11 (2005).

Cannizzaro, E., 'The Scope of EU Foreign Power: Is the EC Competent to Include Human Rights Clauses in Agreements Concluded with Third States?', in E. Cannizzaro (ed.), *The European Union as an Actor in International Relations*, 2002, The Hague and London, Kluwer Law International, 297–319.

Capotorti, F., 'Human Rights the Hard Road towards Universality', in R.St.J. Macdonald and D.M. Johnston (eds), *The Structure and Process of International Law: Essays in Legal Philosophy, Doctrine and Theory*, 1983, Leiden Nijhoff, 977–1000.

Cassel, D., 'Corporate Initiatives: A Second Human Rights Revolution?' (1996) 19 *Fordham International Law Journal* 1963–84.

Cassese, A., *Human Rights in a Changing World*, 1990, Cambridge, Polity Press.

Cassese, A., *International Law in a Divided World*, 1989, Oxford, Oxford University Press.

Cassin, R., 'From Ten Commandments to the Rights of Man', in H.H. Cohn and S.G. Shoham (eds), *Essays in Honour of Haim Cohen*, 1971, Tel Aviv and New York, 13–26.

Chandler, J., 'Keynote Address: Crafting a Human Rights Agenda for Business', in M. Addo (ed.), *Human Rights Standards and the Responsibility of Transnational Corporations*, 1999, The Hague, Kluwer Law International, 36–45.

Chirwa D.M., 'Obligations of Non-State Actors in Relation to Economic, Social and Cultural Rights Under the South African Constitution' (2003) 7 *Mediterranean Journal of Human Rights* 29–68.

Choucri, N., 'Corporate Strategy Towards Sustainability', in W. Lang (ed.), *Sustainable Development and International Law*, 1995, London and Boston, Graham & Trotman and M. Nijhoff, 189–201.

Clapham, A., *Human Rights Obligations of Non-State Actors*, 2006, Oxford, Oxford University Press.

Clapham, A. 'The Question of Jurisdiction under International Criminal Law over Legal Persons: Lessons from the Rome Conference on an International Criminal Court', in M.T. Kamminga and S. Zia Zafiri, *Liability of Multinational Corporations under International Law*, 2000, The Hague, Kluwer Law International, 139–95.

Clapham, A., 'Where is the EU Human Rights Common Foreign Policy and How is it Manifested in Multilateral Fora?', in P. Alston et al. (eds), *The EU and Human Rights*, 1999, Oxford, Oxford University Press, 627–83.

Clapham, A. and S. Jerbi, 'Categories of Corporate Complicity in Human Rights Abuses' (1994) 24 *Hastings International and Comparative Law Review* 339–49.

Clapham, A., *Human Rights in the Private Sphere*, 1993, Oxford, Clarendon Press.

Cleveland, S. H., 'Human Rights Sanctions and International Trade: A Theory of Compatibility' (2002) 5 *Journal of International Economic Law* 133–89.

Conforti, B., 'Decisioni Del Consiglio Di Sicurezza e Diritti Fondamentali, in Una Bizzarra Sentenza del Tribunale Comunitario di Primo Grado' (2006) 2 *Il Diritto dell'Unione Europea* 333–54.

Conforti, B., 'Reflections on State Responsibility for the Breach of Positive Obligation: The Case of the European Court of Human Rights' (2003) 13 *Italian Yearbook of International Law* 3–10.

Conforti, B., *Diritto Internazionale*, 2002, Naples, Editoriale Scientifica.

Cosgrove, C., 'Has the Lomé Convention Failed ACP Trade?' (1994) 48 *Journal of International Affairs* 223–49.

Crawford, J., 'The UN Human Rights Treaty System: A System in Crisis?', in P. Alston and J. Crawford (eds), *The Future of UN Human Rights Treaty Monitoring*, 2000, Cambridge, Cambridge University Press, 1–12.

Cremona, M., *External Relations of the EU and the Member States: Competence, Mixed Agreements, International Responsibility, and Effects of International Law*, EUI Working Paper Law, 22 (2006).

Cremona, M., 'The European Neighbourhood Policy: Partnership, Security and the Rule of Law', in N. Copsey and A. Mayhew (eds), *Ukraine and the European Neighbourhood Policy*, 2005, Brighton, Sussex European Institute.

Cremona, M., 'The Draft Constitutional Treaty: External Relations and External Action' (2003) 40 C.M.L.R. 1347–66.

Cremona, M., 'A Policy of Bits and Pieces? The Common Commercial Policy After Nice' (2002) *Cambridge Yearbook of European Legal Studies* 61–91.

Cremona, M., 'The EU and the External Dimension of Human Rights Policy', in S.V. Konstadinidis (ed.), *A People's Europe Turning a Concept Into a Content (EC/International Law Forum III)*, 1998, Ashgate and Dartmouth, Aldershot, 155–81.

Crook, C. 'A Survey of Corporate Social Responsibility' [2005] 374 *The Economist,* 3–18.

CSR Europe & Ashridge Center for Business and Society, *Exploring Business Dynamics. Mainstreaming Corporate Social Responsibility in a Company's Strategy, Management and Systems* (2002).

Daugareilh, I., 'La Negoziazione Collettiva Internazionale' (2005) 19 *Lavoro e Diritto* 599–629.

De Búrca, G., *EU Law, Text, Cases and Materials,* 2003, Oxford, Oxford University Press.

De Búrca, G., *Setting Constitutional Limits to EU Competence*, Francisco Lucas Pires Working Papers Series, Universidade Nova de Lisboa (2001), available at: http://www.fd.unl.pt/je/wpflp02a.doc.

de Franchis, F., *Dizionario Giuridico* [Law Dictionary] 1996, Milan, Giuffrè.

de Haan, E. and J., Oldenziel, *Labour Conditions in IKEA's Supply Chain. Case Studies in India Bulgaria and Vietnam*, 2003, Amsterdam, SOMO, available at: http://www.somo.nl/html/paginas/pdf/IKEA_eindrapport_2003_NL.pdf.

de la Rosa, S., '*Observations après le rapport du groupe spécial "communautés européennes – conditions d'octroi de préférences tarifaires aux pays en développement." Vers une remise en couse du SPG communautaire a la carte?*' (2003) 15 *Revue de l'association Française pour les Nations Unies – Section Aix en Provence, Dossiers Spécial – l' Asie, redécouverte d' un continent* 2.

de Schutter, O., *Corporate Social Responsibility European Style*, Paper presented at the conference 'Corporate Social Responsibility in the EU-10: Expectations vs. Reality', organized in Prague as part of the GARDE programme of EPS, with the Czech League of Human Rights on 15 September 2006, available at: http://www.responsibility.cz/.

de Schutter, O., 'The Challenge of Imposing Human Rights Norms on Corporate Actors,' in O. De Schutter, *Transnational Corporations and Human Rights*, 2006, Oxford and Portland, Or., Hart, 1–39.

de Schutter, O., 'Mainstreaming Human Rights in the European Union', in P. Alston and O. de Schutter, *Monitoring Fundamental Rights in the EU: The Contribution of the Fundamental Rights Agency*, 2005, Oxford and Portland, Or., Hart, 37–72.

de Schutter, O., 'Transnational Corporations as Instruments of Human Development', in P. Alston and M. Robinson (eds), *Human Rights and Development: Towards Mutual Reinforcement*, 2005, Oxford, Oxford University Press, 403–44.

de Schutter, O., 'The Implementation of the Charter of Fundamental Rights through the Open Method of Coordination', in O. de Schutter and S. Deakin (eds), *Social Rights and Market Forces. The Open Method of Coordination of Employment and Social Policies the Future of Social Europe?*, 2004, Brussels, Bruylant, 279–343.

de Schutter, O., *The Accountability of Multinationals for Human Rights Violation in European Law*, Center for Human Rights and Global Justice Working Paper, 1 (2004).

de Witte, B., and G.N. Toggenburg, 'Human Rights and Membership of the European Union', in S. Peers and A. Ward (eds), *The European Charter of Fundamental Rights*, 2004, Oxford, Hart, 59–69.

de Witte, B., 'The Past and Future Role of the European Court of Justice in the Protection of Human Rights', in P. Alston et al. (eds), *The EU and Human Rights*, 1999, Oxford, Oxford University Press, 859–97.

Devillechabrolle, V., 'Ces groupes qui jouent la carte du dialogue social au niveau mondial' (Avril 2005) *Liaisons Sociales* 52–4.

Dine, J., 'Human Rights and Company Law', in M. Addo (ed.), *Human Rights Standards and the Responsibility of Transnational Corporations*, 1999, The Hague, Kluwer Law International, 209–37.

Dommen, C., 'Raising Human Rights Concerns In The World Trade Organization: Actors, Processes And Possible Strategies' (2002) 24 *Human Rights Quarterly* 1–50.

Donnelly, J., *Universal Human Rights in Theory and Practice*, 2003, Ithaca, Cornell University Press.

Donnelly, J., 'Human Rights as Natural Rights' (1982) 4 *Human Rights Quarterly* 391–405.

Douma, W., 'Evolution of Sustainable Development in the European Union', in F. Weiss, E. Denters and P. de Waart (eds), *International Economic Law With a Human Face*, 1998, The Hague and Cambridge, Mass., Kluwer Law International, 271–87.

Draetta, U., 'La Società Europea e il Federalismo Strisciante del Diritto Comunitario', in U. Draetta and F. Pocar (eds), *La Società Europea. Problemi di Diritto Societario Comunitario*, 2002, Milan, Egea, 1–4.

Drezewicki, K., 'Internationalization and Juridization of Human Rights', in R. Hanski and M. Suksi, (eds), *An Introduction to the International Protection of Human Rights: A Textbook,* 1999, Turku/Åbo, Institute for Human Rights, Åbo Akademi University, 25–48.

Dubin, L., 'The Direct Application of Human Rights Standards to, and by Transnational Corporations' (1991) 61 *The Review of the International Commission of Jurists* 35–66.

Dupuy, P.M., *Droit International Public,* 2002, Paris, Dalloz.

Dupuy, P.M., *L'Unité de l'Ordre Juridique International, Cours Général de Droit International Public Recueil des Cours 2002,* 2003, Académie de Droit International de la Hague.

Eeckhout, P., *External Relations of the European Union: Legal and Constitutional Foundations*, 2004, Oxford, Oxford University Press.

Eeckhout, P., 'The EU Charter of Fundamental Rights and the Federal Question' (2002) 39 C.M.L.R. 945–94.

Eide, A. et al. (eds), *Human Rights and the Oil Industry,* 2000, Antwerp, Groningen and Oxford, Intersentia.

Eide, A. et al. (eds), *Economic, Social and Cultural Rights*, 1995, The Hague and Boston, M. Nijhoff.

Errol, M. and M. Ozay, *Global Governance, Economy and Law: Waiting for Justice,* 2003, London and New York, Routledge.

European University Institute, *Leading by Example: A Human Rights Agenda for the European Union for the Year 2000. Agenda of the Comité de Sages and Final Project Report*, 1998, Florence, European University Institute.

Fierro, E., *The EU's Approach to Human Rights Conditionality in Practice,* 2003, The Hague and London, M. Nijhoff.

Fisse, B. and J. Braithwaite, 'The Allocation of Responsibility for Corporate Crime: Individualism Collectivism and Accountability' (1998) 11 *Sydney Law Review* 468–513.

FitzGerald, E.V.K., *Regulating Large International Firms. United Nations Research Institute for Social Development*, United Nations Research Institute for Social Development, UNRISD PB/04/1, Geneva (19 March 2004).

Forcese, C., *Putting Conscience into Commerce: Strategies for Making Human Rights Business as Usual*, International Centre for Human Rights and Democratic Development, 1997, Montreal, available at: http://www.ichrdd.ca/flash.html.

Fox, T. and H. Ward, 'Moving the Corporate Citizenship Agenda to the South', in *Words into Action,* International Institute for Environment and Development (IIED), (2002), available at: www.iied.org.

Fox, T. et al., *Public Sector Roles in Strengthening Corporate Social Responsibility: A Baseline Study*, The World Bank (October 2002).

Francioni, F., 'Alternative Perspectives on International Responsibility for Human Rights Violations by Multinational Corporations', in W. Benedek et al. (eds), *Economic Globalisation and Human Rights*, 2007, Cambridge, Cambridge University Press, (forthcoming).

Francioni, F., 'The Role of the EU in Promoting Reform of the UN in the Field of Human Rights and Enviromental Protection' (2005) 78 *Chaillot Paper* 31–48.

Francioni, F., 'International "Soft Law:" A Contemporary Assessment', in V. Lowe and M. Fitzmaurice (eds), *Fifty Years of the international Court of Justice: Essays in Honour of Sir Roberts Jennings*, 1996, Cambridge, Cambridge University Press, 167–78.

Francioni, F., 'Exporting Environmental Hazard through Multinational Enterprises: Can the State of Origin be Held Responsible?', in F. Francioni and T. Scovazzi, *International Responsibility for Environmental Harm*, 1991, London and Boston, Graham & Trotman; Norwell, Kluwer, 275–98.

Francioni, F., 'International Law Aspects of the Control of MNEs in the ECC', (1983) 95 *Studi Senesi* 450–71.

Francioni, F., *Imprese Multinazionali, Protezione Diplomatica e Responsabilità Internazionale*, 1979, Naples, Giuffré.

Friedman, M., 'The Social Responsibility of Business is to Increase its Profits', (1970) 13/9 *New York Times Magazine* 122–6.

Friedmann, W., *The Changing Structure of International Law*, 1964, London, Stevens.

Gaja, G., 'Casenote: Accession by the Community to the European Convention for the Protection of Human Rights and Fundamental Freedoms – Opinion 2/94' (1996) 33 C.M.L.R. 973–89.

Gamboa, M.J., *Dictionary of International Law and Diplomacy*, 1973, Quezon City, Phoenix.

Gatto, A., 'The Integration of Social Rights Concerns in the External Relations of the European Union', in G. de Búrca, B. de Witte and L. Ogertschnig (eds), *Social Rights in Europe,* 2005, Oxford, Oxford University Press, 339–65.

German Development Institute, *Evaluation on EC Positive Measures in Favour of Human Rights And Democracy (1991–1993)*, Berlin, May 1995.

Hammer, N., *International Framework Agreements: Global Union Federations and Value Chains*, Paper Presented at the International CRIMT Colloquium, 'Union Renewal: Assessing Innovations for Union Power in a Globalised Economy', HEC Montréal, 18–20 November 2004.

Hammer, N., *International Framework Agreements: Overview and Key Issues*, Paper presented at the Industrial Relations in Europe Conference, Utrecht, (August 2004).

Hanley, C., 'The Abuse of Human Rights by European-Based Multinational Corporations: Effective Control Mechanisms for the EU' (LLM thesis on file at the European University Institute, Florence, 2002).

Harrison, J., 'Incentives for Development: The EC's Generalized System of Preferences, India's WTO Challenge and Reform' (2005) 42 C.M.L.R. 1663–89.

Harrison, J., 'The Impact of the World Trade Organisation on the Protection and Promotion of Human Rights', (Ph.D. thesis on file at the European University Institute, Florence, 2005).

Hart, H.L.A., 'Positivism and the Separation of Law and Morals' (1955) 71 *Harvard Law Review* 593–629.

Hart, H.L.A., *The Concept of Law*, 1994, Oxford and New York, Clarendon Press and Oxford University Press.

Henkin, L., *International Law: Politics and Values*, 1995, Dordrecht and Boston, M. Nijhoff.

Higgins, R., *Problems and Processes: International Law and How We Use It*, 1999, Oxford, Oxford University Press.

Holdcroft, J., 'International Framework Agreements: A Progress' (2006) 3 *Metal World* 18–22.

Horn, N., 'Codes of Conduct for MNEs and Transnational Lex Mercatoria: An International Process of Learning and Law Making', in N. Horn (ed.), *Legal Problems of Codes of Conduct for Multinational Enterprises*, 1980, Deventer, Kluwer, 45–81.

Howse, R., 'India's WTO Challenge to Drug Enforcement Conditions in the European Community Generalized System of Preferences: A Little Known Case with Major Repercussions for "Political" Conditionality in US Trade Policy', available at: http://faculty.law.umich.edu/rhowse/Drafts_and_Publications/Howse3.pdf.

International Council on Human Rights Policy, *Beyond Voluntarism-Human Rights and the Developing International Legal Obligations of Companies*, February 2002, available at: www.ichrp.org.

International Peace Academy and Fafo AIS, *Business and International Crimes: Assessing the Liability of Business Entities for Grave Violations of International Law*, September 2004.

Jägers, N., 'Multinational Corporations under International Law', in M. Addo (ed.), *Human Rights Standards and the Responsibility of Transnational Corporations*, 1999, The Hague, Kluwer Law International, 259–70.

Jägers, N., *Corporate Human Rights Obligations: in Search of Accountability*, 2002, Antwerp and Oxford, Intersentia.

Jonathan, G.C., 'Human Rights Covenants', in R. Bernhardt et al. (eds), *Encyclopaedia of Public International Law*, 2000, Amsterdam and New York, North-Holland and Elsevier, 915–22.

Jones, G., *Multinationals and Global Capitalism: from the Nineteenth to the Twenty-First Century*, 2005, Oxford, Oxford University Press.

Joseph, S., 'An Overview of the Human Rights Accountability of Multinational Enterprises', in M.T. Kamminga and S. Zia Zafiri, *Liability of Multinational Corporations under International Law*, 2000, The Hague, Kluwer Law International, 75–93.

Joseph, S., 'Taming the Leviathans: Multinational Enterprises and Human Rights' (1999) 46 *Netherlands International Law Review* 171–203.

Joseph, S., *Corporations and Transnational Human Rights Litigation*, 2004, Oxford, Hart.

Jungk, M., 'A Practical Guide to Addressing Human Rights Concerns for Companies Operating Abroad,' in M. Addo (ed.), *Human Rights Standards and the Responsibility of Transnational Corporations*, 1999, The Hague, Kluwer Law International, 171–86.

Kabeer, N., 'Globalisation, Labour Standards and Women's Rights: Dilemmas of Collective (In)action in an Interdependent World' (2004) 10 *Feminist Economics* 3–35.

Kamminga, M.T., 'Holding Multinational Corporations Accountable for Human Rights Abuses: A Challenge for the EC', in P. Alston et al. (eds), *The EU and Human Rights*, 1999, Oxford, Oxford University Press, 554–69.

Kelsen, H., *Principles of International Law*, 1959, New York, Rinehart.

Kinley, D. and J. Tadaki, 'From Talk to Walk: the Emergence of Human Rights Responsibilities for Corporations at International Law' (2004) 44 *Virginia Journal of International Law Association* 931–1024.

Kinley, D., 'Human Rights as Legally Binding or Merely Relevant?', in S. Bottomley and D. Kinley (eds), *Commercial Law and Human Rights*, 2002, Aldershot, Ashgate, 25–45.

Kolben, K., 'Trade, Monitoring, and the ILO: Working to Improve Conditions in Cambodia's Garment Factories' (2004) 7 *Yale Human Rights & Development Law Journal* 79–107.

Korah, V., *An Introductory Guide to EC Competition Law and Practice*, 2000, Oxford and Portland, Or., Hart.

Kunzlik, P., 'Environmental Issues in International Procurement', in S. Arrowsmith and A. Davies, *Public Procurement: Global Revolution*, 1998, London and Boston, Kluwer, 199–217.

Langille, B., 'Core Labour Rights – The True Story (Reply to Alston)' (2005) 16 *European Journal of International Law* 409–37.

Leino, P., 'European Universalism? The EU and Human Rights Conditionality', in P. Leino (ed.), *Particularity vs. Universality: The Politics of Human Rights in the European Union*, 2005, Helsinki, Erik Castrén Institute, Hakapaino, 237–302.

Liubicic, R., 'Corporate Codes of Conduct and Product Labelling: the Limits and Possibilities of Promoting International Labour Rights Through Private Initiatives' (1998) 1 *Law and Policy in International Business* 111–48.

Lowe, V., 'Corporations as International Actors and International Law Makers' (2004) 14 *Italian Yearbook of International Law* 23–38.

Lucchetti, D., *Il Buco Nero Della RSI. Un commento alla Comunicazione della Commissione EU sulla Responsabilità Sociale d'Impresa e sul rapporto del Rappresentate Speciale dell'ONU John Ruggie sulle Norme per le imprese*, available at: http://www.faircoop.it/PDF/Il_buco_nero_della_Rsi.pdf.

Maduro, M.P., 'Europe and the Constitution: What if This is as Far as It Gets?', Constitutionalism Web Papers 5 (2000).

Maduro, M.P., 'Striking the Elusive Balance Between Economic Rights and Social Rights in the EU,' in P. Alston et al. (eds), *The EU and Human Rights*, 1999, Oxford, Oxford University Press, 449–72.

Malanczuk, P., 'Globalization and the Future Role of Sovereign States', in F. Weiss, *et al.* (eds), *International Economic Law with a Human Face*, 1998, The Hague, Kluwer, 45–65.

Malatesta, A., 'Il Regolamento CE 21 57/2001 sulla Società Europea', in U. Draetta and F. Pocar, *La Società Europea. Problemi di Diritto Societario Comunitario*, 2002, Milano, Egea, 5–21.

Manzella, L.M., *Ominous Outlook for the UN Norms*, 22 March 2006, available at: http://www.earthrights.org/legalfeature/ominous_outlook_for_the_un_norms.html.

Maritain, J., *The Rights of Man and Natural Law*, 1980, London, UMI.

Marx, K., *Economic and Philosophic Manuscripts of 1844*, 1977, Moscow.

McCorquodale, R., 'Human Rights and Global Business', in S. Bottomley and D. Kinley (eds), *Commercial Law and Human Rights*, 2002, Aldershot, Ashgate, 89–114.

McCrudden C., 'International Economic Law and the Pursuit of Human Rights: a Framework for Discussion of the Legality of "Selective Purchasing" Laws Under the WTO Government Procurement Agreement' (1999) 2 *Journal of International Economic Law* (1999) 3–48.

McDougal, M.S., 'Some Basic Theoretical Concepts about International Law: A Policy-Oriented Framework of Inquiry' (1960) 4 *The Journal of Conflict Resolution* 337–54.

McGoldrick, D., 'Sustainable Development and Human Rights an Integrated Conception' (1996) 45 *International and Comparative Law Quarterly* 796–818.

McLean, A., 'The European Union Code of Conduct on Arms Exports' in M. Addo (ed.), *Human Rights Standards and the Responsibility of Transnational Corporations*, 1999, The Hague, Kluwer Law International, 115–22.

Meeran, R., *Access to Courts for Corporate Accountability: Recent Developments*, available at: http://www.johnpickering.co.uk.

Meeran, R., *The Unveiling of Transnational Corporations* in M.T. Kamminga and S. Zia Zafiri (eds), *Liability of Multinational Corporations under International Law*, 2000, The Hague, Kluwer Law International, 251–64.

Michalet, C.A., *Qu'Est-Ce Que la Mondialisation?* 2004, Paris, La Découverte.

Moreau, M.A., 'Le Territoire – Aspects Européens et Internationaux – Des Rattachements Territoriaux Nationaux à la Transnationalité des Normes du Travail' (2003) 1140 *Semaine Sociale Lamy* 82–7.

Moreau, M.A. and G. Trudeau, *The Social Effects of Globalization on Labour Law International*, in Industrial Relations Association, Global Integration and Challenges for Industrial Relations and Human

Resource Management in the Twenty-First Century, World Congress on Industrial Relations, Tokyo, May 2000.

Moreau, M.A., G. Trudeau and G. Murray, *Peut-on déceler une dynamique spécifique de regulation de l'enterprise mondialisée dans l'Union européenne?*, Conference organised by the CRIMT, Toward a Social Regulation of a Global Firm, Montreal, Canada.

Morici, P. and E. Shultz, *Labour Standards in the Global Trading System*, 2001, Washington, Washington Economic Strategy Institute.

Morth, U. (ed), *Soft Law in Governance and Regulation: An Interdisciplinary Analysis*, 2004, Cheltenham, Edward Elgar.

Mosler, H., 'Subjects of International Law', in R. Bernhardt et al. (eds), *Encyclopaedia of Public International Law*, 2000, Amsterdam and New York, North-Holland and Elsevier, 710–27.

Muchlinski, P., 'Human Rights Social Responsibility and the Regulation of International Business: the Development of International Standards by Intergovernmental Organisations' (2003) 3 *Non-State Actors and International Law* 123–52.

Muchlinski, P., *Multinational Enterprises and the Law*, 1999, Oxford, UK and Cambridge, Mass., Blackwell.

Muchlinski, P., 'A Brief History of Business Regulation', in S. Picciotto and R. Mayne (eds), *Regulating International Business. Beyond Liberalisation*, 1999, London, Macmillan Press, 47–59.

Noortmann, M., 'Non-State Actors in International Law', in B. Arts et al. (eds), *Non State Actors in International Relations,* 2001, Aldershot and Burlington, Vt., Ashgate, 59–76.

O' Brien, R., 'NGOs, Civil Society and Global Economic Regulation', in S. Picciotto and R. Mayne (eds), *Regulating International Business. Beyond Liberalisation*, 1999, London, Macmillan Press, 257–72.

Oxford Dictionary of English, 2003, Oxford, Oxford University Press.

Papaioannou, A.M., 'The Illegal Exploitation of Natural Resources in the Democratic Republic of Congo: A Case Study on Corporate Complicity in Human Rights Abuses' in O. de Schutter (ed), *Transnational Corporations and Human Rights*, 2006, Oxford and Portland, Or., Hart, 263–86.

Parekh, B., *Rethinking Multiculturalism: Cultural Diversity and Political Theory*, 2000, London, Macmillan.

Partsch, K.J., 'Individuals in International Law', in R. Bernhardt et al. (eds), *Encyclopaedia of Public International Law,* 2000, Amsterdam and New York, North-Holland and Elsevier, 957–62.

Pasqualucci, J.M., *The Practice and Procedure of the Inter-American Court of Human Rights*, 2003, Cambridge, Cambridge University Press.

Ratner, R., 'Corporations and Human Rights: A Theory of Legal Responsibility' (2001) 3 *Yale Law Journal* 443–545.

Reinisch, A., 'The Changing International Legal Framework for Dealing with Non-State Actors', in P. Alston (ed.), *Non-State Actors and Human Rights*, 2005, Oxford, Oxford University Press, 37–89.

Rickford, J., 'The European Company', in J. Rickford (ed), *The European Company. Developing Community Law of Corporations*, 2003, Antwerp, Intersentia, 26–38.

Riedel, E. and W. Martin, 'Human Rights Clauses in External Agreements of the EC', in P. Alston *et al.* (eds), *The EU and Human Rights*, 1999, Oxford, Oxford University Press, 723–54.

Riisgaard, L., *The IUF/COLSIBA – CHIQUITA Framework Agreement: a Case Study*, ILO Working Paper, 94 (2004).

Rosas, A. and M. Sheinin, 'Economic and Social Rights as Legal Rights', A. Eide et al. (eds), *Economic, Social and Cultural Rights*, 2001, The Hague and Boston, M. Nijhoff, 29–54.

Rosas, A. and M. Sheinin, 'Categories and Beneficiaries of Human Rights', in R. Hanski and M. Suksi (eds), *An Introduction to the International Protection of Human Rights: A Textbook,* 1999, Turku/Åbo, Institute for Human Rights, Åbo Akademi University, 49–62.

Sadurski, W., 'The Role of the EU Charter of Rights in the Process of Enlargement', in G. Bermann and K. Pistor (eds), *Law and Governance in an Enlarged European Union*, 2004, Oxford, Hart, 61–95.

Salcedo, J.C., 'Human Rights Universal Declaration', in R. Bernhardt et al. (eds.), *Encyclopaedia of Public International Law,* 2000, Amsterdam and New York, North-Holland and Elsevier, 922–6.

Sarna, R., *The Impact of Core Labour Standards on Foreign Direct Investment in East Asia*, 2005, Tokyo, The Japan Institute for Labour Policy and Training.

Schmid, D., *The Use of Conditionality in Support of Political Economic and Social Rights: Unveiling the Euro-Mediterrean Partnership's True Hierarchy of Objectives?*, paper presented at the Fifth Mediterranean Social and Political Research Meeting of the Mediterranean Programme of the Robert Schuman Centre for Advanced Studies at the European University Institute, Florence and Montecatini Terme, 24–28 March 2004. Workshop No. 14 'Economic and Social Rights in the Euro-Mediterranean Area and the Impact of the Euro-Mediterranean Free Trade Areas', jointly organised with the Euro-Mediterranean Human Rights Network (EMHRN).

Schumacher, T., *Survival of the Fittest: the First Five Years of the Euro-Mediterranean Economic Relations*, EUI Working Paper RSCAS (2004).

Seidermann, I.D., *Hierarchy in International Law: The Human Rights Dimension,* 2001, Antwerp, Intersentia.

Sheehy, O., *The Positive Application of Human Rights within EU–ACP Development Co-operation*, Conference Proceedings, 'The Relationship between Africa and the European Union', organised by ECSA of South Africa, University of the Western Cape, 22–23 January 2004, available at: http://www.uwc.ac.za/ECSA-SA/conf2004_prog.htm.

Shestack, J.J., 'The Jurisprudence of Human Rights', in T. Meron (ed), *Human Rights in International Law: Legal and Policy Issues*, 1984, Oxford, Oxford Clarendon Press, 69–113.

Simma, B., J.B. Aschenbrenner and C. Shulte, 'Human Rights Considerations in the Development Co-operation Activities of the EC', in P. Alston et al. (eds), *The EU and Human Rights*, 1999, Oxford, Oxford University Press, 571–626.

Simma, B., 'International Human Rights and General International Law: A Comparative Analysis' (1993) 4 *Collected Courses of the Academy of European Law* 153–256.

Simma, B. and P. Alston, 'The Sources of Human Rights Law: Custom, Jus Cogens and General Principles', (1992) 12 *Australian Year Book of International Law* 82–108.

Skogly, S.I., 'Economic and Social Human Rights, Private Actors and International Obligations', in M. Addo (ed.), *Human Rights Standards and the Responsibility of Transnational Corporations*, 1999, The Hague, Kluwer Law International, 239–58.

Smith, K.E., 'The Outsiders: The European Neighbourhood Policy' (2005) 81/4 *International Affairs* 757–73.

Sornarajah, M., *The Settlement of Foreign Investment Disputes*, 2000, The Hague, Kluwer.

Spar, D., 'The Spotlight on the Bottom Line: How Multinational Export Human Rights' (1988) 77 *Foreign Affairs* 7–12.

Spicher, P., *Les Droits de l'Homme dans les Chartes d'étique Economique*, 1996, Bern and Fribourg, Commission Nationale Suisse pour l'Unesco, Institut Interdisciplinaire d'Etique et des Droits de l'Homme de l'Université de Fribourg-Centre Info.

Steiner, H.J. and P. Alston, *International Human Rights in Context: Law, Politics, Morals*, 2000, Oxford and New York, Oxford University Press.

Stephens, B., 'Corporate Liability: Enforcing Human Rights Through Domestic Litigation' (2001) 24 *Hastings International and Comparative Law Review* 401–13.

Stokke, O. (ed), *Aid and Political Conditionality,* 1995, London, Frank Cass.

Sudre, F., *Droit Communautaire des Droits Fondamentaux: Recueil de Décisions de la Cour de Justice des Communautés Européennes*, 1999, Bruxelles, Bruylant.

Sullivan, R. and D. Hogan, 'The Business Case for Human Rights – The Amnesty International Perspective', in S. Bottomley and D. Kinley (eds), *Commercial Law and Human Rights*, 2002, Aldershot, Ashgate, 69–87.

Supiot, A., 'Du Nouveau au Self-Service Normatif: la Responsabilité Sociale des Entreprises', in *Etudes Offerts à Jean Pélissier, Analyse Juridique et Valeurs en Droit Social*, 2004, Paris, Dalloz, 541–58.

Sykes, A., 'International Trade and Human Rights: an Economic Prospective', in F.M. Abbott et al. (eds), *International Trade and Human Rights. Foundations and Conceptual Issues*, 2006, Ann Arbor, The University of Michigan Press, 69–92.

Teubner, G. (ed), *Global Law Without a State*, 1997, Aldershot, Brookfield, Dartmouth.

Thürer, Daniel. 'Soft Law', in R. Bernhardt et al. (eds), *Encyclopaedia of Public International Law*, 2000, Amsterdam and New York, North-Holland and Elsevier, 452–60.

Tófalo, I., 'Overt and Hidden Accomplices. Transnational Corporations' Range of Complicity for Human Rights Violations', in O. de Schutter, *Transnational Corporations and Human Rights*, 2006, Oxford and Portland, Or., Hart, 335–57.

Tomuschat, C., Case T-306/01, *Ahmed Ali Yusuf and Al Barakaat International Foundation v Council and Commission*; Case T-315/01, *Yassin Abdullah Kadi v Council and Commission* (2006) 43 C.M.L.R. 537–51.

Tomuschat, C., 'The International Responsibility of the European Union', in E. Cannizzaro (ed), *The European Union as an Actor in International Relations*, 2002, The Hague and London, Kluwer Law International, 177–91.

Tomuschat, C., 'Is Universality of Human Rights Standards an Outdated and Utopian Concept?', in B. Roland and D. Nickel (eds), *Das Europa der zweiten Generation: Gedachtnisschrift für Christoph Sasse*, 1981, Kehl am Rein, NP Engel Verlag, 585–609.

Torremans, P., 'Extraterritoriality and Human Rights', in N. Neuwahl and A. Rosas (eds), *The European Union and Human Rights,* 1995, The Hague, M. Nijhoff, 281–96.

Trebilcock, M.J. and R. Howse, 'Trade Policy and Labor Standards' (2005) 14 *Minnesota Journal of Global Trade* 261–300.

Tridimas, Takis, 'Liability for Breach of Community Law: Growing Up and Mellowing Down?' (2001) 38 C.M.L.R. 301–32.

Tsogas, G., 'Labour Standards in the General System of Preferences of the European Union and The United States' (2000) 6 *European Journal of Industrial Relations* 349–70.

Tsogas, G., 'Labour Standards in International Trade Agreements: an Assessment of the Arguments' (1999) 2 *International Journal of Human Resource Management* 351–75.

Tully, S., 'The 2000 Review of the OECD Guidelines for Multinational Enterprises' (2001) 50 I.C.L.Q. 394–403.

Uriz-Hernandez, G., 'Human Rights as the Business of Business. The Application of Human Rights Standards to the Oil Industry', (Ph.D. thesis on file at the European University Institute, Florence, 2005).

Urminsky, M., *Self-Regulation in the Workplace: Codes of Conduct, Social Labelling and Socially Responsible Investment*, MCC Working Paper, 1 Series on Management Systems and Corporate Citizenship, International Labour Organization (2001).

Vagts, D., 'The Multinational Enterprise: A New Challenge For Transnational Law' (1970) 83 *Harvard Law Review* 739–92.

Van Boven, T., 'General Course on Human Rights' (1993) 4 *Collected Courses of the Academy of European Law* 1–106.

Vazquez, C.M., 'Trade Sanctions and Human Rights – Past, Present and Future' (2003) 6 *Journal of International Economic Law* 797–840.

Vicuña, F.O., *International Dispute Settlement in an Evolving Global Society: Constitutionalization, Accessibility, Privatization*, 2004, Cambridge, Cambridge University Press.

Von Bogdandy, A., 'The European Union as Human Rights organization? Human Rights and the Core of the European Union' (2000) 37 C.M.L.R. 1307–38.

Ward, H., *Governing Multinationals: the Role of Foreign Direct Liability*, The Royal Institute of International Affairs, Briefing Paper, No. 18 (2001).

Weiler, J.H.H. and S. C. Fries, 'A Human Rights Policy for the European Community and Union: The Question of Competences,' in P. Alston et al. (eds), *The EU and Human Rights*, 1999, Oxford, Oxford University Press, 147–66.

Weissbrodt, D. and M. Kruger, 'Norms on the Responsibilities of Transnational Corporations and Other Bussiness Enterprises with Regard to Human Rights' (2003) 97 *American Journal of International Law* 901–22.

Williams, A., *EU Human Rights Policies: A Study in Irony*, 2004, Oxford, Oxford University Press.

Winter, J., 'EU Company Law on the Move' 31/2 *Legal Issues of Economic Integration*, (2004) 97–114.

Winter, J., *The Future of European Company Law*, speech delivered at the Conference European Company Law Company – Law in Europe, 22 May 2002, Law Faculty, University of Maastricht, The Netherlands.

Woodroffe, J., 'Regulating Multinational Corporations in a World of Nation States', M. Addo, *Human Rights Standards and the Responsibility of Transnational Corporations*, 1999, The Hague, Kluwer Law International, 131–42.

Wouters, J., L. de Smet and C. Ryngaert, *Tort Claims Against Multinational Companies for Foreign Human Rights Violations Committed Abroad: Lessons from the Alien Tort Claims Act?*, K.U. Leuven Faculty of Law Institute for International Law, Working Paper, 46 (2003).

Zeisel, K., 'The Promotion of Human Rights by Selective Public Procurement Under International Trade Law', in O. de Schutter, *Transnational Corporations and Human Rights*, 2006, Oxford and Portland, Or., Hart, 361–92.

Zubaidur, M.R. 'The Local Value Added Statement: a Reporting Requirement of Multinationals in Developing Host Countries', 25 *International Journal of Accounting* (1990) 87–98.

II. EU DOCUMENTS AND LEGISLATION

Agreement establishing an association between the European Community and its Member States, of the one part, and the Republic of Chile, of the other part [2002] OJ L 352/3, 30 December 2002.

Agreement on Extradition between the United States of America and the European Union, of 25 June 2003 (2004) 43 *International Legal Materials* 749.

ACP-EEC Convention [1991] OJ L 229/3, 17 August 1991.

Charter of Fundamental Rights of the European Union [2000] OJ C 364/1, 18 December 2000.

Code of Conduct for Community Companies with Subsidiaries, Branches or Representation in South Africa of 16 November 1985 (1985) 24 *International Legal Materials* 1477.

Commission Staff Working Document, European Initiative for Democracy and Human Rights Programming Document 2002–04, REV 1, Final, Brussels, 20 December 2001.

Common Position 2001/758/CFSP of 29 October 2001 on combating the illicit traffic in conflict diamonds, as a contribution to prevention and settlement of conflicts [2001] OJ L 286/2, 30 October 2001.

Common Position of 28 October 1996 defined by the Council on the basis of Article J.2 of the Treaty on European Union, on Burma/Myanmar (96/635/CFSP) [1996] OJ L 287/1, 8 November 1996.

Common Strategy of the European Union of 4 June 1999 on Russia (1999/414/CFSP) [1999] OJ L 157/1, 24 June 1999.

Communication from the Commission to the Council and the European Parliament on Strengthening the European Neighbourhood Policy COM (2006) 726 final, 4 December 2006.

Communication from the Commission to the European Parliament, the Council and the European Economic and Social Committee, Implementing the Partnership for Growth and Jobs: Making Europe a Pole of Excellence on Corporate Social Responsibility COM (2006) 136 final, 22 March 2006.

Communication from the Commission to the Council and the European Parliament on the Instruments for External Assistance under the Future Financial Perspective, 2007-2013 COM (2004) 626 final, Brussels, 29 September 2004.

Communication from the Commission, European Neighbourhood Policy. Strategy Paper COM (2004) 373 final, 15 May 2004.

Communication from the Commission to the Council and the European Parliament Reinvigorating EU actions on Human Rights and Democratisation with Mediterranean Partners, Strategic guidelines COM (2003) 294 final, Brussels, 21 May 2003.

Communication from the Commission to the Council, the European Parliament and the Economic and Social Committee of 7 November 2002: Participation of non-state actors in EC development policy COM (2002) 598 final, 7 November 2002.

Communication from the Commission to the Council and the European Parliament, Trade and Development Assisting Developing Countries to Benefit from Trade of 18 September 2002 COM (2002) 513 final.

Communication from the Commission on The Charter of Fundamental Rights of the European Union COM (2002) 559 final, 13 September 2002.

Communication from the Commission Concerning Corporate Social Responsibility: a Business Contribution to Sustainable Development COM (2002) 347 final, 2 July 2002.

Communication from the Commission to the Council, the European Parliament and the Economic and Social Committee, Towards a Global Partnership for Sustainable Development COM (2002) 82, final, 13 February 2002.

Communication from the Commission on the Community Law Applicable to Public Procurement and the possibilities for Integrating Social

Considerations into Public Procurement COM (2001) 566 final, 15 October 2001.

Communication from the Commission of the European Communities, Green Paper – Promoting a European Framework for Corporate Social Responsibility COM (2001) 366 final, 18 July 2001.

Communication from the Commission to the Council, the European Parliament and the Economic and Social Committee, Promoting Core Labour Standards and Improving Social Governance in the Context of globalisation COM (2001) 416 final, 18 July 2001.

Communication from the Commission to the Council and the European Parliament, The European Union's Role in Promoting Human Rights and Democratisation in Third Countries COM (2001) 252 final, 8 May 2001.

Communication from the Commission to the Council, the European Parliament and the Economic and Social Committee, Social Policy Agenda COM (2000) 379 final, 28 June 2000.

Communication from the Commission, The Trading System and Internationally Recognized Labour Standards COM (96) 402 final, 24 July 1996.

Communication from the Commission to the Council, Multinational Undertakings and the Community Bulletin of the European Communities, Supplement 15/73, 8 November 1973.

Consolidated version of the Treaty establishing the European Community, in European Union Consolidated Treaties (1997) Luxembourg, Office for Official Publications of the European Communities.

Corporate Social Responsibility. National Public Policies in the European Union, European Commission, Employment and Social Affairs (January 2004).

Council Regulation (EC) 732/2008 of 22 July 2008 applying a scheme of generalised tariff preferences for the period from 1 January 2009 to 31 December 2011 and amending Regulations (EC) 552/97, (EC) 1933/2006 and Commission Regulations (EC) 1100/2006 and (EC) 964/2007 [2008] OJ L 211, 6 August 2008.

Council Regulation (EC) 1933/2006 of 21 December 2006 Temporarily Withdrawing Access to the Generalised Tariff Preferences from the Republic of Belarus, [2006] OJ L 405/35, 30 December 2006.

Council Regulation (EC) 1889/2006 establishing a Financing instrument for cooperation with industrialised and other high-income countries and territories [2006] OJ L 386/1, 29 December 2006.

Regulation (EC) 1905/2006 of the European Parliament and of the Council of 18 December 2006 establishing a financing instrument for development cooperation, [2006] OJ L 378, 27 December 2006.

Council Regulation (EC) 1085/2006 establishing an Instrument for Pre-Accession Assistance (IPA) for Community assistance to candidate and potential candidate countries [2006] OJ L 210/82, 31 July 2006.

Council Regulation (EC) 980/2005 of 27 June 2005 Applying a Scheme of Generalized Tariff Preferences [2005] OJ L 169/1, 30 June 2005.

Council Regulation (EC) 2242/2004 of 22 December 2004 amending Regulation (EC) No 976/1999 laying down the requirements for the Implementation of Community operations, other than those of development cooperation, which, within the framework of Community cooperation policy, contribute to the general objective of developing and consolidating democracy and the rule of law and to that of respecting human rights and fundamental freedoms in third countries [2004] OJ L 390/21, 31 December 2004.

Council Regulation (EC) No 552/97 of 24 March 1997 temporarily withdrawing access to generalized tariff preferences from the Union of Myanmar [1997] OJ L 085, 27 March 1997.

Directive 2004/18/EC of the European Parliament and of the Council of 31 March 2004 On the coordination of procedures for the award of public works contracts, public supply contracts and public service contracts [2004] OJ L 134/114, 30 April 2004.

Council Regulation (EC) 139/2004 of 20 January 2004 on the Control of concentrations between undertakings (the EC Merger Regulation) [2004] OJ L 24/1, 29 January 2004.

Council Directive 2003/123/EC of 22 December 2003 amending Directive 90/435/EEC on the Common system of taxation applicable in the case of parent companies and subsidiaries of different Member States [2004] OJ L 7/ 41, 13 January 2004.

Directive 2003/51/EC of the European Parliament and of the Council of 18 June 2003 Amending Directives 78/660/EEC, 83/349/EEC, 86/635/EEC and 91/674/EEC On the Annual and Consolidated Accounts of Certain Types of Companies, Banks and Other Financial Institutions and Insurance Undertakings [2003] OJ L 178/16, 17 July 2003.

Council Regulation (EC) 2211/2003 of 15 December 2003 amending Regulation (EC) 2501/2001 Applying a Scheme of Generalised Tariff Preferences for the Period from 1 January 2002 to 31 December 2004 and Extending It to 31 December 2005 [2003] OJ L 332/1, 19 December 2003.

Council Regulation (EC) 1/2003, of 16 December 2002 on the Implementation of the rules on competition laid down in Articles 81 and 82 of the Treaty [2003] OJ L 1/1, 4 January 2003.

Directive 2002/14/EC of the European Parliament and of the Council of 11 March 2002 establishing a General framework for informing and consulting employees in the European Community – Joint declaration of the European Parliament, the Council and the Commission on employee representation [2002] OJ L 80/29, 23 March 2002.

Council Regulation 2501/2001 of 10 December, 2001 applying A Scheme of Generalised Tariff Preferences for the Period from 1 January 2002 to 31 December 2004 [2001] OJ L 346/1, 31 December 2001.

Council Directive 2001/86/EC of 8 October 2001 supplementing the Statute for a European company with regard to the involvement of employees, [2001] OJ L 294, 10 November 2001, 22–32.

Council Regulation (EC) 2157/2001 of 8 October 2001 on the Statute for a European company (SE) [2001] OJ L 294/1, 10 November 2001.

Council Regulation (EC) No 44/2001 of 22 December 2000 on Jurisdiction and the Recognition and Enforcement of Judgments in Civil and Commercial Matters [2001] OJ L 12/1, 16 January 2001.

Council Regulation (EC) 2698/2000 of the November 2000 amending regulation (EC) No. 1488/96 of 23 July 1996 on Financial measures to accompany (MEDA) the reform of economic and social structures in the framework of the Euro-Mediterranean partnership [2000] OJ L 311/1, 12 December 2000.

Council Directive 2000/78/EC of 27 November 2000 Establishing a General Framework for Equal Treatment in Employment and Occupation [2000] OJ L 303/16, 2 December 2000.

Council Directive 2000/43/EC of 29 June 2000 Implementing the Principle of Equal Treatment Between Persons Irrespective of Racial or Ethnic Origin [2000] OJ L 180/22, 19 July 2000.

Council Joint Action 2000/298/CSFP of 13 April 2000 on a European Union assistance programme to support the Palestinian Authority in its efforts to counter terrorist activities emanating from the territories under its control [2000] OJ L 097/4, 19 April 2000.

Council Regulation (EC, EURATOM) 99/2000 of 29 December 1999 Concerning the Provision of Assistance to the Partner States in Eastern Europe and Central Asia [2000] OJ, L 12/1, 18 January 2000.

Council Regulation (EC) 1216/1999 of 10 June 1999 amending Regulation No 17: first Regulation implementing Articles 81 and 82 of the Treaty [1999] OJ L/5 148, 15 June 1999.

Council Regulation (EC) 975/1999, of 29 April 1999 laying down the requirements for the Implementation of development cooperation operations which contribute to the general objective of developing and consolidating democracy and the rule of law and to that of respecting human rights and fundamental freedoms and the rule [1999] OJ L 120/1, 8 May 1999.

Council Regulation (EC) 976/1999 of 29 April 1999 laying down the requirements for the Implementation of Community operations, other than those of development cooperation, which, within the framework of Community cooperation policy, contribute to the general objective of developing and consolidating democracy and the rule of law and to that of respecting human rights and fundamental freedoms in third countries [1999] OJ L 120/8, 8 May 1999.

Council Directive 98/59/EC of 20 July 1998 on the Approximation of the laws of the Member States relating to collective redundancies [1998] OJ L 225/16, 12 August 1998.

Council Directive 98/50/EC of 29 June 1998 amending Directive 77/187/EEC on the approximation of the laws of the Member States relating to the safeguarding of employees' rights in the event of transfers of undertakings, businesses or parts of businesses [1998] OJ L 20/88, 17 July 1998.

Council Directive 97/74/EC of 15 December 1997 extending, to the United Kingdom of Great Britain and Northern Ireland, Directive 94/45/EC on the establishment of a European Works Council or a procedure in Community-scale undertakings and Community-scale groups of undertakings for the purposes of informing and consulting employees [1998] OJ L 254/64, OJ L 10/22, 16 January 1998.

Council Regulation 552/97 of 27 March 1997 on temporarily withdrawing Access to generalised system of preferences from the Union of Myanmar Burma [1997] OJ L 85/8, 27 March 1997.

Council Regulation (EC) 1488/96 of 23 July 1996 on Financial measures to accompany (MEDA) the reform of economic and social structures in the framework of the Euro-Mediterranean partnership [1996] OJ L 189/1, 30 July 1996.

Council Directive 94/45/EC of 22 September 1994 on the Establishment of a European Works Council or a procedure in Community-scale undertakings and Community-scale groups of undertakings for the purposes of informing and consulting employees [1994] OJ L 254/64, 30 September 1994.

Council Regulation (EC) 3286/94 of 22 December 1994, laying down Community procedures in the field of the common commercial policy in order to ensure the exercise of the Community's rights under international trade rules, in particular those established under the auspices of the World Trade Organization [1994] OJ L 349/71, 31 December, 1994.

Council Regulation (EEC) 443/92 of 25 February 1992 on Financial technical assistance to and cooperation with developing countries in Asia and Latin America (the ALA Regulation) [1992] OJ L 52/1, 27 February 1992.

Council Directive 77/187/EEC of 14 February 1977 on the Approximation of the laws of the Member States relating to the safeguarding of employees' rights in the event of transfers of undertakings, businesses or parts of businesses [1977] OJ L 61/26, 5 March 1977.

Council Directive 75/129/EEC of 17 February 1975 on the Approximation of the laws of the Member States relating to collective redundancies [1975] OJ L 48/29, 22 February 1975.

Council Joint Action 2005/643/CFSP of 9 September 2005 on the European Union Monitoring Mission in Aceh (Indonesia) (Aceh Monitoring Mission) [2005] OJ L 234/13, 10 September 2005.

Council Joint Action 2005/557/CFSP of 18 July 2005 on the European Union civilian-military supporting action to the African Union mission in the Darfur region of Sudan, OJ L 188/46, 20 July 2005.

EU Annual Report on Human Rights 1998/99–2006, Office for Official Publications of the European Community, Luxembourg, 1999–2006.

European Commission Directorate-General for Trade Directorate F – WTO. *Sustainable Development, Investment, Standards, Intellectual Property, New Technologies. Bilateral Trade Relations Investments, Standards & Certification, TBT, Note to 133 Committee, Corporate Social Responsibility and Trade Policy – Implementing CSR Practices and the OECD Guidelines for Multinational Enterprises in Developing Countries* Brussels, 7 June 2004.

European Commission, *Euro–Med Partnership, Regional Strategy Paper 2002–2006 & Regional Indicative Programme 2002–2004.*

European Commission, *Explanatory Memorandum to the Proposal for a Council Regulation*, COM (2004) 699 final, 20 October 2004.

European Commission, Proposal for a Council Directive on the *Establishment of a European Works Council in Community-Scale Undertakings or Group of Undertakings for the Purposes of Informing and Consulting Employees*, COM (90) 581 final, OJ C 39/10, 15 February 1991.

European Commission, Proposal for a Council Directive on *Procedure for Informing and Consulting Employees of Undertakings with a Complex Structure in Particular Transnational Undertakings (so called 'Vredeling Proposal')* [1989] OJ (1980) C 297/13, 25 November 1989.

European Commission, *Proposal for a Council Regulation applying a scheme of generalised tariff preferences for the period 1 January 2002 to 31 December 2004* COM (2001) 293 final, Brussels, 12 June 2001.

European Commission, *Proposal for a Council Regulation establishing a European Union Agency for Fundamental Rights and Proposal for a Council Decision, empowering the European Union Agency for Fundamental Rights to pursue its activities in areas referred to in Title VI of the Treaty on European Union* COM (2005) 280 final, 30 June 2005.

European Commission, Proposal for a Fifth Directive on the Coordination of Safeguards Which for the Protection of the Interests of Members and Outsiders, are Required by Member States of Companies within the Meaning of Article 59, Second Paragraph, with Respect to Company Structure and to the Power and Responsibilities of Company Boards [1972] OJ C 131/49, 13 December 1972.

European Commission, *Regional Strategy Document Latin America for 2002–2006*, adopted by the European Commission in April 2002.

European Commission, *Report from the Commission to the Council and the European Parliament, Parliament Annual Report of the MEDA programme 2000*, Brussels COM (2001).

European Multi-Stakeholder Forum on Corporate Social Responsibility – Final Report, July 2004, available at: http://forum.europa.eu.int/irc/empl/csr_eu_multi_stakeholder_forum/info/data/en/csr%20ems%20forum.htm.

European Parliament, A6 – Committee on Employment and Social Affairs Rapporteur: Richard Howitt 0471/2006 Final, *Report on corporate social responsibility: a new partnership*, 006/2133(INI), 20 December 2006.

European Parliament, Resolution on EU standards for European enterprises operating in developing countries: Towards a European Code of Conduct, adopted by the European Parliament on 15 January 1999, A4-0508/1998 [1999] OJ C 104/176, 14 April 1999.

European Parliament, Resolution on a code of conduct for arms exports (B4-0502, 0505, 0520, 0522, 0529 and 0546/98) at point C, OJ C 167/226, 1 June 1998.

European Parliament and the Council, Regulation (EC) 1889/2006 of the European Parliament and of the Council of 20 December 2006 on Establishing a Financing Instrument for the Promotion of Democracy and Human Rights Worldwide [2006] OJ L 386/1, 29 December 2006.

European Parliament and the Council, Regulation (EC) 1717/2006 establishing a Financing Instrument for Stability [2006] OJ L 327/1, 24 November 2006.

European Parliament and the Council, Regulation (EC) 1638/2006 of the European Parliament and of the Council of 24 October 2006 Laying Down General Provisions Establishing a European Neighbourhood and Partnership Instrument [2006] OJ L 310/1, 9 November 2006.

European Parliament and the Council, Regulation (EC) 2240/2004 of the European Parliament and of the Council of 15 December 2004 amending Council Regulation (EC) 975/1999 laying down the requirements for the Implementation of development cooperation operations which contribute to the general objective of developing and consolidating democracy and the rule of law and to that of respecting human rights and fundamental freedoms [2004] OJ L 390/3, 31 December 2004.

European Parliament and the Council, Regulation (EC) 761/2001 of the European Parliament and of the Council of 19 March 2001 Allowing Voluntary Participation by Organisations in a Community Eco-Management and Audit Scheme (EMAS) [2001] OJ L 114 / 1, 24 April 2001.

Evaluation of Community Aid Concerning Positive Measures in the Field of Human Rights and Democracy in the ACP Countries, 1995–1999, Synthesis Report Phase 3, SCR Evaluation, 951518, 28 August 2000.

Joint Declaration signed by the President of the European Council M. José María Aznar, the President of Chile, M. Ricardo Lagos, and the President of the European Commission, M. Romano Prodi, Madrid, 17 May 2002.

Meeting of Heads of State and Government from Mercosur and Chile & from the EU Joint Communiqué of Rio de Janeiro – 28 June 1999 – 9410/99 (Press 207), available at: http://europa.eu.int/comm/external_relations/chile/assoc_agr/pol.htm.

Partnership Agreement between the members of the African, Caribbean and Pacific Group of States (ACP) of the one part, and the European Community and its Member States, of the other part, signed in Cotonou on 23 June 2000, 2000/483/EC [2000] OJ L 317, 15 December 2000.

Report on the proposal for a Council Decision concerning the conclusion of the Framework Agreement for trade between the European Community and its member States, of the one part and the republic of South Korea on the other part COM (96) 0141- C4-0073/97 – 96/0098 (CNS), A4- 0445/98.

Resolution of the Council and of the Member States Meeting in the Council on Human Rights, Democracy and Development, 28 November 1991, *Bulletin of the European Communities,* 1991, 122.

Roundtable on the Development Aspects of Corporate Social Responsibility, available at: http://forum.europa.eu.int/irc/empl/csr_eu_multi_stakeholder_forum/info/data/en/CSR Forum roundtables meetings.htm.

Strategy Paper and Indicative Programme for Multi-Country Programmes in Asia 2005–2006.

Strategy Paper and Indicative Programme 2004–2006, Tacis Regional Cooperation.

Sustainable Impact Assessment (SIA) of the trade aspects of negotiations for an Association Agreement between the European Communities and Chile (Specific agreement No. 11) Final Report October 2002, at 217, available at: http://www.planistat.com/sia/report/SA%20nbr1%20final%20Oct%202002.pdf.

Third ACP–EEC Convention signed at Lomé on 8 December 1984 [1986] OJ L 86/3, 31 March 1986.

Treaty of Lisbon [2007] OJ C306 17 December 2007.

User's Guide to the European Union's Scheme of Generalised Tariff Preferences
P5 (2003), http://europa.eu.int/comm/trade/gsp/gspguide.htm.

III. OTHER INTERNATIONAL ORGANIZATIONS' DOCUMENTS

A/HRC/8/5, *Protect, Respect and Remedy: a Framework for Business and Human Rights Report of the Special Representative of the Secretary-General on the issue of human rights and transnational corporations and other business enterprises* John Ruggie, 7 April 2008.

African [Banjul] Charter on Human and Peoples' Rights, 27 June 1981, preamble and Article 28, OAU Doc. CAB/LEG/67/3 rev. 5 (1982) 21 *International Legal Materials* 58.

African Charter on Human and Peoples' Rights, adopted 27 June 1981, O.A.U. Doc. CAB/LEG/67/3 rev. 5 (1982) 21 *International Legal Materials* 58.

African Charter on the Rights and Welfare of the Child, OAU Doc. CAB/LEG/24.9/49 (1990).

American Convention on Human Rights, *Organisation of American States (O.A.S). Treaty Series* No. 36, 1144 UNTS 123 (entered into force 18 July 1978), reprinted in *Basic Documents Pertaining to Human Rights in the Inter-American System*, OEA/Ser.L.V/II.82 doc.6 rev.1 (1992).

American Declaration of the Rights and Duties of Man, *O.A.S. Res.* XXX, adopted by the Ninth International Conference of American States (1948), reprinted in Basic Documents Pertaining to Human Rights in the Inter-American System, OEA/Ser.L.V/II.82 doc.6 rev.1 at 17 (1992).

Basel Convention on the Control of Transboundary Movements of Hazardous Wastes and Their Disposal, 22 March 1989 [1989] 28 *International Legal Materials* 657.

Charter of the International Military Tribunal (Annex to the 8 August 1945 London Agreement establishing an ad hoc International Military Tribunal, 28 UNTS 284).

Comprehensive Anti Apartheid Act of 1986 (1987) 26 *International Legal Materials* 79.

Convention on Civil Liability for Oil Pollution Damage Resulting from Exploration for and Exploitation of Seabed Mineral Resources, 17 December 1976, in Intergovernmental Conference on the Convention on Civil Liability for Oil Pollution Damage from Offshore Operations: Final Act and Text of Convention, opened for signature 1 May 1977 (1977) 16 *International Legal Materials* 1450.

Convention Relating to Civil Liability in the Field of Maritime Carriage of Nuclear Material, 17 December 1971, 974 U.N.T.S 255.

Criminal Law Convention on Corruption, 27 January 1999 (2000) 38 *International Legal Materials* 505.

E/CN.4/2006/97 Report of the Special Representative of the Secretary-General on the issue of human rights and transnational corporations and other business enterprises.

European Convention for the Protection of Human Rights and Fundamental Freedoms, (ETS 5), 213 United Nations Treaty Series (UNTS) 222 (entered into force 3 September 1953, as amended by Protocols Nos 3, 5, and 8 which entered into force on 21 September 1970, 20 December 1971 and 1 January 1990 respectively).

'Final Report of the Panel of Experts on the Illegal Exploitation of Natural Resources and Other forms of Wealth of the Democratic Republic of the Congo', S/2003/1027, 23 October 2003.

General Agreement on Tariffs and Trade (GATT), 30 October 1947, 61 Stat. A3, 55 UNTS 188.

Geneva Convention for the Amelioration of the Condition of the Wounded and Sick in Armed Forces in the Field, 12 August 1949, art. 3, 6 U.S.T. 3114, 3116-18, 75 UNTS 31, 32.

Geneva Convention for the Amelioration of the Condition of Wounded, Sick and Shipwrecked Members of Armed Forces at Sea, 12 August 1949, art. 3, 6 U.S.T. 3217, 3220-22, 75 UNTS 85, 86.

Geneva Convention Relative to the Protection of Civilian Persons in Time of War, 12 August 1949, art. 3, 6 U.S.T. 3516, 75 UNTS 287.

Geneva Convention Relative to the Treatment of Prisoners of War, 12 August 1949, art. 3, 6 U.S.T. 3316, 75 UNTS 135.

Government Procurement Agreement (GPA) of the World Trade Organisation, 15 April 1994, LT/UR/A-4/Pluri/2.

Human Rights Committee, General Comment 10, Article 19 (19 session, 1983), Compilation of General Comments and General Recommendations Adopted by Human Rights Treaty Bodies, UN Doc. HRI/GEN/1/Rev.6 at 132 (2003).

Human Rights Committee, General Comment 17, Article 24 (35th session, 1989), Compilation of General Comments and General Recommendations Adopted by Human Rights Treaty Bodies, UN Doc. HRI/GEN/1/Rev.6 at 144 (2003).

Human Rights Committee. General Comment 28, Equity of Rights between Man and Women (Article 3) 29/03/ 2000, CCPR/C/21/Rev.1 Add. 10, CCPR.

Human Rights Committee, The Right to Life (Article 6) General Comment 6, (Sixteenth session, 1982), Compilation of General Comments and General Recommendations Adopted by Human Rights Treaty Bodies, UN Doc. HRI\GEN\1\Rev.1 at 6 (1994).

Human Rights Committee, The Right to Respect Family Privacy, Family, Home Correspondence and Protection of honour and reputation (Article 17), General Comment 16, (Twenty-third session, 1988), Compilation of General Comments and General Recommendations Adopted by Human Rights Treaty Bodies, UN Doc. HRI\GEN\1\Rev.1 at 21 (1994).

Inter-American Commission on Human Rights, Organization of American States. Report on the Situation of Human Rights in Ecuador, 24 April 1997; OEA/Ser. L/V/II.96 Doc. 10 rev.1. (VIII-IV).

International Centre for the Settlement of Investment Disputes (ICSID). *Convention on the Settlement of Investment Disputes between States and Nationals of Other States*, Washington, 18 March 1965 (entered into force 14 October 1966).

International Commission of Jurists, Rijksuniversiteit Limburg, Centre of Human Rights and Urban Morgan Institute for Human Rights, 'The Maastricht Guidelines on Violations of Economic Social and Cultural Rights' (1998) 81 *Human Rights Quarterly* 87.

International Labour Organisation (ILO), Tripartite Declaration of Principles concerning Multinational Enterprises and Social Policy, adopted by the Governing Body of the International Labour Office at its 204th Session (Geneva, November 1977) as amended at its 279th (November 2000) and 295th Session (March 2006).

ILO Convention concerning Occupational Safety and Health and the Working Environment, 11 August 1983.

ILO Eighth Synthesis Report on the Working Conditions Situation in Cambodia's Garment Sector, available at: http:// www.ilo.org/public/ english/dialogue/ifpdial/publ/cambodia8.htm.

Organisation for Economic Cooperation and Development (OECD), *The OECD Guidelines for Multinational Enterprises*, OCDE/GD 97/40 (2000), 2000, Paris, OECD Publications.

OECD, Convention on Combating Bribery of Foreign Public Officials in International Business Transactions, 17 December 1997 (1999) 37 *International Legal Materials* 1.

OECD, *Voluntary Approaches for Environmental Policy: an Assessment,* 1999, Paris, OECD Publications.

OECD, *Trade, Employment and Labour Standards: A Study of Core Workers' Rights and International Trade*, 1996, Paris, OECD Publications.

OECD, *Declaration on International Investment and Multinational Enterprise,* 1976, Paris, OECD Publications.

Organization of American States, Inter-American Convention Against Corruption, 29 March 1996 (1996) 35 *International Legal Materials* 724.

Protocol Additional to the Geneva Conventions of 12 August 1949, and Relating to the Protection of Victims of Non-International Armed Conflicts, 8 June 1977, art. 13, 1125 UNTS 609.

Report of the Sub-commission on the Promotion and Protection of Human Rights, Report of the United Nations High Commissioner on human rights, on the Responsibilities of Transnational Corporations and Related Business Enterprises with Regard to Human Rights, UN Document E/CN/.4/2005/91.

Rules Governing Additional Facilities for the Administration of Proceedings by the Secretariat of the ICSID, available at: http://www.worldbank.org/icsid/facility/3htm.

South African Truth and Reconciliation Commission. *Report of the South African Truth and Reconciliation Commission*, Vol. 4, Chapter 2, *Institutional Hearings, Business and Labour*, 1998, Cape Town, Juta.

The African Commission on Human and Peoples' Rights, Decision on Communication 155/96, 30th Ordinary Session, Banjul, The Gambia, 13–17 October 2001.

United Nations (UN), UN Doc.A/CN.4/532, Third Report on Responsibility of International Organizations, G. Gaja, A/CN 4/553, 26 March 2003.

UN, *UN Norms on the Responsibilities of Transnational Corporations and Other Business Enterprises with Regard to Human Rights*, UN Doc. E/CN.4/Sub.2/2003/12/Rev.2 (2003). Approved August 13, 2003, by UN Sub-Commission on the Promotion and Protection of Human Rights Resolution 2003/16, U.N. Doc. E/CN.4/Sub.2/2003/L.11, 52 (2003).

UN Committee on Economic, Social and Cultural Rights. General Comment 7, Forced Evictions, and the right to adequate housing (16session, 1997), UN Doc. E/1998/22, annex IV, at 113 (1998), reprinted in Compilation of General Comments and General Recommendations Adopted by Human Rights Treaty Bodies, UN Doc. HRI/GEN/1/Rev.6, 45 (2003).

UN Convention Against Corruption, UN GAOR, 58th Sess., Supp. No. 49, UN Doc. A/Res/58/4 (2003).

UN, 'Security Council resolution 1499 (2003) adopted by the Security Council at its 4807th meeting, on 13 August 2003', SC Res. 1499 (2003).

UN, 'Final Report of the Panel of Experts on the Illegal Exploitation of Natural Resources and Other Forms of Wealth of the Democratic Republic of the Congo', S/2002/1146, (2002).

UN, 'Draft Fundamental Human Rights Principles for Business Enterprises', Addendum 1, UN Doc. E/CN.4/Sub.2/2002/X/Add.1, E/CN.4/Sub.2/2002/WG.2/WP.1/Add.1 (Draft for Discussion, November 2001).

UN, Convention against Transnational Organized Crime defines the crimes of participation in an organised criminal group, money laundering, corruption and obstruction of justice, all of which apply to corporations as well as natural persons. GA Res. 55/25, UN GAOR, 55th Sess., 62d plen. mtg., Annex 1 at arts. 5, 6, 8 & 23, UN Doc. A/Res/55/25 (2001).

UN Commission on Human Rights, Draft Universal Human Rights Guidelines for Companies, Addendum 1, UN Doc. E/CN.4/Sub.2/2001/WG.2/WP.1/Add.1 (2001).

UN, *Guidelines for Cooperation between the United Nations and the Business Community*, Issued by the Secretary-General of the United Nations 17 July 2000.

UN, *UN World Conference on Human Rights: Vienna Declaration and Programme of Action*, A/CONF.157/23 (1993).

UN, Convention on the Elimination of All Forms of Discrimination against Women, GA Res. 34/180, 34 UN GAOR Supp. (No. 46), A/34/46, at 193 (entered into force 3 September 1981).

UN, *Universal Declaration of Human Rights,* GA Res. 217a (III), UN Doc. A/180 (1948).

United Nations Conference on Trade and Development (UNCTAD). *World Investment Report – FDI from Developing and Transition Economies: Implications for Development*, 2006, Geneva, United Nations Publications.

IV. DOMESTIC LEGISLATION

'An Act Regulating Contracts with Companies Doing Business with or in Burma (Myanmar)', Ch. 130, 1996 Session Laws, Massachusetts General Laws, Ch. 7. 223 (West 1997).

Agreement Relating to Trade in Cotton, Wool, Man-made Fiber, Non-Cotton Vegetable Fiber and Silk Blend Textiles and Textile Products Between the Government of the United States of America and the Royal Government of Cambodia, signed on January 20, 1999, and renewed in December 2001.

Crimes Amendment (Corporate Manslaughter) Bill 2003 (New South Wales, Australia).

Proposal to amend the administrative code of the city of New York, in relation to Procurement of Apparel and Textile Services by City Agencies. Proposed Int. No 693-A.

UNITE, Memorandum on Proposals for Bilateral Trade Agreement by/from UNITE (Nov. 19, 1998).

V.   ECJ AND CFI CASES AND OPINIONS

Ahlström Osakeyhtiö v Commission (Wood Pulp) Cases 89/85, 114/85, 116-117/85, 125-129/85 [1988] ECR 5193.

Bosphorus [1996] Case C-84/95ECR I-3953.

Commission of the European Communities v Council of the European Communities (GSP) Case 45/ 86 [1987] ECR 1493.

Commission of the European Communities v Council of the European Communities. – European Agreement on Road Transport (ERTA) Case C-22/70 [1971] ECR 263.

Commission of the European Communities v French Republic Case C-225/98 [2000] ECR I-7445.

Commission v Council (GSP case) Case 45/86 [1987] ECR 1493.

Concordia Bus Finland Oy Ab (previously Stagecoach Finland) v Helsingin Kaupunki Case C-513/99 [2002] ECR I-7213.

Coöperative Vereniging UA and Others v Commission (The Sugar Cartel) Joined cases 40–48, 50, 54 to 56, 111, 113 and 114–73, [1975] ECR 1663.

Defrenne v Société Anonyme Belge de Navigation Aérienne Sabena Case 43/75 [1976] ECR 445.

Eugen Schmindberger, Internationale Transporte und Planzüge v Austria Case C-112/00 [2003] ECR I-5659.

Europemballage and Continental Can v Commission Case 6/72 [1973] ECR 215.

Gebroeders Beentjes BV v State of the Netherlands, Case 31/87 [1988] ECR 4635.

Grant v South-West Trains Case C-249/95 [1998] ECR I-621.

Istituto Chemioterapico Italiano Commercial Solvents Co v Commission, Cases 6&7/73 [1974] ECR 223.

Kadi v Council and Commission Case T- 315/01 (not yet published).

Opel Austria GmbH v Council Case T-115/94 [1997] ECR II-39.

Opinion 1/94 [1994] ECR I-5267.

Opinion 1/78 [1979] ECR-2871.

Opinion 2/94 [1996] ECR I-1061.

Portuguese Republic v Council of the European Union – Cooperation Agreement between the European Community and the Republic of India Case C-268/94 [1996] ECR I-6177.

Poulsen and Diva Navigation Case C-286/90 [1992] ECR I-6019.

Racke GmbH & Co v Hauptzollant Mainz Case C-162/96 [1998] ECR I-3655.

Van Gend en Loos v Nederlandse Administraties Der Belastingen Case 26/62 [1963] ECR 3.

Viho Europe BV v Commission, Case C-73/95 [1996] ECR I-5457.

Walrave v Association Union Cycliste Internationale Case 36/64 [1974] ECR 1405.

Yusuf & Al Barakaat International Foundation v Council of the European Union and Commission of the European Communities Case T-306/01 [2005] ECR II-3533.

Yassin Abdullah Kadi and Al Barakaat International Foundation v Council of the European Union and Commission of the European Communities, Joined cases C-402/05 P and C-415/05 P, 2008 [ECR] I-6351.

VI. INTERNATIONAL COURTS CASES AND OPINIONS

A. v United Kingdom, Judgment of 23 September 1998, ECHR 1998-VI, 2699.

Advisory Opinion of 20 December 1980 on the Question Concerning the Interpretation of the Agreement of 25 March 1951 between the World Health Organisation and Egypt (1980) ICJ Reports 73.

Amco Asia Corporation v Republic of Indonesia, 1 ICSID Reports 389, [1984] 23 *International Legal Materials,* 351.

Anglo Iranian Oil (United Kingdom v Iran), Judgement, (1952) ICJ Reports 96.

Asian Agricultural Products Ltd v Sri Lanka, ICSID Case No. ARB/87/3, 4 [1991] ICSID Reports 245.

Autronic AG v Switzerland ECHR (1990) Series A, No. 178, 12, EHRR 485.

Barcelona Traction, Light and Power Co., Limited (Belgium v Spain) (1970) ICJ Reports 3.

Bosphorus Hava Yollari Turizm Ve Ticaret Anonim Şirketi v Ireland ECHR (2005), VI [n. 45036/98].

Casado Coca v Spain [1994] IIHRL 10 (24 February 1994), ECHR Series A, No. 285.

De Geïllustreerde Pers. N.V. v The Netherlands ECHR, report of 6 July 1976, D. R. 8.

Dombo Beheer v Netherlands ECHR (1993) Series A, 274.

Ethyl Corporation v Canada (NAFTA-UNCITRAL Case) (1999) 38 *International Legal Materials* 700.

Godínez Cruz Case, Order of the Court of September 10, 1996, reprinted in 1996 *Annual Report of the Inter-American Court of Human Rights* (IACHR), [213], OEA/Ser.L/V/III.35, doc. 4 (1997).

Guerra v Italy (1998) ECHR 777.

Hatton and Others v The United Kingdom, ECHR Application 3602/77.

Inter-American Commission on Human Rights, *Resolution 38/81, Case 4425 (Guatemala) (25 June 1982)*; IACHR (1980–81), OEA/ Ser. L/V/ II.54; Doc. 9 rev. 1, 16 October 1981.

Kadic v Kardžić case [1995] 70 F 3d 232 2nd Cir.

Loizidou v Turkey, Case 40/1994/435/541, Judgment of 23 March 1995, ECHR (A) 310.

Matthews v United Kingdom, App. No. 24833/94, Judgment of 18 February 1999, 28 EHRR (1999), 361.

Mayagna Awas Tingni Community v Nicaragua, Judgment of 31 August 2001, IACHR Decisions and Judgments, (ser. C) N. 79 (2001).

Military and Paramilitary Activities in and Against Nicaragua, Case *Nicaragua v USA*, Judgment of 27 June 1986, ICJ Rep. 14.

Naviflora Sweden AB v Sweden EHRR (1993) 15, CD 6.

Osman v United Kingdom, Case 23452/94, 28 October 1998, (1998) ECHR 101.

Plattform Ärtze für das Leben v Austria, Judgment of 21 June 1988, ECHR (1991) Series A, No. 191.

Prosecutor v Dusko Tadic Case IT 94-I-T.

Re Union Carbide Corp. gas Plant Disaster 809 F. 2d 195.

Reparations from Injuries Suffered in the Service of the United Nations, Advisory Opinion (1949) ICJ Reports 174.

Request for Consultations by India, WT/DS246/1, 12 March 2002, 174.

Trial of Friedrich Flick and Five Others (1947), Case 48, 9 *Law Reports of the Trials of War Criminals* 1, reproduced in (1947) 14 *International Law Reports*.

United States v Carl Krauch, et al., *IC Farben*, Case 6, Nurberg Military Tribunals, vol. VII–VIII.

Velásquez Rodríguez case, Inter-Am. C.T.H.R. 8 (ser C) No 4 (1998).

World Trade Organisation (WTO), WTO, *European Communities – conditions for the granting of tariff preferences to developing countries* WT/DS246/AB/R, 7 April 2004.

WTO, *Notification of an appeal by the European Communities*, WT/ DS246/7, 8 January 2004.

WTO, *European Communities – conditions for the granting of tariff preferences to developing countries*, WT/ DS246/R, adopted by the special group on 28 October 2003, 1 December 2003.

WTO, WT/DS88/1, GPA/D2/126 *United States – Measure Affecting Government Procurement. Request for Consultations by the European Communities*, June 1997.

WTO, *Decision on Differential and More Favourable Treatment Reciprocity and Fuller Participation of Developing Countries*, GATT document L/4903, 28 November 1979, BISD 26S/203.

X and Y v The Netherlands (1985) ECHR Series A, No. 91.
X and Church of Scientology v Sweden 7805/77 [1979] ECHR 9.
Yanomami v Brazil, Case 7615, 5.3.1985, Res. No 12/85, IACHR (1985).

VII.   DOMESTIC CASES

Burma v Unocal Inc. 176 FRD 329, 345.
Lubbe and Others v Cape plc [2000] 4 All ER 268, [2000] 1 WLR 1545, [2000] 2 Lloyd's, Rep 383.
Spiliada Maritime Corporation v Cansulex Ltd. [1987] AC 460.
Wiva Royal Dutch Shell Petroleum, Co. 226 F. 3d, 88 (2d Cir. 2000).

VIII.   INTERVIEWS

Prof. Mark Barenberg, Columbia University Law School, in New York, (November 2005).
Dominique Be, European Commission, Directorate General, Employment and Social Affairs (February 2003).
Andrea Mogni, European Commission, Directorate General, External Relations, Brussels (June 2002).
Geoffrey Peeters, European Commission, Directorate General, External Trade, Brussels (July 2001.)
Giusy Chiovato Rambaldo, European Commission, Directorate General, Employment and Social Affairs, Brussels (March 2002).

IX.   INTERNET SOURCES

http://ec.europa.eu/comm/external_relations/belarus/intro/#prospects.
http://ec.europa.eu/comm/external_relations/consultations/cswp_tacis. htm.
http://ec.europa.eu/comm/external_relations/delegations/intro/web.htm.
http://europa.eu.int/comm/.
http://europa.eu.int/comm/internal_market/smn/smn29/s29mn22.htm.
http://europa.eu/publicprocurement/index_en.htm.
http://www.europa.eu.int/ comm//employment_social/soc-dial/csr.
http://www.globalreporting.org/.
http://www.icftu.org.
http://www.tcc.mac.doc.gov/cgi-bin/doit.cgi?204:64:189233445:25.
http://www.unglobalcompact.org/Portal/Default.asp.

http://www.worldbank.org/icsid/cases/cases.htm.http://www.worldbank.
  org/icsid/constate/c-states-en.htm.
http://www.worldbank.org/icsid/treaties/treaties.htm.

Index

Abi-Saab, G. 54
Abrami, R. 264, 265
access to company records, public 21
access to justice 25
accountability 16–17, 27, 47, 78
  European Union: MNEs 103,
    104–13, 135–6, 143, 288
    EU competence in human rights
      field 113–21, 133, 195–204,
      278–9, 283–4, 285–7
    EU and international human
      rights law 32–4, 121–9,
      133–5, 216, 283
    MNEs in EU law 129–33, 135
  informal 18
  interaction between binding and
    non-binding instruments 27–9,
    275–6, 277, 280, 282, 284,
    287–8
  legal responsibility 24–7
  self-regulation 6, 15–16, 18–24, 179,
    276
activism, grassroots 18
Addo, M. 46, 58
addressees of international law, MNEs
  as 15–16, 26–7, 61–3, 81, 93,
  281–2, 284
  from rights to obligations 28, 53–61,
    240
  legal personality 48–53, 62
African, Caribbean and Pacific (ACP)
  countries 32, 191, 218, 269
  Cotonou Agreement 168, 193, 204,
    229–33, 238, 239, 270, 281,
    283
African Charter on Human and
  Peoples' Rights (1981) 42, 71,
  73–4
African Charter on Rights and Welfare
  of the Child (1990) 73–4
Aguirre, D. 44

Ahmed, T. 128
ALA programme 207, 226–9, 238, 239
Alston, P. 90, 111, 116, 117, 120, 121,
  128, 192, 200, 211, 251, 255,
  256–7, 260, 262
American Convention on Human
  Rights (1969) 42
American Declaration of the Rights
  and Duties of Man (1948) 73–4
annual accounts/reports
  corporate governance 21
  social statements 15
  value-added statements 20, 21–2
Anzilotti, D. 53
apartheid 85, 92, 176
Arangio-Ruiz, G. 49
arbitration 57, 62
  ICSID (International Centre for
    Settlement of Investment
    Disputes) 55–7, 62
  treaties 27
armed conflict 179
arms 247
  export: EU code of conduct 175,
    177–8, 187, 207, 282
  proliferation 206
Arnull, A. 198
Arrowsmith, S. 153, 154, 155
Arts, K. 269
Asian Human Rights Charter 73–4
Asian and Latin American (ALA)
  countries 191, 218
  ALA programme 207, 226–9, 238,
    239
association, freedom of 19, 69–70, 79,
  81, 95, 184, 214
  trade and human rights 244
    EU–GSP scheme 252, 253, 261
Association Agreement between EU
  and Chile 31, 182, 228, 266–71
Atkinson, B. 252